AI, DATA AND PRIVATE LAW

This book examines the interconnections between artificial intelligence, data governance and private law rules with a comparative focus on selected jurisdictions in the Asia-Pacific region. The chapters discuss the myriad challenges of translating and adapting theory, doctrines and concepts to practice in the Asia-Pacific region given the differing circumstances, challenges and national interests. The contributors are legal experts from the UK, Israel, Korea, and Singapore with extensive academic and practical experience.

The essays in this collection cover a wide range of topics, including data protection and governance, data trusts, information fiduciaries, medical AI, the regulation of autonomous vehicles, the use of blockchain technology in land administration, the regulation of digital assets and contract formation issues arising from AI applications.

The book will be of interest to members of the judiciary, policy makers and academics who specialise in AI, data governance and/or private law or who work at the intersection of these three areas, as well as legal technologists and practising lawyers in the Asia-Pacific, the UK and the US.

This research is supported by the National Research Foundation, Singapore under its Emerging Areas Research Projects (EARP) Funding Initiative. Any opinions, findings and conclusions or recommendations expressed in this material are those of the authors and do not reflect the views of National Research Foundation, Singapore.

AI, Data and Private Law

Translating Theory into Practice

Edited by
Gary Chan Kok Yew
and
Man Yip

•HART•
OXFORD • LONDON • NEW YORK • NEW DELHI • SYDNEY

HART PUBLISHING
Bloomsbury Publishing Plc
Kemp House, Chawley Park, Cumnor Hill, Oxford, OX2 9PH, UK
1385 Broadway, New York, NY 10018, USA
29 Earlsfort Terrace, Dublin 2, Ireland

First published in Great Britain 2021
First published in hardback, 2021
Paperback edition, 2023

A catalogue record for this book is available from the British Library.

Library of Congress Cataloging-in-Publication data

Names: Chan, Gary Kok Yew, editor. | Yip, Man, editor.

Title: AI, data and private law : translating theory into practice / edited by Gary Chan Kok Yew and Man Yip.

Other titles: Artificial intelligence, data and private law.

Description: Oxford ; New York : Hart, 2021. | Includes bibliographical references and index.

Identifiers: LCCN 2021030048 (print) | LCCN 2021030049 (ebook) | ISBN 9781509946839 (hardback) | ISBN 9781509946822 (paperback) | ISBN 9781509946853 (pdf) | ISBN 9781509946846 (Epub)

Subjects: LCSH: Data protection—Law and legislation—Asia. | Artificial intelligence—Law and legislation—Asia. | Internet—Law and legislation—Asia.

Classification: LCC KNC646 .A3 2021 (print) | LCC KNC646 (ebook) | DDC 343.509/99—dc23

LC record available at https://lccn.loc.gov/2021030048

LC ebook record available at https://lccn.loc.gov/2021030049

ISBN: PB: 978-1-50994-682-2
ePDF: 978-1-50994-685-3
ePub: 978-1-50994-684-6

Typeset by Compuscript Ltd, Shannon

TABLE OF CONTENTS

List of Contributors vii
Table of Cases ix
Table of Legislation xv

1. *AI, Data and Private Law: The Theory-Practice Interface* 1
Gary Chan Kok Yew and Man Yip

PART I
DATA PROTECTION, GOVERNANCE AND PRIVATE LAW

2. *How to De-identify Personal Data in South Korea: An Evolutionary Tale* 25
Haksoo Ko and Sangchul Park

3. *Data Trusts for Lawful AI Data Sharing* 47
Chris Reed

4. *The Future of Personal Data Protection Law in Singapore: A Role for the Use of AI and the Propertisation of Personal Data* 69
Warren Chik

5. *Personal Data as a Proprietary Resource* 91
Pey Woan Lee

6. *Transplanting the Concept of Digital Information Fiduciary?* 117
Man Yip

PART II
AI, TECHNOLOGY AND PRIVATE LAW

7. *Regulating Autonomous Vehicles, Liability Paradigms and Value Choices* 147
Chen Siyuan

8. *Medical AI, Standard of Care in Negligence and Tort Law* 173
Gary Chan Kok Yew

9. *Contractual Consent in the Age of Machine Learning* 199
Goh Yihan

10. *Digital Assets: Balancing Liquidity with Other Considerations* 225
Gal Acrich, Katia Litvak, On Dvori, Ophir Samuelov and Dov Greenbaum

11. *Blockchain in Land Administration? Overlooked Details in Translating Theory into Practice* 253
Alvin W-L See

Index 277

LIST OF CONTRIBUTORS

Gal Acrich is Research Fellow at the Zvi Meitar Institute for Legal Implications of Emerging Technologies, IDC Herzliya, Israel.

Gary Chan Kok Yew is Professor of Law at the Yong Pung How School of Law, Singapore Management University, Singapore.

Warren Chik is Associate Professor and Deputy Director of the Centre for AI and Data Governance, Yong Pung How School of Law, Singapore Management University, Singapore.

On Dvori is Research Fellow at the Zvi Meitar Institute for Legal Implications of Emerging Technologies, IDC Herzliya, Israel.

Dov Greenbaum is Professor of Law and Director of the Zvi Meitar Institute for Legal Implications of Emerging Technologies, IDC Herzliya, Israel.

Haksoo Ko is Professor at Seoul National University, South Korea.

Katia Litvak is Research Fellow at the Zvi Meitar Institute for Legal Implications of Emerging Technologies, IDC Herzliya, Israel.

Sangchul Park is Professor at Seoul National University, South Korea.

Pey Woan Lee is Professor of Law and Vice Provost (Faculty Matters) at the Yong Pung How School of Law, Singapore Management University, Singapore.

Chris Reed is Professor of Electronic Commerce Law at the Centre for Commercial Law Studies, Queen Mary University of London, UK.

Ophir Samuelov is Research Fellow at the Zvi Meitar Institute for Legal Implications of Emerging Technologies, IDC Herzliya, Israel.

Alvin See is Associate Professor of Law (Education) at the Yong Pung How School of Law, Singapore Management University, Singapore.

Chen Siyuan is Associate Professor of Law and Director (Moots) at the Yong Pung How School of Law, Singapore Management University, Singapore.

Goh Yihan is Professor of Law and the Dean of the Yong Pung How School of Law, Singapore Management University, Singapore.

Man Yip is Associate Professor of Law at the Yong Pung How School of Law, Singapore Management University, Singapore.

TABLE OF CASES

Australia

Bahr v Nicolay (No 2) (1988) 164 CLR 604 266–67
Breen v Williams (1996) 186 CLR 71 140
Dwan v Farquhar [1988] 1 Qd R 234 186
Hospital Products Pty Ltd v United States Surgical Corporation (1984) 156 CLR 42 133
Maloney v Commissioner for Railways (1978) 18 ALR 147 182
Moorgate Tobacco Co Ltd v Philip Morris Ltd (1984) 156 CLR 414 94
P & V Industries v Porto (2006) 14 VR 1 141
Rogers v Whitaker [1992] 175 CLR 479 190
Rosenberg v Percival [2001] HCA 18 182

Canada

Bergen v Sturgeon General Hospital (1984) 38 CCLT 155 186
Douez v Facebook Inc 2017 SCC 33 119
Financial Management Inc v Associated Financial Planners Ltd (2006) 367 WAC 70 133
Lac Minerals Ltd v International Corona Resources Ltd (1989) 61 DLR (4th) 14 133
McInerney v MacDonald (1992) 137 NR 35 .... 94, 100
Norberg v Wynrib [1992] 2 SCR 226 140
R v Stewart [1988] 1 SCR 963 .... 93, 99

EU

Case C-203/02 British Horseracing Board Ltd and Others v William Hill Organization Ltd Case C-203/02, 9 November 2004 [2005] RPC 260 (ECJ) 49
Case C-507/17 Google Inc v Commission nationale de l'informatique et des libertes (CNIL) (ECJ, 24 September 2019) 75, 86
Case C-131/12 Google Spain SL and Google Incorporated v Agencia Española de Protección de Datos (AEPD) and Costeja González (ECJ, 13 May 2014) 75, 85

Case C-5/08 Infopaq International A/S v Danske Dagblades Forening [2009] ECR I-6569 48

Malaysia

Ahmad Zubir bin Zahid (suing by himself and as the administrator of the estate of Fatimah bt Samat, deceased) v Datuk Dr Zainal Abidin Abdul Hamid & Ors [2019] 5 MLJ 95 190
Dr Kok Choong Seng and Sunway Medical Centre Berhad v Soo Cheng Lin [2018] 1 MLJ 685 196
Dr Hari Krishnan v Megat Noor Ishak bin Megat Ibrahim [2018] 3 MLJ 281 ....190, 194, 196
Foo Fio Na v Dr Soo Fook Mun [2007] 1 MLJ 593 ....190, 192
John Dadit v Bong Meng Chiat [2015] 1 LNS 1465 121
Kee Boon Suan and Others v Adventist Hospital & Clinical Services (M) and Others and Other Appeals [2018] 5 MLJ 321 196
Oh Hiam v Tham Kong [1980] 2 MLJ 159 267
Zulhasnimar bt Hasan Basri and Another v Dr KuppuVelumani P and Others [2017] 5 MLJ 438 190

New Zealand

Dixon v R [2015] NZSC 147 95–97
Henderson v Walker [2019] NZHC 2184 96–97
Ruscoe v Cryptopia Ltd [2020] NZHC 728 ....18–19, 96, 98
Smith v Auckland Hospital Board [1965] NZLR 191 140

Singapore

Asia Pacific Publishing Pte Ltd v Pioneers & Leaders (Publishers) Pte Ltd [2011] 4 SLR 381 48
B2C2 Ltd v Quoine Pte Ltd [2019] 4 SLR 17 98
Bakery Mart Pte Ltd (In Receivership) v Sincere Watch Ltd [2003] 3 SLR(R) 462 205
BNM v National University of Singapore [2014] 4 SLR 931 185
Centre for Laser and Aesthetic Medicine Pte Ltd v GPK Clinic (Orchard) Pte Ltd [2018] 1 SLR 180 141
Chwee Kin Keong v Digilandmallcom Pte Ltd [2005] 1 SLR(R) 502 222
Cooperatieve Centrale Raiffeisen-Boerenleenbank BA (Trading as Rabobank International), Singapore Branch v Motorola Electronics Pte Ltd [2011] 2 SLR 63 205

Global Yellow Pages Ltd v Promedia Directories Pte Ltd [2017] 2 SLR 185..........48
Grace Electrical Engineering Pte Ltd v Te Deum Engineering Pte Ltd [2018] 1 SLR 76 166
Gobinathan Devathasan v SMC [2010] 2 SLR 926 180
Hii Chii Kok v Ooi Peng Jin London Lucien [2016] 2 SLR 544 ....184, 196–97
Hii Chii Kok v Ooi Peng Jin London Lucien [2017] 2 SLR 492 ...... 181–82, 190–92
I-Admin (Singapore) Pte Ltd v Hong Ying Ting [2020] 1 SLR 1130..........98
Khoo James v Gunapathy d/o Muniandy [2002] 1 SLR(R) 1024..........179, 191–92
Lim Siong Khee v Public Prosecutor [2001] 1 SLR(R) 631..........81
My Digital Lock Pte Ltd, Re [2018] SGPDPC 3 ....121–22, 124
National University of Singapore, Re [2017] SGPDPC 5..........80
Ng Huat Seng v Munib Mohammad Madni [2017] 2 SLR 1074..........196
Noor Azlin bte Abdul Rahman v Changi General Hospital Pte Ltd and Others [2019] 1 SLR 834..........179
Ooi Han Sun v Bee Hua Meng [1991] 1 SLR(R) 922..........166
Pang Ah San v SMC [2014] 1 SLR 1094 181
Quoine Pte Ltd v B2C2 Ltd [2020] 2 SLR 20 220–23
Rathanamalah d/o Shunmugam v Chia Kok Hoong [2018] 4 SLR 159..........180
Re My Digital Lock Pte Ltd [2018] SGPDPC 3 111
Shanghai Turbo Enterprises Ltd v Liu Ming [2019] 1 SLR 779..........227
Skandinaviska Enskilda Banken AB (Publ), Singapore Branch v Asia Pacific Breweries (Singapore) Pte Ltd [2011] 3 SLR 540 194
Tan Siok Yee v Chong Voon Kee Ivan [2005] SGHC 157..........166
TV Media Pte Ltd v De Cruz Andrea Heidi [2004] 3 SLR(R) 543..........183
United Overseas Bank Ltd v Bebe bte Mohammad [2006] 4 SLR(R) 884.......... 267, 274
Vinmar Overseas (Singapore) Pte Ltd v PTT International Trading Pte Ltd [2018] 2 SLR 1271 227

South Korea

Case No 99-Heonma-513, Korean Constitutional Court, 26 May 2005..........26

UK

AA v Persons Unknown [2020] 4 WLR 35 .... 18, 98
Armstrong GmbH v Winnington Networks Ltd [2012] 3 WLR 835 269
Biffa Waste Services Ltd v Maschinenfabrik Ernst Hese GmbH [2009] QB 725..........193
Bolam v Friern Hospital Management Committee [1957] 1 WLR 582 .... 14, 178–82, 189–91

Bolitho v City and Hackney Health Authority
[1998] AC 232 .... 14, 178–82, 189–90, 192
Boardman v Phipps [1967] 2 AC 46 93
Bristol and West Building Society v Mothew [1998] Ch 1 .... 133, 138
British Horseracing Board Ltd and Others v William Hill Organization Ltd
[2001] EWHC 516 (Pat) (High Court) 49
British Horseracing Board Ltd and Others v William Hill Organization Ltd
[2001] EWCA Civ 1268 (CA) 49
The British Horseracing Board Ltd v William Hill Organisation Ltd [2005]
EWCA Civ 863 49
Bumper Development Corp Ltd v Metropolitan Police Commissioner
[1991] 1 WLR 1362 21
Campbell v MGN [2004] 2 AC 457 121
Carlill v Carbolic Smoke Ball Company [1893] 1 QB 256 211
Cassidy v Ministry of Health [1951] 2 KB 343 .... 194, 196
Computer Associates UK Ltd v The Software Incubator Ltd [2018] FSR 25 97
Crawford v Charing Cross Hospital, The Times, 8 December 1953 186
De Freitas v O'Brien and Connolly [1995] 6 Med LR 108 179
Donoghue v Stevenson [1932] UKHL 100 198
Douglas v Hello! Ltd (No 3) [2006] QB 125 121
English v Dedham Vale Properties Ltd [1978] 1 WLR 93 131
Fairstar Heavy Transport NV v Adkins [2012] EWHC 2952 .... 94, 100
Fairstar Heavy Transport NV v Philip Jeffrey Adkins, Claranet Ltd
[2014] FSR 8 94
Farraj v King's Healthcare NHS Trust [2010] 1 WLR (CA) 2139 196
First Energy UK Ltd v Hungarian International Bank
[1993] 2 Lloyd's Rep 194 217
Force India Formula One Team Ltd v 1 Malaysia Racing Team Sdn Bhd
[2010] RPC 757 93
Frazer v Walker [1967] 1 AC 569 267
GHLM Trading Ltd v Maroo [2012] EWHC 61 (Ch) 141
Gold v Essex County Council [1942] 2 KB 293 194
Hely-Hutchinson v Brayhead Ltd [1968] 1 QB 549 217
Hepworth v Kerr [1995] 6 Med LR 139 180
Hunter v Hanley [1955] SLT 213 178
Imerman v Tchenguiz [2011] Fam 116 121
Item Software (UK) Ltd v Fassihi [2004] EWCA Civ 1244 141
Maple Leaf Macro Volatility Master Fund v Rouvroy [2009] EWHC 257 220
McKennitt v Ash [2008] QB 73 121
Meridian Global Funds Management Asia Ltd v Securities Commission
[1995] 2 AC 500 21
Montgomery v Lanarkshire Health Board [2015] UKSC 11 190
Morgans v Launchbury [1973] AC 127 193

Mosley v News Group Newspapers [2008] EWHC 1777 121–23
Murray v Big Pictures (UK) Ltd [2009] Ch 481 121
National Provincial Bank Ltd v Ainsworth [1965] AC 1175 .... 18, 83, 254
Naylor v Preston Health Authority [1987] 1 WLR 958 141
OBG Ltd v Allan [2008] 1 AC 1 123
ODL Securities Ltd v McGrath [2013] EWHC 1865 (Comm) 141
One Step (Support) Ltd v Morris-Garner [2018] 2 WLR 1353 95–96
Oxford v Moss [1978] 68 Cr App 183 .... 58, 93
Phillips v News Group Newspapers Ltd [2013] 1 AC 1 93
R v Department of Health [2001] QB 423 93
R v Mid-Glamorgan FHSA ex parte Martin [1993] PIQR 426 139
Regina (Veolia ES Nottinghamshire Ltd) v Nottinghamshire County Council [2012] PTSR 185 94
Richard Lloyd v Google LLC [2018] EWHC 2599 95
Richard Lloyd v Google LLC [2019] EWCA Civ 1599 .... 94–95, 112
Roe v Minister of Health [1954] 2 QB 66 178
SAS Institute Inc v World Programming Ltd [2013] EWCA Civ 1482 48
Sidaway v Bethlem Royal Hospital Governors [1985] AC 871 139
Smith v Salford HA [1994] 5 Med LR 321 186
St Albans City and District Council v International Computers Ltd [1996] 4 All ER 481 97
Stupples v Stupples & Co (High Wycombe) Ltd [2012] EWHC 1226 (Ch) 141
Thompson v Smiths Shipbuilders (North Shields) Ltd [1984] QB 405 185
Toyota Motor Corp Unintended Acceleration Marketing, Sales Practices, and Products Liability Litigation, In Re [2013] WL 5763178 166
Vidal-Hall v Google Inc [2015] EWCA Civ 311 121
Your Response Ltd v Datateam Business Media Ltd [2014] 3 WLR 887 93
Wainwright v Home Office [2004] 2 AC 406 121
Woodland v Swimming Teachers Association and Others [2013] 3 WLR 1227 .... 196, 198

US

Ajemian v Yahoo!, Inc, 83 Mass App Ct 565, 987 NE 2d 604 (App Ct 2013) 235
Ajemian v Yahoo!, Inc, 478 Mass 169, 84 NE 3d 766, 171 (2017) 235
Atlantic Marine Construction Co v US Dist Court for W Dist of Tex, 571 US 49 (2013) 227
Brittain v Twitter, Inc, No 19-cv-00114-YGR (ND Cal Mar 15, 2019) 228
Ellsworth, In Re (No 2005-296, 651-DE, Mich Prob Ct 2005) 235
Facebook, Inc, In Re, 923 F Supp 2d 1204 (ND Cal 2012) 239
Feist Publications, Inc v Rural Telephone Service Co, 499 US 340, 111 S Ct 1282, 113 L Ed 2d 358 (1991) 244

Frederick Hsu Living Trust v ODN Holding Corp, No 12108-VCL 2017 WL 1437308 at 17 (Del Ch Apr 24, 2017) 129
Haelen Laboratories v Topps Chewing Gum, Inc 202 F 2d 866 (2nd Cir, 1953)....78
Heidbreder v Epic Games, Inc, No 19-348 (EDNC Feb 3, 2020)....227
Johnson v Kokemoor 545 NW2d 495, 498 (Wis 1996)....191
Lerman v Chuckleberry Pub Inc 521 F Supp 228 (1981)....78
M/S Bremen v Zapata Off-Shore Co, 407 US 1, 10 (1972)....227
Moore v Regents of the University of California (1990) 793 P 2d 479....140
Scherk v Alberto-Culver Co, 417 US 506 (1974)....227
Sorrell v IMS Health, Inc et al, 131 S Ct 2653, (2011)....93
Sunrise Medical HHG, Inc v Health Focus of NY, 278 F App'x 80, 81 (2d Cir 2008)....227
The Bremen v Zapata Off-Shore Co, 407 US 1 (1972)....227
The TJ Hooper 60 F 2d 737 (2d Cir 1932)....185
Thyroff v Nationwide Mutual Insurance Co 8 NY 3d 283 (NY 2007)....96
We are the People Inc v Facebook 19-CV-8871 (2020)....227
Zacchini v Scripps-Howard Broadcasting 433 US 562 (1977)....78

TABLE OF LEGISLATION

Australia

Real Property Act 1858 (South Australia)....................266

EU

Council Directive (EC) 85/374 on the approximation of the laws, regulations and administrative provisions of the Member States concerning liability for defective products [1985] OJ L210/29....................162–64, 168

Directive 96/9 on the legal protection of databases, OJ L77/20 27 March 1996....................49

Directive 1999/93/EC on a Community framework for electronic signatures [2000] OJ L13/12....................55

Directive 2000/46/EC of the European Parliament and of the Council on the taking up, pursuit of and prudential supervision of the business of electronic money institutions, [2000] OJ L275/39....................54–55

Directive 2009/110/EC of the European Parliament and of the Council of 16 September 2009 on the taking up, pursuit and prudential supervision of the business of electronic money institutions amending Directives 2005/60/EC and 2006/48/EC and repealing Directive 2000/46/EC, [2009] OJ L267/7....................55

Payment Services Directive (Directive 2007/64/EC of the European Parliament and of the Council on payment services in the internal market amending Directives 97/7/EC, 2002/65/EC, 2005/60/EC and 2006/48/EC and repealing Directive 97/5/EC, [2007] OJ L319/1....................55

Regulation (EU) No 2016/679 of the European Parliament and of the Council of 27 April 2016 on the protection of natural persons with regard to the processing of personal data and on the free movement of such data, and repealing Directive 95/46/EC, [2016] OJ L119/1....................10, 26, 29–31, 34–38, 40, 44, 53–54, 64–67, 72–75, 79–81, 84–87, 91, 108–09, 112, 114, 121, 125, 134, 136–39, 142, 164

Regulation (EU) No 910/2014 of the European Parliament and of the Council of 23 July 2014 on electronic identification and trust services for electronic transactions in the internal market and repealing Directive 1999/93/EC, [2014] OJ L257/73 55
Regulation (EU) 2016/679 of 27 April 2016 on the protection of natural persons with regard to the processing of personal data and on the free movement of such data, and repealing Directive 95/46/EC [2016] OJ L119/1 164

India

Land Titling Bill 2011 .... 262, 266–67
Transfer of Property Act 1882 260–61
Rajasthan Urban Land (Certificate of Titles) Act 2016 262
Registration Act 1908 260

Malaysia

Personal Data Protection Act 2010 .... 122, 124, 137

New Zealand

Crimes Act 1961 96

People's Republic of China

General Provisions of the Civil Law of the People's Republic of China 232

Philippines

Data Privacy Act 2012, Republic Act No 10173 86

Singapore

Business Trusts Act 2005 (Cap 31A, Rev Ed 2005) 58–59
Civil Law (Amendment) Bill No 33/2020 189
Computer Misuse Act (Cap 50A, 2007 Rev Ed) 71, 80–82, 88
Copyright Act (Cap 63, 2006 Rev Ed) 78, 80

Criminal Law Reform Act 2019 82
Health Products Act (Cap 122D, 2008 Rev Ed) 183
Health Products (Medical Devices) Regulations 2010 183
Land Titles Act (Cap 157, 2004 Rev Ed) 267, 274
Land Titles Ordinance (No 21 of 1956)....................267, 273
Personal Data Protection Act 2012 ....8, 71, 73, 86, 91, 106–10, 123–24, 137
Protection from Harassment Act (Cap 256A)....................79
Road Traffic Act (Cap 276, 2004 Rev Ed)....................150–51
Road Traffic (Amendment) Act 2017 (Bill 10 of 2017) 150
Road Traffic (Autonomous Motor Vehicles) Rules 2017....................150

South Korea

Act on the Promotion of Information and Communications Network Utilization and Information Protection, Act No 16955 25
Act on the Protection and Utilization of Credit Information, Act No 16957 ....25–29, 31, 34–35, 37–41
Act on the Protection and Utilization of Location Information, Act No 17347 27–29
Bioethics and Safety Act, Act No 17472 ....27, 42
Contagious Disease Prevention and Control Act, Act No 17491 ....27, 43
Enforcement Decree for the Credit Information Act, Presidential Decree No 30893 41
Enforcement Decree for the Personal Information Protection Act, Presidential Decree No 30892 ....37, 41
Personal Information Protection Act, Act No 16930 ....25–32, 34–43

UK

Automated and Electric Vehicles Act 2018....................13, 20, 149, 159–61, 169, 171

US

California Code, Civil Code – CIV s 33441....................236
Federal Stored Communications Act....................235
Fiduciary Access to Digital Assets Act 238
Internal Revenue Code....................248
Revised Uniform Fiduciary Access to Digital Assets Act (Act 72 of 2020) (July 23, 2020)....................16, 238, 252
Securities Exchange Act of 1934....................241

1

AI, Data and Private Law

The Theory-Practice Interface

GARY CHAN KOK YEW AND MAN YIP*

I. Introduction

The growing importance of artificial intelligence (AI) and big data in modern society, and the potential for their misuse as a tool for irresponsible profit[1] call for a constructive conversation on how the law should direct the development and use of technology. This collection of chapters, drawn from the Conference on 'AI and Commercial Law: Reimagining Trust, Governance, and Private Law Rules',[2] examines the interconnected themes of AI, data protection and governance, and the disruption to or innovation in private law principles.[3] This collection makes two contributions. First, it shows that private law is a crucial sphere within which that conversation takes place. To borrow from the extra-judicial comments of Justice Cuéllar of the Supreme Court of California, private law 'provides a kind of first-draft regulatory framework – however imperfect – for managing new technologies ranging from aviation to email'.[4] As this collection demonstrates, private law furnishes a first draft regulatory framework by directly applying or gently extending existing private law theory, concepts and doctrines to new technological

* This research is supported by the National Research Foundation, Singapore under its Emerging Areas Research Projects (EARP) Funding Initiative. Any opinions, findings and conclusions or recommendations expressed in this material are those of the authors and do not reflect the views of National Research Foundation, Singapore.

[1] F Pasquale, 'Data-Informed Duties in AI Development' (2019) 119 *Columbia Law Review* 1917, 1918.

[2] This conference, which was organised by the Centre for AI and Data Governance (CAIDG), was held at the School of Law of Singapore Management University on 5–6 December 2019.

[3] In this collection, 'private law' and 'private law principles' are widely defined and principally comprise the law of torts, contract law, property law, the principles of equity and trusts, and the law of succession. Further, reference to private law or private law principles in this volume, unless otherwise stated, generally refers to the private law principles developed in case law.

[4] M Cuéllar, 'A Common Law for the Age of Artificial Intelligence: Incremental Adjudication, Institutions and Relational Non-arbitrariness' (2019) 119 *Columbia Law Review* 1773, 1780. In this article, Justice Cuéllar used the term 'common law', which comprises private law doctrines of contract law, tort law, property law, etc.

phenomena and, more markedly at times, by creating new principles or inspiring a new regulatory concept. This is not to say that private law is superior to or replaces legislation. This collection asks that we consider more deeply the potential and limits of private law regulation of AI and data use, as well as its co-existence and interface with legislations.

Second, the chapters, individually and/or collectively, explore existing legal frameworks and innovative proposals from a 'theory meets practice' angle. They offer insights into the challenges of translating theory, doctrines and concepts to practice. Some of these challenges may arise from a general disconnect between a proposed theory, concept and doctrine on the one hand, and the practical reality on the other. For example, is the proposed solution consistent with the pre-existing legislative regime, whether it amounts to a regulatory overkill and therefore is inimical to innovation, and whether it is conceived based on a full appreciation of the technical aspects of the underlying technology? Other challenges may arise from the inherent limits of existing theories, doctrines and concepts which were developed for non-technological or non-big data phenomena. For instance, is the existing private law doctrine sufficient to deal with the new legal issues (most notably, the absence or remoteness of human involvement) brought to the fore by technological developments? In taking this 'theory meets practice' line of inquiry, the chapters adopt a degree of comparative focus on selected jurisdictions in the Asia-Pacific region, with the aim of capturing some of the unique challenges confronting countries in this part of the world in terms of practical implementation.

II. AI, Big Data and Trust

In order to enable a meaningful conversation on how private law can and should direct AI and big data developments, we must first unpack what these labels mean in theory and in practice, as well as highlight the important theme of building trust in the use of new technologies and data.

A. Artificial Intelligence

The term 'AI' does not lend itself to a singular monolithic definition. Broadly speaking, AI refers to the use of machines to imitate the ability of humans to think, make decisions or perform actions.[5] The definition of AI proposed by the European Commission further highlights as follows:

> AI-based systems can be purely software-based, acting in the virtual world (e.g. voice assistants, image analysis software, search engines, speech and face recognition systems)

[5] See T Rothkegel, 'What Characterises Artificial Intelligence and How Does it Work?' (2016) 22 *Computer and Telecommunications Law Review* 98; Infocomm Media Development Authority, 'Artificial Intelligence' (9 December 2020), www.imda.gov.sg/infocomm-media-landscape/SGDigital/tech-pillars/Artificial-Intelligence.

> or AI can be embedded in hardware devices (e.g. advanced robots, autonomous cars, drones or Internet of Things applications).[6]

Given the above broad understanding of AI, we propose to discuss AI from three interrelated perspectives. The first focuses on AI as a means (or technology) to achieve certain goals. In this regard, AI may refer to the technologies that produce outputs or decision-making models, such as predictions or recommendations from AI algorithms, together with computer power and data.[7]

Second, the term invites comparisons with humans and human intelligence in the achievement of certain goals. AI technologies may thus involve the simulation of human traits such as knowledge, reasoning, problem solving, perception, learning and planning in order to produce the output or decision.[8] Examples of these human traits are evident in machine learning, deep learning, computer vision and natural language processing. The Turing test[9] requires AI to 'act humanly' so as to fool a human interrogator into thinking it is human. Russell and Norvig's 'rational agent' approach[10] is premised on AI acting rationally in order to achieve the 'best outcome or, when there is uncertainty, the best expected outcome'.

AI has improved significantly in terms of its efficiency and speed of analysis, capacity to read and decipher patterns from voluminous documents and images, and enhanced reliability and accuracy in generating outputs. In many respects, it is becoming superior to humans in performing specific tasks, even though it is not error-free. Clarke[11] refers to the concept of 'intellectics' that goes beyond 'machines that think' to 'computers that do' in which artefacts 'take autonomous action in the real world'.

Third, AI may be defined in part at least by how it interacts with humans. Implicit in the first and second perspectives of AI is the human–AI interface that we should not overlook. Clarke conceives of AI as 'Complementary Artefact Intelligence' that '(1) does things well that humans do poorly or cannot do at all; (2) performs functions within systems that include both humans and artefacts; and (3) interfaces effectively, efficiently and adaptably with both humans and artefacts'.[12] Indeed, AI technologies such as self-driving vehicles, medical treatment, self-performing contracts and AI-driven management of digital assets exhibit human traits in their interactions with humans, generating practical consequences in the real world. The human-like aspect of AI invites debates as to whether AI should be attributed personhood for liability, and the better-than-human performance of AI prompts

[6] 'Communication from the Commission to the European Parliament, the European Council, the Council, the European Economic and Social Committee and the Committee of the Regions on Artificial Intelligence for Europe, Brussels' COM (2018) 237 final, 25 April 2018.

[7] See European Commission, 'White Paper on Artificial Intelligence: A European Approach to Excellence and Trust' (19 February 2020) 2; Infocomm Media Development Authority and Personal Data Protection Commission, *Model Artificial Intelligence Governance Framework*, 2nd edn (2020) 21.

[8] Infocomm Media Development Authority and Personal Data Protection Commission (n 7) 21.

[9] A Turing, 'Computing Machinery and Intelligence' (1950) LIX(236) *Mind* 433.

[10] S Russell and P Norvig, *Artificial Intelligence: A Modern Approach*, 3rd edn (Prentice Hall, 2010) 4–5.

[11] R Clarke, 'Why the World Wants Controls over Artificial Intelligence' (2019) 35 *Computer Law & Security Review* 423, 430.

[12] ibid.

us to assess whether standards and liability rules should differ where intelligent machines are used.

As AI continues to evolve in terms of its functions and advances in its capabilities, its role in society will become more pervasive. This gives rise to the question as to whether humans can trust AI. For example, it has been reported that machine-learning algorithms (most notably, face recognition technologies) have racial, gender and age biases.[13] The complexity, unexplainability and incomprehensibility of AI is also emerging as a key reason why people do not trust AI decisions or recommendations.[14] Building trust is thus a priority agenda for AI innovation and regulation going forward.

B. Big Data

The proliferation of data is a global phenomenon. Information on citizens is constantly collected by organisations through websites, mobile phones, smart watches, virtual personal assistants, drones, face recognition technologies, etc.[15] The term 'big data' refers to very large datasets that are often complex, varied and generated at a rapid speed.[16] As the McKinsey Global Institute Report on 'Big Data: The Next Frontier for Innovation, Competition, and Productivity' points out: 'The use of big data will become a key basis of competition and growth for individual firms.'[17] Information is value in itself. Big data in particular creates tremendous value because it is an enormous volume of information from which new insights can be drawn. The McKinsey Report highlights that big data creates value in various ways: it creates informational transparency; enables experimentation to discover needs, exposes performance variability and improves performance; allows segmentation of the population to customise actions (eg, for interest-based advertising); substitutes/supports human decision-making with automated algorithms; and facilitates the invention of new business models, products and services or the enhancement of existing ones.[18] In this connection, the reciprocal relationship between data and AI should not be missed. The value in big data is unlocked by AI, which provides us with the capability to analyse these enormous datasets to

[13] BBC, 'Facial Recognition to "Predict Criminals" Sparks Row over AI Bias' (24 June 2020), www.bbc.com/news/technology-53165286.

[14] PwC, 'AI and Trust: What Businesses Fear about AI – and How to Trust it' (2019), http://explore.pwc.com/c/pw-c-2019-artificial-2?eq=CT13-PL1300-DM2-CN_ai2019-ai19-info foot&utm_campaign=ai2019&utm_medium=org&utm_source=pwc_ai2019&x=ae-asK. These qualities of AI make it difficult for people to control the AI or to assess the quality of the AI output.

[15] See a detailed discussion on this in P Keller and S Ross, 'Risks in AI over the Collection and Transmission of Data' (2018) 1 *Journal of Robotics, Artificial Intelligence & Law* 161.

[16] See, for example, J Gurin, 'Big Data and Open Data: How Open Will the Future Be?' (2015) 10 *Journal of Law and Policy for the Information Society* 691.

[17] J Manyika et al, 'Big Data: The Next Frontier for Innovation, Competition, and Productivity' (1 May 2011), www.mckinsey.com/business-functions/mckinsey-digital/our-insights/big-data-the-next-frontier-for-innovation (hereinafter 'McKinsey Report').

[18] ibid 5–6.

derive trends and patterns more quickly or in a way that was not possible before. The input of data to AI technologies improves the latter's performance; in other words, the technology gets better with more data.

Nevertheless, the concentration of data in the hands of corporate titans raised deep suspicions as to how the consumers' data is being collected and used by such corporations. In fact, data scandals involving tech giants (such as Google and Facebook) have dampened public confidence and trust in companies.[19] More recently, contact tracing technological applications created to monitor and control the COVID-19 virus outbreak have also sparked privacy concerns as these applications enable governments to gain control over citizens' location-based data and biometric data.[20]

Clear lines of tension have thus developed in the context of data: the tension between privacy/data protection[21] and economic value; the tension between privacy/data protection and innovation; the tension between privacy/data protection and public health; and the tension between business facilitation and consumer protection. How should the law balance between these competing concerns? How does the law catch up with the pace of technological developments and business model transformations? And, most importantly, how can the law help to restore public trust and confidence in companies and governments?[22]

C. Trust

Trust is a multi-faceted concept. It involves a relation importing some risk to or vulnerability of the trustor who nonetheless chooses to place trust in the

[19] NBC News, 'Trust in Facebook Has Dropped by 66 Percent since the Cambridge Analytica Scandal' (19 April 2018), www.nbcnews.com/business/consumer/trust-facebook-has-dropped-51-percent-cambridge-analytica-scandal-n867011.

[20] Organisation for Economic Co-operation and Development, 'Tracking and Tracing COVID: Protecting Privacy and Data While Using Apps and Biometrics' (23 April 2020), www.oecd.org/coronavirus/policy-responses/tracking-and-tracing-covid-protecting-privacy-and-data-while-using-apps-and-biometrics-8f394636. In Singapore, the 'TraceTogether' contact tracing app stirred controversy when it was discovered that the data collected by the app could be used by the police for criminal investigations. The Singapore government, in response, will be passing a law to formalise assurances that the data can only be used by police for the investigation of serious crimes, including murder, terrorism and rape (see *Straits Times*, 'S'pore Govt to Pass Law to Ensure TraceTogether Data Can Be Used Only for Serious Crimes' (9 January 2021), www.straitstimes.com/singapore/legislation-to-be-passed-to-ensure-tracetogether-data-can-only-be-used-for-serious-crimes).

[21] Privacy and data protection are different concepts: the former is concerned with the right/ability to be left alone, while the latter is concerned with protecting one's personal data from illegal collection and use by others. The two concepts overlap significantly in the age of AI as '[t]he uncontrolled use of AI to process data will invade the most intimate parts of our personal life' (see R Genderen, 'Privacy and Data Protection in the Age of Pervasive Technologies in AI and Robotics' (2017) 3 *European Data Protection Law Review* 338, 342).

[22] In a 2014 survey involving 900 people in five countries (the US, the UK, Germany, China and India), it was found that 97 per cent of people surveyed 'expressed concern that businesses and the government might misuse their data': see 'Customer Data: Designing for Transparency and Trust' *Harvard Business Review* (May 2015).

trustee. The bases of trust are varied: the trustor's rational self-interests and goals (cognitive),[23] emotions and attitudes towards the trustee (affective) and socio-normative considerations.[24] From a stakeholder perspective, trust may be reposed in an individual or organisation such as the AI developer or user, the technology itself, the socio-technical systems,[25] and social and legal institutions, including the government. The trustor–trustee relationship may be reciprocal, though not necessarily so (eg, humans placing trust in AI, but not the reverse).[26] Serious deviations or aberrations can occur, resulting in trust being inadequate or absent (distrust), abused by the trustee (mistrust) or so excessive as to cause the trustor to be exploited (over-trust).

On a practical level, trust may be regarded as a 'process'[27] encompassing multiple 'trusting' concepts (eg, trusting dispositions, attitudes, beliefs, expectations and behaviours), and their commonalities and differences. The level of human trust in AI is mediated by a myriad of factors: the personal characteristics of the trustor, knowledge of the technology[28] and its potential errors,[29] and perceptions of the positive or negative attributes of the technology.[30] Furthermore, trust in the technology alone may not be adequate without considering trust in the innovating firm and its communication to third parties. This 'dichotomous constitution of trust in applied AI'[31] is also tied to the ideas and practices of stakeholder alignment, transparency and proactive communication. According to the 2019 Edelman AI survey, which compiled responses from 1,000 members

[23] M Taddeo, 'Modeling Trust in Artificial Agents: A First Step toward the Analysis of E-trust' (2010) 29(2) *Mind and Machines* 243.

[24] M Tuomela and S Hofmann, 'Simulating Rational Social Normative Trust, Predictive Trust, and Predictive Reliance between Agents' (2003) 5 *Ethics of Information Technology* 163.

[25] European Commission's High-Level Expert Group on AI (HLEG), 'Ethics Guidelines for Trustworthy AI' (8 April 2019) 5.

[26] See M Ryan, 'In AI We Trust: Ethics, Artificial Intelligence, and Reliability' (2020) 26 *Science and Engineering Ethics* 2749 (that trust in AI is a form of reliance instead of trust because it only covers rational trust, but not the affective and normative accounts of trust).

[27] LM PytlikZillig and CD Kimbrough, 'Consensus on Conceptualizations and Definitions of Trust: Are We There Yet?' in E Shockley et al (eds), *Interdisciplinary Perspectives on Trust* (Springer International Publishing Switzerland, 2016) 17–47.

[28] T Araujo, N Helberger, S Kruikemeier and CH de Vrees, 'In AI We Trust? Perceptions about Automated Decision-Making by Artificial Intelligence' (2020) 35 *AI & Society* 611, https://doi.org/10.1007/s00146-019-00931-w (finding that people with more knowledge were more optimistic about automated decision-making when it comes to its usefulness, whereas knowledge mattered less for perceptions of fairness or of risk (at 618)).

[29] MT Dzindolet, SA Peterson, RA Pomranky, LG Pierce and HP Beck, 'The Role of Trust in Automation Reliance' (2003) *International Journal of Human-Computer Studies* 697 (knowledge as to why the automation might lead to errors increases trust and automation reliance).

[30] The people's trust in relation to interpretable Machine Learning was affected by the stated accuracy as well as observed accuracy (M Yin, JW Vaughan and H Wallach, 'Understanding the Effect of Accuracy on Trust in Machine Learning Models' CHI 2019, 4–9 May, Glasgow, UK, https://dl.acm.org/doi/10.1145/3290605.3300509.

[31] M Hengstler, E Enkel and S Duelli, 'Applied Artificial Intelligence and Trust: The Case of Autonomous Vehicles and Medical Assistance Devices' (2016) 105(c) *Technological Forecasting & Social Change* 105.

of the US general population and 300 technology executives, over 70 per cent of respondents in both groups took the view that technology companies have an obligation to use AI to improve societies.[32] Also, over 70 per cent of respondents in both groups were concerned that the technology companies were not spending sufficient time contemplating the long-term AI consequences.[33]

As for trust in data collection and use, according to an online survey conducted by Wakefield Research in early 2020, which gathered responses from 5,000 adults across six countries (Australia, Germany, Japan, New Zealand, the UK and the US), the institutions which consumers trust most with their data are banks (48 per cent), healthcare providers (40 per cent) and government agencies (39 per cent).[34] Social media companies (48 per cent), cryptocurrency providers (23 per cent) and smart-home device companies (23 per cent) emerged as the least trustworthy organisations in this survey. It has been proposed that companies should be transparent about the exchange in order to build consumer trust – that is, companies should be proactive to communicate to consumers what data is being collected and used for what purposes.[35] Such communication should go beyond clear stipulation in disclosures and end-user licensing agreements for regulatory compliance, and could take the form of more proactive public education.[36] Studies have also revealed that consumer data that is being collected for improving services and products would generally be considered a fair trade by the consumers.[37] On the other hand, where consumer data is collected for targeted advertising/marketing and for generating profits for the company through the sale of data to third parties, consumers would expect more value in return for such trades.

The role of the wider community and the institutional framework must be borne in mind in the preservation of trust in the AI and data ecosystem. Studies have been conducted on trust in democracy[38] and its contributions to democratic governance.[39] Trust in the government may depend on the trustworthiness of its agents and the knowledge of the citizens about such trustworthiness.[40] The building of social trust and trust in the government can take root and find expression in a nation's policy to the extent that the latter respects certain cultural values and rights (eg, through information security, transparency in AI literacy education

[32] See *2019 Edelman AI Survey* (March 2019), 30: https://www.edelman.com/sites/g/files/aatuss191/files/2019-03/2019_Edelman_AI_Survey_Whitepaper.pdf.

[33] See ibid.

[34] PR Newswire, 'Survey Shows Banks, Healthcare Providers and Government Remain Most Trusted by Consumers, Despite Lack of Transparency and Data Security Breaches' (11 June 2020), https://www.prnewswire.com/news-releases/survey-shows-banks-healthcare-providers-and-government-remain-most-trusted-by-consumers-despite-lack-of-transparency-and-data-security-breaches-301074053.html.

[35] 'Customer Data: Designing for Transparency and Trust' *Harvard Business Review* (May 2015).

[36] ibid.

[37] ibid.

[38] G Brennan, 'Democratic Trust: A Rational-Choice Theory View' in V Braithwaite and M Levi (eds) *Trust and Governance* (Russell Sage Foundation, 2003) 197–217.

[39] TR Tyler, 'Trust and Democratic Governance' in Braithwaite and Levi (n 38) 269–94.

[40] R Hardin, 'Trust in Government' in Braithwaite and Levi (n 38) 9–27, 12.

and clear algorithmic decision-making, and openness through data trusts).[41] With a commitment to rationality, consistency and justice as its defining characteristics, the law can generate positive effects on cognitive and social trust by building social and not merely financial capital.[42] As we will see below, private laws play an important role in enabling and maintaining public trust through the protection of personal data, the institution of data trusts and the implementation of blockchains.

III. Data Protection, Governance and Private Law

Part I of this volume, 'Data Protection, Governance and Private Law', consists of five chapters addressing the theme of data protection and governance innovation. All five chapters speak to the theme of finding the balance between ensuring data protection on the one hand and promoting the beneficial utilisation of personal data on the other, through a detailed analysis of the existing or proposed legal approach and its practical implications. All chapters recognise that personal data, if used and managed responsibly, can generate massive economic, intellectual or public benefits. In particular, the sharing of datasets between data controllers can yield valuable insights which would not be available if the datasets were analysed separately on their own. Reed's chapter on 'Data Trusts for Lawful AI Data Sharing' (Chapter 3) discusses how to facilitate lawful and responsible data sharing.

More generally, the responsible use and management of data is not necessarily based on or ensured by obtaining data subjects' consent. To rely solely on the principle of consent is to place too onerous a burden on data subjects to look out for their own interests, given their position of informational disadvantage and inferior bargaining power. And in practice, it is difficult to ensure that a data subject's consent to collection and use of his or her personal data is informed, voluntary and meaningful.[43] A data subject's personal data (and his or her privacy) can still be adequately protected if proper safeguards are introduced. Ko and Park's contribution on 'How to De-identify Personal Data in South Korea: An Evolutionary Tale' (Chapter 2) discusses the Korean concept of data pseudonymisation, which allows pseudonymised data to be processed, in the absence of data subjects' consent, for archiving, scientific research or statistical purposes.

Significantly, all five chapters, for different reasons and commenting on different contexts, acknowledge the insufficiency and/or inadequacy of legislative

[41] SC Robinson, 'Trust, Transparency, and Openness: How Inclusion of Cultural Values Shapes Nordic National Public Policy Strategies for Artificial Intelligence (AI)' (2020) 63 *Technology in Society* 101421.

[42] FB Cross, 'Law and Trust' (2005) 93 *Georgetown Law Journal* 5.

[43] See BW Shermer et al, 'The Crisis of Consent: How Stronger Legal Protection May Lead to Weaker Consent in Data Protection' (2014) 16 *Ethics and Information Technology* 171, 176–79; M Yip, 'Personal Data Protection Act 2012: Understanding the Consent Obligation' [2017] *Personal Data Protection Digest* 266.

regulation. Reed argues in Chapter 3 that data sharing may be better governed by 'private sector' regulation through the mechanism of a data trust, instead of a formal and general legislative system which may result in over-regulation and under-regulation, fits poorly with the different data-sharing instances and is generally incapable of adapting quickly to new developments. In Chapter 2, Ko and Park point out that there are clear gaps in the recent legislative amendments that introduced the Korean regime for data pseudonymisation. Of the five chapters, four consider the value (if any) of borrowing/introducing private law concepts to enhance data protection. Reed's chapter on data trusts as a facilitative vehicle for lawful data sharing recommends against using the traditional trust as the underlying legal form, principally on the basis that information is not regarded as 'property' at common law.[44] Nevertheless, the equitable concept of trust has clearly inspired the concept of data trust (based on whichever other legal form), which is underlined by the idea of using an independent, third-party data steward to manage the datasets pooled together from different data controllers. Taking a contrary stand to Reed, Chik in Chapter 4, 'The Future of Personal Data Protection Law in Singapore: A Role for the Use of AI and the Propertisation of Personal Data', and Lee in Chapter 5, 'Personal Data as a Proprietary Resource', propose regulating personal data as property.[45] Chik and Lee, proceeding from different perspectives, argue that data can be treated as property[46] and that this proprietary characterisation can enhance the level of data protection.[47] Finally, in Chapter 6, 'Transplanting the Concept of Digital Information Fiduciary?', Yip explores the feasibility of transplanting the concept of 'information fiduciary', championed by US scholars, to regulate digital businesses' collection and use of consumer data in Asian common law jurisdictions such as Singapore and Malaysia, which generally apply the English doctrine of fiduciary law. The chapters by Chik, Lee and Yip plainly demonstrate that the common law concepts of property and fiduciary are sufficiently flexible to enable their application to new contexts. Indeed, the common law concept of property has been described as 'messy' and 'ambiguous', with its meaning changing depending on the context.[48]

To varying degrees, all five chapters adopt a comparative focus. In part, this is because any serious discussion of data protection and governance, even

[44] *cf* J Lau, J Penner and B Wong, 'The Basics of Private and Public Data Trusts' (2020) 1 *Singapore Journal of Legal Studies* 90.

[45] They are not alone in their views: see, for example, J Ritter and A Mayer, 'Regulating Data as Property. A New Construct for Moving Forward' (2018) 16 *Duke Law & Technology Review* 220. *cf* Law Reform Committee, Singapore Academy of Law, 'Report on Rethinking Database Rights and Data Ownership in an AI World' (July 2020), www.sal.org.sg/sites/default/files/SAL-LawReform-Pdf/2020-09/2020%20Rethinking%20Database%20Rights%20and%20Data%20Ownership%20in%20an%20AI%20World_ebook_0_1.pdf, [3.34]–[3.36].

[46] cf ibid.

[47] In ch 4 of this volume, Chik also argues that AI can be utilised to manage and protect personal data, for example, through developing privacy by design AI models.

[48] K Low, 'Trusts of Cryptoassets' (2021) 34(4) *Trust Law International* 191. *cf* PW Lee, 'Inducing Breach of Contract, Conversion and Contract as Property' (2009) 29 *Oxford Journal of Legal Studies* 511.

in relation to the domestic laws of a non-European Union (EU) Member State, would entail some reference to the General Data Protection Regulation (GDPR), which provides a harmonised and robust framework for data protection across the EU Member States. The GDPR is touted as the 'new global digital gold standard' for data protection and prescribes many obligations/rights which are adopted/adapted in other jurisdictions.[49] The GDPR implementation experience also provides a useful reference for other jurisdictions.[50] Ko and Park's chapter on data pseudonymisation in Korea highlights that the Korean concept of data pseudonymisation was inspired by the provisions of the GDPR, but appears to differ from the European concept in some important ways. Reed's chapter on data sharing through data trusts examines how law and regulation in both the EU and Singapore will affect the operation of data trusts. Chik and Lee's respective chapters on enhancing data protection through data propertisation, whilst anchoring their analysis in the Singaporean context, make reference to the GDPR for further support that the concept of treating data as property is consistent with the data protection legislative regime. Yip's chapter on the transplant of the concept of information fiduciary draws heavily from American literature, given the origin of concept, but still makes some reference to the GDPR in posing the wider question as to whether legislative regulation is the best and only way forward. The comparative reference to the GDPR in these chapters also exposes the weaknesses/disadvantages of the EU approach to data protection. Hence, whilst the GDPR is certainly an international benchmark and the source of inspiration for the data protection laws of many jurisdictions, it is not necessarily the best or only sensible legislative approach.

Finally and most importantly, these chapters on data protection bring to the fore the challenges of translating theory into practice and discuss how these challenges may be overcome. On data pseudonymisation, Ko and Park in Chapter 2 highlight that the relevant pieces of Korean legislation fail to deal with the multitude of scenarios that can arise in practice. They are drafted based on one particular type of situation in which an original dataset is pseudonymised to produce a new dataset and to which a particular mode of reconstruction of the original dataset is thus explicitly referred to in the ensuing guidelines. These pieces of legislation therefore do not address the risks of constructing the original dataset through other means. Further, the laws are unclear as to how the legal requirements of data pseudonymisation are satisfied in practice (for example, by what precise processes).

Reed, who gave an illuminating and pragmatic analysis of the data trust as a 'private sector' regulatory format for lawful data sharing in Chapter 3, points

[49] See G Buttarelli, 'The EU GDPR as a Clarion Call for a New Global Digital Gold Standard' (1 April 2016), www.edps.europa.eu/press-publications/press-news/blog/eu-gdpr-clarion-call-new-global-digital-gold-standard_fr.

[50] See, for example, B Tan, 'Lessons on Managing Breaches in Singapore from One Year of the General Data Protection Regulation' [2020] *Personal Data Protection Digest* 120.

out that the most important question concerning the data trust is not what legal form it should take – that is, whether it is a trust, a company, a contract or some other legal form. The data trust can take a variety of legal forms, depending on the specific instance of data sharing, although Reed is generally disinclined against using the common law trust. According to him, the more pertinent practical issues that require working out are: constitutional governance, operational governance and regulatory compliance. These three matters, if thoughtfully worked out in practice, will ensure the data trust's success as well as enabling it to generate trust and confidence.

As mentioned above, Chik and Lee, writing in their separate chapters, argue for treating data as property. Chik compares data to copyright and argues for the creation of a *sui generis* property right. Lee, on the other hand, proceeds from a more theoretical perspective and argues that personal data is an excludable proprietary resource, and there are cogent policy reasons justifying its excludability. In particular, their respective lines of analysis require them to consider whether a property classification of data is compatible with and/or supported by the rights and obligations prescribed in the national legislative regime on data protection. As both authors base their discussion in the Singaporean context, they address the compatibility issue by reference to the Personal Data Protection Act, which does not explicitly confer proprietary status on personal data. Both Chik and Lee offer clear analysis as to how the generally agreed characteristics of property rights are reflected in the legislative regime. Further, Chik points out that treating data as property has practical benefits, as a proprietary understanding of data can provide useful guidance on the interpretation and application of data regulation concepts. Lee, on the other hand, reflects that the propertisation of data restores real control to consumers over their own data which has been harvested by business operators.

Finally, Yip unpacks the American idea of 'information fiduciary' in Chapter 6 into its key attributes and assesses whether these attributes can be mapped onto the more traditional English doctrine of fiduciary for the development of a category of fiduciaries called 'information fiduciary' in Singapore and Malaysia. On accepting that such an endeavour is conceptually possible, Yip further analyses the interplay between the common law doctrine of 'information fiduciary' and the pre-existing data protection legislative framework, which is a key practical challenge arising from the legal transplant. Unlike the US, which adopts a patchwork, sector-specific approach towards data protection, Singapore and Malaysia (and many other jurisdictions) have respectively enacted a comprehensive general data protection legislation, which makes it more difficult to justify and/or adopt an equitable conception of 'information fiduciary' as a parallel system of regulation. Yip ultimately concludes that the equitable doctrine has the merit of articulating standards in general terms, which may be better able to deal with new risks and unforeseen scenarios than the legislative regime of 'hard and fast' rules.

IV. AI, Technologies and Private Law

Part II of this volume, 'AI, Technologies and Private Law', traverses a wide range of AI-related technologies and jurisdictions: autonomous vehicles in New Zealand, Australia, the UK, the EU, Singapore and Japan, medical AI in Singapore and Malaysia, automated contracts in Singapore and beyond, digital assets in the US, and blockchain technology for land administration in India, Singapore and Georgia. The examination cuts across several categories, areas and issues within the private law domain, such as:[51]

- the law of property (including succession, copyright law and security over land);
- the law of obligations (contract, tort, agency, equitable wrongs and insurance); and
- the law of persons (which may include issues as to proprietary rights of next-of-kin, the protection of the owner's privacy interests and the legal personality of artificial persons).

Theory, in both legal and technological fields, can interact with practice in myriad ways. New technologies may in their implementation introduce fresh challenges or amplify existing challenges, whether these relate to theoretical foundations, legal rules and principles or societal values. How private law responds to AI technologies in the face of present and future challenges will be central to the discussion. Part II thus investigates the following theory–practice interactions:

(a) What are the relevant legal and wider societal considerations in our search for an appropriate liability framework (whether fault-based, strict liability or no-fault regimes) applicable to autonomous vehicles (see Chapter 7, 'Regulating Autonomous Vehicles: Liability Paradigms and Value Choices', by Chen Siyuan).
(b) How common law rules on standard of care for medical doctors and hospitals which have been derived partly from the West may be adapted to the use of medical AI (see Chapter 8, 'Medical AI, Standard of Care in Negligence and Tort Law', by Gary Chan).
(c) How a theory of consent underlying the formation of conventional contracts and the associated doctrine of mistake may be applicable in the real world of automated contracts (see Chapter 9, 'Contractual Consent in the Age of Machine Learning', by Goh Yihan).
(d) Whether private laws (on property, inheritance and privacy) may be subject to challenges and conundrums in the face of newly created digital assets (see Chapter 10, 'Balancing Liquidity with Other Considerations', by Gal Acrich, Katia Litvak, On Dvori, Ophir Samuelov and Dov Greenbaum).

[51] See generally the coverage of private law in A Burrows, *English Private Law*, 3rd edn (Oxford University Press, 2013).

(e) How can the implementation of the ideology underlying the blockchain technology (distributed nature and immutability) be mediated or influenced by (property) laws and the levels of trust in different jurisdictions (see Chapter 11, 'Blockchain in Land Administration? Overlooked Details in Translating Theory into Practice', by Alvin See).

These theory–practice interactions will become more apparent as we briefly introduce the core ideas in these chapters. This will be followed by an examination of a few broad intersecting themes, legal doctrines and legal concepts that apply to issues discussed in two or more of the chapters.

In Chapter 7, Chen examines the civil liability regimes for regulating autonomous vehicles, including the negligence, strict liability, and no-fault compensation regimes from a plethora of jurisdictional experiences in the Asia-Pacific region, the UK and the EU. With respect to negligence claims, he discusses the difficulties in proving breach on the part of manufacturers due in part to complications associated with the AI-driven software. There are also significant evidential obstacles in demonstrating that the design was defective for the purpose of establishing product liability. Furthermore, product liability laws are heavily dependent on the interpretation of product defects (eg, whether it includes software defects) and the state of scientific and technical knowledge at the time when the product was put into circulation. In contrast to negligence and to some extent product liability, the plaintiff's burden is considerably lighter in a no-fault compensation system (such as in New Zealand) as he or she is only required to show that an accident resulting in the harm suffered by him or her had taken place. This approach may prioritise compensation for traffic accident victims, but may not offer, in Chen's view, sufficient incentives for manufacturers to take care in avoiding or minimising the risks of accidents. Moreover, the practical matter of who should fund such a system (whether manufacturers or the government) cannot be ignored.

Insurance – an area of private law – serves as a legal and operational tool to advance the objective of compensation for accident victims. As Chen notes, Singapore has approved driverless vehicles with mandatory insurance in place for trials on public roads without enacting specific legislation to deal with the liability issue thus far. On the other hand, the UK Automated and Electric Vehicles Act 2018 (AEVA) has imposed liability on the insurers for damage and, where there is no insurer, on the vehicle owner, without the need for the victim to prove fault against the driver. The insurer or vehicle owner may then claim against the 'person responsible for [the] accident'.[52] The insurance system thus appears to take centre stage in the UK in the absence of a definitive choice-of-liability regime.[53]

[52] Automated and Electric Vehicles Act 2018, s 5 (UK).

[53] For a critique of the UK Automated and Electric Vehicles Act 2018, see J Davey, 'By Insurers, for Insurers: The UK's Liability Regime for Autonomous Vehicles' (2020) 13(2) *Journal of Tort Law* 163; however, see Law Commission Consultation Paper No 253 Scottish Law Commission Discussion Paper No 171, 'Automated Vehicles: Consultation Paper 3 – A Regulatory Framework for Automated Vehicles: A Joint Consultation Paper' (18 December 2020), Chapter 16 on 'Civil Liability' (that the current legislation is 'good enough for now' (at 277)).

In comparison, Chan's chapter has a narrower remit as it focuses on the legal standard of care under the tort of negligence which we should expect from doctors and hospitals utilising medical AI in the delivery of medical services to patients. Without discounting other liability regimes or compensation approaches,[54] Chan observes that the tort of negligence for assessing medical liability has been 'firmly established' in Singapore and Malaysia, and seeks to assess the applicability of standard of care principles to medical AI. Legal principles on the medical standard of care such as the famous twin cases of *Bolam*[55] (on the judicial deference to the opinions of the defendant's medical peers) and *Bolitho*[56] (on the requirement that the opinion be scrutinised for logic) supplemented by more recent case law and statutory developments are examined. In his chapter, we see an important intersection between negligence and the *ex ante* regulatory framework pertaining to the use of medical innovations and AI-driven medical devices as well as the hospitals' internal quality assurance mechanisms. The discussion is also juxtaposed against wider policy considerations such as efficiency in the delivery of medical services, promoting innovations, and safeguarding patient welfare and the ethics of the medical profession.

The tort liability system based on the negligent conduct of doctors and hospitals will inevitably involve some uncertainty as to the expected standards in utilising emerging technology and may also generate more costs than, for instance, a no-fault system. Yet, the tort of negligence is able to prioritise accountability of the medical profession based on the professional ethical code and guidelines and legal precedents, as argued by Chan. Furthermore, it seeks to balance the competing interests of innovation promotion and ensuring patient safety and welfare.

Moving to another area of private law, Goh examines how the legal theory underlying the concept of contractual consent and the associated doctrine of mistake may apply to algorithmic contracts. The precise application, he argues, depends on the design of the algorithms. For 'deterministic' algorithms, the user stipulates the parameters of the algorithm as well as their corresponding weights in a manner that reflects the user's deliberate choice vis-à-vis the contract. In contrast, the 'non-deterministic' algorithm does not follow decisional parameters based on the user's choice to generate a fixed output. Instead, such an algorithm has a margin of discretion when predicting user preferences from various sources of user data.

With regard to contractual consent, Goh separately analyses the three concepts of objectively ascertained assent to an agreement, the state of mind of the user at the time of employing the algorithm, and the content of the choice made by the user. When applied to algorithmic contracts, these concepts remain applicable,

[54] See H Smith and K Fotheringham, 'Artificial Intelligence in Clinical Decision-Making: Rethinking Liability' (2020) 20(2) *Medical Law International* 131 (on the possibility of compensation to injured patients via insurance based on risk pooling and shared responsibility between clinicians and software development companies).

[55] *Bolam v Friern Hospital Management Committee* [1957] 1 WLR 582.

[56] *Bolitho v City and Hackney Health Authority* [1998] AC 232.

albeit with modifications or extensions to accommodate the new contexts.[57] Hence, for deterministic algorithms,[58] Goh suggests that the notion of 'assent' should be sufficiently elastic to allow the user to give assent *in advance* to the algorithmic contract. For non-deterministic algorithms, Goh examines agency principles where computers are likened to agents who exercise discretion and judgement for the purpose of contracting on behalf of human principals.[59]

With regard to the doctrine of mistake, Goh referred to the landmark Singapore Court of Appeal decision in *Quoine Pte Ltd v B2C2 Ltd*,[60] in which glitches in Quoine's trading platform resulted in the matching of trades in cryptocurrencies between B2C2 and counterparties at abnormal prices. Those trades were subsequently cancelled by Quoine upon discovery. Notably, Quoine was not entitled to cancel the trading contracts that had been formed between B2C2 and counterparties in line with the analysis on deterministic algorithms. There was also no operative mistake on the part of the counterparties that could have resulted in the vitiation of the trading contracts.[61] The Singapore Court of Appeal[62] opined that, assuming there was a mistake as to a term of the contract, the proper legal approach was to assess the programmer's (ie, the director of B2C2) state of knowledge of the mistake from the time of programming up to the time of formation of the relevant contract.

The above case also concerned the question of whether cryptocurrencies amounted to property that could form the subject matter of a trust. This segues nicely to Acrich et al's chapter on US perspectives regarding issues of ownership and inheritance to digital assets (consisting of virtual currencies, video game assets, emails and personal digital files, and social media accounts) by the next-of-kin. On the other side of the coin, the law would have to contend with the privacy rights of the deceased owners, especially with regard to social media accounts and personal emails. The chapter also examines public law responses such as the tax and criminal laws in the US.

The digitalised nature of newly created assets has given rise to new legal challenges and uncertainties.[63] With respect to the right of inheritance to video game

[57] See also the UK Jurisdiction Taskforce's Legal Statement on Cryptoassets and Smart Contracts (that smart contracts have contractual force (at para 18) and normal contractual principles for formation of conventional contract should generally apply to smart contracts (at paras 136–41): https://35z8e83m1ih83drye280o9d1-wpengine.netdna-ssl.com/wp-content/uploads/2019/11/6.6056_JO_Cryptocurrencies_Statement_FINAL_WEB_111119-1.pdf.

[58] Such was the nature of trading algorithms employed in *Quoine Pte Ltd v B2C2 Ltd* [2020] SGCA(I) 2 [97]–[98].

[59] For another contractual analysis of automated contracts, see V Ooi, 'Contracts Formed by Software: An Approach from the Law of Mistake', *Journal of Business Law* (forthcoming), https://papers.ssrn.com/sol3/papers.cfm?abstract_id=3322308.

[60] *Quoine Pte Ltd v B2C2 Ltd* (n 58). For a case commentary, see A Loke, 'Mistakes in Algorithmic Trading of Cryptocurrencies' (2020) 83(6) *Modern Law Review* 1343.

[61] *Quoine Pte Ltd v B2C2 Ltd* (n 58) [7].

[62] Mance IJ dissenting on the point of unilateral mistake.

[63] See N Cahn, 'Probate Law Meets the Digital Age' (2014) 67(6) *Vanderbilt Law Review* 1697 (on the Stored Communications Act in the US and the uncertainties generated by digital assets on the question

virtual assets, there exists the problem of ambiguity as to the scope and interpretation of legislation and the terms of service governing the assets. As for personal emails, the next-of-kin may resort to copyright law in support of their right to inherit the items. Yet, email platforms have countered that the protection of privacy rights of the deceased as specified in certain terms of service should be respected. For social media accounts of celebrities and social influencers that may contain information that are personal and yet socially valuable, issues relating to privacy interests, the rights of online platforms, their terms of service and the creative content generated under intellectual property laws come to the fore.

The legal uncertainties are marked as much by the conflicts between different areas of private law (property and privacy laws) governing the issue as by the clashes between the commercial interests of platform owners and operators and the more personal and sentimental interests of next-of-kin. To ameliorate the ambiguities, legislation such as the Revised Uniform Fiduciary Access to Digital Assets Act (RUFADAA) in Pennsylvania[64] may be needed to lay out some general rules – for example, by putting the onus on the deceased to stipulate in advance how the digital assets will be distributed after death, failing which the terms of service of the online platforms may apply.

See's chapter explores the viability of employing blockchain technology in land administrations to protect land rights with reference to the experiences in India, Singapore and Georgia. He distinguishes blockchains that are available publicly from private blockchains that serve particular institutional needs. Whilst a public blockchain prioritises immutability without the need for trust in an intermediary (ie, no central land registry), the private blockchain emphasises control based on trust and pre-agreed rules in lieu of immutability.

Given the varied situations in the abovementioned jurisdictions, there is clearly no 'one-size-fits-all' solution. Notwithstanding the Digital India Land Records Modernization Programme since 2016, India's attempts to introduce blockchain-based land-registers have generally been unsuccessful.[65] The country has faced practical impediments to ensuring the comprehensiveness and quality of both textual and spatial land records – a prerequisite for conversion into digital form for the successful implementation of blockchain technology. In contrast, the good quality of electronic land records and infrastructure in the Republic of Georgia has enabled the country to transition to blockchain for land administrations.

On the issue of compatibility of blockchain land registers with the law, See observes that the public blockchain ideology of immutability is not entirely reflected in the land law registration system. Nor should it be. For instance, the

of access by personal representatives of the estate to the decedent's communications) and the subsequent commentary by D Horton, 'The Stored Communications Act and Digital Assets' (2014) 67(6) *Vanderbilt Law Review* 1729.

[64] Revised Uniform Fiduciary Access to Digital Assets Act (Act 72 of 2020) (23 July 2020) (US).

[65] The exception was the state of Andhra Pradesh, which initiated fresh land titling in the state capital Amaravati in 2014 and placed land records on a blockchain.

Torrens system of land registration, which is based on the concept of indefeasibility of title, is subject to certain exceptions such as fraud and forgery. A completely immutable blockchain-based land register would not allow for the rectification of fraudulent and erroneous land records. Furthermore, See notes that the shift to a public decentralised blockchain for land registrations can address the issue of public trust by minimising the threat of bureaucratic corruption, but may at the same time entail a loss of control by the authorities. Ironically, where the people trust the land administration authorities (as is the case in Singapore), there may be little incentive to migrate to a completely trustless system such as the public blockchain.[66]

As mentioned, the chapters in Part II involve intersecting themes and overlapping legal theories, doctrines and concepts as applied to different types of AI technology. The main issues for discussion may be categorised as follows:

(a) how AI and related technologies can prompt and influence the development of private laws (primarily tort, contract and property);
(b) the need to consider the benefits of AI and technological innovations, and the competing interests of stakeholders (such as privacy and safety); and
(c) the interconnected concepts of autonomy and legal personality of AI both present and future.

A. How AI and Technology Can Prompt and Influence the Development of Private Law

Autonomous vehicles, medical AI and automated contracts employ machine learning, deep learning, computer vision and other AI technologies to power the software as discussed by Chen, Chan and Goh, respectively. Acrich et al refer to AI digital asset management (DAM) systems that utilise deep learning and natural language processing to identify, curate and extract content in order to monetize the value of the digital assets. See observes the potential contributions of AI towards enhanced blockchain land administration – for example, a private sector AI-driven legal process automation[67] that facilitates the establishment of clear title for lands and the possibility of determining land boundaries based on a machine learning and images collected from satellites, planes and drones. Further, facial or image recognition technology might aid in validating identity and documentation in land transactions to reduce human errors and prevent fraud.

Chan and Goh are both inclined towards adapting existing common law principles (the tort of negligence and contractual consent) to novel AI technologies.

[66] M Basu, 'Exclusive: AI Takes over Singapore's Property Estate' *GovInsider* (8 March 2017), www.govinsider.asia/digital-gov/ai-takes-over-singapores-property-estate (cited by See in ch 11 of this volume).

[67] This automation was developed by a company (Terra Adriatica) in Croatia.

Even so, the manner of adaptations have to be tailored to the particular AI functioning and its effects. Unlike certain conventional medical tools, medical AI can generate output in ways that are not obvious even to the medical experts, much less the patients. Potential problems with bias in training datasets may taint the AI output. Would the doctor or hospital then be reasonably justified in relying on (or overriding) the AI output in these circumstances? As we have seen, automated contracts that rely on deterministic or non-deterministic algorithms, though they are both capable of forming legal contracts as argued by Goh, may entail different contractual analyses based on assent in advance and agency principles, respectively.

On the proprietary status of digital assets, in tandem with the analysis of Acrich et al on the US position, courts, expert bodies and academics and researchers[68] in other jurisdictions are also grappling with this novel issue. According to the UK Jurisdiction Taskforce's Legal Statement on Cryptoassets and Smart Contracts, one type of digital assets namely cryptoassets[69] should be treated as property[70] and can therefore be subject to succession upon death. Thorley IJ, sitting in the Singapore International Commercial Court case of *B2C2 Ltd v Quoine Pte Ltd*,[71] regarded cryptocurrencies as property by reference to the House of Lords' decision of *National Provincial Bank v Ainsworth*[72] that property 'must be definable, identifiable by third parties, capable in its nature of assumption by third parties and having some degree of permanence or stability'.[73] On appeal, the Singapore Court of Appeal,[74] whilst it noted that '[t]here may be much to commend the view that cryptocurrencies should be capable of assimilation into the general concepts of property', decided to leave the issue open, noting the 'different questions as to the type of property that is involved'.

Where the digital assets contain or involve personal data, we have seen in Chapters 4 and 5 by Chik and Lee respectively in Part I (see above) the discussions

[68] See D Fox, 'Cryptocurrencies in the Common Law of Property' in D Fox and S Green, *Cryptocurrencies in Public and Private Law* (Oxford University Press, 2019) 139–76 (on accommodating cryptocurrencies within the common law concept of property); K Low and E Teo, 'Bitcoins and Other Cryptocurrencies as Property?' (2017) 9(2) *Law, Innovation and Technology* 235, DOI: 10.1080/17579961.2017.1377915; and J Bacon et al, 'Blockchain Demystified: A Technical and Legal Introduction to Distributed and Centralised Ledgers' (2018) 25(1) *Richmond Journal of Law & Technology*, https://jolt.richmond.edu/files/2018/11/Michelsetal-Final-1.pdf.

[69] The UK Jurisdiction Taskforce's Legal Statement on Cryptoassets and Smart Contracts defined cryptoassets as having certain features of intangibility, cryptographic authentication, use of a distributed transaction ledger, decentralisation and rule by consensus; see n 57 at para 31.

[70] ibid para 15.

[71] *B2C2 Ltd v Quoine Pte Ltd* [2019] SGHC(I) 03.

[72] *National Provincial Bank v Ainsworth* [1965] 1 AC 1175.

[73] See also *AA v Persons Unknown* [2020] 4 WLR 35 [59]–[61] (cryptocurrencies held with the operators of the exchange constituted property following the *Ainsworth* criteria and capable of being the subject matter of a proprietary injunction); and *Ruscoe v Cryptopia Ltd* [2020] NZHC 728 [102], [120] and [187] (cryptocurrencies of a trading exchange, ie, the company in liquidation are property based on *Ainsworth* criteria and constituted the subject matter of trusts held by the company for its account holders).

[74] *Quoine Pte Ltd v B2C2 Ltd* (n 58) [144].

on some form of propertisation of personal data based on certain features such as non-rivalry and non-excludability. Nonetheless, it must be highlighted that there is still a conceptual distinction between the asset and the recorded data pertaining to the asset,[75] even if the significant commercial value of certain digital assets may be derived from the data itself.[76] In this regard, Acrich et al have discussed the tax implications of regarding digital assets (including cryptocurrencies) as property.

B. AI, Promoting Innovations and Other Competing Interests and Considerations

How private law responds to nascent developments in AI can indeed affect the dissemination of the technology. First, are there technological benefits that provide the impetus for dissemination to the wider society? Second, how does private law deal with questions of potential risks and losses, enable trust in the technology or legal framework, or accommodate societal values and choices?

As we have seen from the chapters in Part II, the socio-economic benefits generated by AI and related technologies are indeed wide-ranging: enhanced accuracy and speed of diagnosis by medical AI, reduced incidence of road accidents and transport time for users of autonomous vehicles, the operations of automated high frequency trading platforms, the advantages of liquidity from digital assets and the use of AI-assisted database management systems to manage these digital assets, and, finally, the implementation of blockchains for land administration that can decrease the time and costs entailed in ownership disputes and can reduce opportunities for bureaucratic corruption.

Chen and Chan discuss the advantages of promoting technological innovations and, at the same time, the need to protect passengers and patients from personal harms. This involves, through the choice-of-liability regimes, not only the setting of legal standards with respect to human conduct but also raising tangential questions about machine standards.

This question of legal standards and responsibility for human actors has been complicated to some extent by the opacity of AI. Chan explores the problem of ascertaining whether a medical doctor or hospital would be negligent in relying on AI that is opaque and incapable of providing human-interpretable explanations for the AI outputs. Chen discusses the evidential obstacles in determining fault and causal responsibility for accidents involving 'blackbox' autonomous vehicles on the part of manufacturers, AI developers and other entities. As for machine standards, the alleged superiority of AI to humans at least in performing particular tasks brings to the fore a fresh legal challenge to ascertain AI's proper standards

[75] *Ruscoe v Cryptopia Ltd* (n 73) [128].
[76] UK Jurisdiction Taskforce's Legal Statement on Cryptoassets and Smart Contracts (n 57) para 60.

(such as the concept of the 'reasonable' AI) and concomitant responsibilities to be attributed to AI, given that the technology may act autonomously, generating unpredictable outcomes.

Innovations in automated contracting and the creation of digital assets are already upon us. The particular risks posed by the operation of automated trading platforms on the owners and users alike necessitate an enquiry into where the loss should lie in normal circumstances, as well as in the event of unexpected glitches and mistakes, whether human or technical. Insofar as automated contracting is concerned, Goh contends that assent and choice should remain paramount considerations. Whilst the innovations from digital assets may be given recognition through the granting of proprietary rights, Acrich et al acknowledge that the law has a role in balancing the inheritance rights of next-of-kin with the owners' privacy and contractual rights.

In order to successfully implement blockchain technology along with its ideology (distributed nature and immutability), See reminds us that societal choices as to the nature and type of land registration system must be taken into account. Even though the blockchain architecture relies on the so-called *lex cryptographia or* 'rule of code',[77] its implementation cannot be completely divorced from the law of the land. Moreover, whilst trust of users in blockchains may be placed in the outputs generated by the system rather than individual actors, the importance of norms, market, law and code in enabling an architecture of trust in commercial transactions cannot be underestimated.[78]

C. Legal Personality and Autonomy

The discussion of the interrelated concepts of legal personality and autonomy is anchored in the present with a foothold in the future. Goh engages briefly in crystal ball-gazing into the future world of computer systems. The algorithmic design of the future may be a fully autonomous algorithm that makes decisions for the user without the latter's intervention. Imbued with Artificial General Intelligence, such AI may in the future be capable of acting autonomously as a contracting party, an independent contractor and one that possesses legal personality.[79] Chen highlights the UK AEVA, which appeared to implicitly recognise that autonomous vehicles may cause accidents and be at fault. Chan refers to autonomous medical AI that may one day function as a 'second doctor' or an independent contractor acting on its own account. Furthermore, he notes that one major obstacle against the strict liability of doctors and hospitals based on existing doctrines of vicarious liability and non-delegable duties is that at present, medical AI, unlike the employee or the independent contractor, does not possess legal personality.

[77] M Zou, 'Code, and Other Laws of Blockchain' (2020) 40(3) *Oxford Journal of Legal Studies* 645, 647.

[78] See K Werbach, *Blockchain and the New Architecture of Trust* (MIT Press, 2018).

[79] L Wein, 'Responsibility of Intelligent Artifacts: Toward an Automation Jurisprudence' (1992) 6 *Harvard Journal of Law & Technology* 103.

The concept of an artificial or legal person seems quite malleable. As stated in court judgments and academic treatises, 'legal persons, being the arbitrary creature of the law, may be of as many kinds as the law pleases'.[80] For example, it is the law manifested by legal rules that dictate whether a company exists and its functional role.[81] Thus, there appears to be no fundamental conceptual objection to AI being granted legal personality. Whether we *should* confer legal personality is another matter.

Corporate separate personality is a useful but imperfect analogy. Unlike AI, corporations are after all made up of human beings (directors and employees). Drawing from more anthropocentric premises, human capacity for reasoning may serve as a theoretical basis for legal personhood. At the moment, such capacity for rationality may be sufficient to establish competence in specific tasks performed by AI systems, even if AI does not possess consciousness[82] and Artificial General Intelligence still lies somewhere in the future. There may be economic reasons, as is the case for corporations, to justify a separate legal personality for AI and robots that generate economic activity and profits. Granting AI legal personality may also allow human actors to shift legal risks to the AI concerned,[83] though this should not result in the arbitrary absolving of human responsibility for human error. If AI were to be granted legal personhood, one practical implication is that AI may have to bear legal responsibility for civil wrongs, such as to make monetary compensation.[84] If so, we may consider instituting a funding mechanism to deal with the adverse consequences of AI errors and enable AI to insure against potential losses.

An entity either possesses legal personality or not, though there may be limits to what a legal person is entitled to do under the law. In comparison, autonomy is a matter of degree. For instance, Clarke[85] refers to (seven) degrees of autonomy corresponding to the different levels connecting the function of the artefact to that of the controller. This concept of calibrated artefact–controller correspondence is

[80] *Bumper Development Corp Ltd v Metropolitan Police Commissioner* [1991] 1 WLR 1362, 1371–72, per Purchas LJ, citing PJ Fitzgerald (ed), *Salmond on Jurisprudence*, 12th edn (Sweet & Maxwell, 1966) 306–08.

[81] *Meridian Global Funds Management Asia Ltd v Securities Commission* [1995] 2 AC 500, 506.

[82] LB Solum, 'Legal Personhood for Artificial Intelligences' (1992) 70 *North Carolina Law Review* 1235, 1281–82.

[83] S Chesterman, 'Artificial Intelligence and the Limits of Legal Personality' (2020) 69 *International & Comparative Law Quarterly* 819, 825.

[84] See European Parliament, 'Civil Law Rules on Robotics', European Parliament Resolution of 16 February 2017 with Recommendations to the Commission on Civil Law Rules on Robotics (2015/2103(INL)), European Parliament (16 February 2017) at para 59(f) (that 'the most sophisticated autonomous robots could be established as having the status of electronic persons responsible for making good any damage they may cause'); however, see Liability for Artificial Intelligence and Other Emerging Digital Technologies, Expert Group on Liability and New Technologies – New Technologies Formation (November 2019) 37-8; Recital 7 of the European Parliament resolution of 20 October 2020 with recommendations to the Commission on a civil liability regime for artificial intelligence (2020/2014(INL); and Recital 6 of the Proposal for a Regulation of the European Parliament and of the Council on liability for the operation of Artificial Intelligence systems.

[85] Clarke (n 11) 427. At the first level, the artefact has no function whilst the controller 'acts'. The roles are reversed at level 7. In between, the function of the artefact becomes more significant as we progress to higher levels ranging from 'analyse options' and 'act and inform'. The function of the controller correspondingly decreases from 'decide among options' to 'interrupt/suspend/cancel an action'.

evident in the levels of autonomy for self-driving vehicles ranging from zero automation (where the human driver performs all the driving tasks) to full automation (where the vehicle is capable of performing all the driving tasks).[86]

Though autonomy is not a proper legal concept, it nonetheless carries with it potentially significant practical consequences that may be manifested in the operations of non-deterministic (versus deterministic) algorithms in automated contracts and fully autonomous contracting systems, unsupervised (versus supervised) machine learning tasks in medical diagnoses and predictions, and in AI systems without human review or with human in-the-loop only for certain stages of decision-making. We also need to consider in this equation, even for supposedly autonomous AI, the human element in the choice of algorithms used and the training data, the state of mind of human actors and their control over the risks of harm. Further, control may be said to be 'distributed' to varying degrees amongst the various stakeholders.[87]

V. Conclusion

AI capacity and data generation share a mutual relationship for value enhancement. With a view to optimising the benefits of these technological innovations and interactions, private laws can play a facilitative and/or regulatory role vis-a-vis their applications and deal with potential legal liabilities. Whether and how private laws – with their underlying theories, doctrines and concepts – can rise to the challenges posed by these technologies in a manner that builds trust and is sensitive to the practical realities will no doubt be closely watched by lawyers, judges, academics and technologists. We hope this book will make a not insignificant contribution to engaging and enduring conversations about the place of private laws in the regulation of AI and data governance.

Postscript

See footnote 20 – pursuant to a recent amendment exercise, section 82(2) of the COVID-19 (Temporary Measures) Act 2020 makes clear that personal contact tracing data can only be used for investigation or criminal proceeding in respect of a serious offence.

[86] Society of Automotive Engineers, 'Taxonomy and Definitions for Terms Related to Driving Automation Systems for On-Road Motor Vehicles' (2018).

[87] For autonomous vehicles, control may be distributed amongst the manufacturers, developers, users and operators (as opposed to focusing solely on the driver or his or her control over the vehicle). For example, the manufacturer exercises control over the hardware and the software developer the design of the automated driving systems: see J Soh, 'Towards a Control-Centric Account of Tort Liability for Automated Vehicles' (2021) 26 *Torts Law Journal* 221.

PART I

Data Protection, Governance and Private Law

2

How to De-identify Personal Data in South Korea

An Evolutionary Tale

HAKSOO KO AND SANGCHUL PARK*

I. Introduction

In early 2020, South Korea's legislature made amendments to major laws in the area of data protection in order to, among other things, promote the utilisation of pseudonymised personal data by allowing the processing of personal data for statistical purposes, scientific research purposes or archiving for public interest purposes, without having to obtain consent from the data subjects. This is the latest attempt by South Korea in its efforts to strike a balance between the proper safeguarding of personal data and fostering of data analytics, and other types of utilisation. The statutes that were amended are as follows: (i) the Personal Information Protection Act (hereinafter 'the PIPA');[1] (ii) the Act on the Protection and Utilisation of Credit Information (hereinafter 'the Credit Information Act');[2] and (iii) the Act on the Promotion of Information and Communications Network Utilisation and Information Protection (hereinafter 'the IC Network Act').[3] These were all

* This chapter is based on Haksoo Ko and Sangchul Park, 'How to De-identify Personal Data in South Korea: An Evolutionary Tale' (2020) 10(4) *International Data Privacy Law* 385, available at https://doi.org/10.1093/idpl/ipaa015. This research is supported by the National Research Foundation, Singapore under its Emerging Areas Research Projects (EARP) Funding Initiative. Any opinions, findings and conclusions or recommendations expressed in this material are those of the authors and do not reflect the views of National Research Foundation, Singapore.

[1] Personal Information Protection Act, Act No 16930 (amended 4 February 2020, effective 5 August 2020).

[2] Act on the Protection and Utilization of Credit Information, Act No 16957 (amended 4 February 2020, effective 5 August 2020).

[3] Act on the Promotion of Information and Communications Network Utilisation and Information Protection, Act No 16955 (amended 4 February 2020, effective 5 August 2020).

amended as of 4 February 2020 and became effective as of 5 August 2020 in South Korea (collectively hereinafter 'the 2020 Amendments').

Paying particular attention to the influence that the General Data Protection Regulation (GDPR) of the European Union (EU)[4] had on the debates in South Korea in areas related to personal data, this chapter explains how the evolution of South Korea's data privacy law reflects efforts to provide useful avenues for data utilisation, while at the same time safeguarding data privacy. The rest of this chapter is organised as follows. Section II discusses the main factors that drove recent major amendments, including the demand for enhanced availability of data that could be used for artificial intelligence (AI). Section III introduces discussions that took place before the 2020 Amendments, which include, most notably, those relating to the de-identification guidelines issued by the government in 2016. We also outline the new rules contained in the 2020 Amendments concerning the use of pseudonymised data. Finally, section IV provides theoretical and practical observations relating to the new rules.

II. The Legal Context

A. The Statutory Framework and Regulatory Governance

South Korea has a stringent legal regime regarding personal data protection. The primary body of legislation is the PIPA, which was enacted in 2011. Prior to the enactment of the PIPA, the Korean Constitutional Court had already declared that there is a constitutional right to data privacy in the form of the self-determination of personal data. The Constitutional Court derived this right in part from the secrecy and freedom of privacy under Article 17 of the Korean Constitution.[5] The PIPA itself does not explicitly mention the right to self-determination of personal data. What is noteworthy from a practical perspective is that the PIPA includes an exceedingly stringent notice-and-consent requirement prior to the collection of personal data. In addition to the PIPA, several other statutes cover specific areas for data protection. The IC Network Act largely governs personal data collected online. However, the 2020 Amendments consolidated most of the relevant provisions into the PIPA and, as such, the role of the IC Network Act as a personal data protection law has been drastically reduced. The Credit Information Act

[4] Regulation (EU) 2016/679 of the European Parliament and of the Council of 27 April 2016 on the protection of natural persons with regard to the processing of personal data and on the free movement of such data, and repealing Directive 95/46/EC (General Data Protection Regulation) [2016] OJ L119/1.

[5] See Korean Constitutional Court, 26 May 2005, 99-*Heonma*-513. Article 17 of the Korean Constitution stipulates that 'no citizen's secrecy and freedom of private lives shall be infringed'.

covers issues relating to financial privacy and contains provisions governing the credit information industry.[6] Also, the Act on the Protection and Utilization of Location Information (hereinafter 'the Location Information Act')[7] is a statute with jurisdiction over issues relating to location information collected from various sources.

Thus, while the PIPA is in principle expected to serve as a general statute governing data protection matters, there are also several other relevant statutes. Depending on the specific circumstances, there could be many additional relevant statutes. For instance, in the realm of health and medical data, the Bioethics and Safety Act[8] is important. This Act governs data processing involving human subjects research. In the context of public health relating to a pandemic, the Contagious Disease Prevention and Control Act (hereinafter 'the CDPCA')[9] is relevant. It includes pandemic-triggered provisions that allow for the tracking and disclosure of data involving confirmed cases. Although these statutes would not have overlapping subject-matter jurisdictions in theory, difficult jurisdictional questions may well be raised in practice. If these practical aspects are considered, Korea's data protection regime can be called a hybrid regime between the EU model of omnibus data protection legislation and the sectoral approach of the US legal regime.[10] With the 2020 Amendments, some of the overlaps have been eliminated, in particular between the PIPA and the IC Network Act.

The data protection laws are enforced by different data protection agencies. Prior to the 2020 Amendments, the Korea Communications Commission (hereinafter 'the KCC') had the power to govern online data protection rules under the IC Network Act. In the case of offline data protection rules under the PIPA, the role of policy-making and coordination lay with the Personal Information Protection Commission (hereinafter 'the PIPC'), while enforcement powers belonged to the Ministry of the Interior and Safety (hereinafter 'the MOIS'). The 2020 Amendments, for the most part, transferred the regulatory power over online data from the KCC to the PIPC. Also, the enforcement authority of the PIPA was transferred from the MOIS to the PIPC. Thus, the PIPC's regulatory and enforcement authority has been reinforced extensively. The Credit Information Act and the Location Information Act will continue to be enforced by the Financial Services Commission (hereinafter 'the FSC') and the KCC, respectively. The following table outlines the changes brought about by the 2020 Amendments.

[6] Pursuant to the Credit Information Act, the Korea Credit Information Services was established in 2016, taking over the tasks that had mostly been conducted by several credit registries.

[7] Act on the Protection and Utilization of Location Information, Act No 17347 (last amended 9 June 2020, effective 9 June 2020).

[8] Act on the Bioethics and Safety Act, Act No 17472 (last amended 11 August 2020, effective 12 September 2020).

[9] Contagious Disease Prevention and Control Act, Act No 17491 (last amended 29 September 2020, effective 29 September 2020).

[10] See P Schwarz, 'Preemption and Privacy' (2009) 118 *Yale Law Journal* 902, 908–15.

Table 2.1 Summary of changes in regulatory governance triggered by the 2020 Amendments

	Financial data	**Other data collected online**	**Other data collected offline**	**Location data**
Existing laws (relevant data protection authority)	Credit Information Act (FSC)	IC Network Act (KCC)	PIPA (PIPC: policy-making and coordination /MOIS: enforcement)	Location Information Act (KCC) (unaffected by the 2020 Amendments)
The 2020 Amendments (relevant data protection authority)	Credit Information Act (FSC)	PIPA (PIPC)		

B. The Consent Principle

A major principle which is commonly observed in Korea's data protection statutes is the consent principle. In other words, in order to collect statutorily defined personal data from a data subject for processing or for transferring to a third party, it is required to obtain prior informed consent from the data subject.[11] On the concept of personal data, identifiability of an individual is used as a key component in all relevant statutes.[12] Regarding the notification that should be given to

[11] Under the PIPA, consent should be obtained after disclosing each notice item so as to be clearly recognisable by the data subject, (i) with certain important notice items (concerning marketing promotion, sensitive personal data, unique identifiers, retention period, and the recipient of data and its purpose of use) being made more conspicuous if consent is obtained in writing or electronic document, and (ii) with consent-requiring items being separated from non-consent-requiring items (arts 22, 15(1)(i) and 17(1)(i)). Under the Credit Information Act, for the transfer of personal credit data, prior consent should be obtained in each case in writing or through digital public key certificate, accredited digital signature, personal password, voice recording or other secure and creditworthy methods, while a lesser degree of formality would apply to the collection and processing of personal credit data (arts 15(2) and 32(1)(2)). The Location Information Act also provides for consent requirements (arts 18 and 19).

[12] Under the PIPA, personal data is defined as any information relating to an individual which can be used to identify the individual alone or when easily combined with other information (which can be interpreted to mean a direct identifier and quasi-identifier, respectively) (art 2(i)). The Credit Information Act uses a similar terminology to define personal credit data (art 2(ii)). The Location Information Act defines personal location data as 'location data relating to a specific individual (including data which can be used to identify the location of the specific individual when easily combined with other data even if the location cannot be identified by the data alone)' (art 2(ii)).

the data subject before obtaining his or her consent, each statute contains provisions with specific requirements.[13]

There are stipulated exceptions to the consent principle that are specifically listed in these statutes. For instance, under the PIPA and the Credit Information Act, personal data may be collected and used without the data subject's consent in the following limited circumstances: when permitted by law or necessary for compliance with a legal obligation; when required to exercise legal authority vested in the public agency; when necessary to enter into or perform a contract to which the data subject is a party; when evidently necessary in order to urgently protect the vital, bodily or pecuniary interests of the data subject or another person (when the data subject or his or her legal custodian is legally incapable, the address is unknown, or otherwise obtaining prior consent is unfeasible); or when necessary for the purposes of the legitimate interests pursued by the data controller,[14] which evidently override the rights of the data subject.[15] These exceptions have similarities to the lawful basis for processing under Articles 6(1)(b)–(f) of the GDPR, except (among other things) that the public interest alone does not constitute a lawful basis[16] and that not only the protection of vital interests but also the evident and urgent protection of bodily or pecuniary interests constitutes a lawful basis.[17] Also, the Credit Information Act includes publicly available data among the exceptions (Article 15(2)(ii)). Further, the 2020 Amendment to the PIPA included an additional list of exceptions to the personal data collected by online service providers (Article 39-3(2)).[18]

[13] Under the PIPA, the data subject must be given notice before giving consent to data collection, including: (i) the purpose of collection and use; (ii) the items of data to be collected; (iii) retention and use period; and (iv) (unless data is collected online) the data subject's right to refuse consent and disadvantages, if any, from the refusal (arts 15(2) and 39-3(1)). The data subject must, before giving consent to a transfer to a third party, be given notice of the recipient and similar items as above (art 17(2)). Under the Credit Information Act, the data subject must, before giving consent to a transfer to a third party, be given notice of: (i) the recipient, (ii) the recipient's purpose of use; (iii) the items of data to be transferred; and (iv) the recipient's retention and use period (art 32(1)). Under the amended Credit Information Act, the data subject must, before giving consent to data collection, be given notice of the same items as set forth under the PIPA (art 34-2). The Location Information Act requires the disclosure of certain items in the standard terms of use before obtaining consent to the collection, use or transfer (arts 18 and 19).

[14] The PIPA defines a data controller as a 'public agency, entity, organization, or individual which processes personal data alone or through another person to administer personal data files for work purposes' (art 2(v)). In fact, the PIPA uses a term that literally translates as 'personal data processor', but it does not distinguish between data controller and data processor as in the GDPR. In this chapter, the term 'controller' is used. Roughly speaking, the controller under the PIPA would serve the combined roles that the controller and processor would serve under the GDPR.

[15] PIPA, art 15(1)(ii)–(vi); Credit Information Act, art 15(2)(i).

[16] GDPR, art 6(1)(e).

[17] ibid art 6(1)(d).

[18] Exceptions are as follows: when it is remarkably difficult, due to economic or technical reasons, to obtain consent, whereas personal data is required in order to perform contract duties in the context of online service; when personal data is needed to settle online service fees; or when other laws permit.

In practice, these exceptions appear to be rarely applied and particularly so in the business context.[19] For instance, although consent is not required when the data controller's legitimate interests evidently override the data subject's interests, it is not clear who is authorised to make the requisite decision and what the applicable criteria would be. In fact, the permissible scope of 'legitimate interests' under this exception is even narrower than the scope of the 'legitimate interests' basis for processing under Article 6(1)(f) of the GDPR, as the former requires the legitimate interests to 'evidently' override the data subject's interests. Thus, in a business context, obtaining consent is commonly perceived to be the only legal way of collecting personal data from data subjects.

C. Reconsideration of the Consent Principle

Unlike the previous generation of AI, including an expert system which often contain many 'if-then' statements, the current generation of AI models (in particular, machine learning models) are statistically and inductively constructed and are heavily reliant on data. Thus, it was natural that the advent of AI and the growing use of big data spurred repeated debates as to how to find legitimate and expedient ways to utilise data without having to obtain consent from data subjects. Early attempts in this context culminated in the 2016 publication of a Personal Data De-identification Guideline by the government (hereinafter 'the 2016 Guideline'). The 2016 Guideline excludes data from the application of the PIPA and other data protection laws if the following requirements are met: the personal data is de-identified, undergoes adequacy assessment and is subject to follow-up control for the prevention of re-identification.[20]

However, even with the publication of the 2016 Guideline, uncertainty remained and controversies continued, in particular, regarding whether de-identification has a legal basis under the then-existing laws. Following further discussions, the 2020 Amendments tried to bring greater clarity and introduced the concept of pseudonymisation explicitly into the relevant statutes. With the 2020 Amendments, personal data under the PIPA has been recategorised into: (i) non-pseudonymised personal data (in general, subject to the consent principle) (Article 2(i)(*ga*)(*na*));[21] (ii) pseudonymised personal data (without consent requirement and subject to *ex post* control for the prevention of re-identification)

[19] The authors' experience suggests that private parties, in their ordinary course of business, almost always obtain consent without resorting to the provisions which allow for the collection of personal data without obtaining consent.

[20] These requirements are discussed below.

[21] This category includes any information relating to an individual which can be used to identify the individual alone or when easily combined with other information (to determine whether it can be 'easily combined', the time, expense, technology etc needed to identify an individual, including availability of other information, should be considered at a reasonable level) (art 2(i)(*ga*)(*na*)).

(Article 2(i)(*da*));[22] and (iii) anonymised or anonymous data (which is not legally deemed personal data) (Article 58-2).[23] The 2020 Amendments also allow the use of personal data without consent if doing so does not impair the interest of a data subject, if appropriate safeguards such as encryption of data are in place, and if it is within the scope reasonably related to the purpose for which the personal data is initially collected.[24] The following section expounds on the debates surrounding the concept and mechanics of de-identification of personal data, which resulted in the 2020 Amendments.

III. Debates on the De-identification of Personal Data Prior to the 2020 Amendments

A. The Need for De-identification

From the perspective of regulatory compliance, it would be best if consent could easily be obtained from every data subject. However, for obvious practical reasons, obtaining consent from all relevant data subjects would be an exceedingly cumbersome process in most circumstances. In particular, if the data to be utilised involve a large number of data subjects, obtaining consent from each of these data subjects would be all but impossible.

One way to solve this conundrum is to de-identify personal data. Personal data, once properly de-identified, would no longer be considered personal data under the PIPA or other statutes. As such, once de-identification is conducted, at least in theory, the various stringent statutory requirements for personal data protection would not have to be complied with. As such, de-identified data can be used without having to consider the consent requirement or the purpose for which the consent was initially obtained. De-identified data may also be transferred to a third party.

[22] Pseudonymised data is explicitly defined as the information which has been pseudonymised so as not to be used to identify an individual without the use of and combination with additional information for the reconstruction of the original data (art 2(i)(*da*)). Pseudonymisation is defined as 'the processing of personal data in such a manner that a specific individual becomes not identifiable without the use of additional information, rendered through deletion of a part of the data or substitution of all or a part of the data' (art 2(i-2)).

[23] The term 'anonymised' or 'anonymous data' is not explicitly referenced in the PIPA, but the amended PIPA provides that the law does not apply to the data when identification cannot take place even through combination with other information and that, in making the decision about identifiability, the reasonableness of the time, cost and technology should be considered (art 58-2).

[24] PIPA, arts 15(3) and 17(4). Article 32(6)(ix-4) of the Credit Information Act also provides for a similar exception. These new broad exceptions are analogous to the concept of 'compatibility with the purpose for which the personal data are initially collected' under art 6(4) of the GDPR, although it remains unclear how this exception will be interpreted. An indication is that this exception will perhaps not be applied frequently in practice.

Prior to the 2020 Amendments, there was already a provision in the PIPA which allowed for the utilisation of de-identified personal data. In other words, Article 18(2)(iv) of the PIPA permitted the use of personal data for purposes other than the initial purposes notified to the data subjects prior to consent or its transfer to a third party, without having to obtain additional consent, to the extent that the following safeguards are satisfied: (i) personal data at issue is de-identified; and (ii) the utilisation of the personal data is limited to statistical purposes or academic research purposes (although it remained unclear whether these purposes would include commercial purposes).

Thus, there were two possible avenues for statutory interpretation related to de-identified data for data utilisation. First, de-identified data would no longer be considered to fall under the legal definition of personal data in all relevant Korean statutory laws. Second, personal data, once de-identified, can satisfy an exception under Article 18(2)(iv) of the PIPA. Either way, for de-identified data, there would be room for manoeuvre and utilisation.

i. *The 2016 Guideline*

The 2016 Guideline was a result of the joint efforts made by the government[25] to create a balance between data utilisation and data protection. The 2016 Guideline did not have the power or authority of a statute because it is simply a government-issued guideline and not even an administrative ordinance. Nonetheless, since it was issued by multiple government agencies, it carried a heavy de facto authority in practice.

The 2016 Guideline offered an explanation on various de-identification techniques and suggested utilising these techniques appropriately as needed. Specifically, it established a four-step approach for de-identifying personal data. First, it should be examined if the given data falls under the legal definition of personal data. Obviously, if deemed personal data, such data should be de-identified prior to engaging in analytics or other utilisation.

Second, actual de-identification is conducted. For de-identification, identifiers should be removed in a given dataset and, as a general rule, attributes should also be eliminated to the extent that they are not needed for the purposes of the proposed analytics. With the remaining data elements, various statistical methods may be applied in order to prevent linkage attacks and other attempts for re-identification. Most notably, the concept of *k*-anonymity is proffered as an important concept to be applied.[26] Further, if needed, the concepts of *l*-diversity[27] and/or *t*-closeness[28]

[25] The agencies involved include the following: the Office for Government Policy Coordination; the Ministry of the Interior (now the MOIS); the KCC; the FSC; the Ministry of Science, ICT, and Future Planning (now the Ministry of Science and ICT); and the Ministry of Health and Welfare.

[26] A release of data is said to satisfy *k*-anonymity if each equivalence class contains at least *k* records (in other words, each person's information is indistinguishable from at least $k - 1$ individuals' information in the release): P Samarati and L Sweeney, 'Protecting Privacy When Disclosing Information: k-Anonymity and its Enforcement through Generalization and Suppression' [1998] *Proceedings of the IEEE Symposium on Security and Privacy* 4–5.

could be applied as well. The 2016 Guideline provides illustrations as to how various statistical methods can be applied, such as pseudonymisation, aggregation, data reduction, data suppression and data masking.

Third, after the de-identification process is finished, an assessment should be made by a panel of experts regarding the adequacy of the de-identification that took place. An important criterion in the assessment process is again the concept of *k*-anonymity.[29]

Fourth, if de-identification is considered to be adequate, de-identified data can then be utilised without obtaining the data subject's consent. At the same time, the data controller is required to assume a duty to prevent the illegitimate use of data – for example, the re-identification of data.

After the 2016 Guideline was issued, several public agencies were designated,[30] with mandates to provide assistance in the process of de-identifying personal data and to carry out tasks of linking or combining datasets that are de-identified. Within a year, pursuant to the 2016 Guideline, certain de-identification and data combination projects were reported to have been carried out involving multiple organisations, including mobile carriers, insurers and credit card companies.[31] Through these projects, companies de-identified part of their data and asked one of the designated agencies to link the data, confirm the de-identification status and return the consolidated dataset. Amid controversies over the validity and legality of carrying out these projects, in November 2017, 11 non-governmental organisations (NGOs)[32] joined forces and filed criminal complaints against four of the

[27] A release of data is said to satisfy *l*-diversity if each equivalence class has at least *l* well-represented values for each sensitive attribute: Ninghui Li et al, '*t*-Closeness: Privacy beyond *k*-Anonymity and *i*-Diversity' [2007] *IEEE 23rd International Conference on Data Engineering* 107–08.

[28] A release of data is said to satisfy *t*-closeness if the distribution of a sensitive attribute in any equivalence class is close (within a threshold *t*) to the distribution of the attribute in the table: ibid, 109–11.

[29] The expert assessment panel thus determines the reference or threshold value of *k*, after taking into consideration various factors such as the number of (quasi-)identifiers, the possibilities of accruing linkable data, the possibilities of re-identification attempts, the potential damage caused by re-identification and the purposes of data utilization. Once the reference value of *k* is determined, among other tasks, the expert panel compares the value of *k*-anonymity achieved through de-identification with the reference value of *k*. In principle, if the level of *k* achieved through de-identification is higher than the reference *k*, de-identification would be considered successful.

[30] They include the Korea Internet & Security Agency (KISA), the National Information Society Agency (NIA), the Korea Credit Information Services (KCIS), the Korea Financial Security Institute (KFSI), the Social Security Information Service (SSIS) and the Korea Education & Research Information Service (KERIS).

[31] It was disclosed in October 2017 by a member of the national legislature, Hyeseon Chu, who obtained the records of de-identification projects from the four designated public agencies in the course of the parliamentary inspection of the administration: J Kim, 'A Surge of Distribution of De-identified Customer Personal Data: 340 Million Items within a Year' *The Hankyoreh* (9 October 2017), www.hani.co.kr/arti/economy/it/813776.html.

[32] They include a lawyer group (Lawyers for a Democratic Society), four healthcare NGOs (the Korean Federation of Medical Activist Groups for Health Rights, the Association of Physicians for Humanism, Korean Pharmacists for Democratic Society and the Association of Korea Doctors for Health Rights), a national trade union centre (the Korean Confederation of Trade Unions) and five other NGOs (People's Solidarity for Participatory Democracy, the Korean Progressive Network Centre, the Citizens' Action Network, the People's Coalition for Media Reform, and Solidarity for Workers' Health).

designated public agencies and the companies which carried out these projects for alleged violations of the PIPA, the Credit Information Act and the IC Network Act.[33] The NGOs contended that the 2016 Guideline was flawed and illegitimate in itself as it infringed data subjects' constitutional right to control personal data, and that any de-identification work conducted following the 2016 Guideline was illegal.[34]

In March 2019, Seoul Central Prosecutors' Office decided not to indict these public agencies and companies on the ground that the consolidated data do not fall under the definition of personal data under the PIPA. More specifically, the following reasons were provided: it would not be possible to re-identify data subjects from the data; the allegedly illegal acts are not punishable as they were conducted pursuant to the direction of relevant public authorities; and the data combination was carried out for research purposes.[35] While the accused public agencies and companies were cleared from possibilities of criminal liability, the mere fact that a criminal complaint was filed had a chilling effect on the business community.

B. Pseudonymisation under the 2020 Amendments

i. Preparation for Legislation

With respect to the 2016 Guideline, a major contentious issue arose in relation to the mechanics which allowed for the combination of datasets from two or more sources. Under this scheme, in order for the combination to take place, organisations holding datasets should transfer their data to one of the designated public agencies so that this public agency can combine the datasets. In that process, data would initially be de-identified, and the data combination would be carried out with such de-identified data. What was not entirely clear was whether such de-identified-and-combined data should legally be deemed personal data.

While controversies surrounding the 2016 Guideline ensued, an argument was made that pseudonymisation could provide a useful alternative to the data de-identification scheme contained in the 2016 Guideline. This argument was in part inspired by the related pseudonymisation provisions contained in the GDPR. In particular, the Presidential Committee on the Fourth Industrial Revolution served as an important venue for public debates.[36] The Committee, among other

[33] T Park, 'Does Common Customer Tendency Analysis Qualify for the Research Purpose? Concerns Raised over Retrogression in Data Protection' *The Hankyoreh* (28 March 2019), www.hani.co.kr/arti/economy/it/887851.html.

[34] ibid.

[35] ibid.

[36] This Committee was established in 2017 with the aim of laying the foundations for the so-called Fourth Industrial Revolution, including AI, and of providing a coordination channel among government agencies in relation to the development and propagation of new policy agenda involving rapid social change: Presidential Committee on the Fourth Industrial Revolution Official Website, https://www.4th-ir.go.kr/home/en.

things, held two 'Hackathon' meetings in 2018 to discuss issues related to personal data.[37]

The first of these Hackathon meetings concluded that legal concepts related to personal data need to be streamlined and that the concept of pseudonymisation needed to be discussed further. At the second Hackathon meeting on personal data, the concept of pseudonymisation was included as a main discussion item and the GDPR's relevant provisions were more extensively discussed. The participants reached the following conclusions regarding pseudonymisation:[38]

- pseudonymised data can be utilised for a purpose other than the initial purpose of collection or can be transferred to a third party to achieve the following purposes: (i) archiving purposes in the public interest; (ii) scientific and/or research purposes; or (iii) statistical purposes;[39]
- during the relevant processes, appropriate safeguards such as technical and organisational measures should be employed;[40] and
- scientific and/or research purposes may include an industrial research purpose, and the statistical purposes may include a commercial purpose.[41]

It was also agreed that the use of personal data for the purposes compatible with the initial purposes should be permitted to the extent that due considerations are made regarding various circumstances, including pseudonymisation.[42]

ii. 2020 Amendments

A key conclusion reached at the end of these Hackathon meetings on personal data was that appropriate statutory amendments were needed. In response, government agencies undertook the task of preparing an amendment proposal. In November 2018, the government submitted to the National Assembly (Korea's legislature) the amendment proposals for the PIPA, the Credit Information Act

[37] One of the authors participated in the Hackathons and the related meetings before and after the Hackathons. While called 'Hackathon', it was in practice akin to a lengthy town hall meeting among relevant stakeholders and experts.

[38] Presidential Committee on the Fourth Industrial Revolution, 'Press Release: Reviewing the Scope and Objective of Utilisation of Pseudonymised Data, the Reform of the Information Rating System for Facilitating the Use of Cloud Computing, and the Alleviation of Difficulties that the Drone Industry Faces' (5 April 2018) 3, 4th-ir.go.kr/hackathon/detail/7?num=03.

[39] Although GDPR provisions were not mentioned in the public announcement, this is arguably modelled after arts 5(1)(b) and 89(1) of the GDPR, which exempts from purpose limitation processing for archiving in the public interest, scientific or historical research, or statistical purposes.

[40] This is arguably modelled after art 89(1) of GDPR, which requires safeguards relating to processing for archiving in the public interest, scientific or historical research, or statistical purposes.

[41] Although GDPR provisions were not explicitly mentioned in the public announcement, this development is arguably inspired by the broad interpretation of scientific research and statistical purposes under Recitals 159 and 162 of the GDPR.

[42] Presidential Committee on the Fourth Industrial Revolution (n 38) 3. The 'EU GDPR' was explicitly referenced in the public announcement in the part where the concept of compatibility was mentioned.

and the IC Network Act.[43] The amendment proposals were finally passed by the legislature on 9 January 2020, promulgated on 4 February 2020, and became effective on 5 August 2020.

The amendments to the PIPA contain several provisions on pseudonymisation. They define pseudonymisation as 'the processing of personal data in such a manner that a specific individual becomes not identifiable without the use of additional information, rendered by removing a part of the data, replacing all or a part of the data, etc'.[44] This definition is somewhat analogous to the definition of pseudonymisation under Article 4(5) of the GDPR.[45] It is yet unclear if the concept of pseudonymisation under Korea's PIPA carries the same meaning as the concept of pseudonymisation under the GDPR. With respect to the concept under Korea's PIPA, the following appears to be noteworthy: data which can be attributed to a specific individual would fail to qualify as pseudonymised data if identification can take place through, for instance, using certain additional data;[46] certain methods of pseudonymisation (ie, removal or replacement) are specifically mentioned in the statute, although these methods are not meant to be exhaustive; and the separation of additional information and technical and organisational measures are not embedded in the definition itself, but instead constitute a part of the legal obligations that should be complied with in the process of collecting and utilising pseudonymised data.

The amendments made clear that pseudonymised data still falls under the definition of personal data (Article 2(i)).[47] Pseudonymised data can be processed without consent from a data subject for: (i) statistical purposes; (ii) scientific research purposes; and (iii) archiving purposes in the public interest (Article 28-2(1)). This is also similar to Article 89(1) of the GDPR, except that 'historical research purposes' are not included. The pseudonymised data to be transferred to a third party should not include identifiers either (Article 28-2(2)).

The PIPA explicitly introduced a scheme for the consolidation of pseudonymised data. Only designated agencies are permitted to link or combine pseudonymised datasets sourced from different data holders and to prepare a

[43] These statutory amendment proposals were submitted by individual law-makers, with the appearance that they were submitted on the law-makers' own initiatives. They were, for all practical purposes, the government's amendment bills.

[44] PIPA, art 2(i-2).

[45] Art 4(5) of the GDPR provides that 'pseudonymisation' means 'the processing of personal data in such a manner that the personal data can no longer be attributed to a specific data subject without the use of additional information, provided that such additional information is kept separately and is subject to technical and organisational measures to ensure that the personal data are not attributed to an identified or identifiable natural person'.

[46] Here, the 'additional data' would include the hash function or mapping table that was used during the process of rendering the original data into a pseudonymised data. It is unclear if the 'additional data' would include the auxiliary information or background knowledge, which was not used in the process of preparing the pseudonymised data.

[47] This is in line with Recital 26 of the GDPR, which provides that: 'Personal data which have undergone pseudonymisation, which could be attributed to a natural person by the use of additional information should be considered to be information on an identifiable natural person'.

combined dataset (Article 28-3). Also, appropriate technical, organisational and physical safeguards should be put in place for the processing of pseudonymised data. These safeguards include the separate storage of additional data which would be needed to reconstruct the original data from the pseudonymised data (Article 28-4(1)). The accompanying amendments to the Enforcement Decree for the PIPA[48] stipulate that the data controller which requested linkage or combination can, after such linkage or combination, make a request to take out the consolidated data from the designated agency, and a separate approval from the agency is required to take out the data (Article 29-3(1) and (3) of the PIPA Enforcement Decree). The data controller should also keep records regarding the history of the processing of pseudonymised data, including its purposes and recipients (Article 28-4(2) of the PIPA). The processing of pseudonymised data is exempted from not only the consent requirement but also various other PIPA rules, such as the data subject's right to access, rectification and erasure, and the data controller's obligation to notify data breaches to data subjects (Article 28-7). The amendments to the PIPA do not make an explicit reference to anonymous or anonymised data, unlike Recital 26 of the GDPR. However, the PIPA contains a provision which can be interpreted to define anonymised data in an indirect way. In other words, the PIPA provides that the law does not apply to certain data when identification cannot possibly take place by being combined with other data and that, in making the decision about identifiability, reasonableness of the time, cost and technology should be considered (Article 58-2).

The amendments to the Credit Information Act also include provisions on pseudonymisation. They define pseudonymisation as 'the processing of personal credit data in such a manner that a specific credit data subject becomes not identifiable without the use of additional information' (Article 2(xv)). Similar to the amendments to the PIPA, the Credit Information Act provides that pseudonymised data may be processed for archiving purposes in the public interest, for research purposes or for statistical purposes (Article 32(6)(ix-2)).[49] This provision, unlike the PIPA, explicitly declares that research purposes include industrial research purposes and that statistical purposes may include commercial purposes such as market survey. The amendments further stipulate that credit bureaus, credit registries, debt collection agencies, 'My Data' service providers,[50] and data furnishers and users (which include banks and other financial institutions)

[48] Enforcement Decree for the Personal Information Protection Act, Presidential Decree No 30892 (amended 4 August 2020, effective 5 August 2020).

[49] While the Credit Information Act provides for an exemption for 'research purposes', the PIPA's exemption refers to 'scientific research purposes'. The difference, if any, between 'research' under the Credit Information Act and 'scientific research' under the PIPA remains unclear.

[50] A 'My Data' service provider may engage in the following: gathering and consolidating a customer's credit data from various sources; giving the customer access to the consolidated data; analysing the customer's credit rating, financial risks and consumption patterns; providing customised financial consulting; and recommending financial products. Overall, providing this line of services is predicated upon the concept of data portability and upon the introduction of credit management business for individuals: Credit Information Act, arts 2(ix-ii) and (ix-iii).

(collectively hereinafter 'creditors') must store additional data that were used for pseudonymisation in a separate place or otherwise erase such data altogether (Article 40-2(1)). Appropriate technical, organisational and physical safeguards must also be put in place for pseudonymised personal credit data. These safeguards include preparing for an internal management plan or a retention system for log records (Article 40-2(2)), and establishing a system to recall pseudonymised data, suspend its processing and immediately erase identifiers if it turns out that an individual is identifiable in the course of using pseudonymised data (Article 40-2(3)).

The amendments to the Credit Information Act also include provisions on the linkage or combination of datasets held by different creditors. Only a designated data agency can link or combine a dataset held by a creditor with another dataset held by another creditor (Article 17-2(1)). A creditor can transfer personal credit data to the data agency for this purpose without obtaining consent from the data subjects (Article 32(6)(ix-3)). The data agency must pseudonymise or anonymise the consolidated dataset before releasing the dataset to the creditor or to a third party (Article 17-2(2)).

With respect to an anonymised dataset, a creditor can further request the data agency to review the adequacy of anonymisation, and the data agency's finding of adequacy would be considered prima facie evidence that personal data has been rendered unidentifiable (Article 40-2(3)–(5)).

IV. Theoretical and Practical Perspectives

A. Overview

Korea does not have a long history of enforcing its legal regime for data protection. The PIPA was enacted in 2011 and, in particular, with regard to data de-identification, it has only been a few years since serious discussions began to take place. Although the government published its 2016 Guideline in order to provide practical guidance regarding de-identification of personal data, due to various legal and other constraints, potential users have not been able to actively embrace the methodology of de-identification contained in the 2016 Guideline.

While debates continued in Korea after the publication of the 2016 Guideline, in the EU, the GDPR was enacted. This led to active discussions in Korea concerning what useful implications could be drawn from the GDPR. As such, some of the concepts and provisions contained in the GDPR had a significant impact in the evolution process of the Korean data protection regime, in particular in the context of developing the concepts of de-identification and pseudonymisation.

The 2020 Amendments, which were introduced to address the limitations of the 2016 Guideline and other related concerns, contain unique features such as provisions on data linkage and on designating agencies for carrying out such linkage.

B. Uncertainties that Remain about the Production, Use and Linking of Pseudonymised Data

Following the 2020 Amendments, preparatory work for issuing subordinate decrees and guidelines has been under way. Through this process, certain issues that have not been resolved or clarified may perhaps need to be addressed, as will be discussed below.

i. Failure to Address Diverse Risks Surrounding Pseudonymised Data

Regarding pseudonymisation, the PIPA and the Credit Information Act appear to postulate a particular type of situation under which data contained in an original dataset is transformed through a pseudonymisation process and a new dataset is created. In other words, in a typical case, there would be an original dataset, which contains personal data, and a transformed dataset, which is derived from the original dataset and contains pseudonymised data. According to the explanatory guidelines that the PIPC and the FSC issued in September and August 2020, respectively,[51] examples of 'additional information' (which could be used for the reconstruction of the original dataset) would include cryptographic keys or functions (as in two-way encryption) or mapping tables (as in one-way encryption or other irreversible substitution) that were used in the process of pseudonymisation (or reconstruction of the original data). Interpreted this way, these statutes arguably fail to explicitly address risks involving: (i) reconstruction of the original dataset by utilising an auxiliary dataset held by a third party (eg, identifying a person by matching the pseudonymised dataset with another firm's customer list); (ii) re-identification of a single individual without reconstructing the whole dataset, perhaps by utilising background knowledge (eg, inferring the identify of a top sports star from an exceptionally high salary disclosed by a news report); or (iii) inadvertent or unintentional re-identification (eg, disclosing disease without the knowledge that it is rare enough to identify the few patients contained in the dataset).[52]

ii. The Scope of 'Scientific Research Purposes'

Amid the debates on pseudonymisation, particular attention was paid to the meaning and scope of 'scientific research purposes' under the PIPA (Article 28-2(1)) or 'research purposes' under the Credit Information Act (Article 32(6)(ix-2)) as

[51] PIPC, Guideline on Processing of Pseudonymised Data (September 2020); FSC, Guide on Pseudonymisation and Anonymisation in the Financial Sector (6 August 2020).

[52] However, there is a requirement: (i) not to process pseudonymised data for purposes of identification; and (ii) to stop processing and to reclaim or discard data if identifiable data is produced while processing pseudonymised data: PIPA, art 28-5.

lawful bases for processing pseudonymised data without the consent of the data subject. The PIPA provides that scientific research means research which applies scientific methodology and that it includes technological development and demonstration, fundamental research, applied research and privately funded research (Article 2(8)). This broad interpretation is modelled after Recital 159 of the GDPR. However, it is not entirely clear whether scientific research would include research with commercial or industrial motivations.

More specifically, while the Credit Information Act made it clear that the research purposes include industrial research purposes, and that the statistical purposes include commercial purposes such as marketing research (Article 32(6)(ix-ii)), the PIPA does not contain an analogous provision. Separate from what is (or is not) provided for in the statutory language, the PIPC's guideline on the PIPA explains that the scientific research purposes include industrial purposes and that the statistical purposes include commercial purposes. Thus, while it is still unclear to what extent, if any, scientific research (under the PIPA) or research (under the Credit Information Act) would be legally interpreted to include commercial research, references from other jurisdictions, such as the UK Information Commissioner's Office (ICO) Anonymisation Code of Practice[53] and the European Data Protection Supervisor's preliminary opinion in 2020,[54] appear to support the argument that the concept is broad enough to encompass commercial motivations.

iii. The Process of Pseudonymisation

As to the concept and methodology of pseudonymisation, the 2020 Amendments did not make clear whether in order to satisfy the legal requirements: (i) it is sufficient to remove or replace only direct identifiers in a given dataset; or (ii) quasi-identifiers and other attributes should also be examined and modified as needed in order to reduce linkability and prevent inference.[55] The former would entail a relatively straightforward, simple and low-cost process, but a downside

[53] The Code of Practice states the UK Data Protection Act makes it clear that 'research purposes include statistical or historical research, but other forms of research, for example market, social, commercial or opinion research, could benefit from the exemption': UK ICO, 'Anonymisation: Managing Data Protection Risk Code of Practice' (2012) 45, ico.org.uk/media/1061/anonymisation-code.pdf.

[54] '[N]ot only academic researchers but also … profit-seeking commercial companies can carry out scientific research': European Data Protection Supervisor (EDPS), 'A Preliminary Opinion on Data Protection and Scientific Research' (2020) 11, edps.europa.eu/data-protection/our-work/publications/opinions/preliminary-opinion-data-protection-and-scientific_en.

[55] This is inherently about the concept of identification and also about how to distinguish between anonymisation and pseudonymisation. In the context of anonymisation, quasi-identifiers and other attributes would need to be considered. 'Data controllers often assume that removing or replacing one or more attributes is enough to make the dataset anonymous. Many examples have shown that this is not the case; simply altering the ID does not prevent someone from identifying a data subject if quasi-identifiers remain in the dataset, or if the values of other attributes are still capable of identifying an individual': EU Data Protection Working Party, Opinion 05/2014 on Anonymisation Techniques [2014] (Opinion 05/2014) 21.

would be that a significant risk of linkage or inference attacks might remain. Such a risk may not be apparent when data that can possibly be used for a linkage or inference attack is hidden in a given dataset outside the identifiers. On the other hand, the opposite would be true with the latter method. The guidelines of the PIPC and the FSC do not appear to take a firm stand on this front. This could imply that, from a practical point of view, it would be safe to erase or replace not only direct identifiers but also quasi-identifiers (including peculiar attributes) in order to minimise the possibility that quasi-identifiers and other attributes could be used to link a record to an individual or to infer an individual from such a record.

iv. The Role of Designated Data Linking Agencies

It had been also unclear under the 2020 Amendments whether designated data-linking agencies would play a relatively limited role as a trusted third party (TTP), mainly linking records from different entities based on common linkage keys,[56] or whether they would assume more active roles like approving and managing the takeout process of a linked dataset. The Enforcement Decrees for the PIPA and the Credit Information Act appear to envision slightly different mechanisms for data linkage between the two laws.[57] For example, a data-linking agency under the Credit Information Act would: (i) receive linkage keys (along with datasets) directly from the entities wishing to combine the datasets that they hold and combine datasets based on the keys; and (ii) before transferring the combined dataset to the requesting entities, be given the authority to further pseudonymise or anonymise the combined dataset if the then level of pseudonymisation is found to be inadequate. On the other hand, a data-linking agency under the PIPA would receive linkage keys from the requesting entities, which would generate linkage keys in consultation with the Korea Internet & Security Agency (KISA). As such, the KISA would assume a special role for the management of linkage keys. A data-linking agency under the PIPA should also: (i) be equipped with a secure research space within its premise where entities can link their datasets based on the connecting key; and (ii) be given the authority to approve or reject the entities' application for takeout of the combined dataset.

v. Failure to Draw a Clear Line between Pseudonymisation and Anonymisation

As mentioned above in section III, while the PIPA does not explicitly employ the concept of anonymised data, it provides that the law would not apply to the data

[56] See European Union Agency for Cybersecurity (ENISA), 'Pseudonymisation Techniques and Best Practices' (2019) 14, enisa.europa.eu/publications/pseudonymisation-techniques-and-best-practices.

[57] Enforcement Decree for the Personal Information Protection Act, Presidential Decree No 30892 (amended 4 August 2020, effective 5 August 2020); Enforcement Decree for the Credit Information Act, Presidential Decree No 30893 (amended 4 August 2020, effective 5 August 2020).

when identification cannot take place even through combination with other data and with reasonable consideration of time, cost and technology (Article 58-2). As a matter of statutory interpretation, this concept arguably overlaps with the definition of pseudonymised data: personal data processed in such a manner that a specific individual becomes unidentifiable 'without the use of and combination with additional information for the reconstruction of the original data' (Article 2(i)(*da*), (i-2)). In other words, if re-identification takes place with certain additional information and only after spending an exorbitant amount of time and efforts, the data at issue would fall under the definitions of anonymised data and, at the same time, of pseudonymised data. However, this cannot be the case since pseudonymised data is, by definition, personal data.

vi. Potential Conflict with Other Legislations

The 2020 Amendments may conflict with what is contained in other special laws and, as such, harmonisation measures may need to be taken. In theory, the 2020 Amendments, as a later general law, does not necessarily repeal an earlier special law (*lex posterior generalis non derogate legi priori speciali*) and, further, the PIPA provides that unless other laws contain specialised provisions, the provisions of the PIPA would apply (Article 6). Notwithstanding the general principles that can be generated from this, there would be situations where clarifications are needed. To illustrate this, in healthcare, de-identification of personal health data takes place on a regular basis, and there are laws and regulations governing such de-identification processes. In particular, the Bioethics and Safety Act defines 'anonymisation' as (i) erasing identifiers or (ii) replacing the whole or part of identifiers with a unique ID used within an institution conducting research (Article 2(19)). This definition of anonymisation is very similar to the definition of pseudonymisation under the newly amended PIPA. On 4 August 2020, the Ministry of Health and Welfare (MOHW) issued a ministerial interpretation that the second part of the definition of anonymisation under the Bioethics and Safety Act encompasses pseudonymisation under the PIPA and that when conducting research involving human subjects, the requisite review and approval process of an Institutional Review Board (IRB) can be exempted if healthcare data are adequately pseudonymised.[58]

C. Additional Notes on Technology-Based Contact Tracing in Response to the COVID-19 Pandemic

In response to the outbreak of the COVID-19 pandemic, various approaches for technology-based contact tracing have taken place around the world. In broad

[58] Ministry of Health and Welfare Official Website, 'Guide on a Ruling on the Bioethics Act-Related Institutions Management Guideline according to Amendments to the PIPA' (5 August 2020), www.mohw.go.kr/react/jb/sjb0406vw.jsp?PAR_MENU_ID=03&MENU_ID=030406&page=1&CONT_SEQ=359711.

terms, many European countries opted for a decentralised, user-centric approach based on the Bluetooth Low Energy (BLE) technology in order to discover and log individuals in proximity. This approach can further be divided into a partially centralised approach and a fully decentralised approach. Examples of a partially centralised approach include PEPP-PT (tried in France, and tested and discarded in the UK) and BlueTrace (deployed in Singapore and Australia). Decentralised approaches include DP3T (adopted in Austria) and the Apple-Google Exposure Notification API (adopted in, among others, Germany, Switzerland, the UK, Estonia and Lithuania). Outside Europe, several states in the US (such as North Dakota and South Dakota) and Japan adopted the Apple-Google Exposure Notification scheme.

However, Korea, alongside Israel, has taken a fully centralised approach. Under Korea's centralised approach, the Korea Disease Control and Prevention Agency (hereinafter 'the KDCA') would gather and compile data from various sources. Data gathered for the purposes of the KDCA include location data that can be extracted using mobile base station data from mobile carriers and payment card transaction records.

Between a decentralised approach and a centralised approach, in general, the former approach would be more privacy-preserving, in part because it employs pseudonymised IDs. On the other hand, the latter approach is more effective in promptly and precisely tracing confirmed cases and those who were in close proximity to the confirmed individuals. This centralised approach is also helpful in saving time and resources that epidemiological investigators need to take for the purposes of interviewing and tracing.[59]

After experiencing the MERS outbreak in 2015, Korea revised the CDPCA and inserted a pandemic trigger provision, which authorised embarking on a centralised contact tracing system once a pandemic breaks out.[60] Also, once a pandemic begins, this Act's provisions on data collection would override the general consent requirement under the PIPA (Article 15(1)(ii) of the PIPA). Despite this statutory basis, legal controversies have arisen. In particular, several activist groups joined forces and filed a constitutional petition seeking the Korea Constitutional Court's decision that the provision, as well as the government's collection of mobile base station data based on this provision of the CDPCA, violates the constitutional right to self-determination of personal data and privacy.

The contact tracing scheme adopted in Korea served as a crucial enabling factor in the implementation of the country's trace, test and treat strategy.[61] However, it also revealed what could possibly go wrong when pseudonymised data change hands and are communicated to the public. In particular, pseudonymisation has often been proved to be insufficient: although names of the confirmed individuals were never revealed, some of them have at times been re-identified based on the

[59] S Park et al, 'Information Technology–Based Tracing Strategy in Response to COVID-19 in South Korea: Privacy Controversies' *JAMA* (23 April 2020), doi:10.1001/jama.2020.6602.

[60] ibid.

[61] ibid.

age, sex, domicile, and other quasi-identifiers and attributes that are exposed in the public disclosure process.

D. Prospects

Pseudonymisation and other de-identification methodologies are not novel concepts in themselves. However, traditionally, they have been implemented under strict control based on stringent professional ethics in highly specialised areas such as the healthcare and pharmaceutical industry. The 2020 Amendments expanded the scope of application to much wider areas, without restriction in principle. This poses daunting new challenges in terms of harmonising conflicting concepts and establishing best practices across different research environments and different industrial sectors. There remain a large number of uncertainties and ambiguities. Experiencing some level of uncertainties and ambiguities may be inevitable in the realm of data simply because enough experiences have not yet been accumulated. It is also expected that there will be continued discussions and debates among various stakeholders, including policy-makers, businesses and civic groups. The introduction of the concept of pseudonymisation in the 2020 Amendments was inspired by the related provisions contained in the GDPR. Yet, obviously, what is contained in the 2020 Amendments in Korea is different from the related GDPR provisions. Among other things, one important difference would be that while pseudonymisation is generally considered as a component of various safeguarding measures in the GDPR for an enhanced level of data protection, in Korea's 2020 Amendments, pseudonymisation is considered as part of the requisite conditions that must be satisfied in order to engage in certain types of data processing activities.

During the course of future discussions, Korea may well pay particular attention to technical alternatives such as differential privacy,[62] homomorphic encryption[63] and federated learning[64] in order to overcome the limitations of the de-identification and pseudonymisation methodologies. However, none of the technical methodologies can be perfect. More importantly, there will always be

[62] Differential privacy is a formally defined concept, but intuitively, it requires the injection of random noise when publishing aggregate data in order to limit the disclosure of each individual's private data. See C Dwork et al, 'Calibrating Noise to Sensitivity in Private Data Analysis' (2016) 7(3) *Journal of Privacy and Confidentiality* 17.

[63] Homomorphic encryption is a 'scheme that allows one to evaluate circuits over encrypted data without being able to decrypt'. See C Gentry, 'Fully Homomorphic Encryption Using Ideal Lattices' in *Proceedings of the 41st ACM Symposium on Theory of Computing* (2009) 169–78, https://doi.org/10.1145/1536414.1536440.

[64] Federated learning enables client systems to collaboratively learn a 'shared prediction model' without uploading the training data to a server, 'decoupling the ability to do machine learning from the need to store the data in the cloud'. See B McMahan et al, 'Federated Learning: Collaborative Machine Learning without Centralized Training Data' *Google AI Blog* (6 April 2017), https://ai.googleblog.com/2017/04/federated-learning-collaborative.html.

a need for relevant social assessments and proper procedural safeguards, even when more reliable technical methodologies are introduced. In other words, if the concept of differential privacy is to be deployed, the value of 'privacy budget' will need to be determined at a social or community level and, depending on the socially determined privacy budget, different sets of data circumstances will be determined under which differential privacy methodologies can safely be deployed. Determining all relevant parameters as well as putting in place proper safeguards will require not just theoretical expertise but also accumulated experiences and know-how. These are difficult challenges to meet. Once the challenges are met, Korea's experience, in particular the trial and error throughout this long evolving legislative history as well as the continuing debates among different stakeholders, may serve as a useful reference for other jurisdictions facing a similar conundrum with the advent of the data-driven society.

In sum, the concept of pseudonymisation was introduced in an effort to strike a balance between conflicting needs for the protection and utilisation of personal data, in particular in the context of developing AI technologies. However, many uncertainties remain as to the details to be adopted in the process of conducting pseudonymisation. These are expected to be clarified as more real-world cases are accumulated and more debates are spurred on the subject of the further development of AI technologies. Korea will perhaps need to pay continuous attention to innovative technical alternatives that might transcend a trade-off between protection and use.

3

Data Trusts for Lawful AI Data Sharing

CHRIS REED*

I. Introduction

Data sharing is never easy. Even a simple sharing relationship, between two entities whose common aims are advanced by that sharing, can be difficult to negotiate. The difficulties grow exponentially as the number of data-sharing partners increases. And these are only the difficulties which arise when negotiating between the data-sharing parties themselves – once we add in the need to respect the interests of those who are external to the data sharing but who nevertheless are impacted by the sharing, we can see that the problem becomes very complex.

Artificial intelligence (AI) or, more accurately, the data analysis and machine learning on which much of AI is based has a real need for data sharing. Machine learning analyses large datasets, and the larger and more comprehensive the dataset, the more likely it is that machine learning will produce 'correct' results. But it is rare to find comprehensive datasets which are under the sole control of one entity. More commonly, data is held by a number of different entities, so that a comprehensive dataset can only be produced if they share data with each other.

A related issue, which is noted but not analysed in this chapter, is that of building up a comprehensive dataset on humans by persuading individuals to contribute their own data.[1] A simple data-sharing agreement cannot cope with this number of parties, for reasons which will become obvious later.

All these are obstacles to data sharing, and will be examined in more detail in section II. Section III explains the fundamental principles which should underpin any system of regulation and governance designed to remove or reduce these obstacles, and section IV discusses why overarching regulation at a national level

* This research is supported by the National Research Foundation, Singapore under its Emerging Areas Research Projects (EARP) Funding Initiative. This research was also supported by the Cloud Legal Project at the Centre for Commercial Law Studies, Queen Mary University of London and the author is grateful to Microsoft for the generous financial support that has made this project possible. Any opinions, findings and conclusions or recommendations expressed in this material are those of the author and do not reflect the views of National Research Foundation, Singapore or of Microsoft.

[1] For example, via researchers soliciting individuals to contribute their personal data for a particular research project, where that data will be shared with other researchers. The UK COVID Symptom Study (see n 17 below and the accompanying text) is an example here.

is unlikely to be successful. This analysis suggests that each data-sharing instance requires its own bespoke system of regulation and governance, and section V introduces data trusts as a potentially useful, private-sector rule-maker for data sharing. Section VI focuses on how a data trust's governance system should be shaped so as to secure the trust of all stakeholders and to generate a system of data-sharing rules which is accepted as legitimate, while section VII identifies data trusts as a potential mechanism to outsource complicated regulatory compliance, using data protection compliance as its illustration. Throughout, examples are taken from EU and Singapore law and regulation, both hard and soft, and these are compared to show how different approaches to regulatory issues can affect the operation and effectiveness of data trusts.

II. Obstacles to Data Sharing

The main obstacle to the kinds of data sharing which AI needs is that for most useful data, there are numerous entities and individuals who have interests in that data. Sharing inevitably has the potential to compromise those interests.

Some players will consider themselves to be owners of the data and thus have an interest in controlling how others use it. They might have a legal ownership right in the form of a copyright and database right or some other form of intellectual property, but such rights are more limited than most dataset owners usually believe. Copyright requires a work of *authorship*, and in many jurisdictions, this is framed in terms of intellectual creativity. For example, in the EU, *Infopaq International A/S v Danske Dagblades Forening*[2] decided that a work should be the author's own intellectual creation in order to qualify for copyright protection. This was explained more fully in *SAS Institute Inc v World Programming Ltd*:

> The essence of the term is that the person in question has exercised expressive and creative choices in producing the work. The more restricted the choices, the less likely it is that the product will be the intellectual creation (or the expression of the intellectual creation) of the person who produced it.[3]

What this means is that although there is no requirement for a work to show artistic or literary merit, the mere effort required to produce it is not enough. Many, perhaps most, datasets will not meet this standard for copyright protection.

Even where, as in Singapore, the required level of creativity is low enough to protect datasets via copyright,[4] that dataset requires a human author. In *Asia Pacific Publishing Pte Ltd v Pioneers & Leaders (Publishers) Pte Ltd*,[5] the Singapore

[2] *Infopaq International A/S v Danske Dagblades Forening* [2009] ECR I-6569.

[3] *SAS Institute Inc v World Programming Ltd* [2013] EWCA Civ 1482 [31].

[4] See *Global Yellow Pages Ltd v Promedia Directories Pte Ltd* [2017] 2 SLR 185, holding that sufficient creativity might be found in the effort, skill and judgement involved in selecting and arranging data, but that this protection could not extend to the factual information contained in the dataset.

[5] *Asia Pacific Publishing Pte Ltd v Pioneers & Leaders (Publishers) Pte Ltd* [2011] 4 SLR 381.

Court of Appeal held that tables of horse-racing information did not attract copyright because none of the individuals who contributed data had made enough of a contribution for any one of them, or group of them, to be identifiable as its author. In Singapore, as elsewhere, data receives a low or non-existent level of legal protection, and the Law Reform Committee of the Singapore Academy of Law has rejected suggestions that the protections offered by property law (of all types) should be extended to provide greater rights of ownership:

> Given the nature of data, there are fundamental difficulties – on grounds of jurisprudential principle and policy – to using ownership and property rights as legal frameworks to control data. In addition, any attempt to create such a right would mean significant disruption to established legal frameworks.[6]

The EU's *sui generis* database right also offers less protection than might be expected. Protection is based on a substantial investment in 'obtaining, verification or presentation of the contents'.[7] But *British Horseracing Board Ltd and Others v William Hill Organization Ltd*[8] decided that the costs of *creating or generating* the data do not count for this purpose, and for many datasets, that will have been almost the entire element of investment.

A bigger obstacle might be the psychological sense of ownership, which leads dataset owners to demand restrictions on use as a precondition for sharing.[9] Psychological research reveals that individuals who believe they own an item exhibit a particularly strong endowment effect, so that they place a value on that item which cannot be explained by economic theories.[10] This is even more true if the individual considers that he or she has earned or deserves, the owned thing,[11] so that creators of works and datasets value their creations even higher than intellectual assets which were purchased from another creator.[12] This sense of ownership applies to information as well as to physical property,[13] even if there are in fact no

[6] Singapore Academy of Law, Law Reform Committee, *Rethinking Database Rights and Data Ownership in an AI World* (July 2020) 3, https://www.sal.org.sg/sites/default/files/SAL-LawReform-Pdf/2020-09/2020%20Rethinking%20Database%20Rights%20and%20Data%20Ownership%20in%20an%20AI%20World_ebook_0_1.pdf.

[7] Directive 96/9 on the legal protection of databases [1996] OJ L77/20, 27 March, art 7(1). See also W Chik and PW Lee, chs 4 and 5 in this volume, respectively.

[8] *British Horseracing Board Ltd and Others v William Hill Organization Ltd* [2001] EWHC 516 (Pat) (High Court); [2001] EWCA Civ 1268 (CA); Case C-203/02, 9 November 2004 [2005] RPC 260 (ECJ); [2005] EWCA Civ 863 (CA).

[9] See C Reed, 'Information Ownership in the Cloud' in C Millard (ed), *Cloud Computing Law*, 2nd edn (Oxford University Press, 2021).

[10] James K Beggan, 'On the Social Nature of Nonsocial Perception: The Mere Ownership Effect' (1992) 62 *Journal of Personality and Social Psychology* 229, suggesting that this is explained by the role which property ownership plays in one's self-image.

[11] G Loewenstein and S Issacharoff, 'Source Dependence in the Valuation of Objects' (1994) 7 *Journal of Behavioral Decision Making* 157, 165.

[12] C Buccafusco and C Sprigman, 'Valuing Intellectual Property: An Experiment' (2010) 96 *Cornell Law Review* 1.

[13] Researchers conducted experiments on personal information stored in Facebook accounts, which found that the more strongly an individual believed they owned that information, the more they would be willing to pay to preserve it from deletion. They also found that knowledge that a third party was

intellectual property rights in it. And of course, individuals believe that they own their personal data, even though in most cases they do not, probably because that information feels like an extension of their personalities and thus themselves.[14]

Whether a dataset 'owner' actually has legally recognised ownership rights in the dataset or merely perceives psychological ownership of it is irrelevant. If that person has exclusive control of the dataset, it will be necessary to protect their 'ownership' in order to persuade them to share the data.

As a separate issue, much of the data which is useful for AI relates to humans or human activities. Those individuals have an interest in protecting their privacy, and there may also be applicable data protection laws which need to be respected.[15] Again, data sharing will have an impact on those interests.

Next, useful data will often contain confidential information about its holder or about others. A simple example might be a corporation's sales data. This obviously contains confidential information about the corporation's business activities. And it also contains information about customers, such as what they buy and when. This too is likely to be confidential.

Third, there may be an element of public interest in the data. This chapter was written at the height of the 2020 COVID-19 pandemic, and in many countries, individuals are being asked to download a tracking and tracing app which will share personal data with national authorities to help control outbreaks of infection. Singapore has developed a contact tracing app[16] to help control the spread of the virus. In the UK, a partnership between a technology company, universities and health charities has developed the COVID Symptom Study App,[17] which asks individuals to record any symptoms they develop in order to create a research dataset. This dataset will be shared among a group of research organisations.[18] There is a clear public interest in the data generated by both apps, and sharing

interested in acquiring the information led individuals to value it even more highly. Interestingly, and perhaps counter to what lawyers have thought in this field, a belief in information ownership was demonstrated experimentally to be far more influential in valuing personal information highly than whether the information was considered private or not. See S Spiekermann, J Korunovska and C Bauer, 'Psychology of Ownership and Asset Defense: Why People Value their Personal Information Beyond Privacy', *International Conference on Information Systems* (ICIS 2012), 16–19 December 2012.

[14] This is Hegel's argument that our intellectual constructions become part of our persona: see Georg Wilhelm Friedrich Hegel, *Philosophy of Right* (1821). See also Spiekermann et al (n 13); RP Abelson and DA Prentice, 'Beliefs as Possessions: A Functional Perspective' in AR Pratkanis, SJ Breckler and AG Greenwald (eds), *Attitude Structure and Function* (Erlbaum, 1989) 361; H Dittmar, *The Social Psychology of Material Possessions: To Have is to Be* (St Martin's Press, 1992); JD Porteous, 'Home: The Territorial Core' (1976) 66 *Geographic Review* 383.

[15] See, eg, Singapore Academy of Law, Law Reform Committee, *Applying Ethical Principles for Artificial Intelligence in Regulatory Reform* (July 2020) 27, https://www.sal.org.sg/sites/default/files/SAL-LawReform-Pdf/2020-09/2020 Applying Ethical Principles for AI in Regulatory Reform_ebook.pdf: 'constant review and finetuning of [data protection] legislation – as well as consideration of other "soft" regulatory mechanisms – will likely be required to ensure that AI system designers and deployers have the regulatory freedom to research, develop and deploy AI systems but remain subject to sufficiently robust safeguards to effectively protect the general public'.

[16] TraceTogether website: www.tracetogether.gov.sg.

[17] COVID Symptom Study: www.covid.joinzoe.com.

[18] COVID Symptom Study, 'Privacy Notice': www.covid.joinzoe.com/privacy.

will need to consider that interest as well as the interests of individuals and researchers.

Finally, there is a range of ethical interests which will need to be considered and accommodated, both for their own sake and to ensure continued public acceptance of data sharing. The Law Reform Committee of the Singapore Academy of Law has identified eight ethical principles which should form part of the regulatory landscape for AI and are therefore also relevant to data sharing for AI research purposes:

> a) respecting fundamental interests; b) considering effects; c) wellbeing and safety; d) managing risks to human wellbeing; e) respect for values and culture; f) transparency; g) accountability; and h) the ethical use of data.[19]

This is by no means a comprehensive list of all the interests which will need to be respected if any planned data sharing is to be successful.

At first sight, it might seem that although the range of interests to be considered is wide and complex, the legal technique for dealing with the problem should be simple. All the necessary interests need to be identified and then a set of rules governing the data sharing needs to be put in place in a legally binding way. These rules might be made binding through simple contract, or through regulation or legislation.

However, there is one further (and vital) point. That legal technique works if the purposes for which the data will be shared can be specified. In that case, it is possible to work out how that sharing might adversely impact each interest and draft a rule to deal with it. But data-sharing purposes can change, particularly where machine learning is to be used. A dataset collected for one purpose might be found to be useful for an entirely new purpose. If so, the rules governing the original data sharing are unlikely to provide adequate protection for some, maybe even most, interests in the context of any new use of the dataset.

As another COVID-19 example, imagine a dataset of public transport journeys which singularises individual passengers by reference to their payment instrument, though without containing their banking details.[20] This dataset will have been collected for the purpose of improving the efficiency of the transport system, and appropriate protections for the interests of the individual passengers should have been built into any sharing. The individualisation of passengers is only important to identify matters such as round trips. But might not that data now be useful to analyse the movement patterns of individuals and how far they have repeat contact with each other, for the purpose of controlling the spread of infection by restricting collective or even individual movements? Analysis for this new purpose will focus more closely on the individuals and thus will create risks to their interests in privacy and freedom of movement which will not have been anticipated in the original data sharing.

[19] Singapore Academy of Law, Law Reform Committee (n 15) 1.

[20] For an understanding of how the data are already shared for analysis, see Fu Kurauchi and J Schmöcke (eds), *Public Transport Planning with Smart Card Data* (CRC Press, 2017).

This is where simple data sharing agreements fall down. If the shared data is used for new purposes, the rules established by that agreement will need to be amended to cover those new purposes. This is not easy. In the case of contractual agreements, such changes require the consent of all the original parties, and the greater the number of parties, the more unlikely it is that agreement will be reached. If the rules are established by regulation or legislation, they will need to be amended or re-enacted, a notoriously slow process.

III. Solving the Data-Sharing Problem

From what has been said above, it should be clear that any substantial data-sharing project will require a suitable regulatory system and also a system of governance which ensures there is sufficient trust from stakeholders that 'their' data will be looked after and used appropriately. The basic principles which should be adopted in setting up this regulation and governance are likely to be quite uncontroversial.

First, data should be shared only for clearly defined purposes. It is deeply problematic if data is shared with a third party in a completely unrestricted way. If personal data is involved, there will almost certainly be a breach of data protection law. And even if not, those with an interest in the data are likely to react unfavourably to sharing without safeguards, thus creating risks for future data sharing.[21] However, the original sharing purposes must not be fixed for all time, because that will prevent shared data from being used for AI research in new areas. The regulation and governance system therefore needs to include a mechanism for changing the purposes of sharing in a way which still respects the interests of those who are stakeholders in the data.

Second, and perhaps most importantly, the regulation and governance system must achieve trust on the part of stakeholders. They need to be convinced that their interests will be protected properly, and this should be a primary role for any form of regulation in this area. In particular, those who currently control datasets and are handing over control to another will want to be assured that the control they retain, in the form of restrictions on the use and onward sharing of those datasets, will be respected.[22]

[21] See, eg, N Kobie, 'Everyone Should Be Worried by Big Tech's NHS Data Grab' *Wired* (16 December 2019), www.wired.co.uk/article/google-apple-amazon-nhs-health-data.

[22] Singapore Academy of Law, Law Reform Committee (n 6) 6 and 46. Thus, the Law Reform Committee identifies that there are two issues of fundamental importance: 'a) who controls or has rights over such "big data" databases, and b) how best to ensure that those who contribute data to those databases retain an appropriate degree of control over, and access, to that data'. The Committee concludes that conferring a property right in data is not the best approach – if rights of control are needed, these should be conferred by specific legislation: 'If conferring a particular right or entitlement over personal data was felt to be sufficiently important, it would be entirely possible to do so specifically through other legal means (e.g. legislation or common law).'

Third, in order to maintain trust, stakeholders must be convinced that the recipients of shared data will respect any restrictions which are placed on the use of such data. Thus, regulation needs an enforcement mechanism.

Finally, some data sharing will enable the recipients of data to develop profitable applications or services. In these circumstances, stakeholders in the data might reasonably wish to receive some share of that profit. Examples might include commercial companies, each of whose datasets is too small for effective machine learning, but that are prepared to pool them on the basis that each contributor will receive some return from successful commercial exploitation, or health organisations that share data with a pharmaceutical company and without whose data a drug treatment could not have been developed.

Although there might be little disagreement about the broad shape of these principles, they remain merely principles. Implementing them in a way which solves the data-sharing problem is more difficult.

IV. Routes to a Regulation and Governance System

The most obvious way of introducing a regulation and governance system for data sharing might appear to be through formal legislation and regulation. This is what the European Commission has proposed in its communication 'A European Strategy for Data'.[23] The solution suggested here is to develop a high-level and cross-sectoral regulatory framework. The communication sets out a vision which 'stems from European values and fundamental rights and the conviction that the human being is and should remain at the centre'.[24] It is clear from this statement and the broader discussion in the document that the regulatory focus would be on individuals and data relating to them, building on and reinforcing the fundamental rights set out in the EU Charter of Fundamental Rights and, more pertinently, the specific rights and obligations in the General Data Protection Regulation (GDPR).[25] Although the communication recognises that business-to-business data sharing is important and requires the creation of trust if it is to be achieved,[26] little additional attention is given to this issue. The assumption seems to be that the GDPR has already achieved 'a solid framework for digital trust'[27] and needs no further consideration. As we shall see in section VII, this might be over-optimistic.

The communication is just the first step towards developing a regulatory framework and so is inevitably light on detail. Some of its proposals, such as developing

[23] European Commission, 'A European Strategy for Data' (Communication) COM (2020) 66 final.

[24] ibid 4.

[25] Regulation (EU) No 2016/679 of the European Parliament and of the Council of 27 April 2016 on the protection of natural persons with regard to the processing of personal data and on the free movement of such data, and repealing Directive 95/46/EC [2016] OJ L119/1.

[26] ibid 7.

[27] ibid 4.

standards and processes to enhance interoperability across different datasets,[28] will clearly be useful. In relation to data sharing for AI research purposes, there are plans to:

- facilitate decisions on which data can be used, how and by whom for scientific research purposes in a manner compliant with the GDPR. This is particularly relevant for publicly held databases with sensitive data not covered by the Open Data Directive;
- make it easier for individuals to allow the use of the data they generate for the public good, if they wish to do so ('data altruism'), in compliance with the GDPR.[29]

If these plans can be implemented without imposing excessive regulatory burdens, they will clearly facilitate more data sharing.

The communication also sets out a menu of possible legislative actions to encourage data sharing between private sector organisations,[30] which might include provisions on rights in co-generated data, reform of the Databases Directive and guidelines on the application of competition law. All these could prove useful. More worrying are the hints at some form of compulsory licensing,[31] based on competition law principles, and at an extraterritorial application of the law.[32] These have the potential to complicate and deter data sharing by non-EU dataset owners.

The vision set out in the European Commission's communication has idealistic aims, in particular that regulation can solve the problems discussed in section II. There are three main risks to any regulatory system of this kind which are likely to be unavoidable, and the communication does not suggest how they are to be avoided.

The first risk is that a regulatory system will achieve both over- and under-regulation. In any system which is high-level and cross-sectoral, it is likely that the obligations which the regulation imposes will in many cases be unnecessary and will thus act as barriers to successful data sharing. An example from another field is the first E-Money Directive 2000,[33] which was interpreted by the UK Financial Services Authority as applying to mobile telephone companies that allowed their customers' prepay float to be used to make payment for non-telephony services such as ringtones and music downloads.[34] These companies were already

[28] ibid 12.
[29] ibid 13.
[30] ibid 13–14.
[31] ibid 13.
[32] ibid, 14: 'The EU should not compromise on its principles: all companies which sell goods or provide services related to the data-agile economy in the EU must respect EU legislation and this should not be compromised by jurisdictional claims from outside the EU.'
[33] Directive 2000/46/EC of the European Parliament and of the Council on the taking up, pursuit of and prudential supervision of the business of electronic money institutions, [2000] OJ L275/39 (hereinafter 'E-Money Directive 2000').
[34] UK FSA, 'Electronic Money: Perimeter Guidance' (February 2003).

heavily regulated under telecommunications regulation schemes and, worse, the two schemes of regulation were so incompatible that it was impossible to comply with both.

Under-regulation occurs when data sharing in a particular sector poses additional risks which were not anticipated in the general scheme of regulation. These can be dealt with by sectoral regulation, but only if that sector is a regulated one. An instructive example might be the pilot project for wildlife data sharing, described in the UK Open Data Institute (ODI) report.[35] The risks identified here included access to data by poachers, smugglers and loggers, and hampering national and cross-border law enforcement activities, among other things.[36] General data-sharing regulation would be unlikely to anticipate and deal with these risks, and of course the production and use of wildlife data is not at present a regulated activity.

Second, general regulation is likely to be a very poor fit with some, perhaps even the majority, of data-sharing instances. This is because general regulation always has a business model embedded in it, in this case the regulator's understanding of who will be sharing and why. The European Commission Communication demonstrates this clearly – the business model which is referred to repeatedly is that of a pan-European data pool which combines public sector data and makes it available more widely. Only a minority of data-sharing relationships are likely to fit this model, and yet all will have to comply with regulation which was developed with a different model in mind.

Finally, legislation and regulation are inflexible. The world changes, but law and regulation remain the same. The first E-Money Directive, some of whose problems have already been mentioned, proved to be a very bad fit with the technology as it developed, but it was nearly ten years before it was reformed.[37] The same was true of the E-Signatures Directive 1999,[38] which had to wait even longer for its defects to be corrected.[39] If, as has been argued above, data sharing for AI research will regularly find new uses for existing data and new sharing partners, flexibility in its regulatory and governance framework will clearly be essential.

[35] Open Data Institute, *Exploring the Potential for Data Trusts to Help Tackle the Illegal Wildlife Trade* (ODI, April 2019), https://theodi.org/?post_type=article&p=7890.

[36] ibid 17–18.

[37] Directive 2009/110/EC of the European Parliament and of the Council of 16 September 2009 on the taking up, pursuit and prudential supervision of the business of electronic money institutions amending Directives 2005/60/EC and 2006/48/EC and repealing Directive 2000/46/EC [2009] OJ L267/7, art 6(1)(b). In theory, this Directive, together with the Payment Services Directive (Directive 2007/64/EC of the European Parliament and of the Council on payment services in the internal market amending Directives 97/7/EC, 2002/65/EC, 2005/60/EC and 2006/48/EC and repealing Directive 97/5/EC [2007] OJ L319/1), creates a coordinated system of regulation for non-credit institution payment services. However, the dividing line between e-money issuers and other payment service providers is by no means clear, and this raises the possibility of further contradiction.

[38] Directive 1999/93/EC on a Community framework for electronic signatures [2000] OJ L13/12.

[39] Regulation (EU) No 910/2014 of the European Parliament and of the Council of 23 July 2014 on electronic identification and trust services for electronic transactions in the internal market and repealing Directive 1999/93/EC [2014] OJ L 257/73.

These risks do not mean that formal regulation is incapable of providing a solution. There is an alternative regulatory model which Singapore has adopted in its Model Artificial Intelligence Governance Framework.[40] This model deliberately eschews detailed regulation and is instead framed in broad and open-textured terms,[41] usually requiring regulatees to act reasonably and fairly. Existing regulation is supplemented by guidelines which are not legally binding, but which help those who are subject to the regulation to decide their best way of achieving compliance. It is noteworthy that the first edition (January 2019) has already been updated as a second edition (January 2020), which clearly shows the flexibility that such an approach can provide.

Of course, neither regulatory model is perfect. The EU tradition is to produce highly detailed regulation, and this makes compliance easy so long as the regulation is practicable for that particular activity and with a compliance burden is not excessive. The Singapore approach has uncertainty built into it, and thus the costs of compliance in terms of management time and external advice could be substantial. It also requires a high degree of trust that the regulator will give credit for best efforts when enforcing the regulation, even if the solution adopted by the regulatee is inadequate in the regulator's view.[42]

So, is there an alternative to statute and regulation? There might be. There is a growing tendency in the field of digital technology for what might be described as 'private sector' regulation which runs as a parallel system to the applicable law, and in some cases in practice ousts its authority.[43] This private sector regulation is most likely to develop where national law is unable to provide suitable regulatory solutions, such as where those who are to be regulated are located in multiple national jurisdictions.[44]

A data trust is one such private sector regulatory mechanism. It works by transferring control of the data that is to be shared to some legal structure or entity which establishes binding rules for the data sharing and has a governance mechanism that meets the principles explained in section III above. Each data trust is established specifically for its own instance of data sharing, and should thus have a regulatory and governance regime which exactly fits the particular needs of that

[40] Personal Data Protection Commission, 'A Proposed Model Artificial Intelligence Governance Framework' (January 2020), www.pdpc.gov.sg/-/media/files/pdpc/pdf-files/resource-for-organisation/ai/sgmodelaigovframework2.pdf.

[41] ibid para 3.1. This covers four broad areas: (a) internal governance structures and measures; (b) determining the level of human involvement in AI-augmented decision-making; (c) operations management; and (d) stakeholder interaction and communication.

[42] This need for trust in the regulator is recognised in the Framework (ibid, para 2.12): 'Adopting this voluntary Model Framework will not absolve organisations from compliance with current laws and regulations. However, as this is an accountability-based framework, adopting it will assist organisations in demonstrating that they had implemented accountability-based practices in data management and protection.'

[43] See C Reed and A Murray, *Rethinking the Jurisprudence of Cyberspace* (Edward Elgar, 2018) ch 2.

[44] See C Reed, 'Cyberspace Institutions, Community and Legitimate Authority' in O Aksell and J Linarelli (eds), *The Future of Commercial Law* (Hart Publishing, 2020) ch 6.

sharing. Because the data trust will have the ability to change its rules as the data sharing by trust members evolves, it has the potential to be a particularly flexible regulatory and governance model.

V. What Does a Data Trust Look Like?

The first characteristic of a data trust is that it has a legal structure which is separate from those who are sharing data with each other. This separation allows control of data to be transferred from the current data 'owner' to the trust.

Transfer of control might be effected via an assignment or licence if the owner has legal rights in the data, or simply by handing over a copy if not. It is even conceivable that the data owner might retain possession of the data on its own servers, granting some element of control to the trust by giving it access remotely. The data owner might retain a copy of the data, and thus keep control over that, or might hand over exclusive possession to the data trust. There is no right answer here – it all depends on the aims and needs of data owners and sharers, and what the trust is aiming to achieve.

Once the data trust has control of the data, it can do useful things with it. For example, it might clean up the data and reformat it to make sharing more effective. It might merge the data with other data to create a bigger dataset which is more useful for machine learning. Most importantly, because the data trust is established to enable data sharing, it can now make that data available to others, subject to their complying with the trust's rules about how they should use that data.

The precise legal structure of the data trust is not its most fundamentally important feature. The initial impetus towards data trusts comes from a perception by Edwards in 2004[45] that if personal data could be conceptualised as trust property, then those who held and processed that data would owe fiduciary duties as trustees which could provide some protection for the privacy and other interests of data subjects. This idea was seized on by Hall and Pessenti[46] in their 2017 report which began the current wave of interest in data trusts. Because Hall and Pessenti began their analysis from a trust law perspective, the legal structure they had in mind was of course a common-law trust. Lau, Penner and Wong have recently analysed this issue and make a convincing argument that there are no insuperable barriers to establishing a data trust under trust law.[47]

[45] L Edwards, 'The Problem with Privacy: A Modest Proposal' (2004) 18 *International Review of Law, Computer, and Technology* 309.

[46] W Hall and J Pesenti, Growing the Artificial Intelligence Industry in the UK' (UK Department for Digital, Culture, Media & Sport and Department for Business, Energy & Industrial Strategy, October 2017), www.gov.uk/government/publications/growing-the-artificial-intelligence-industry-in-the-uk.

[47] J Lau, J Penner and B Wong, 'The Basics of Private and Public Data Trusts' [2020] *Singapore Journal of Legal Studies* 90.

However, there are reasons why trust law might not offer the most suitable structure for a functional data trust.[48] Data is information, and the law in most countries is reluctant to treat it as property.[49] Data might be capable of being trust property,[50] but this has not yet been established by the courts, and if it is not trust property, then its trustees owe no fiduciary duties to anyone in respect of it. Even if data could be trust property, the fiduciary duties of trustees would be owed only to the beneficiaries of the trust. This could prevent the trust from sharing data for a publicly beneficial purpose which was not in the interests of some or all of the defined beneficiaries, who will likely include data owners and individuals whose data is controlled by the trust.

A data trust which shared data for publicly beneficial purposes could be established as a charitable trust, but the restrictions in charity law are likely to make that an unattractive choice for data trusts where providers of datasets wish to receive some payment if their datasets are exploited commercially.[51] And finally, the apparent protections for those with interests in the data which are provided by the trustees fiduciary duties would in practice prove to be illusory. No prudent and appropriately qualified potential trustee would agree to act if faced with unlimited personal liability for breach of duty, and so the trust deed would inevitably relieve trustees of liability to a large extent. The liability insurance which trustees would demand would further reduce the theoretical deterrent effect of a trustee's personal liability for any breach. In effect, a trustee of a data trust would in practice have no greater level of liability than a director of a limited company does.

Equally suitable legal structures can be found in the corporate law of most countries. Where the law recognises cooperatives, these might also be appropriate legal structures. Both of these are easier to set up, more flexible in operation and in practice far more workable. The duties of those who are what will now be described as *custodians* of the data, ie, the officials of the data trust, can be prescribed in the constitution of that legal structure, and could be as stringent as those of a legal trustee or not, depending on the needs of the data trust. Different legal systems may have other structures which are appropriate for a data trust – for example, a business trust under the Singapore Business Trusts Act 2005[52] might be suitable for data trusts which aimed to make a profit from the data sharing and distribute that profit amongst those who contributed the data. The owners of such a trust are called unit-holders, but they do not control the day-to-day operations

[48] See, eg, NA Tiverios and MJR Crawford, 'Equitable Property and the Law of the Horse: Assignment, Intermediate Securities and Data Trusts' (2020) 14 *Journal of Equity* 272; C Reed, BPE Solicitors, Pinsent Masons, *Data Trusts: Legal and Governance Considerations* (Open Data Institute, 2019) 14–19, https://theodi.org/article/data-trusts-legal-report (hereinafter 'ODI report').

[49] See, eg, *Oxford v Moss* [1978] 68 Cr App R 183. For further discussion, see Reed (n 9).

[50] See Lau, Penner and Wong (n 47).

[51] See, eg, UK Charity Commission, 'Conflicts of Interest: A Guide for Charity Trustees' (May 2014), www.gov.uk/government/publications/conflicts-of-interest-a-guide-for-charity-trustees-cc29/conflicts-of-interest-a-guide-for-charity-trustees.

[52] (Cap 31A, Rev Ed 2005). See further HW Tang, 'The Resurgence of "Uncorporation": The Business Trust in Singapore' [2012] *Journal of Business Law* 683.

of the trust.[53] These are undertaken by the 'trustee-manager', which must be a corporation.[54] The duties of the trustee-manager are based on those of trustees of a legal trust, and the business trust must be managed for the interests of the unit-holders as a whole.[55] This creates an obvious drawback of the Singapore business trust for some kinds of data sharing because the interests of the unit-holders will always prevail over the interests of any other stakeholders. Thus, if personal data is involved, some alternative legal structure will be needed if the interests of individuals in their data are to be protected beyond what is required for data protection compliance.

The constitution of any data trust is its most important element. It will define the purposes for which the data trust can take control of and subsequently share data, and limitation of recipients' activities to those purposes is the main way in which the interests of those who are stakeholders in the data will be protected. This protection will be supplemented by the trust's rules on data sharing, which might also be set out in its constitution. The constitution will also make provision for the governance of the data trust and its operational processes (see section VI below).

Achieving trust in the control and use of data is the primary aim of any data trust. This does not mean that it has to host the data. Building infrastructure to host data securely and control access by others is an expensive business. There are numerous cloud providers to which this activity could be outsourced and that will do it more cheaply and more effectively. Or, as already mentioned, the data might remain in the possession of the entity which provided it to the trust, with the data trust accessing and sharing that data remotely.

Although data trusts need not be creations of trust law and, as has been argued above, probably should not be for practical reasons, their primary aim must be to *achieve* trust. Data owners will not transfer data to the trust if they do not believe that it will only be shared and used in accordance with the trust rules. Other stakeholders, such as individuals represented in the dataset, will require a similar level of trust or they may exercise their legal rights in an attempt to prevent 'their' data from being used.

This essential element of trust is achieved through the governance mechanisms of the data trust, which is the subject of the next section.

VI. Governance to Achieve Trust

Trust is a complex phenomenon[56] and it comes in several broad flavours. The first kind of trust is based on close relationships – family, friends and work colleagues.

[53] Section 2 of the Singapore Business Trusts Act 2005, which defines a 'business trust'.
[54] ibid s 6.
[55] ibid s 10.
[56] For a detailed discussion of the trust concepts explained here, see EL Khalil (ed), *Trust* (Edward Elgar, 2003).

This kind of trust might be described as emotionally based. We believe that the other will do what they ought to do because of the nature of the relationship and because of our past dealings with them in the relationship.

In dealings with those with whom we do not have this kind of relationship, the origins of trust are different. Here it is based on some kind of external regulation which gives us confidence that the other will do what they ought to do. In a business dealing, the law of contract gives us confidence that the other party will perform their promises (or, more accurately, that either they will perform or the law will provide us with a remedy if they do not). If we visit a new dentist, we trust the dentist because their training has been certified and their performance is overseen by a regulatory body. In both cases, the knowledge that external regulation is likely to be enforced is what achieves trust. Of course, repeated dealings can lead to the kind of relationship which engenders the first kind of trust, so that long-term business partners will often rely on each other's promises even in the absence of a contract.

A successful data trust will clearly need to engender this second type of trust in order to persuade data owners to hand over control of their data and to persuade individuals to allow their data to be processed and shared. This means that each data trust must have its own system of governance and regulation whose primary aim is to achieve that kind of trust. This system will have two main elements: the constitution of the data trust; and its operational rules and oversight mechanisms.

A. Constitutional Governance

Some parts of the constitution will be dictated by the legal structure adopted – the memorandum and articles or other corporate documents in the case of a company, or the trust deed in the case of a legal trust. But the constitution will also need to address two important issues which are essential if the trust of stakeholders is to be achieved.

First, the constitution must define the data-sharing purposes for which the trust is established, and also any broad limitations on how shared data can be used. In the case of the wildlife data trust discussed in the ODI report, its overriding purpose would be to share data to improve the protection of wildlife, and sharing would likely be limited to organisations and individuals who would use it only to further that aim.

As already explained, one of the main reasons for using a data trust is to allow the aims and purposes of the sharing to evolve over time. So, the wildlife data trust might initially be established by researchers to share wildlife data with each other, and later be extended for sharing with law-enforcement bodies to assist their activities. This would require a change to that part of the constitution which sets out the data-sharing purposes, and so the constitution also needs to establish an appropriate mechanism to make such a change. Initially, sharing for commercial purposes might be forbidden, but might later be relaxed if it became clear that there were some commercial uses of the data which might improve wildlife protection.

The mechanism for changing these aims and purposes therefore needs to be set out in the constitution. It will be extremely important for that mechanism to be perceived by stakeholders as making legitimate decisions about change. Legitimacy is fundamental to trust and will be explained further below.

The second constitutional element which is needed to engender trust is that those who are in charge of the data trust should be suitable and appropriately qualified persons. These are the custodians of the data. When the trust is first set up, it will be the public profile and reputation of those custodians which gives them what might be described as 'charismatic authority'[57] and thus leads stakeholders to trust them as custodians. Over time, though, custodians will leave and new custodians will be appointed, and a self-perpetuating group can easily lack perceived legitimacy. It is therefore important for the constitution to have a mechanism for appointing new custodians which deals with that legitimacy question.

Data trusts have no inherently legitimate claim to any authority to regulate data sharing. That authority can only be achieved through acceptance by its stakeholders, who constitute its legitimating community.[58] A constitution which appears to take the interests of stakeholders properly into account will go a long way towards achieving that acceptance. And an important element in acceptance will be suitable stakeholder representation in the trust's decision-making and the appointment of the custodians.

A particular difficulty here, which the constitution will need to solve, is identifying who belongs to the legitimating community, and appointing suitable members of the legitimating community to represent each category of stakeholders. Data providers will need to be represented, as will those with whom data is shared. This is comparatively easy to arrange when the data trust is set up, as the initial data providers will already be identified. As the number of those with whom data is shared grows, a mechanism will be needed which will enable them to agree on representatives to either act as custodians or, more likely, to help choose the custodians. Representing the public interest will be important to some data trusts, so this also needs to be dealt with. And the hardest question is how to represent individuals whose data forms part of the trust's datasets – in many cases, there may be representative organisations, such as patient groups in the medical sector, which might be suitable sources of representation.

The precise way in which these issues are dealt with will vary from data trust to data trust because of the differences in their aims and purposes. A solution which

[57] M Weber, *Economy and Society: An Outline of Interpretive Sociology* (University of California Press, 1968) 1139 –41.

[58] Reed and Murray (n 43) 59–63.

is likely to be commonly adopted might be an appointments board on which all stakeholders have appropriate representation. This is the solution which the Internet Corporation for Assigned Names and Numbers (ICANN), the autonomous non-state regulator of all internet domains and numbering, adopted in order to enhance its own legitimacy.[59]

In addition to the kind of legitimacy already discussed, data trusts will also want to achieve legitimacy in their decision-making which relates to the trust's fundamental policies, such as who is entitled to participate in data sharing and the rules which govern that sharing. Changes to those policies will need to achieve a different kind of legitimacy, described by Paiement as input, throughput and output legitimacy.[60]

Input legitimacy derives from the participatory nature and inclusiveness of the rule-making and decision-making process, which is normally achieved through stakeholder representation. But it also focuses on the factors which were considered when establishing rules and making decisions about data sharing, and in the case of data trusts, this would primarily require taking proper account of all the stakeholder interests which are engaged in the proposal. This is related to Brownsword's conception of a 'community of rights' approach,[61] in which purely utilitarian decision-making based on the benefit to the greatest number is eschewed in favour of a commitment to respecting individual or minority rights, even if in the end they are overridden:

> [M]embers will need to be satisfied that the regulators have made a conscientious and good faith attempt to set a standard that is in line with their best understanding of the community's rights commitments. Regulators do not have to claim that the standard set is right; but, before a procedural justification is accepted, regulators must be demonstrably trying to do the right thing relative to the community's particular moral commitments.[62]

Such an approach might be embedded expressly in a data trust's decision-making processes or be achieved as a matter of throughput legitimacy via decision-making processes which exhibit procedural fairness and impartiality. And the outcome of decisions, as perceived by stakeholders, is the source of a data trust's output legitimacy, which is based on the quality of the rules and decisions themselves, particularly in terms of achieving their desired outcomes.

[59] See ICANN, 'Accountability & Transparency Frameworks and Principles' (January 2008), www.icann.org/en/system/files/files/acct-trans-frameworks-principles-10jan08-en.pdf. For further discussion of how ICANN achieves legitimacy, see Reed (n 44), 137–39.

[60] P Paiement, 'Paradox and Legitimacy in Transnational Legal Pluralism' (2013) 4 *Transnational Legal Theory* 197, 213–15.

[61] D Beyleveld and R Brownsword, 'Principle, Proceduralism, and Precaution in a Community of Rights' (2006) 19 *Ratio Juris* 141.

[62] R Brownsword, *Rights, Regulation and the Technological Revolution* (Oxford, Oxford University Press, 2008) 127.

B. Operational Governance

The custodians of the data trust will be in charge of its day-to-day operational decisions, and of course it is not possible for them to consult stakeholders before making every decision. This means that stakeholders will need to trust that the custodians are making those decisions properly.

In order to bolster that trust, data trusts should aspire to offer their stakeholders the greatest possible transparency in operational decision-making. One mechanism for doing so is to make all decisions available to stakeholders, but this risks overwhelming them and also gives them only a fragmentary review of how the custodians are operating the trust. A more accessible option might be to establish an oversight board which reviews the custodians' decisions periodically and provides to stakeholders a report focusing on the main trust issues. A second mechanism for achieving trust would be a periodic audit of all the decisions which the custodians have made and of the operational processes of the trust. For many data trusts, both these mechanisms might be appropriate.[63]

Oversight and audit reports should focus on the issues which are relevant to trust, and also on the input, throughput and output legitimacy of the custodians' activities. There are five main areas on which report needs to be made:

(a) Identifying the reasoning behind important decisions which affect the interests of one or more groups of stakeholders. Stakeholders need to be reassured that those decisions have been taken fairly and that their interests have been properly considered, even if the final decision was against their interests.
(b) Providing assurance that the custodians have been competent in their management of the data with which they have been entrusted and in the financial affairs of the trust. This is very much the kind of reporting and audit which is required from public companies.
(c) Providing information about how effectively the custodians have enforced limitations and restrictions on the use of data by those with whom it has been shared. In order to satisfy themselves about these matters, the custodians might well demand a similar level of transparency and audit from data recipients.
(d) Providing assurance that the trust's regulatory obligations, such as those under data protection law, have been complied with.
(e) Information and assurance about the data security precautions which the trust has adopted, and how it has dealt with any data security breaches. This will be particularly important if the data relates to individuals or contains commercially sensitive or other confidential information.

Stakeholders will also want to know about any problems which have occurred in relation to these matters and how the custodians resolved them.

[63] See ODI report (n 48) 8, 39 and 50.

VII. Outsourcing Regulatory Compliance to Data Trusts

Data sharing and use is subject to an increasing volume of regulation, both generally under data protection laws and specifically via sectoral regulation. Drafting a data-sharing agreement which ensures that all this regulation is complied with once the data has been shared is a complex task. A common difficulty is that the recipient of the data may have little experience of compliance with that regulation. An example in the AI research field might be the provision of patient data by a health authority to an AI technology company. This data will be subject to regulation specific to the medical sector, and so the data-sharing agreement will need complex and explicit provisions about what the AI company must do to maintain compliance. Educating the AI company about how medical regulation works will be time-consuming and expensive.

This is the kind of situation which might create an incentive to establish a data trust or to engage in data sharing via an already established trust. Because the trust will have clear data-sharing aims and purposes – in this case, sharing for medical research purposes – it can focus its energies and resources on developing systems which ensure that the data sharing is regulatorily compliant. Such a data trust might also be able to gain access to the medical regulator, to engage in regulatory conversations[64] about the nuances of medical regulation and appropriate means of compliance, whereas mere recipients of shared data might find that the regulator has inadequate resources or is unwilling to engage.

In effect, data sharers will be outsourcing the compliance issues which arise from data sharing to a third party, the data trust, which has expertise in that area. This could be cost-effective for data sharers and could also lead to improved levels of compliance. However, data trusts cannot solve all compliance issues. In particular, data protection law is a major obstacle to data sharing because of its fundamental mismatch with the very concept of data sharing.

The EU's data protection law is found in the GDPR, which provides that data may only be collected 'for specified, explicit and legitimate purposes and not further processed in a manner that is compatible with those purposes'.[65] This is where the mismatch with AI data mining and machine learning research occurs. The fundamental assumption of the GDPR is that data should not be allowed to be used for

[64] These kinds of regulatory conversations are a hallmark of complex regulatory systems. See J Black, 'Talking about Regulation' [1998] *Public Law* 77. In those conversations, regulatees negotiate the content and application of the rules with the regulator. The regulatory model generates an interpretive community (J Black, *Rules and Regulators* (Clarendon Press, 1997) 30–37) which consists of the regulator together with those specialists within each regulated entity who work on regulatory compliance. The conversational model of regulation works with open-textured rules and sees the achievement of the regulatory objectives as a moving target which requires constant adjustment of the rules to take account of new behaviours and other relevant factors.

[65] GDPR, art 5(1). See also recital 39: 'In particular, the specific purposes for which personal data are processed should be explicit and legitimate and *determined at the time of the collection of the personal data*' (emphasis added).

any purpose other than that for which it was originally collected (with some exceptions, which will be explained below). The purpose of processing should match the expectations of the data subject.[66] In contrast, the fundamental assumption underlying data mining and machine learning is that data often contains hidden knowledge which can be extracted by processing that data – in other words, the purpose of processing here is to discover unexpected things. By definition, this kind of processing cannot have been expected by the person collecting the data or, more importantly, by the data subject when the data were collected.

In part, the GDPR recognises that the reuse of personal data will often be desirable, and so it makes provision in Article 6(4) for such reuse:

> Where the processing for a purpose other than that for which the personal data have been collected is not based on the data subject's consent or on a Union or Member State law … the controller shall, in order to ascertain whether processing for another purpose is compatible with the purpose for which the personal data are initially collected, take into account, *inter alia*: [five factors].

The five factors are not discussed here because they are not relevant to the point at issue, which is that the new purpose must be *compatible* with the original purpose. Although compatibility is undefined, it would seem there must be some connection between the original and new purposes. An unconnected purpose might be *not incompatible*, but this is not what the wording says. So, it seems unlikely that data sharing for a new purpose which has no connection with the original purpose can ever be compatible, no matter how socially desirable it is.

To continue the COVID-19 theme, it appears that there is a correlation between suffering from diabetes and susceptibility to suffering severe consequences from a COVID-19 infection.[67] It would seem likely that deep analysis of the health records of diabetes sufferers might generate new insights into their infection susceptibility and perhaps even possible treatments. But the original data in those records were collected for the purpose of treating diabetes patients for their diabetes. Analysing that data to discover knowledge about infectious diseases, and particularly a disease which was unknown when the data was collected, is so different in nature that it is hard to argue that it is a compatible purpose.

[66] This is made clear by recital 50 of the GDPR, which provides that: 'In order to ascertain whether a purpose of further processing is compatible with the purpose for which the personal data are initially collected, the controller, after having met all the requirements for the lawfulness of the original processing, should take into account, inter alia: any link between those purposes and the purposes of the intended further processing; the context in which the personal data have been collected, in particular the reasonable expectations of data subjects based on their relationship with the controller as to their further use.' See also recital 47: 'the expectations of the data subject also play an important role determining whether, in the absence of consent, a data controller can use its legitimate interest as a ground of processing'.

[67] C Arnold, 'Why is Coronavirus Deadly for Some, But Harmless in Others?' *New Scientist* (6 May 2020), www.newscientist.com/article/mg24632811-300-why-is-coronavirus-deadly-for-some-but-harmless-in-others.

One author, writing from a medical science perspective, has suggested that researchers should consider the five factors listed and that:

> Where the results of the test shows that none of these elements has significantly changed in a way that would make the further processing unfair or otherwise illicit, the compatibility test is satisfied and no legal basis separated from that which allowed the initial collection of the personal data is required.[68]

But this suggested approach seems to ignore the need to assess positively for compatibility, instead asking researchers only to identify that the new purpose is not incompatible. This may not be enough to comply with the GDPR.

If the reuse of the data is not for a compatible purpose, some further ground of legitimate processing under Article 6(1) of the GDPR will be necessary, or the processing will need to be legitimated under one of the exceptions set out in the GDPR or in national law. It is usually suggested that consent will need to be obtained,[69] but the practical problems of contacting all those represented in a dataset, let alone obtaining the kind of properly informed consent which the GDPR envisages,[70] seem insurmountable.

Article 89(2) contains a specific exemption which allows Member States to derogate from some of the rights given to data subjects.[71] These are the rights of access, rectification, restriction of processing and to object to automated decision-making. Useful though this derogation might be, it does not legitimate the repurposing of data. The same seems to be true of the derogation in respect of academic publication.[72]

Therefore, it seems that data trusts will need to engage in regulatory conversations with national data protection supervisors, aiming to persuade them to adopt a very broad interpretation of compatibility under Article 6(4). Some are likely to be more receptive than others, which may lead data trusts to establish themselves in the most helpful jurisdictions.

Singaporean data protection law is more helpful in this respect. Unlike the GDPR, the sole ground on which personal data may be collected and processed is the consent of the data subject, unless the collection and processing is otherwise authorised by law.[73] In obtaining that consent, the purposes of collection, use or disclosure must be communicated to the data subject.[74] When data is shared, the disclosee must be sufficiently informed about the purposes for which consent

[68] Gauthier Chassang, 'The Impact of the EU General Data Protection Regulation on Scientific Research' (2017) 11(709) *Ecancermedicalscience* 1, 9.

[69] ibid.

[70] See GDPR, art 7.

[71] Specifically, to derogate from arts 15, 16, 18 and 21.

[72] For a detailed discussion of both derogations, see M Mourby, H Gowans, S Aidinlis, H Smith and J Kaye, 'Governance of Academic Research Data under the GDPR: Lessons from the UK' (2019) 9 *International Data Privacy Law* 192.

[73] Singapore Personal Data Protection Act 2010 (as amended 2021) (PDPA), s 13.

[74] ibid s 20. Unless there is deemed consent (s 15), deemed consent by notification (s 15A) or collection, use or disclosure without consent is permitted by s 17.

was originally given so that the disclosee can ensure that the new processing is undertaken in accordance with the provisions of the Singapore Personal Data Protection Act 2010 (PDPA).

The big difference from the GDPR lies in section 17 of the PDPA. This permits collection, use or disclosure without consent if it is in accordance with Schedules 2–4, respectively. Data trusts are not concerned with the initial collection of data, but their entire purpose is to disclose data to others so that it can be used, in the context of the discussion in this chapter, for research purposes.

Schedule 4, paragraph 1(q) permits disclosure without consent for a research purpose, subject to the conditions in paragraph 4, and Schedule 3, paragraph 1(i) permits the recipient of the data to use it for that research purpose subject to the conditions in paragraph 2 of that Schedule.

The first four conditions are common to each Schedule:

(a) the research purpose cannot reasonably be accomplished without the personal data being provided in an individually identifiable form;
(b) it is impracticable for the organisation to seek the consent of the individual for the disclosure;
(c) the personal data will not be used to contact persons to ask them to participate in the research;
(d) linkage of the personal data to other information is not harmful to the individuals identified by the personal data and the benefits to be derived from the linkage are clearly in the public interest.

In addition, Schedule 4, paragraph 4 requires the recipient of the data to sign an agreement with the discloser which imposes obligations to comply with the PDPA, to maintain security and confidentiality of the data, to destroy individual identifiers as soon as is reasonably possible, and not to use the data outside the research purpose without the authorisation of the discloser.

These provisions are well adapted to data trusts, though two uncertainties remain. First, 'research purpose' is undefined, which leaves some uncertainty as to whether commercial research falls within the exception. It is likely that it does so, because the much stricter GDPR makes it clear that 'the processing of personal data for scientific research purposes should be interpreted in a broad manner including for example technological development and demonstration, fundamental research, applied research and privately funded research'.[75] However, any uncertainty can act as a barrier to data trust activity, and formal guidance would be useful here. Second, because the obligations of those involved in data sharing are set out in the Schedules in broad, open textured terms, translating them into operational processes and the data trust's rules will inevitably require much thought. Official guidance would make this rather easier. The Singapore Personal Data Protection Commission (PDPC) has issued guidelines on data sharing for

[75] ibid recital 50.

research purposes, but only for the healthcare sector.[76] These guidelines do not map easily to non-medical data sharing, and the other sectoral guidance documents and the general guidance do not cover this specific issue. More generic guidelines on data sharing for research purposes would clearly encourage the formation of data trusts.

VIII. Conclusion

By now, it should be clear that a data trust is, at heart, a governance mechanism for data-sharing relationships. This governance mechanism will establish the rules for data sharing and enforce them. The appropriate rules for data sharing cannot be set out generically, as a template for data trusts to follow, because each individual data trust has a different set of stakeholder interests which need to be respected and thus needs a bespoke regulatory regime. The first task of any data trust is to establish that regime.

Once established, a data trust's focus on governance needs to focus on two main issues. The first is gaining the trust of its stakeholders that its custodians, rules and operating procedures will, in combination, achieve the protection of stakeholder interests, which is the trust's main purpose. Transparency will be key here, as will cementing and enhancing the trust's legitimacy as a decision-maker about data sharing. The second is operating in a way which secures compliance with the trust's rules by data sharers and compliance with the wider regulatory landscape in which it operates. As a private-sector regulator, a data trust's authority over data sharers rest entirely on the acceptance of that authority by its stakeholders and regulators, which in turn rests on trust in the data trust.

Much of the literature on data trusts focuses on their 'proper' legal structure and, in particular, on whether they should, or should not, be established as legal trusts. This is something of a side issue because the important question is whether a data trust can be an effective regulator of data sharing and not what legal structure it should adopt to do so. It might even be argued that the name 'data trust' is unfortunate precisely because it focuses attention on structure above substance.

But maybe not. Even if data trusts are not most appropriately established as legal trusts, their role in establishing and maintaining trust between all those with an interest in data sharing means that they are, indeed, aptly named.

[76] PDPC, 'Advisory Guidelines for the Healthcare Sector' (2017) 4–16, www.pdpc.gov.sg/-/media/Files/PDPC/PDF-Files/Sector-Specific-Advisory/advisoryguidelinesforthehealthcaresector-28mar2017.pdf?la=en.

4

The Future of Personal Data Protection Law in Singapore

A Role for the Use of AI and the Propertisation of Personal Data

WARREN CHIK*

I. Introduction

Data has emerged as the most important driver for modern economic change and development. New industries have emerged from the use of data with personal information as the core asset, while many traditional models of business have been 'disrupted' or drastically transformed due to the changes in the forms of communication, the format of products, the nature of services, and innovation in relation to methods of delivery. Personal data is an important category of data as it involves issues of privacy and an individual's rights to self. At the same time, the consumer's personal profile is integral to digital information capitalism[1] and for a more efficient sale (and effective marketing) strategy for commercial organisations.

Artificial intelligence (AI) has become an integral tool for the management and processing of data, including personal data, as it provides greater accuracy and capability. This provides challenges for regulators, as AI gives rise to potential lack of transparency and oversight, and to potentially wide-ranging and damaging abuse, especially with the shadow of cybersecurity breach that may follow any valuable set of data. The use of AI by data controllers in relation to data management (ie, collection, use and disclosure) has not been a common feature

* This research is supported by the National Research Foundation, Singapore under its Emerging Areas Research Projects (EARP) Funding Initiative. Any opinions, findings and conclusions or recommendations expressed in this material are those of the author(s) and do not reflect the views of National Research Foundation, Singapore.

[1] This term is more neutral, whereas 'surveillance capitalism' has been used as an alternative, but with negative connotations.

of data protection laws for many years, but it is increasingly becoming the focus of general principles and guidelines relating to the development of 'trust' and 'ethics' in its use. It is inevitable that some of these principles and guidelines will be transposed into data protection legislation. At the same time, AI can also be a useful regulatory tool to ensure more compliance and accountability, and to further personal data rights and interests (eg, through data portability and privacy by design requirements), given its potential for greater efficiency and accuracy in performance.

'Coding' ethics into law must be done at the sectorial level, because the nature and type of the information concerned, and the objectives of every industry differs. Each industry – such as the finance industry or the health industry – must select an appropriate model of ethical decision-making to be consistently applied in constructing a suitable framework for data governance. This should be supported by clearer and more detailed guidelines issued by trade and professional associations for their members to follow in order to ensure standardisation across the industry and the maintenance of industry-wide standards. This will then strengthen the robustness of the system and instil the trust of consumers – itself an important component for the successful development and deployment of AI solutions.

Meanwhile, 'data proliferation' also leads to social problems that require regulatory and legal solutions that will involve private-sector organisations and particularly internet intermediaries such as search engines and social media platforms. Examples of social issues include online defamation and harassment as well as online falsehoods and social or political manipulation.

Regulations have evolved from being mainly focused on content-based regulations (ie, the nature of the information and its potential impact on the individual and on society) to data per se as a value. Increasingly, personal data is viewed as an asset or 'currency' by organisations that require regulatory intervention and guidance. Although it is stated by the Singapore Personal Data Protection Commission (PDPC) that the 'PDPA does not specifically confer any property or ownership rights on personal data per se to individuals or organisations and also does not affect existing property rights in items in which personal data may be captured or stored',[2] perhaps it may be appropriate – with the increasing use of AI and the commoditisation of personal information by data controllers – to consider whether certain types of personal information should be imbued with proprietary rights and interest not unlike that which is extended to copyright (and personality or publicity) rights.[3] At the very least, certain characteristics of property rights will provide useful ideas, and a different perspective, to strengthen the personal data

[2] See PDPC, *Advisory Guidelines on Key Concepts in the PDPA* (revised 2 June 2020) para 5.30.

[3] See V Bergelson, 'It's Personal But is it Mine? Towards Property Rights in Personal Information' (2003) 37 *UC Davis Law Review* 379, 429–32, where the author refers to the 'personality theory' of property.

rights of individuals as well as to revisit how these rights can be expressed and should be enforced. This is both in reaction to AI as the data controller's tool for data collection and use, as well as AI as the data subject's instrument for control and protection.

In section II, I will first examine the scope and nature of AI generally and its effects on society, followed by the concerns over its use in relation to personal data. I will examine how data protection laws are evolving and how policy-makers and law-makers are approaching the issue of AI in the data processing activities of organisations in order to address concerns such as the lack of oversight by organisations, the lack of awareness on the part of consumers (and the potential impact or weakening of the access, correction and accuracy obligations), and the role of the regulator in balancing the policy interest of technological innovation against data protection. The legislative response in the European Union (EU), and the government and industry response in Singapore, to the ethical use of AI will also be examined.

In section III, the proposal will be made to elevate personal data to a form of property. I will analyse the Singapore legislation that treats data as a form of property. A comparison will be made to the development of 'intellectual property', specifically copyright and the proprietary rights attached to it, and reference will also be made to the treatment of data in the Computer Misuse Act (CMA)[4] and the Singapore Personal Data Protection Act (PDPA).[5]

Finally, in section IV, I will explain how the propertisation of personal data can strengthen the individual's control over his or her personal data in response to the deployment of AI in relation to the collection of personal data and its use. This will in turn justify the role of AI in relation to personal data and allay any lingering ethical and security concerns over its use.

II. AI: Trust, Security and Regulation

A. What is AI?

There have been a range of AI-related governance and strategic frameworks and guidelines released in recent years that focus on ethics and trust issues. For example, the European Commission High-Level Expert Group on Artificial Intelligence (AI HLEG) released the 'Ethics Guidelines for Trustworthy Artificial Intelligence' on 8 April 2019[6] and the Singapore Ministry for Communications and Information

[4] Computer Misuse Act 2007.
[5] Personal Data Protection Act 2012.
[6] The AI HLEG website is accessible at: www.ec.europa.eu/digital-single-market/en/high-level-expert-group-artificial-intelligence.

(MCI), with the involvement of the PDPC, presented its 'Model AI Governance Framework' on 23 January 2019.[7]

These are living documents that form the basis for more refined sector-specific rules and implementation. A core component of these documents is a human-centric approach to the development and use of AI, which will create a trustworthy environment and inculcate consumer trust in AI.

There is no consistent definition of AI. Generally, AI is an area of computer science relating to the creation of intelligent machines that can work and act/react like humans.[8]

B. The Insidious Nature of AI and its Effects

Ensuring consumer trust is the ultimate goal, and transparency and explicability are important to the successful development and deployment of AI into society for diverse functions. It is reasonable to say that there is a general distrust of AI by the public, stemming from a general lack of understanding of AI as well as the regular diet of 'killer robots' in the media. Also, because of expectations that AI should outperform the fallible human, AI is often expected to meet a higher standard of care than its human counterpart in the performance of any function for which it was created. For example, autonomous vehicles are expected to pass more stringent safety tests and to react faster and with greater care and consideration than the natural person before regulators allow them on the roads. They are also required to go through a longer and stricter pilot-testing phase than a human driver when getting his or her driving licence. This 'default of distrust' and the requirement of greater care in AI use sometimes translate into law. In the General Data Protection Regulation (GDPR), for example, there is a general prohibition on the use of AI for human profiling, which will be considered in more detail later.

AI can have 'internal' and 'external' effects on the individual, a class or group of individuals, and on society as a whole. For example, it has the potential to be used for social and political manipulation through the biased curation and distribution of news reports to individuals and segments of the online community. In other words, it can cause 'information disorder' that in turn can lead to socio-political problems. AI can also influence societal behaviour and attitudes by pushing certain types of information, products or services to consumers, thereby moulding habits and interests, thoughts and actions, which are in turn facets of 'personal data'. Another example is the impact that algorithmic bias in AI decision-making by governments and organisations can have on an individual.

[7] The Model Artificial Intelligence Governance Framework is now in its second edition, which was released on 21 January 2020: www.pdpc.gov.sg/-/media/files/pdpc/pdf-files/resource-for-organisation/ai/sgmodelaigovframework2.pdf.

[8] See, eg, the current definition of AI in the EU in the AI HLEG at n 6.

Thus, the potential for such effects and discrimination is another reason for concern.

C. Concerns for the Data Subject, the Regulator and the Data Controller

For the individual data subject, although AI can be programmed to simulate a human, which has many benefits for social interaction and business transactions, the natural person should always be made aware that he or she is dealing with AI. There should also be awareness or knowledge of what an AI is doing with personal data or information that can affect a person. Furthermore, consumers should also be able to trust that concerns relating to fairness and security surrounding the use and storage of their personal information are addressed.

The government as regulator must set the rules for private-sector companies to meet their ethical obligations and to put in place industrial standards and practices, reinforced through law and regulations where necessary, to ensure that the above-mentioned problems are eliminated or the risks are reduced and contained. Policy-makers and law-makers must balance the benefits and interests in the use of AI against the potential problems that can ensue.

Last but not least, for the technology users in any industry, ethical considerations should be made at every point in the process and should be embedded and integrated into the culture of the organisation. This is not just a matter of social responsibility, but is also integral to the economic success and reputation of the organisation itself.

D. AI, Ethics and the EU's GDPR

Before going into the issue of ethics, the Singapore PDPA and the future direction that data protection law should take in Singapore, it will be useful to first consider how the EU's GDPR, as the leading data protection regime in the world, is dealing with the issues surrounding AI. The EU's GDPR entered into force on 25 May 2018, and almost a year later, on 8 April 2019, the 'Ethics Guidelines for Trustworthy Artificial Intelligence' was released by the AI HLEG. The EU Commission also released the 'European Approach to Artificial Intelligence'.[9] It was noted that some AI applications raise ethical and legal questions on the liability or fairness of AI decision-making and that legal clarity in such application is required in order for the GDPR to build trust among data subjects.

[9] European Commission (EC), 'Digital Single Market: Artificial Intelligence Policy', available at: www.https://ec.europa.eu/digital-single-market/en/artificial-intelligence.

Currently, the GDPR contains provisions that have a direct and indirect impact on AI in data management and the legality of such practices. The two provisions that have the most direct application to the use of AI are: (a) Article 5 and the requirement of transparency; and (b) Article 22 and the right not to be subject to *solely* automated decision-making.

These provisions relate to the importance of oversight and openness. From one perspective, it could be viewed as a regulator's distrust of AI; from another, it is a precaution to maintain the fragile trust that consumers may have in the use of AI in relation to personal data.

In order for the data subject to be equipped to make decisions about his or her personal data, awareness of the collection and use is essential. That is the reason for the transparency principle (and the basis for consent and notification of purpose requirements under data protection laws). In the GDPR, transparency is provided for through Chapter 3 (Rights of the Data Subject), which includes the transparency of information and communication, and modalities for the exercise of the data subject's rights.[10]

The most direct reference to AI in the GDPR relates to its use for personal profiling, which may have fairness and accuracy concerns. Article 22 provides as a general rule that:

> The data subject shall have the right not to be subject to a decision based solely on automated processing, including profiling, which produces legal effects concerning him or her or similarly significantly affects him or her.

There are limited and strict exceptions, including authorisation based on the data subject's explicit consent,[11] and the authorisation by Member State with suitable measures for safeguarding the data subject's rights, freedoms and 'legitimate interests'.[12]

The GDPR obliges the data controller to ensure fair and transparent processing by providing the data subject with 'meaningful information about the logic involved, as well as the significance and the envisaged consequences of such processing for the data subject'.[13] This requires an organisation to inform an individual of the reasons for an automated decision to be taken in relation to that person and at least a basic explanation of the technical process, as well as the impact on that person.

[10] GDPR, art 12.
[11] ibid art 22(2)(c).
[12] ibid art 22(2)(b). See also Directive (EU) 2016/680 of the European Parliament and of the Council of 27 April 2016 on the protection of natural persons with regard to the processing of personal data by competent authorities for the purposes of the prevention, investigation, detection or prosecution of criminal offences or the execution of criminal penalties, and on the free movement of such data, and repealing Council Framework Decision 2008/977/JHA, L 119, 4 May 2016 (Data Protection in Criminal Matters).
[13] GDPR, arts 13(2)(f), 14(2)(g), and 15(1)(h). See also M Brkan, 'Do Algorithms Rule the World? Algorithmic Decision-Making and Data Protection in the Framework of the GDPR and Beyond' (2019) 27(2) *International Journal of Law and Information Technology* 91.

There are also some GDPR provisions that are indirectly relevant to AI that serve to encourage the use of AI to support the rights of data subjects and empower the individual to better control the use and dissemination of his or her personal information. These provisions deal with:

a. Privacy by Design, which includes the implementation of 'appropriate technical measures' designed to implement data protection principles in an effective manner, integrate necessary safeguards into the data processing;[14] and to ensure that, by default, only personal data necessary for each specific purpose of the processing are processed;[15]
b. The Right to be Forgotten, which refers to the right of erasure and/or to block public accessibility to personal data such as through search engine indexing and results;[16] and
c. The Data Portability right for the convenient transfer of personal data from one organisation to another at the behest of the individual concerned.[17]

Concomitantly, there is a right to fairness and transparency, which is the data subject's *right to be informed* about 'the existence of the right to request from the controller access to and rectification or erasure of personal data or restriction of processing concerning the data subject or to object to processing',[18] as well as 'the right to data portability'.[19]

E. The Protection of Personal Data under the PDPA and AI

The PDPA may not contain many of the GDPR provisions that are relevant to the use of AI. However, the Act does contain the openness obligation in the form of the requirements for organisations to develop and implement data protection policies and practices necessary to meet their obligations under the Act.[20] The move towards greater accountability measures will also involve greater transparency and scrutiny of the use of AI as a tool for data collection and use, as well as for data analytics.

The PDPC's powers of investigation also extend to the legality and propriety in the use of AI in any form (eg, the Internet of Things (IoT)), and whether it is

[14] GDPR, art 25(1).
[15] ibid art 25(2). This can be supported by an 'approved certification mechanism' established at the regulatory level. See also art 25(3), referencing art 42 of the GDPR.
[16] ibid art 17. See also *Google Spain SL and Google Incorporated v Agencia Española de Protección de Datos (AEPD) and Costeja González*, Judgment, reference for a preliminary ruling, Case C-131/12, ECLI:EU:C:2014:317, 13 May 2014; and *Google Inc v Commission nationale de l'informatique et des libertes (CNIL)*, Case C-507/17, ECLI:EU:C:2019:772, 24 September 2019.
[17] GDPR art 20. It is the right to receive and transfer (where technically feasible) personal data 'in a structured, commonly used and machine-readable format' where 'the processing is carried out by automated means'.
[18] GDPR, arts 13(2)(b), 14(2)(b) and 15(1)(e).
[19] ibid arts 13(2)(b) and 14(2)(b).
[20] PDPA, s 11. This includes designating an individual such as a Data Protection Officer to ensure compliance and to meet specific obligations such as to respond to access and correction requests. See also PDPC, *Advisory Guidelines on Key Concepts in the PDPA* (revised 9 October 2019) at ch 20.

in compliance with the Act.[21] What is reasonable and appropriate in the circumstances for the purpose of compliance with the Act can take into account the nature and use of AI, such as the lack of sufficient explainability and awareness (ie, notice), and the requirement of specific permission through the appropriate channels (ie, consent).

Moreover, the deemed consent provision in the PDPA can extend to the 'sharing' of personal data with AI for the purpose of data processing if it is 'reasonable' in relation to the purpose for which it was voluntarily provided by the data subject.[22] Furthermore, the access, correction and accuracy obligations also provide greater transparency and control over one's personal data, and the power to 'correct' or ensure the accuracy of such information in the possession and control of an organisation.[23] This can also provide individuals with the ability to check on the fairness (or otherwise) of decisions made based on the personal data in question, including opinions of the person and individual profiling based on interests, habits and other attributes.[24] As the PDPA evolves, it will gradually include additional rights, such as the right to data portability introduced in the 2021 amendments to the Act, which will be relevant to AI use.[25] It is this expected evolution of the PDPA that takes into account AI concerns and issues, which can benefit from the propertisation of personal data, which will be examined in section IV.

As noted above in section II.A, the Model Artificial Intelligence Governance Framework was developed and released by the PDPC,[26] clearly evidencing the importance of ethics specifically in the area of personal data management.

The use of AI extends to many different economic sectors with their own needs and interests. For example, AI-powered advisors are used in the financial industry and AI-powered gadgets and machines are mobilised in the health industry. These developments also present new and unique challenges to privacy concerns, data protection issues and ethical dilemmas that are unique to each industrial sector as they deal with very different types of data, including sensitive information, that can also have public policy and security concerns, such as where they relate to 'essential services' and the 'critical information infrastructure'. Even though the discussion on these challenges is cross-sectorial, regular sectorial-specific dialogue is also needed, given that the considerations and concerns, as well as solutions, are different in each sector.[27]

[21] See, eg, the PDPC Administrative Decision in *Actxa Pte Ltd* [2018] SGPDPC 5.

[22] PDPA, s 15.

[23] ibid ss 21–23.

[24] Subject to statutory exceptions to the access and correction obligations under the Fifth and Sixth Schedules to the PDPA.

[25] See PDPC, *Discussion Paper on Data Portability* (issued 25 February 2019).

[26] See n 7 above. See also the PDPC website on the Model Framework and the Implementation and Self-Assessment Guide for Organisations (ISAGO), which was developed with the private (industry) sector: www.pdpc.gov.sg/Help-and-Resources/2020/01/Model-AI-Governance-Framework.

[27] On 12 November 2018, the Monetary Authority of Singapore (MAS) issued a set of principles known as FEAT to promote fairness, ethics, accountability and transparency in the use of AI and data analytics in the finance industry. See *Principles to Promote Fairness, Ethics, Accountability and Transparency (FEAT) in the Use of Artificial Intelligence and Data Analytics in Singapore's Financial*

III. The Case for the Propertisation of Personal Data

A. The Fourth Industrial Revolution

The Third Industrial Revolution, which started in the second half of the twentieth century, saw the creation and use of electronics leading to the evolution of smart devices like personal computers and gadgets. The changes in communications technology also led to faster, cheaper and eventually wireless forms of transmitting messages.

We are now experiencing the Fourth Industrial Revolution which started with the introduction of the internet and the World Wide Web (WWW), leading to the emergence of new economies, including the creation of disruptive innovations for businesses. The common feature among them is the increasing utility and use of data, which heightens issues of privacy, value and security (which are also features of property law). Data, in particular personal data, is being used to enhance a sharing economy with social media supplanting mass media and the rise of new stakeholders and giant corporations that provide new forms of product, service and information delivery. These include organisations like Google (search engines), Facebook (social media platforms), Uber and Grab (ride-sharing apps), Airbnb and Booking.com (accommodation sharing apps), and the trend towards a gig economy such as in logistics (eg, Deliveroo and NinjaVan). Existing corporations in retail and entertainment have also greatly modified the content delivery and format of their businesses to survive in this new environment.

Although property law has its roots in land ownership, which is tangible and immovable, it was followed by the recognition of ownership over personal property. The concept of 'property' further evolved to cover intangible forms of property including rights under intellectual property law. As noted above, data per se, which is also intangible, is increasingly given attributes of property to enhance rights protection for data ownership.

'Property' and 'property law' need not fit into any one rubric; rather, there can be some common core features and characteristics that render them 'property' for the purposes of legal rights and remedies for the 'owner'.[28] This can include data per se.[29]

Sector (MAS, 2018), www.mas.gov.sg/~/media/MAS/News%20and%20Publications/Monographs%20and%20Information%20Papers/FEAT%20Principles%20Final.pdf. On 13 November 2019, the MAS announced that it is working with financial industry partners to create a framework, 'Veritas', for financial institutions to promote the responsible adoption of Artificial Intelligence and Data Analytics (AIDA) by incorporating the FEAT principles into the AIDA practices. The same approach is urgently required in other sectors such as the healthcare sector. See, eg, D Schonberger, 'Artificial Intelligence in Healthcare: A Critical Analysis of the Legal and Ethical Implications' (2019) 27(2) *International Journal of Law and Information Technology* 171.

[28] There is no one-size-fits-all solution for one type of data (ie, personal data), much less for all forms of data, tangible or otherwise. Exclusive property rights can, for instance, also be used to ringfence and protect sensitive data (eg, through data localisation laws).

[29] See Sjef van Erp, 'Ownership of Data: The Numerus Clausus of Legal Objects' (2017) 6 *Property Rights Conference Journal* 235.

B. The PDPA, Copyright Law and Comparisons on the Propertisation of Data

The treatment of information under copyright law can make a good comparison to the proposed propertisation of data under the data protection regime.

First, there are similar stakeholders and an 'interest-balancing' approach to both sets of laws, as well as schemes to maximise protection for the 'owner' of data while providing relief to other interested 'users' of the data. Second, the originality and distinctiveness of the information in question also feature in both regimes. Third, the digitisation of information has led to non-rivalry in personal data and intellectual property protected content, offering similar challenges to their protection.

Some commentators have pointed out that a property rights approach to personal property only makes sense if personal data is commoditised in the first place.[30] Professor Jessica Litman argued that: 'We deem something property in order to facilitate its transfer. If we don't intend the item to be transferred, then we needn't treat it as property at all.'[31]

Nevertheless, commercial exploitation need not be the main impetus to treat personal data as property. For example, property rights can provide a data subject with the tools to control personal data that has been leaked to the public by empowering the individual to bring an action to prohibit the collection or use, and to stop access to and the dissemination of such information. It can be used to justify and determine what exceptions can and should be permitted to consent and/or notification, as well as what conditions should be put in place for those that may have 'legitimate' grounds for doing so. For example, there are prerequisites or factors to determine whether a proposed 'legitimate interest' exception applies,[32] just as there are factors laid out for the 'fair dealing' defence in copyright law.[33] After all,

[30] The right of an individual to control how his or her identity is commercially used is widely recognised in the US. See, eg, *Zacchini v. Scripps-Howard Broadcasting* 433 US 562 (1977), where the US Supreme Court explained that the right to publicity is meant to provide an economic incentive for the plaintiffs to make the investment required to entertain the public. Moreover, the right does not arise unless it is shown that the individual has commercially exploited his or her image or likeness; *Lerman v Chuckleberry Pub Inc.* 521 F. Supp. 228 (1981) at 232. See also the US Court of Appeal (Second Circuit) case of *Haelen Laboratories v Topps Chewing Gum, Inc* 202 F 2d 866 (2nd Cir, 1953), 868, where the court stated that: 'Whether it be labelled a "property" right is immaterial; for here, as often elsewhere, the tag "property" simply symbolizes the fact that courts enforce a claim which has pecuniary worth. This right might be called a 'right of publicity.'

[31] Jessica Litman, 'Information Privacy/Information Property' (2000) 52(5) *Stanford Law Review* 1283, at 1296.

[32] This is a new exception in the 2021 amendments to the Act. It is a prerequisite that 'the benefit to the public' must be 'greater than any adverse effect on the individual'. The assessment of 'adverse effect in the individual' is also a prerequisite to a new provision allowing for deemed consent by notification (s 15A).

[33] See s 35(2) of the Copyright Act 2006. The factors assist the assessor to consider what is fair, including the extent to which unauthorised use can adversely affect or impact the interests of the copyright owner, including the market and commercial value of the work concerned.

the reasonableness criteria in PDPA already address the issue to some extent, even though it may benefit from a clearer set of criteria for assessment.[34] The reasons for treating personal data as property will be explored in more detail below.

Although there is no publicity right in Singapore law, a comparison of the personal data protection regime to publicity rights is likewise elucidating, as a person's identity and image is a form of personal data. The consent, notification and purpose limitation obligations under the PDPA (in relation to an organisation's collection, use and disclosure of personal data), and the right of private action for any person who suffers loss or damage as a result of the breach of those obligations in a civil proceeding,[35] provide a similar recourse for a wider range of personal data than that accorded to the specific form of personal data under the law on publicity rights.[36]

C. The Purpose and Objective of the PDPA and the GDPR

The PDPA is not recognised as a privacy protection law in Singapore.[37] This was made clear in both the drafting and parliamentary processes, and the fact that 'privacy' does not appear anywhere in the Act. Instead, the objective and purpose in the long title and the purpose provision clearly state that the Act is enacted:

> 'To govern the collection, use and disclosure of personal data by organisations' and '[t]he purpose of this Act is to govern the collection, use and disclosure of personal data by organisations in a manner that recognises both the right of individuals to protect their personal data and the need of organisations to collect, use or disclose personal data for purposes that a reasonable person would consider appropriate in the circumstances'.[38]

However, there is also no evidence that property law was ever a consideration in the development of the Act. As such, any possible relation of its provisions to property law is based on legislative interpretation only.[39]

Possession and control are key to an organisation's obligation under the PDPA,[40] and this can be interpreted liberally.[41] Although nothing is stated about

[34] See, eg, s 11(1) of the PDPA, which states in relation to compliance with the Act that: 'In meeting its responsibilities under this Act, an organisation shall consider what a reasonable person would consider appropriate in the circumstances.'

[35] ibid s 32.

[36] ibid ss 13, 18, 20, and 32, respectively.

[37] On the other hand, the Protection from Harassment Act (Cap 256A) (PHA) is more of a privacy rights piece of legislation. In the 2019 amendment (Act 17 of 2019), which entered into force on 1 January 2020, the offence of intentional harassment extends to doxxing through the publication of identity information of a target person or a related person (PHA, s 3(1)(c)).

[38] PDPA, long title and s 3 respectively.

[39] However, the PDPC has stated that the PDPA 'does not specifically confer any property or ownership rights on personal data per se to individuals or organisations'. See PDPC, *Advisory Guidelines on Key Concepts in the PDPA* (revised 9 October 2019), para 5.30.

[40] See s 11 of the PDPA, which states that '[a]n organisation is responsible for personal data in its possession or under its control' and section 24 of the PDPA, which states that '[a] organisation shall

the 'ownership' of the data in question and where it lies, the 'interest' in the collection, use and disclosure of personal data lies with both the individual and the organisation (based on its need).[42] This differs from the current treatment of these concepts under the CMA[43] and the Copyright Act.[44]

Practically speaking, one can look at data as a form of 'asset' or 'currency' and not merely one of privacy concern. Data controllers or organisations often 'buy' or obtain personal data as part of a transaction, 'buy' or 'trade' personal data in exchange for providing online services (eg, social media accounts or email accounts) or collect personal data in exchange for goods or opportunities (eg, free products or a chance to win a contest). Organisations also buy and sell datasets such as marketing lists and job application/profiles (eg, job search sites). By perceiving data as something of value or as a 'currency', it is not unreasonable to view such data as a form of property. However, it is not necessary that the 'value' ascribed to personal data must have some direct and tangible commercial value.

Where data is treated as an asset or representation of an asset or interest, whether of commercial value or not, it is easier to treat it (including by law) as a form of property to protect and apportion rights in a way not unlike intellectual property or other forms of movable property (including virtual currency).

It has been asserted that the GDPR 'includes three elements in particular that lend themselves to a property-based conception: Consumers are granted clear entitlements to their own data; the data, even after it is transferred, carries a burden that "runs with" it and binds third parties; and consumers are protected through remedies grounded in "property rules"'.[45] Some US academics also favour a property or market-based approach.[46]

protect personal data in its possession or under its control'. The same phrase appears in the sections on access and correction of personal data (ie, ss 21 and 22), respectively.

[41] In the PDPC Administrative Decision in *National University of Singapore* [2017] SGPDPC 5, the National University of Singapore's responsibility extended to personal data handled by its student organisations even though it was not data that it shared with the students or that the latter collected from or used the personal data in relation to the University's primary purpose (unlike, for example, an agent or employee of the University).

[42] PDPA, s 3.

[43] Computer Misuse Act 2007.

[44] Copyright Act 2006.

[45] JM Victor, 'The EU General Data Protection Regulation: Toward a Property Regime for Protecting Data Privacy' (2013) 123 *Yale Law Journal* 513, 515. See also PM Schwartz, 'Property, Privacy, and Personal Data' (2004) 117 *Harvard Law Review* 2055.

[46] See, eg, P Samuelson, 'Cyberspace and Privacy: A New Legal Paradigm?' (2000) 52 *Stanford Law Review* 1125, 1127–28, where the author proposed one of several alternative solutions to a property-based and human rights/regulatory approach, which is the adaptation of trade secrecy licensing default rules. See also G Malgieri, '"Ownership" of Customer (Big) Data in the European Union: Quasi-property as Comparative Solution?' (2016) 20(5) *Journal of Internet Law* 2, which advocates trade secret requirements to personal data based on a 'quasi-propertisation of personal data' approach; *cf* D Beldiman, 'An Information Society Approach to Privacy Legislation: How to Enhance Privacy While Maximizing Information Value' [2002] *John Marshall Review of Intellectual Property Law* 71, 86–89. See also SA Elvy, 'Commodifying Consumer Data in the Era of the Internet of Things' (2018) 59(2) *Boston College Law Review* 423, 463–72, which examines data ownership vis-a-vis rights in data, and that canvasses the often conflicting and mixed approaches taken by the legislature and courts

The trajectory of data protection developments in the EU have been to embrace a more proprietary approach to the protection obligations in its Member States through the newer rights that the GDPR espouses, like the right to be forgotten and the data portability right. This approach makes sense as it serves to entrench and strengthen the defences to personal data privacy, which is the objective of the EU in updating its provisions and by changing the law from a Directive to a Regulation.[47]

D. Protection of Computer Material in Singapore, AI and Data as Property

The treatment of data and computer material under the CMA is based on ownership and control.[48] The Act defines the data owner whose authority is required for access or modification as someone entitled to control access and who is himself or herself entitled to decide who has permission to do so under sections 3 and 5, respectively.[49] It is this person whose consent to access or modify is required for a defence to an offence under the respective provisions.[50] 'Data' in the CMA is defined as 'representations of information or of concepts that are being prepared or have been prepared in a form suitable for use in a computer'.[51]

In the case of *Lim Siong Khee v Public Prosecutor*,[52] where there was unauthorised access to an email account and its contents, the court determined that based on a common clause in the agreements of the free web-based email systems (in this case, a clause on the Lycos Network Privacy Policy for Mailcity.com, which was part of the Lycos Network), the ownership of the data belonged to the registered user-subscriber, even though it was clearly stated (and more technically accurate) that the control (and possession) of the data was (also and mainly) with the server belonging to the email service provider. Here, a distinction is made between ownership and *legal* entitlement to control on the one hand and possession (and *technical* control) on the other. In fact, the password itself is protected as an asset and '[i]t is possible for a system administrator to sell passwords to unauthorized

alike, as well as the diversity in academic thought on the subject. See also M Blass, 'The New Data Marketplace: Protecting Personal Data, Electronic Communications, and Individual Privacy in the Age of Mass Surveillance through a Return to a Property-Based Approach to the Fourth Amendment' (2015) 42(3) *Hastings Constitutional Law Quarterly* 577.

[47] (EU) 2016/679. The previous permutation was the Data Protection Directive 95/46/EC. The EU is also looking to 'upgrade' the ePrivacy Directive 2002/58/EC to a Regulation.

[48] Computer Misuse Act 2007.

[49] One can perhaps view a computer as a place and the data or program contained in it as a form of movable or personal property. Access without permission is a form of criminal trespass.

[50] CMA, ss 2(5) and (8).

[51] ibid s 2.

[52] *Lim Siong Khee v Public Prosecutor* [2001] SGHC 69, [2001] 1 SLR(R) 631. Unauthorised access can also be viewed as a form of computer trespass.

users to enable free access and usage'.[53] Similarly, access to Wi-Fi, modification of a webpage or the contents of a website, and unobstructed (and 'peaceful') use of one's computer are also protected under the CMA.

The definition of a 'computer' refers to 'an electronic, magnetic, optical, electrochemical, or other data processing device, or a group of such interconnected or related devices, performing logical, arithmetic, or storage functions, and includes any data storage facility or communications facility directly related to or operating in conjunction with such device or group of such interconnected or related devices'.[54] This can potentially cover AI, although perhaps a more unambiguous redefinition can be made. An AI can also be covered by the reference to the performance of any function by a computer.[55]

Specifically, in relation to personal data, the CMA also makes it an offence to use illegally obtained personal data to further offences in any other written law.[56] This provision was added in an amendment in 2017 to supplement and complement the protection of personal data by the PDPA. A similar provision relating to the facilitation or commission of such an offence relating to illegally obtained personal information was included in the Penal Code on 1 January 2020.[57]

IV. The Usefulness of Property Rights in Personal Data and to the Deployment of AI

A. Strengthening the Rights of the Data Subject and Control Over Personal Data

It is possible to interpret relevant PDPA rights as proprietary rights to reinforce their protections. The fundamental basis that can be taken is that the '[u]se and disclosure of private information specifically related to a person (or company)

[53] See ibid para 13, where the then Chief Justice Yong Pung How cited the speech of the then Minister for Home Affairs, Wong Kan Seng, at the Second Reading of the Computer Misuse (Amendment) Bill 1998 on s 8(1) of the CMA.

[54] CMA, s 2. A 'computer service' includes 'data processing', which can also extend to the main function of an AI.

[55] See CMA, ss 3 and 4.

[56] See ibid s 8A. 'Illegally obtained' means obtained in contravention of ss 3–6 of the CMA. Furthermore, another new provision, s 8B, makes it an offence for a person to obtain or retain any item intending to (or with a view to it being supplied or made available to) commit or facilitate the commission of ss 3–7 offences under the Act as well as make, supply, offer to supply or make available any item to do the same. An 'item' includes a 'computer program' that is 'designed or adapted primarily, or is capable of being used, for the purpose of committing the above-mentioned offences'. This can also potentially extend to the programme and use of AI for the purpose of a CMA offence.

[57] Criminal Law Reform Act 2019, s 135, which inserted s 416A into the Penal Code. Section 416A is wider as it is not restricted to personal information obtained through one of the offences in the CMA, but rather without the data subject's consent.

should be controlled by that entity unless a compelling public interest shifts this control to other parties'.[58]

Even though property is difficult to define,[59] there are some attributes that academics generally agree upon as being characteristic of property rights. The first is that a property right is a right *in rem*. It is a right that is enforceable against the world at large (ie, the principle of *erga omnes*). Currently, existing data legislation imposes civil liability on the errant data controller or processor, which means that privacy rights are a right *in personam* (a right enforceable only against particular persons). However, it is arguable that privacy rights have characteristics of a right *in rem*. If we consider personal data to be the *res*, privacy rights follow the personal data as it is shared from one organisation to another. When an organisation transfers personal data to another organisation, the recipient organisation has a duty to ensure that the individual data user has given his or her consent for the transfer,[60] otherwise the recipient organisation will be liable for the unauthorised collection and use of the personal data. The recipient organisation is obliged to respect the rights of the individual, even though it has contracted only with the disclosing organisation (where personal rights result), and there is no relationship formed between the individual and the recipient organisation.[61] The *erga omnes* principle allows a data subject to determine the use of his or her data by any organisation that may come into its possession. At the same time, it gives the greatest effect to data protection as organisations have to observe the obligations under the data protection law concerned.

Another area where the *erga omnes* effect can be useful is when considering the statutory exceptions that may inadvertently dilute or weaken the data subject's rights under a data protection law. Take, for example, the 'publicly available' personal data exception to consent under the PDPA.[62] When personal data is

[58] RT Nimmer and PA Krauthaus, 'Information as Property Databases and Commercial Property' (1993) 1 *International Journal of Law and Information Technology* 3, 4. The authors noted that: 'Property rights in information focus on identifying the right of a company or individual to control disclosure, use, alternation and copying of designated information. The resulting bundle of rights and limits comprises a statement of what property exists in information' (at 5 and 6); see also at 7, which states that '[a] property analysis speaks in terms of transferable assets and fixed zones of legally enforceable control'.

[59] Property is ubiquitous yet difficult to define. In *National Provincial Bank v Ainsworth* [1965] 1 AC 1175 at 1248, for example, Lord Wilberforce stated that property rights must be definable, identifiable by third parties, capable in their assumption by third parties and have some degree of permanence or stability. However, this may not describe all forms of 'property'. It is because of the ambiguity and fluidity in what constitutes 'property' that allows the concept to evolve and possibly extend to new forms, like personal data.

[60] PDPA, s 20(2), which states that: 'An organisation, on or before collecting personal data about an individual from another organisation without the consent of the individual, shall provide the other organisation with sufficient information regarding the purpose of the collection to allow that other organisation to determine whether the disclosure would be in accordance with this Act.'

[61] Similarly, in relation to rights to privacy, Warren and Brandeis stated that they are 'not rights arising from contract or from special trust, but are rights as against the world'. See S Warren and L Brandeis, 'The Right to Privacy' (1890) 4 *Harvard Law Review* 193, 213.

[62] See PDPA, s 17, read with para 1(c) of the Second and Third Schedules and para 1(d) of the Fourth Schedule.

made publicly available by an individual willingly, there may be implicit consent or licence to collect it, and perhaps it may also be reasonable to use it in relation to the context in which it was shared. However, if it was made publicly available through a data breach or leak, then if the exception exempts any organisation from seeking consent for collection, use and disclosure,[63] the data subject's rights are effectively curtailed to a large extent, especially since there is no right of withdrawal of consent under such circumstances. This cannot be consistent with the objective of the Act. The remedy of an injunction can be a very powerful tool against the exploitation of personal data. Thus, applying the principles of property law and the *erga omnes* principle, the exception should be amended thus: first, the right to the use of publicly available personal data without consent or any other valid exception should be removed; and, second, in relation to the collection of publicly available personal data, the exception should be qualified, perhaps to the extent that the personal data was made public by the individual concerned. As for the exception in relation to the disclosure of personal data already made publicly available, the exception may remain as it is since it is already publicly available, unless and until it is the subject of a right of erasure (which does not as yet exist under the PDPA).[64] Similar considerations should be given to the other (presently unqualified) exceptions, where perhaps there should be more clearly defined conditions or factors to be considered in order for them to apply.

Ownership over property has often been described as a bundle of rights.[65] These rights include the right to possess, use or enjoy, alienate, transmit after death, and to exclude others from enjoyment or possession.[66] Individuals have the right to possess, use or enjoy their personal data, and they have the ability to transfer these rights. Under current legislation, an individual exercises his or her right by giving or refusing consent to the collection, use and disclosure of personal information by an organisation.

The inalienable rights under the PDPA and the person's control over his or her personal data in the possession of another can also be found in the right of access and correction, and the obligation on organisations to maintain accuracy of personal data. However, due to the commoditisation of personal data, there is also a market for the partial alienability of rights, such as through legal agreements (which is similar to copyright law).

[63] ibid, respectively.

[64] In this regard, it is of interest to note that under the GDPR, for fairness and transparency, the data controller must provide the data subject with information as to 'which source the personal data originate, and if applicable, whether it came from publicly accessible sources' (art 14(2)(f)) and 'where the personal data are not collected from the data subject, any available information as to their source' (art 15(1)(g)). This allows the individual to investigate further and/or lodge a complaint with (and seek the assistance of) the relevant supervisory authority to enforce his or her rights under the Act, such as the right of access, correction and erasure (arts 15–17, respectively).

[65] See, eg, PM Schwartz, 'Property, Privacy and Personal Data' (2004) 117 *Harvard Law Review* 2056, 2095, where the author refers to it as a 'bundle of sticks' that includes inalienability, default, exit, damages and institutions.

[66] SY Tan, HW Tang and KFK Low, *Tan Sook Yee's Principles of Singapore Land Law*, 4th edn (LexisNexis, 2019) at 9.

As a property right, one owns one's personal data and one also has commercial rights in one's personal information.[67] This recognises personal data as an asset that can generate monetary value (but that is not limited to it). This can also indirectly strengthen the awareness and the exercise of personal data rights, and incentivise data subjects to monitor the use of their data by organisations to ensure that their ownership rights have been complied with.

Hence, the ability to 'trade' (through consent) and retract (through withdrawal of consent), and the requirement of extending rights over disseminated personal data (to third parties) are similar to property rights. Meanwhile, the retention of residual rights that 'runs with' the data wherever it is transferred and to third parties is essential to protect interests relating to personal data (which can be compared to the retention of moral rights in the law of copyright in some jurisdictions).

Retaining control (and the right to assert it) over one's personal information even after transfer is also important, whether or not one's personal data was shared by the data subject, obtained through a third party, or even extrapolated or deduced from increasingly innovative forms of data analysis, including through the use of AI. Hence, perhaps there should not be a test of 'practicability' (to 'directly or indirectly ascertain') or 'reasonable likelihood' assigned to the test of 'identifiable' personal data, as is the case in the data protection legislation of some countries.[68]

The right to control and alienate personal data can also be found in the right of data portability.[69] Under the GDPR, individuals have the right to direct the transfer of personal data from one organisation to another.[70] When the data portability provisions are included in the PDPA, it can bring with it the possibility of the transfer (and sale) of personal data by the data subject from one organisation to another.

The right to exclude others from enjoyment or possession can be found in the consent regime as well as the right to erasure.[71] Individuals can exclude organisations from possessing personal data, either by refusing to give consent in the first place or by sending a deletion request.[72] It is also important to note that exclusivity

[67] See, eg, SE Gindin, 'Lost and Found in Cyberspace: Informational Privacy in the Age of the Internet' (1997) 34 *San Diego Law Review* 1153. See also P Mell, 'Seeking Shade in a Land of Perpetual Sunlight: Privacy as Property in the Electronic Wilderness' (1996) 11(1) *Berkeley Technology Law Journal* 1.

[68] See the definition of personal data in s 2 of the Hong Kong Personal Data (Privacy) Ordinance (Cap 486) as well as recital 26 and art 4(1) of the GDPR, respectively.

[69] See n 7 above, 10. Singapore will include the data portability provisions in the 2021 amendments to the PDPA.

[70] GDPR, recital 68.

[71] As noted above, the right to be forgotten can extend the control and reach of an individual to personal information that is in the possession of another or that can determine the removal of access to it (eg, if it is publicly available information that is indexed by a search engine and displayed on an online platform or website). Personal data as property can explain and guide the development of these concepts in the Singapore context.

[72] Such a request can extend to blocking access through search engines as in Case C-131/12 *Google Spain SL and Google Incorporated v Agencia Española de Protección de Datos (AEPD) and Costeja González*, Judgment, reference for a preliminary ruling, ECLI:EU:C:2014:317, 13 May 2014. The court held that the right to be forgotten applies to search engine results. The indexing and web-crawling carried out by a search engine like Google could be considered a data processing act, with Google as

does not necessarily require the personal data to be fully erased from the organisation's memory bank, which may be impossible in some cases.[73] Anonymisation is a solution. In the same way, exclusivity in privacy rights could simply refer to a right to prevent use by or disclosure to third parties.

The 'extended' suite of rights in the GDPR such as the right to be forgotten and data portability seems to treat data as something that is more tangible that can be erased or transferred in a defined 'form'.[74] They further strengthen the perception of data as belonging to the individual or data subject and that is merely 'shared' with data controllers for limited purposes. The Singapore PDPA contains a retention limitation obligation that provides a more limited right than the right of erasure, and a data portability provision is in the works, as noted above.

The PDPA provides that any person who suffers loss or direct damage as a result of a contravention of the data protection obligations in relation to personal data under the Act shall have right of relief in civil proceedings in a court that can come in the way of damages, injunctions, declarations or such other relief as the court deems fit.[75] It will be interesting to see whether and how this will be used in practice. However, it is likely limited by what constitutes 'loss or direct damage'. A civil right of action to enforce one's proprietary rights (with the possibility of equitable remedies like injunctions) is an important component of property law. Perceiving personal data as a form of property with proprietary characteristics can lead to a greater role and significance as well as more appropriate forms of remedies in *ex post* private actions that will complement the PDPA's primary focus on *ex ante* compliance and accountability obligations.

Finally, although not all jurisdictions recognise this, in some cases the right to personal data can be 'inherited' or transmitted after an individual's death under some data protection laws. For instance, section 17 of the Data Privacy Act of the Philippines states that the 'lawful heirs and assigns of the data subject may invoke the rights of the data subject … at any time after the death of the data subject'.[76] As a form of property, the deceased can also leave a 'digital legacy' to his or her personal data and the PDPA recognises a limited range of rights for data of the

a data controller. In deciding whether to grant a data subject's request to remove a search result link, Google had to carry out a balancing exercise to determine whether there are overriding 'compelling legitimate grounds' against the right to erase personal data. If not, Google had an obligation to remove links to webpages containing personal data. In Case C-507/17 *Google Inc v Commission nationale de l'informatique et des libertes (CNIL)*, ECLI:EU:C:2019:772, 24 September 2019, particularly at para 74, it was further determined that Google's obligation to de-reference extended to all versions of its search engine in the EU Member States but not beyond, although it should take measures to ensure effective protection of data subject's rights, for example, by discouraging Internet users from gaining access to the links in question outside the EU.

[73] In the case of intellectual property, exclusivity refers to the right to control use by others and it is not a right to remove or erase the information altogether. See above n 58, 11.

[74] See European Commission Joint Research Centre, *The Economics of Ownership, Access and Trade in Digital Data* (2017), 17, where it was stated that the GDPR gives data subjects 'no full ownership rights, only certain specific rights'. Instead, it is the data controller who has intellectual property ownership over the databases that it creates out of personal information, although it has a civil and criminal responsibility to respect the data user's specific rights.

[75] PDPA, s 32.

[76] Data Privacy Act 2012, Republic Act No 10173 (the Philippines).

deceased within 10 years of death – the disclosure and protection obligations.[77] In Singapore, a designated individual in a will or the nearest relative of a deceased can exercise limited rights relating to protection and disclosure or transmission of his or her personal data.[78] Such 'digital legacy' data provisions treat personal data as assets and like transferrable property.

B. Data as Property and its Effects on the Use of AI in Relation to Personal Data

The following quote summarises the benefits and challenges of AI to data protection:

> AI requires a vast amount of data to help train and advance its algorithms. Yet the amassing of data poses significant risks to our personal and collective freedoms. By contrast, data protection laws generally advocate minimising the collection and retention of personal data. The advent of AI therefore dictates a review of the traditional approach in personal data protection.[79]

Property rights in personal data can actually promote trust and accountability in the use and adoption of AI by consumers and organisations, respectively. In fact, the GDPR (and PDPA) provisions relating to the use of AI also have 'property traits'.

In the GDPR, the following rights of the data subject treat their personal data like personal property:

(a) The right to be informed[80] and to 'lawfulness, fairness and transparency',[81] that is, the fair processing of personal information through a privacy notice. As noted above, the awareness of what is being done to personal data is an important start to any exercise of personal rights in relation to its management by a third party, hence the importance of notice as well as openness and transparency. The reference to fair processing also relates to, for example, meeting reasonable expectations in the handling of personal data, no unjust

[77] PDPA, s 2(4)(b); and Personal Data Protection Regulations 2014, reg 11 ('Exercise of rights under the Act in respect of deceased individuals'). This can be loosely analogised to the approach to a transfer of assets to descendants after death by statute (ie, compare the 'nearest relative' list under the Personal Data Protection Regulations 2014 (First Schedule) read with s 11 of the Act to the distribution list under s 7 of the Intestate Succession Act or through a will); and also the ownership in a deceased's asset in his or her estate for the purpose of copyright protection. Facebook uses a 'legacy contract' for the personal data of deceased for the selection of someone to look after one's personal account if it is memorialised after death.

[78] PDPA, s 4(b), read with the Personal Data Protection Regulations 2014, reg 11 and First Schedule.

[79] SKY Wong, Privacy Commissioner for Personal Data, Hong Kong, *The Privacy Implications of Artificial Intelligence* (Hong Kong Lawyer, April 2019), www.hk-lawyer.org/content/privacy-implications-artificial-intelligence.

[80] GDPR, arts 13 and 14.

[81] ibid art 5(1)(a). The transparency and effective communication obligations are linked to the notice requirement; see art 12.

adverse effects, no deception in the collection of personal data and no biasness in decision-making based on the personal data of the individual, such as through false assessment or stereotyping by attributes.

(b) The rights of access and rectification (and to accuracy) of personal data, which include active rights to check and correct (and to require accuracy) of personal data.[82]

(c) The right to erasure (ie, to the deletion or removal of personal data when there is no compelling reason or purpose for its retention or processing) and to restrict or suppress the processing of personal data in certain circumstances.[83] Again, these are rights that the data subject can actively seek to enforce against the controller, with or without the assistance of the relevant authority. There is also the right to object to certain forms of processing, such as for direct marketing, scientific or historical research and statistics, and based on 'legitimate interests' or the performance of a task in the public interest or in the exercise of official authority.[84]

(d) The rights to data portability, automated decision-making and profiling,[85] which have been noted above in relation to the use of AI specifically.

How do we operationalise the personal-data-as-property model and how can AI be useful in this exercise? A Personal Information Management System (PIMS) for personal data can be useful in this regard as it can allow individuals to store and manage their personal data in secure (local or online) storage systems and control who they share it with.[86] Unauthorised access is prohibited by law under the CMA, and online service providers and advertisers will have to interact with the data subject through PIMS in order to access and use his or her personal data. This offers a more human-centric approach to personal information.

Another interesting new technology-based approach is the ongoing study on data trusts by Element AI, which just announced a strategic partnership with Mozilla.[87] The German Data Ethics Commission has proposed, among other things, a mandatory labelling scheme applicable to algorithmic systems that may pose a threat to human rights or have the potential for harm (a level of 'system criticality'), such as biased pricing for different people based on their profiles, or where there is a risk of confusion between human and machine (eg, 'social bots').[88]

[82] ibid arts 15 and 16.

[83] ibid arts 16 and 17, respectively.

[84] ibid art 21.

[85] ibid arts 20 and 22, respectively.

[86] See, eg, the European Data Protection Supervisor's (EDPS) Opinion on Personal Information Management Systems (PIMS), available at: www.edps.europa.eu/data-protection/our-work/publications/opinions/personal-information-management-systems_en.

[87] 'Element AI and Mozilla Foundation Partner to Build Data Trusts and Advocate for the Ethical Data Governance of AI', www.elementai.com/press-room/element-ai-and-mozilla-foundation-partner-to-build-data-trusts-and-advocate-for-the-ethical-data-governance-of-ai.

[88] See www.fortune.com/2019/10/24/german-eu-data-ethics-ai-regulation and www.bmjv.de/DE/Themen/FokusThemen/Datenethikkommission/Datenethikkommission_EN_node.html.

As noted in relation to privacy by design, AI can be used to protect a data subject's interest rather than pose a threat to it.[89] AI can be used to prevent crimes against an individual based on personal information such as identity theft and fraud. AI tools can be developed to, for example, recognise privacy preferences and remind, recommend or alert users to promote a consistent approach to data collectors. AI can also serve as a privacy policy scanner that reads and simplifies complicated privacy policies. For example, 'Polisis' ('privacy policy analysis') is an AI that uses machine learning to 'read a privacy policy it's never seen before and extract a readable summary, displayed in a graphic flow chart, of what kind of data a service collects, where that data could be sent, and whether a user can opt out of that collection or sharing'.[90]

V. Final Remarks

Data generally falls within a spectrum of what can be considered property, given the many different forms of property today (such as intellectual property). In some cases, for example, in the law on data protection (even in a country like Singapore that may not have adopted all the 'features' of a property right) and computer crimes, data has been treated as such under legislation and as interpreted by the courts and relevant authorities. From the above assessment, it seems that data can be (and have in some contexts been) treated as a form of property, whether by itself (such as for its marketing potential) or as a representation of something else (such as monetary funds).

The effect and impact of cognising personal data as a *sui generis* form of property goes beyond the doctrinal and can have real and practical implications. Recognising personal data as a form of property can influence and guide the interpretation of such concepts as data portability and help determine the enforcement of an individual's right to seek such a transference of data from one data controller to another, as well as to define the rules and regulations relating to such practices. It can determine whether and to what extent an individual can control his or her personal data in the hands of another party in the context of a right to be forgotten (should it ever be included in the PDPA) and how it is treated vis-a-vis other 'interests' such as the right to free speech.[91] Even in the current implementation of the obligations, perceiving personal data as property can have an impact

[89] See S Stalla-Bourdillon, 'Data Protection by Design and Data Analytics: Can We Have Both?' (2019) 19(5) *Privacy & Data Protection*, 8.

[90] A Greenberg, 'An AI That Reads Privacy Policies So That You Don't Have to' *Wired* (9 February 2018), https://www.wired.com/story/polisis-ai-reads-privacy-policies-so-you-dont-have-to.

[91] See K O'Hara, N Shadbolt and W Hall, 'A Pragmatic Approach to the Right to Be Forgotten' (March 2016) Paper Series No 26, *Global Commission on Internet Governance*, www.cigionline.org/sites/default/files/gcig_no26_web_1.pdf. See also I Stupariu, 'Defining the Right to Be Forgotten: A Comparative Analysis between the EU and the US', LLM thesis (2015), Central European University eTD Collection, www.etd.ceu.hu/2015/stupariu_ioana.pdf.

on the general 'reasonableness test' of compliance and give greater weight to the rights and interests of the individual in any given situation that involves setting the threshold where consent must be sought, notification must be given and the limitation as to the use purpose for the personal data collected. This is even more important given the widening of the deemed consent provision and the exceptions to obtaining real and actual consent in the latest amendments to the PDPA.

Treating and perceiving personal data as a form of property can also be useful when finding solutions to deal with the increased collection and use of personal information, especially through AI technology. The future of data collection and management will increasingly involve AI. The inclusion of AI in the equation can potentially affect the individual's control over his or her personal data and identification. Giving proprietary rights to the data subjects can adjust the possible imbalance and allow them to take back some control over their personal data. It can guide the development of a system of checks and balances and can engender greater acceptance of the use of AI in relation to the use of personal data.

A. Postscript

In the recently released report by the Singapore Academy of Law (SAL) Law Reform Committee entitled 'Rethinking Database Rights and Data Ownership in an AI World',[92] the Committee noted the increasing interest in applying a property rights regime towards data protection and acknowledged the usefulness of granting property rights over personal data.[93] However, the Committee did not recommend 'shifting from an information custodian approach to a property rights regime' due to 'conceptual difficulties' and 'policy risks' that it has identified (and that have also been considered in this book and other legal literature).[94] The Committee preferred an incremental approach to conferring greater rights or entitlements over personal data, citing the impending data portability provision (as well as the data innovation provision), and postulated that the statutory obligations and entitlements in the PDPA already address many of the concerns driving the push for data ownership.[95] Perhaps the arguments put forward in this chapter and other proponents of such a normative shift[96] can find some traction in the future development of the PDPA, such as when concepts like the right to be forgotten are considered for inclusion in the Act.

[92] 'Rethinking Database Rights and Data Ownership in an AI World' (July 2020), https://www.sal.org.sg/Resources-Tools/Law-Reform/AI_database_rights_and_data_ownership.
[93] ibid 37–38, paras 3.17–3.20.
[94] ibid 45–47, paras 3.33–3.36 and 47–48, paras 3.37–3.38.
[95] ibid 40–44, paras 3.25–3.31.
[96] See also Lee Pey Woan, ch 5 in this volume.

5

Personal Data as a Proprietary Resource

PEY WOAN LEE*

I. Introduction

Modern living is increasingly quantified. From wearable fitness trackers to e-shopping, Instagramming and commuting with GPS-enabled devices, our activities are continually being measured and monitored by smart devices from which we are now inseparable. But even as we relish the lifestyle enhancements made possible by technology, we are unwittingly also ceding control of vast amounts of personal information to suppliers of digital devices and services. Important insights gleaned from data analytics empower businesses, enable innovation and development, and alter consumer and market behaviour. An entire data economy has emerged as businesses rush to clinch a slice of this newfound wealth. In the meantime, consumers remain generally unappreciative of the growing surveillance to which they are subject as technology infiltrates their lives. Indeed, as technology marches on, businesses will no doubt continue to push out services and products with data-tracking abilities such that consumers are increasingly at risk of becoming 'digital peasants'[1] with little or no say over their terms of use. To be sure, governments have responded to the threat on information privacy through legislation. The General Data Protection Regulation[2] promulgated by the European Parliament is an instance of a comprehensive attempt at regulating the way in which personal data is processed, stored and transmitted. In Singapore, Parliament enacted the Personal Data Protection Act 2012[3] (hereinafter PDPA or 'the Act') 'to ensure a baseline standard of protection for personal data across the economy'.[4] Such legislative instruments are significant milestones in the recognition of the

* This research is supported by the National Research Foundation, Singapore under its Emerging Areas Research Projects (EARP) Funding Initiative. Any opinions, findings and conclusions or recommendations expressed in this material are those of the author(s) and do not reflect the views of National Research Foundation, Singapore.

[1] J Fairfield, *Owned: Property, Privacy and the New Digital Serfdom* (Cambridge University Press, 2017), 3.

[2] (EU) 2016/679.

[3] Act 26 of 2012.

[4] Singapore Parliament Reports (Hansard) (15 October 2012) 'Personal Data Protection Bill', vol 89 (Associate Professor Dr Yaacob Ibrahim, Minister for Information, Communications and the Arts).

individual's privacy interests, but their efficacy is largely dependent on state actions and sanctions.

In this chapter, I revisit the debate on the conception of personal data as a proprietary resource to augment the personal rights of data subjects under the PDPA. I begin by considering the position at common law and the common objections raised against the conception of information or data as property. I observe that although judicial authorities have largely declined to analyse information as property, more recent decisions have nevertheless exhibited greater willingness to countenance such arguments. While it is often said that information (including data) cannot constitute property because it is non-rivalrous (in that it is not consumed by use) and non-excludable (if it is impossible or too costly to prevent access by others), the true objections lie in, first, the need to safeguard public interests in the free dissemination of information and, second, the difficulty of applying property concepts (such as ownership, title and alienation) to informational assets. However, these difficulties are not insuperable if propertisation is effected by legislation within the PDPA framework. Ultimately, property is a conceptual tool that regulates social relations in respect of valuable resources. To designate a resource as someone's property is to make a baseline allocation of that resource – the owner acquires the right to exclude others from the resource, whilst non-owners bear the burden of demonstrating why they should not be so excluded. A new resource may therefore be regulated as property if it is excludable and there are cogent policy reasons why a specific class should have exclusive right to that resource.

In this chapter, I venture the view that both of these conditions are satisfied with respect to personal data. With the enactment of the PDPA, personal data may now be regarded as an excludable resource since the Act is founded on the central premise that the collection, use and disclosure of data is presumptively subject to the consent of data subjects and are to be used only for appropriate purposes notified to them. Supplementing the PDPA with a property framework is also justified by the need to safeguard the individual's interests in informational privacy. Such a development would augment the rights of data subjects, enable the award of property-based remedies for contraventions, provide clarity on the ownership of residual interests, and foster a culture that respects the individual's interests in informational privacy and self-determination.

II. The Position at Common Law

The suggestion that data could be understood as 'property' is controversial because data is usually analysed as a collection of facts or information. At common law, attempts to 'propertise' pure information[5] have traditionally been viewed

[5] 'Data' and 'information' are used interchangeably in this chapter, although the two terms are conceptually distinct in the context of informational science: see, eg, S Baskarada and A Koronios,

with scepticism. In a frequently cited passage in *Boardman v Phipps*,[6] Lord Upjohn observed that '[in] general, information is not property at all. It is normally open to all who have eyes to read and ears to hear'. This may suggest that information is not property only because it is readily observable and accessible, yet courts have been equally wary even in respect of *confidential* information. In *OBG v Allen*,[7] Lord Walker was categorical that 'information, even if it was confidential, cannot properly be regarded as a form of property'. Hence, even as equity restrains a breach of confidence, it is not a jurisdiction founded on the conceptualisation of confidential information as property (although proprietary remedies may sometimes follow such a breach).[8] This aversion to proprietary analysis is also observed in cases involving personal information. In *R v Department of Health*,[9] the English Court of Appeal held that patients have no proprietary claims to the personal information contained in medical prescription forms handed to pharmacists.[10] As such, the pharmacists were free to sell the information (on an anonymised basis) to data miners to help pharmaceutical companies effect targeted promotion of their products. In *Your Response Ltd v Datateam Business Media Ltd*,[11] a differently constituted Court of Appeal held that a possessory lien could not be asserted over an electronic database because '[p]ossession is concerned with the physical control of tangible objects'.[12] Crucially, the Court also rejected the claimant's suggestion that the database constitutes a form of intangible property distinct from a chose in action. In the lead judgment, Moore-Bick LJ was of the view that the common law recognises only two types of personal property – chattels and choses in action.[13] A third category of personal property that can be 'stolen' does not exist at common law. Indeed, it is well established in the criminal context that one who dishonestly gains access to confidential information is not thereby liable for theft.[14] But lest it be thought that such antipathy is unique to English law, other leading common law jurisdictions have likewise declined to characterise information as property. In *R v Stewart*,[15] the Supreme Court of Canada held that confidential information

'Data, Information, Knowledge, Wisdom (DIKW): A Semiotic Theoretical and Empirical Exploration of the Hierarchy and its Quality Dimension' (2018) 18(1) *Australasian Journal of Information Systems* 5.

[6] *Boardman v Phipps* [1967] 2 AC 46, 127.

[7] *OBG v Allen* [2008] 1 AC 1 [275].

[8] *Boardman v Phipps* (n 6) 127–28, cited with approval in *OBG v Allen* [2008] 1 AC 1 [276]; *Phillips v News Group Newspapers Ltd* [2013] 1 AC 1 [20]; and *Force India Formula One Team Ltd v 1 Malaysia Racing Team Sdn Bhd* [2010] RPC 757 [376].

[9] *R v Department of Health* [2001] QB 424.

[10] ibid [34]. In the US, a similar outcome is achieved, but on the ground of freedom of speech: see *Sorrell v IMS Health, Inc et al*, 131 S Ct 2653 (2011). For a discussion on the complex interaction of medical, ethical and economic concerns in relation to the commercial uses of medical data, see B Kaplan, 'How Should Health Data Be Used? Privacy, Secondary Use and Big Data Sales' (Institute for Social and Policy Studies-Bioethics Working Paper, 7 October 2014).

[11] *Your Response Ltd v Datateam Business Media Ltd* [2014] 3 WLR 887.

[12] ibid [23].

[13] ibid [25]–[26].

[14] *Oxford v Moss* (1979) 68 Cr App R 183.

[15] *R v Stewart* [1988] 1 SCR 963 (SCC).

is not 'property' that can be the subject of theft. In *McInerney v MacDonald*,[16] the same court confirmed that a patient did not own the medical records kept by her physician. They (and the information therein) remain the property of the physician although the latter is obliged, by reason of the physician's fiduciary duty of good faith, to disclose such information upon request. In a similar vein, the Australian High Court has clarified that equity's jurisdiction in protecting confidences is founded on an obligation of conscience rather than the conceptualisation of information as property.[17]

Despite 'the preponderance of authority'[18] pointing against the reification of information, the law remains unsettled as judicial dicta favouring proprietary analyses has persisted.[19] Recognising data's vital role as the new 'oil'[20] of a fast-expanding digital economy and its threat to personal privacy, courts are more ready to countenance property as a conceptual tool for safeguarding such interests. In England, this attitude was apparent in *Regina (Veolia ES Nottinghamshire Ltd) v Nottinghamshire County Council*,[21] where the English Court of Appeal held that a local authority was not obliged to grant interested persons access to contracts containing commercially confidential information. In the main judgment, Rix LJ reached this conclusion through a process of statutory interpretation, but was clearly influenced by the supposition that commercial confidential information, 'the lifeblood of an enterprise', is a 'well-recognised species of property'.[22] This attempt to analogise confidential information with property has been forcefully criticised,[23] but subsequent courts have continued to affirm the possible application of proprietary analyses to informational assets. In *Fairstar Heavy Transport NV v Philip Jeffrey Adkins, Claranet Limited*,[24] the Court of Appeal held that a company (as principal) was entitled to access the emails of its former CEO (as agent). The application of agency principles obviated the need to consider if the company also had property rights to the emails, but Mummery LJ thought it unwise to foreclose the possibility that some types of information may give rise to property rights. Much will depend, in his view, on 'the nature of the information in dispute and the circumstances in which a property right was being asserted'.[25]

Robust endorsement of this stance is also evident in *Richard Lloyd v Google LLC*.[26] In this case, the claimant had brought a representative action on behalf of

[16] *McInerney v MacDonald* (1992) 137 NR 35 (SCC).

[17] *Moorgate Tobacco Co Ltd v Philip Morris Ltd* (1984) 156 CLR 414, 438.

[18] *Fairstar Heavy Transport NV v Adkins* [2012] EWHC 2952 (TCC) [58].

[19] For examples of dicta found in earlier decisions, see P Kohler and N Palmer, 'Information as Property' in N Palmer and E McKendrick (eds), *Interests in Goods*, 2nd edn (Lloyds of London Press, 1998) 6–7.

[20] 'The world's most valuable resource is no longer oil, but data' (*The Economist*, 6 May 2017), www.economist.com/leaders/2017/05/06/the-worlds-most-valuable-resource-is-no-longer-oil-but-data.

[21] *Regina (Veolia ES Nottinghamshire Ltd) v Nottinghamshire County Council* [2012] PTSR 185.

[22] ibid [111].

[23] See Tanya Aplin, 'Confidential Information as Property' (2013) 24(2) *King's Law Journal* 172.

[24] *Fairstar Heavy Transport NV v Philip Jeffrey Adkins, Claranet Ltd* [2014] FSR 8 139.

[25] ibid [48].

[26] *Richard Lloyd v Google LLC* [2019] EWCA Civ 1599.

4 million Apple iPhone users against Google LLC, a Delaware corporation, for infringements of the UK Data Protection Act (DPA). The factual background was that Google had tracked and collated Browser Generated Information (BGI) of iPhone users without their prior knowledge and consent, and sold the information to enable the display and delivery of interest-based advertisements by third parties. However, the claimant had to prove that the represented class had suffered 'damage' as a result of the infringement in order to effect service out of jurisdiction. At first instance,[27] Warby J held that the claimant had failed to prove that the users had suffered any damage compensable under section 13 of the DPA in the absence of any material loss or emotional harm. The mere fact that the users had 'lost control' of their personal data did not invariably justify an inference of material damage.[28] However, the Court of Appeal disagreed. In its view, control of one's personal data clearly has economic value, so it must follow that the loss of such control is compensable.[29] To the extent that *Datateam* suggests otherwise (that data could not count as an asset for the purposes of establishing possessory security), it is a decision that 'may in due course need to be revisited'.[30] Recognising that such loss of autonomy is compensable would also bring the statutory remedies in line with those at common law, since both the DPA and the common law action for misuse of private information are fundamentally concerned with the protection of privacy.[31] Pertinently, Chancellor Geoffrey Vos (who delivered the court's judgment) also thought that the damage in question could, in principle, also be recoverable as 'user damages'.[32] In his view, such damages could be justified because the infringement was tantamount to taking 'something for nothing, for which the owner was entitled to require payment'.[33] Implicit in this reasoning is the conception of data as a 'thing' despite its allegedly non-rivalrous nature.

The reasoning in *Google* is consistent with the reification of data at least in the specific context of the DPA, but it is by no means certain that the UK Supreme Court would endorse such a development if and when the decision is heard on appeal. In contrast, the Supreme Court of New Zealand had taken a more definitive step in that direction in *Dixon v R*,[34] where it accepted that while pure information could not constitute property, digital files were 'property' for purposes of a criminal offence. In this case, the defendant (Dixon) had unlawfully made copies of his employer's CCTV footage with a view to selling it to media interests. When no such sale materialised, however, he posted the footage on YouTube to ensure that no one else could profit from the use of the files. Dixon was charged and

[27] *Richard Lloyd v Google LLC* [2018] EWHC 2599 (QB).
[28] ibid [58], [59].
[29] *Richard Lloyd v Google LLC* (n 26) [46], [47].
[30] ibid [46].
[31] ibid [57].
[32] ibid [68].
[33] ibid [68], citing Lord Reed in *One Step (Support) Ltd v Morris-Garner* [2018] 2 WLR 1353 [91].
[34] *Dixon v R* [2015] NZSC 147.

convicted under section 249(1)(a) of the Crimes Act 1961 for dishonestly accessing a computer and 'thereby … without any claim of right, obtains any property, privilege, service, pecuniary advantage, benefit, or valuable consideration'. The question that arose was whether he had obtained 'property' in the form of digital files. The Supreme Court held that he did. This conclusion was justified as the definition of 'property' in the Act was sufficiently broad to encompass digital files.[35] The Court also adopted a functionalist conception of property: 'the fundamental characteristic of "property" is that it is something capable of being owned and transferred'.[36] Indisputably, the 'compilation of digital files [that Dixon copied] had an economic value and was capable of being sold'.[37] This outcome was, in the Court's view, fortified by New York Court of Appeals decision in *Thyroff v Nationwide Mutual Insurance Co*.[38] There, the Court held that digital records were 'property' that could be the subject of conversion, for '[a] document stored on a computer hard drive has the same value as a paper document kept in a file cabinet'.[39] *Dixon* was followed more recently by *Henderson v Walker*,[40] a decision of the High Court of New Zealand. Here, Thomas J likewise endorsed the position in *Thyroff*, observing (obiter) that digital assets were property that could be protected by the tort of conversion.[41] In so concluding, the learned judge accepted Green and Randall's arguments that intangibles could be the subject of 'possession' if they were excludable and exhaustible.[42] Digital assets are excludable as they alter the physical medium in which they reside.[43] They are also exhaustible as 'they can be deleted or modified so as to render them useless or inaccessible'.[44] Thus, a person may tortiously interfere with another's possession of a digital asset by deleting the information from the medium in which it is stored. Merely taking copies of the digital information would not, however, be so serious an encroachment as to constitute conversion. In the even more recent decision of *Ruscoe v Cryptopia Ltd*,[45] the High Court of New Zealand applied, inter alia, the reasoning in *Henderson* to justify the characterisation of virtual currencies as property.

These decisions demonstrate growing judicial support for deploying property concepts to protect digital assets. However, academic as well as judicial opposition

[35] ibid [11], [37], [46]. Section 2 of the Crimes Act 1961 (NZ) defines 'property' to include 'real and personal property, and any estate or interest in real or personal property, money, electricity, and any debt, and any thing in action, and any other right or interest'.

[36] *One Step (Support) Ltd v Morris-Garner* (n 33) [38].

[37] ibid [39].

[38] *Thyroff v Nationwide Mutual Insurance Co* 8 NY 3d 283 (NY 2007); 864 NE 2d 1272 (NY 2007).

[39] ibid 1278.

[40] *Henderson v Walker* [2019] NZHC 2184.

[41] Thomas J defined digital assets to include 'all forms of information stored digitally on an electronic device, such as emails, digital files, digital footage and computer programmes': ibid [263].

[42] ibid [264], [265], citing S Green and J Randall, *The Tort of Conversion* (Hart Publishing, 2009) 109–11 and 118–19.

[43] *Henderson v Walker* (n 40) [265].

[44] ibid [266].

[45] *Ruscoe v Cryptopia Ltd* [2020] NZHC 728.

against such development remains palpable and formidable. The common reasons for such opposition are considered below.

III. Objections to Property Analysis

In some contexts, the intangible nature of information is cited as a reason for denying property status to information. We have seen,[46] for instance, that it has been held that pure information cannot be stolen because it is intangible, though a book or a disc containing the same information can undoubtedly be the subject of theft. In *St Albans City and District Council v International Computers Ltd*,[47] Sir Glidewell distinguished (obiter) between information and the physical medium in which it resides, such that a disc on which a computer program is written is a 'good' for purposes of the Sale of Goods Act 1979, but the program itself (apart from the disc) is not.[48] According to Low and Llewelyn, the New Zealand Supreme Court erred in *Dixon* when it failed to draw this distinction, for '[n]o one considers words written on a piece of paper to be property separate from the paper itself'.[49]

However, it is clear that tangibility is not an essential element of property. Intangibles such as shares and statutory intellectual property have long been accepted as types of personal property. In determining the legal effects of digital assets, it is often misleading to focus on the tangible/intangible distinction, as that would tend to create 'false categories unrelated to legal significance' that may 'hinder the ability of commercial law to expand to adequately accommodate electronic assets'.[50] Why, for instance, should a purchaser be accorded different or less protection only because the product was supplied through an electronic rather than a physical platform?[51] Where an intangible asset or product is functionally

[46] See the text accompanying n 14 above.

[47] *St Albans City and District Council v International Computers Ltd* [1996] 4 All ER 481. But the correctness of this distinction has been doubted: see *Watford Electronics Ltd v Sanderson CFL Ltd* [2000] 2 All ER (Comm) 884 [59]; *Amlink Technologies Pty Ltd v Australian Trade Commission* (2005) 86 ALD 370 [26]–[43].

[48] [1996] 4 All ER 481, 493.

[49] K Low and D Llewelyn, 'Digital Files as Property in the New Zealand Supreme Court: Innovation or Confusion?' (2016) 132 *LQR* 394, 396. But see *Henderson v Walker* (n 40) [265], where Thomas J opined that the analogy with ink and paper was flawed 'because the ink cannot be obtained separately from the paper in the way that digital assets can be obtained from a digital device'.

[50] J Moringiello, 'False Categories in Commercial Law: The (Ir)Relevance of (In)Tangibility' (2007) 35 *Florida State University Law Review* 119, 120.

[51] In *Computer Associates UK Ltd v The Software Incubator Ltd* [2018] FSR 25 [50]–[55], Gloster LJ considered the tangible/intangible distinction to be arbitrary and unprincipled, but nevertheless felt bound by the 'weight of judicial authority' to maintain it. Indeed, it is 'surprising that the presence of a physical tangible product would be a defining attribute of information products, as the physical embodiment is the ancillary part of the product'; see P Chapdelaine, 'The Undue Reliance on Physical Objects in the Regulations of Information Products' (2015) 20 *Journal of Technology Law & Policy* 65, 74. See also B Haywood, 'What's in a Name? Software, Digital Products and the Sale of Goods' (2016) 38 *Sydney Law Review* 441, 457–58.

equivalent to another asset or product that has a physical manifestation, there is in principle no reason why the former should not be treated as 'property' if the latter is so characterised.[52] Growing judicial acceptance of virtual currencies as a form of property[53] also points to the inevitable expansion of the concept in the intangible and virtual realm.[54]

A second, more significant reason for rejecting property analysis is that information is generally non-rivalrous and non-excludable. In economic terms, a good or service is rivalrous if its consumption prevents another person from consuming it. Information is non-rivalrous because its disclosure does not dispossess the disclosing party of the same information. Information is also (largely) non-excludable. Excludability is the ability to prevent strangers from accessing the benefits inherent in a resource. A non-excludable resource – such as 'the beam of light thrown out by a lighthouse' – cannot, by reason of its very nature, be 'propertised'.[55] Information is often thought to be non-excludable because it is either practically difficult or prohibitively expensive to prevent access by others.[56] However, these features do not completely bar the possibility of propertisation because access to information or its benefits may be excluded by legal means. Confidential information, for instance, does enjoy a 'weak form of excludability' through the equitable action for breach of confidence.[57] Likewise, copyright and patent proprietors may exclude strangers from exploiting their work or invention through the exercise of statutory rights. Crucially, exclusivity in this context (ie, in relation to intellectual property rights) is conferred in relation to the *use* of information rather than cognition or awareness of its content. Someone who owns the copyright to an article does not seek to prevent others from reading (even memorising) the article, but only to reserve to himself or herself the right of

[52] This can be illustrated by the common characterisation of money as 'property,' despite its preponderant manifestation in an incorporeal form. See, eg, David Fox, *Property Rights in Money* (Oxford University Press, 2008) [1.111], where the author argued that 'any asset which may be made the subject of economic exchange and which is given legal protection against infringement by third parties is at least capable of being treated as property and the standard concepts of the law of property may usefully apply to it. Assets which function as generally accepted media of exchange, means of payment, stores of economic purchasing power and units of account should be treated as money'.

[53] See eg, *B2C2 Ltd v Quoine Pte Ltd* [2019] 4 SLR 17; *Ruscoe v Cryptopia Ltd* [2020] NZHC 728 and *AA v Persons Unknown* [2020] 4 WLR 35.

[54] See the UK Jurisdiction Taskforce's Legal Statement on Cryptoassets and Smart Contracts, cited in both *Cryptopia* (n 53) and *AA v Persons Unknown* (n 53), which concludes (at [83]) that 'a cryptoasset might not be a thing in action on the narrower definition of the term does not in itself mean that it cannot be treated as property'.

[55] K Gray, 'Property in Thin Air' (1991) 50 *Cambridge Law Journal* 252, 268–69.

[56] Aplin (n 23) 193. But see the arguments in text accompanying notes 169–71 below on the possible conception of personal data as rivalrous.

[57] Aplin (n 23) 194. In *I-Admin (Singapore) Pte Ltd v Hong Ying Ting* [2020] 1 SLR 1130 [61], the Singapore Court of Appeal held that a breach of confidence action is constituted once it is shown that confidential information has been accessed without the owner's knowledge or consent. No proof of use by the defendant is required. To defeat the action, the onus is on the defendant to show this his or her conscience had not been affected. It is arguable that this modified approach may have strengthened the 'excluability' of confidential information.

reproduction. Therefore, the fact that information is non-rivalrous is not in and of itself a sufficient reason for precluding the application of property analysis.

Beyond the mere ease or practicality of limiting access to information, the non-rivalrous and non-excludable nature of information points to a further and more fundamental objection to privatising information – information being a 'public good' is best left 'in the commons, available for use and exploitation by all'.[58] Or, as economists would put it, it is a resource that is most efficiently utilised when it is accessible to all.[59] That society at large is able to 'free ride' on information generated by private actors is crucial to its progress.[60] This was acknowledged, for instance, by Lamer J in *R v Stewart*:

> From a social point of view, whether confidential information should be protected requires a weighing of interests much broader than those of the parties involved. As opposed to the alleged owner of the information, society's best advantage may well be to favour the free flow of information and greater accessibility by all. Would society be willing to prosecute the person who discloses to the public a cure for cancer, although its discoverer wanted to keep it confidential?[61]

Societal interests in the free flow and dissemination of information thus militate against the privatisation of information for the benefit of the exclusive few. More debatable, however, is the assertion that this should also bar the propertisation of valuable confidential information.[62] To the extent that such information is the result of considerable skill, labour and resources, there is a case for granting exclusivity to those who have laboured to create the information and to preserve incentives for optimising the value of the information in question.[63] Where the information comprises personal data, there can be no question that considerations of public interests are highly pertinent. Nowhere is this more visible than the COVID-19 pandemic battlefield. Even as critics bemoan the resultant privacy intrusions, it is clear national authorities must have access to vast amounts of movement data in order to anticipate, and curb, the spread of the disease.[64] But while the exigencies of public health and other crises may, exceptionally, require the subordination of privacy concerns, the individual's interests

[58] Gray (n 55) 268.

[59] J Stiglitz, 'Knowledge as a Global Public Good' in I Kaul, I Grunberg and M Stern (eds), *Global Public Goods: International Cooperation in the 21st Century* (Oxford Scholarship Online, 2003) 2.

[60] A Weinrib, 'Information and Property' (1998) 38 *University of Toronto Law Journal* 117, 124.

[61] *R v Stewart* (n 15).

[62] Confidential information and trade secrets may encompass personal data, but not all personal data is confidential. The PDPA regulates the collection, use and disclosure of personal data, whether confidential or not.

[63] Weinrib (n 60) 126–27. This is similar to the justification for protecting copyright: see W Cornish, D Llewelyn and Tanya Aplin, *Intellectual Property: Patents, Copyright, Trademarks & Allied Rights*, 8th edn (Sweet & Maxwell, 2013) [1-42].

[64] M Ienca and E Vayena, 'On the Responsible Use of Digital Data to Tackle the COVID-19 Pandemic' (2020) 26 *Nature Medicine* 463, https://doi.org/10.1038/s41591-020-0832-5; F Ventrella, "Privacy in Emergency Circumstances: Data Protection and the COVID-19 Pandemic" *ERA Forum* (2020), https://doi.org/10.1007/s12027-020-00629-3.

of privacy and self-determination – namely, the right to maintain secrecy and control of information relating to the self – remain elemental and deserving of high protection.[65]

Admittedly, even if it is possible to restrict access to a class of information, there are practical difficulties in identifying the owners and what ownership should entail in this context. This issue is particularly vexed when the information in question is digitally generated by two or more parties. In *Fairstar Heavy Transport NV v Adkins*,[66] Edwards-Stuart J considered whether, and how, property could reside in the content of emails. Should title vest in the sender or the recipient or in both of them jointly? What does it mean for an owner to assert title against the whole world? If the creator owned the email, can he or she then require recipients – however far down the chain – to delete the emails? If title should vest in the recipient and the email has been sent or forwarded to numerous recipients, would not the question of title be 'hopelessly confused'?[67] In view of these complex and unrealistic ramifications, Edwards-Stuart J concluded there was no practical basis for analysing the content of emails as property. These difficulties are also true of personal data, which is usually 'co-created' when individuals transact with service providers (so the data is descriptive of *both* the individual and the service provider).[68] Therefore, it cannot be assumed that one would necessarily 'own' information pertaining to oneself. As we have seen in the case of *McInerney*,[69] the patient did not have property interests in her own medical history even though she might have had a right of access on other grounds. Uncertainties as to what title and ownership means in relation to information are further compounded when we consider how the 'alienation' of information differs from that of other property. Because information is non-excludable or only partially excludable by contract, the purchaser or assignee of information does not obtain title in the usual way since he or she may not be able to enjoin the seller or third parties from exploiting the same information. Thus, notions of exchange and alienation can only (at best) apply to information in a manner that is 'contorted and strained'.[70]

[65] For example, the Organisation for Economic Co-operation and Development (OECD) reiterates the need to observe data protection principles even as governments adopt extraordinary measures to fight COVID-19; see 'Ensuring Data Privacy as We Battle Covid-19', OECD Policy Responses to Coronavirus (COVID-19) (14 April 2020), www.oecd.org/coronavirus/policy-responses/ensuring-data-privacy-as-we-battle-covid-19-36c2f31e.

[66] *Fairstar Heavy Transport NV v Adkins* (n 18) [61]–[69].

[67] ibid [66].

[68] 'Data Ownership, Rights and Contracts: Reaching a Common Understanding: Discussions at a British Academy, Royal Society and techUK Seminar on 3 October 2018' British Academy (Policy and Research) 5, www.thebritishacademy.ac.uk/publications/data-ownership-rights-controls-seminar-report. Indeed, one could imagine a range of 'ownership paradigms', each adopting a different rationale for according ownership (or control); see the helpful discussion in D Loshin, *Enterprise Knowledge Management: The Data Quality Approach* (Academic Press, 2001) ch 2.

[69] *McInerney* (n 16) 16.

[70] Aplin (n 23) 196.

These difficulties cast further doubt on the usefulness of characterising information as property.

To sum up, the real objections to treating information as property are twofold. First, the free flow of information is of paramount importance, so informational access should not be curtailed as a general rule. Second, information has a poor fit with conventional concepts of ownership, title and transfer because of its fluidity and variability in function and conception. These are serious hurdles, but they are by no means absolute impediments. As alluded to above, the individual's interests in privacy and self-determinacy are significant counterweights that may justify some curtailment of access to information. While it is true that information should not, in general, be privatised, personal data may warrant special treatment as a means of augmenting the data subject's legal rights and control. Of course, information being intangible and non-rivalrous is not, in its natural state, an excludable resource. Such exclusivity, if desired, can only be artificially constructed by legal means.[71] In respect of personal data, one may query whether the enactment of the PDPA has had such effects or has at least paved the way for such development. We will turn to examine that question below but first, it is necessary to embark on a brief excursion to consider what 'property' means as the question whether personal data can be analysed or analogised with 'property' will depend on how that term is conceptualised.

IV. Conceptions of Property

A. Rights in Relation to 'Things'

Academic discourse on the theoretical foundation of property is vast, varied and contested. This section therefore seeks to do no more than sketch the dominant approaches and their possible application to personal data. A useful point to start is the lay conception of property as 'things' or as relationships that are mediated through 'things'. This approach finds support in Blackstone's explication of property as 'that sole and despotic dominion which a man claims and exercises over the external things of the world, in total exclusion of the right of other men'.[72] Although it is sometimes argued that 'things' must, for this purpose, be confined to physical things,[73] the more prevalent view is that both physical and non-physical

[71] See M Madison, 'Law as Design: Objects, Concepts and Digital Things' (2005) 56 *Case Western Reserve Law Review* 381, analysing 'things' as a broad and varied phenomenon encompassing things found in nature, those created by design and those created by contracts or simply by public policy.

[72] Herbert Broom and Edward A Hadley, *Commentaries on the Laws of England*, vol 2 (Albany, 1875) 423.

[73] See, eg, S Douglas and B McFarlane, 'Defining Property Rights' in JE Penner and HE Smith (eds), *Philosophical Foundations of Property Law* (Oxford University Press, 2014).

objects could count as 'things'. Blackstone himself contemplated 'things' to include intangibles such as choses in action, though he did not explain why they should be so reified.[74] Other jurists have attempted to fill this gap.

Penner, for example, theorised that 'the right to property is a right to exclude others from things which is grounded by the interest we have in the use of things'.[75] For this purpose, a 'thing' can be an object of property if it is 'separable' from the owner. The condition for separability is satisfied when 'a different person who takes on the relationship to the thing stand[s] in essentially the same position as the first person'.[76] Penner's scheme clearly admits of intangibles, such as choses in action and intellectual property rights, as 'property'. Specifically, he conceives of intellectual property – such as patent rights – as property in a monopoly right rather than property in the underlying information. Unlike property in land, the patent holder does not own the idea as such, but 'the exclusive right to a particular use of the invention or idea, that is, working it to produce goods for sale in the market'.[77] This reasoning obviously assumes that the monopoly power to exploit an idea or an invention is a 'thing' that is separable from the patent holder. On this approach, whether a new source constitutes 'property' would depend on the extent to which it is excludable and separable from the owner.

B. A Bundle of Rights

Commentators who favour the analysis of personal data as property often adopt the alternative, and contrasting, conception of property as a 'bundle of rights'.[78] This approach explicates property not as rights to things, but as a complex set of legal relations between persons. Its conceptual foundation is traced to Wesley Hohfeld's account of property as 'a complex aggregate of rights (or claims), privileges, powers and immunities'.[79] Thus conceived, property is not reducible to a single relation with a 'thing', but comprises multiple jural relations with multiple persons. What therefore distinguishes property from personal rights is not the unique relation that an owner bears to an object, but the fact that they are *erga omnes* (good against

[74] Hence, 'Blackstone's conception of property as dominion over things was maintained at the expense of intellectual integrity'; see K Vandevelde, 'The New Property of the Nineteenth Century: The Development of the Modern Concept of Property' (1980) 29 *Buffalo Law Review* 325, 332.

[75] J Penner, *The Idea of Property in Law* (Oxford University Press, 1997), 71.

[76] ibid 114.

[77] ibid 120.

[78] For example, Nimmer and Krauthaus explicate property rights as a 'bundle of privileges, powers and rights that law recognises with respect to particular subject matter': see R Nimmer and P Krauthaus, 'Information as Property Databases and Commercial Property' (1993) 1 *International Journal of Law & Information Technology* 3, 5. Schwartz similarly utilises the 'bundle of sticks' conception to unpack the property elements of personal information. He argues that these elements may be shaped by focusing on five relevant aspects, viz inalienabilities, defaults, a right of exit, damages and institutions; see P Schwartz, 'Property, Privacy and Personal Data' (2004) 117 *Harvard Law Review* 2056, 2095.

[79] WN Hohfeld, 'Fundamental Legal Conceptions as Applied in Judicial Reasoning II' in W Cook (ed), *Fundamental Legal Conceptions as Applied in Judicial Reasoning* (Yale University Press, 1919) 96.

everyone). The bundle metaphor builds upon this schema to explain property as a collection of distinct and independent legal relations. This makes property a flexible concept since it is not defined by fixed criteria, but may comprise different bundles of legal incidents in different contexts. Unsurprisingly, advocates of propertisation adopt this flexible concept to argue that data may constitute property even if they do not entail all the legal incidents applicable to conventional property (eg, land). For example, Nimmer and Krauthaus contend that property in information is that which enables its owner to 'control disclosure, use, alteration and copying of the designated information'.[80] In a similar vein, Schwartz argues that free alienability is not an inexorable aspect of property, so the data subject's access to his or her personal data (after having assigned the same to others) is not, by itself, a sufficient reason for rejecting property analysis.[81] In all these instances, the bundle metaphor is invoked for its ability to explicate property as a complex legal phenomena rather than a unitary, monistic 'thing'. However, this fluidity is also its weakness. At its broadest, the bundle approach is completely malleable and policy-driven, so that 'it explains everything and explains nothing'.[82] Likewise, Grey has declared that: 'The substitution of a bundle of rights for a thing-ownership conception of property has the ultimate consequence that property ceases to be an important category in legal and political theory.'[83] These criticisms notwithstanding, the bundle-of-sticks metaphor remains a dominant and influential account of property as it brings to light the complex relations encapsulated by property and its function in regulating allocation of valuable resources.

C. Economic Analyses

From a law and economics perspective, the institution of property is justified where it serves as an efficient means of regulating the use of resources. Since efficiency (or the obverse concepts of utility and welfare) is ultimately an empirical determination that is context specific, theorists who espouse this view have typically favoured the bundle conception of property.[84]

However, more recently, a competing utilitarian approach has emerged that seeks to defend property as a unique institution characterised by its *in rem* quality.

[80] Nimmer and Krauthaus (n 78) 6.
[81] Schwartz (n 78) 2092.
[82] H Smith, 'Property as the Law of Things' (2012) 125 *Harvard Law Review* 1691, 1697.
[83] T Grey, 'The Disintegration of Property' in J Pennock and J Chapman (eds), *Ethics, Economics and the Law of Property* (New York Press, 1980); republished in T Grey, *Formalism and Pragmatism in American Law: Formalism and Pragmatism in American Law* (Brill, 2014) 44. Likewise, Penner has criticised the bundle concept as a 'little more than a slogan' that provides no obvious means of resolving the problem at hand: J Penner, 'The Bundle of Rights Picture of Property' (1996) 43 *UCLA Law Review* 711, 714. For a more recent and comprehensive critique of the bundle metaphor, see J Penner, *Property Rights: A Re-examination* (Oxford University Press, 2020).
[84] See, eg, the summary of this tendency in T Merrill and H Smith, 'What Happened to Property in Law and Economics?' (2001) 111 *Yale Law Journal* 357, 366–83.

In this vein, Smith theorises that property law is justifiable and distinguished by its ability to minimise information costs in organising the use of resources. According to Smith, the essence of property law is its 'exclusion strategy'.[85] Through exclusion, an owner controls access to a resource using rough proxies such as boundaries and fences.[86] This strategy incurs low informational costs as its message (eg, 'keep off' or 'don't take' (without permission))[87] to outsiders is simple to produce and process, and also simple for third parties to observe. The exclusion strategy is contrasted with the governance strategy, which regulates by defining the permitted uses and users of resources in greater detail – a much more cost-intensive approach that is more suited for situations involving a smaller group of duty holders.[88] Although governance strategies (such as the tort of nuisance) are sometimes needed to resolve particular types of conflicts,[89] the exclusion strategy is at the 'core'[90] of property's architecture by reason of its significant cost advantages. That explains why property rights are largely *in rem* in character.[91] Importantly, the primacy of the exclusion strategy also supports the conception of property as 'things'. Things, according to Smith, are resources that can be bounded as 'modules' that have intense interactions within but interact with other modules in a relatively sparse and standardised manner.[92] A resource only constitutes a thing or module if it can be delineated by exclusion. By necessary implication, a resource is unsuited for regulation as 'property' if it cannot be bounded in a way that allows it to interact with other modular units in a relatively simple and standardised way.

This particular utilitarian account provides important insights into the relevance of information costs and property's unique design in minimising such costs. Its conception of property as modularised 'things' also furnishes a sophisticated framework for extending property beyond tangibles to more complex legal constructs.[93] Thus, this framework could support the understanding of personal data as 'property' if the exclusion of personal data in favour of data subjects would result in lower information costs and greater benefits than adopting the alternative governance approach of enumerating permitted uses of such data. However, it is important to note that the question whether to categorise a resource under an exclusion or a governance regime ultimately requires a normative assessment of

[85] Smith (n 82) 1704–1705.

[86] H Smith, 'Exclusion versus Governance: Two Strategies for Delineating Property Rights' (2002) 32 *Journal of Legal Studies* S453, S468.

[87] H Smith, 'Property is Not Just a Bundle of Rights' (2011) 8 *Econ Journal Watch* 279, 282.

[88] Smith (n 86) S455.

[89] Smith (n 82) 1714.

[90] ibid 1705.

[91] ibid 1706.

[92] H Smith, 'Intellectual Property as Property: Delineating Entitlements in Information' (2007) 116 *Yale Law Journal* 1742, 1742–43.

[93] Smith argues, for example, that the information cost account could explain why the law of patents adopts a more property-like approach to coordinate the attribution of outputs to rivalrous inputs; see generally ibid.

the outcomes of the rules.[94] Cost-effectiveness is the emblem of a superior outcome only to the extent that it adequately assimilates the moral and social values that conduce towards a fair and just outcome.

D. An Integrated Perspective

This chapter does not seek to resolve the jurisprudential debate on the nature of property. It proceeds on the basis that each theoretical approach illuminates an essential dimension of the institution of property and these different dimensions collectively inform our assessment of whether to regulate personal data as property. For Penner and Smith, the emphasis is on exclusion as property's definitive trait. Their accounts cohere well with the traditional conception of property as rights *in rem* in relation to 'things', which must at the very least be some form of excludable resource. This starting point is uncontroversial and is accepted even by bundle theorists, who typically analogise with conventional forms of property as the baseline. However, bundle theorists differ from the exclusion theorists in their focus on the social relations that property regulates. Because a resource can be owned by different people at the same time, the interests of the owners will invariably conflict. Property law is tasked to resolve such conflicts and in so doing, courts are inevitably required to make value choices between competing interests. The bundle theory is significant for making explicit such value choices.[95] Seen in this light, the bundle theory is not opposed to, but complements, exclusionary accounts. Exclusionary accounts justify the juridical form or structure of property rights, but the bundle theory explains 'how property law functions to enable the exercise of an open-ended set of privileges and entitlements in an object or resource'.[96] This view of property does not lead to its disintegration;[97] rather, 'property' remains significant as a legal and political category because it is the conceptual tool by which to set the *baseline* entitlement to valuable resources. When the law decides that a resource is 'owned' by someone, it creates a presumption of entitlement in favour of the owner, which a non-owner may seek to displace by demonstrating that there are overriding public interests or values which justify the limitation of the owner's rights. The designation of a resource as property is therefore a conscious and evaluative decision to place the 'burden of persuasion' on non-owners.[98]

[94] P Gerhart, *Property and Social Morality* (New York: Cambridge University Press, 2013) 43–44; and G Alexander and E Peñalver, *An Introduction to Property Theory* (Cambridge University Press, 2012) 139–40.

[95] D Johnson, 'Reflections on the Bundle of Rights' (2007) 248 *Vermont Law Review* 248, 251–52.

[96] J Wall, 'Taking the Bundle of Rights Seriously' (2019) 50 *Victoria University of Wellington Law Review* 733, 736.

[97] As Gerhart ((n 94) 38) explained, bundle theorists did not set out 'to disaggregate law for its own sake, but to build our understanding of law around the justifications for the law that explain why the law should take one shape rather than another'.

[98] J Singer, *Entitlement: The Paradoxes in Property* (Yale University Press, 2000) 62.

Together, the exclusionary and bundle views of property suggest that a new resource could be regulated as a form of property if it is an excludable resource and there are cogent policy reasons for conferring the right to exclude on a specific class of persons. Therefore, the objects of property are not fixed, but may expand in tandem with changing social and moral conceptions of value. This dynamic process is evident, for instance, in the evolution of money from metallic coins to bank deposits. Though the precise analysis of their proprietary effects differ, few would disagree that both are established forms of property.[99] What is property in one epoch (eg, slaves) may not be so in another.[100] Technological and scientific developments may transform hitherto valueless objects into valuable property. Dead bodies were worthless prior to developments in anatomy science, but calls to regulate them as property have risen in tandem with the rise in their commercial value.[101] These examples exemplify property's role in regulating social relations with respect to the control of valuable resources.[102]

In the following sections, we turn to consider whether the PDPA has had the effect of rendering personal data a type of excludable resource and what, if any, policy reasons may justify characterising such a resource as property.

V. The Personal Data Protection Act 2012

The PDPA was enacted in 2012 amidst concerns over abuse and the excessive collection of data fuelled by rapid growth in e-commerce, social networking and technological innovation. Although data protection laws do protect an individual's interests in informational privacy, which is in turn a critical aspect of personal privacy, it is clear that the PDPA is not designed to protect privacy per se.[103] Rather, its impetus lies in the recognition of *both* the need to 'safeguard the individual's personal data against abuse' *and* to 'enhance Singapore's competitiveness and strengthen our position as a trusted business hub'.[104] The need to *balance* these competing interests is underlined by section 3 of the Act, which states that:

> The purpose of this Act is to govern the collection, use and disclosure of personal data by organisations in a manner that recognises both the right of individuals to protect their personal data and the need of organisations to collect, use or disclose personal data for purposes that a reasonable person would consider appropriate in the circumstances.

[99] Fox (n 52) [1.73]–[1.77].

[100] R Nwabueze, *Biotechnology and the Challenge of Property: Property Rights in Dead Bodies, Body Parts and Genetic Information* (Routledge, 2016) 13–14.

[101] ibid 17.

[102] Singer (n 98) 134.

[103] L Goh and J Aw, 'Data Protection Law and Privacy in Singapore' in S Chesterman (ed), *Data Protection Law in Singapore: Privacy and Sovereignty in an Interconnected World*, 2nd edn (Academy Publishing, 2018) [4.19]–[4.21].

[104] Singapore Parliamentary Reports (Hansard) (15 October 2012) 'Personal Data Protection Bill', vol 89 (Associate Professor Dr Yaacob Ibrahim, Minister for Information, Communications and the Arts).

This provision thus makes it clear that the individual's informational privacy interests is an integral, but not an overriding, part of the equation. Given its focus on the *collection, use and disclosure of personal data*, the Act is 'better understood as a pragmatic attempt to regulate the flow of information, moderated by the touchstone of reasonableness'.[105]

Under the PDPA, 'personal data' is defined as 'data, whether true or not, about an individual who can be identified (a) from that data; or (b) from that data and other information to which the organisation has or is likely to have access'.[106] The Personal Data Protection Commission (PDPC) clarified in its guidelines that this definition should not be narrowly construed and would cover different types of data that enable the individual to be identified.[107] An 'individual', for purposes of the Act, refers to natural persons, whether living or deceased.[108] The inclusion of deceased persons is interesting as it is unclear what interests of the deceased persons are being protected.[109] One possibility is that the estate of the deceased may have interests in controlling the use or commodification of data relating to the deceased, which (if true) may lend some implicit support to the conception of personal data as property.

Given its objective of regulating the 'collection, use and disclosure' of personal data by organisations,[110] the focus of the Act is to articulate the obligations of organisations that engage in these activities (as opposed to the rights of data subjects). At first sight, a number of the obligations appear to have the effect of conferring a significant measure of control on the data subject that is analogous to an *in rem* right. Most significantly, the Act provides that organisations may only collect, use or disclose data from individuals with their prior consent.[111] By conferring on data subjects default or residual control over the use of their personal data, the principle of consent could be understood to be suggestive of a propertisation strategy. Further fortifying this understanding is the requirement for the data collected to be used only for purposes that a reasonable person would consider appropriate in the circumstances.[112] Moreover, data subjects must be notified of those purposes at the point of collection,[113] may request to access their data,[114] or correct errors

[105] S Chesterman, 'From Privacy to Data Protection' in Chesterman (n 103) [2.49].
[106] PDPA, s 2(1).
[107] PDPC, *Advisory Guidelines on Key Concepts in the Personal Data Protection Act* (issued 23 September 2013, revised 9 October 2019) [5.2] (hereinafter *Advisory Guidelines*). See also W Chik and KYJ Pang, 'The Meaning and Scope of Personal Data under the Singapore Personal Data Protection Act' (2014) 26 *Singapore Academy of Law Journal* 354.
[108] PDPA, s 2(1).
[109] Chesterman (n 105) [2.53]. However, as Chesterman notes, the protection is limited to deceased persons who have been dead for 10 years or less: PDPA, s 4(b).
[110] An 'organisation' includes individuals, companies, associations and body of persons (incorporated or unincorporated); see PDPA, s 2(1).
[111] ibid s 13.
[112] ibid s 18.
[113] ibid s 20.
[114] ibid s 21.

or omissions in the data,[115] and withdraw their consents to the collection, use and disclosure of the data.[116] More recently, the PDPA has been amended to introduce data portability.[117] With this amendment, data subjects will be able to request one organisation to transmit a copy of their personal data to another organisation. This can be seen as a further step that is consistent with propertisation as it enhances the data subject's autonomy and control.[118]

However, upon a closer look, the actual control of the individual appears more limited. An organisation is not required, for instance, to seek consent in a broad range of circumstances set out in the first and second schedules to the Act. These include situations where the use or disclosure affects the vital interests of individuals,[119] affects the public,[120] is necessitated by business asset transactions,[121] is justified by the legitimate interests of the collecting organisation[122] or is reasonably needed for improving an organisation's products, services and processes.[123] Of these, the 'legitimate interests' exception appears to be the broadest since it is not tied to a particular purpose, but permits a collecting organisation to identify any purpose that it may demonstrate to be legitimate.[124] Moreover, the PDPA accepts that consent may be deemed in situations where an individual voluntarily provides personal data for a purpose, or where he or she consents, or is deemed to have consented, to the disclosure by one organisation to another.[125] Deemed consent may also arise by way of contractual necessity[126] or by notification.[127] Further, the

[115] ibid s 22.

[116] ibid s 16.

[117] ibid pt VIB, as enacted by s 14 of the Personal Data Protection (Amendment) Act 2020 (hereinafter 'PDPA (Amendment) Act 2020').

[118] PDPA, s 26G(a). However, it has been argued, in the context of the General Data Protection Regulation, that data portability does not seek to confer property-like control, but is intended more as a regulatory tool to stimulate competition and innovation; see I Graef, M Husovec and N Purtova, 'Data Portability and Data Control: Lessons for an Emerging Concept in EU Law' (2018) 19 *German Law Journal* 1359, 1363 and 1368.

[119] For example, where the use and disclosure are clearly in the interests of the individual, but consent cannot be obtained in a timely manner or is needed to respond to an emergency or other situations that threaten the health or safety of the individual: see PDPA, pt 1, sched 1 (as amended by the PDPA (Amendment) Act 2020).

[120] This includes situations where the data in question was already publicly available, or which affects national interest, or is used solely for artistic or literary purposes, or for historical or archival purposes, or is collected by a news organisation solely for its news activity: see PDPA, pt 2, sched 1 (as amended by the PDPA (Amendment) Act 2020).

[121] PDPA, pt 4, sched 1 (as amended by the PDPA (Amendment) Act 2020).

[122] PDPA, pt 3, sched 1 (as amended by the PDPA (Amendment) Act 2020).

[123] PDPA, pt 5, sched 1 (as amended by the PDPA (Amendment) Act 2020).

[124] Although the organisation is also constrained by the need to carry out an assessment to determine the possible adverse effects on the individual and how such effects may be mitigated or eliminated.

[125] PDPA, s 15(1) and (2).

[126] ibid s 15(3), enacted by s 6 of the PDPA (Amendment) Act 2020. In essence, this provision deems an individual to have consented to the collection, use or disclosure of personal data by one organisation as well as downstream organisations if such collection, use or disclosure is reasonably necessary for the performance of the contract between the individual and the first-mentioned organisation.

[127] PDPA, s 15A, enacted by s 6 of the PDPA (Amendment) Act 2020. Under this provision, an individual is deemed to have consented if he or she has been notified of the collection, use and disclosure

Act does not prescribe the manner by which consent may be obtained. Hence, the possibility remains that consent may be secured by way of a failure to opt out in some circumstances.[128] The fact that an individual could withdraw consent upon giving notice[129] and request to access as well as correct his or he personal data[130] may also suggest that the information in question is inalienable and hence inconsistent with property rights.

There can be no doubt that even whilst it confers upon data subjects a measure of control over the collection, use and disclosure of their personal data, the PDPA was not intended to institute a statutory framework of data ownership. The PDPC made this clear in its advisory guidelines:

> Personal data, as used in the PDPA, refers to the information comprised in the personal data and not the physical form or medium in which it is stored, such as a database or a book. The PDPA does not specifically confer any property or ownership rights on personal data per se to individuals or organisations and also does not affect existing property rights in items in which personal data may be captured or stored.[131]

This approach is unsurprising as it reflects the legislature's conception of privacy as a balance of competing interests rather than a fundamental human right.[132] Also noteworthy is the fact that it is consistent with other major data protection statutes such as the General Data Protection Regulation (GDPR). Even though the GDPR is in many ways more protective of data subjects than the PDPA,[133] the rights it accords to data subjects are generally viewed as falling short of property rights.[134] One may therefore reason that the proprietary foundation of the PDPA is even weaker.

of personal data and has not objected to the same within a reasonable time. However, deemed consent under this provision is subject to an assessment confirming that the collection, use and disclosure is unlikely to have an adverse effect on the individual.

[128] *Advisory Guidelines* (n 107) [12.10]–[12.11].

[129] PDPA, s 16.

[130] ibid ss 21 and 22.

[131] *Advisory Guidelines* (n 107 [5.30].

[132] See Singapore Academy of Law Law Reform Committee (SAL LRC), 'Rethinking Database Rights and Database Ownership in an AI World' (July 2020), https://www.sal.org.sg/sites/default/files/SAL-LawReform-Pdf/2020-09/2020%20Rethinking%20Database%20Rights%20and%20Data%20Ownership%20in%20an%20AI%20World_ebook_0_1.pdf, [3.24].

[133] Salient distinctions between the two regimes include the fact that the GDPR does not permit deemed or implied consent (art 4) and it grants subjects a right to erasure (art 17), whilst the PDPA does not. The GDPR is also underpinned by the principle of data minimalisation, limiting data collection, use and disclosure to that which is 'necessary' for the purposes for which it is processed (art 5). For a helpful and succinct discussion of the difference between the two regimes, see H Lim, 'GDPR Matchup: Singapore's Personal Data Protection Act' *IAPP* (14 June 2017), www.iapp.org/news/a/gdpr matchup-singapores-personal-data-protection-act.

[134] 'From a legal perspective, the GDPR gives data subjects no full ownership rights, only certain specific rights including the right not to be subject to data processing without a legal basis (eg 'informed consent'), access, limited re-purposing, the right to be forgotten and the right to data portability': N Duch-Brown, B Martens and F Mueller-Langer, 'The Economics of Ownership, Access and Trade in Digital Data', European Commission Joint Research Centre Digital Economy Working Paper 2017-01, 2017, 17. See also C Fernández, 'When GDPR is Not Enough: Who Owns the Data?' *Scrypt* (3 April 2019), www.scrypt.media/2019/04/03/when-gdpr-is-not-enough-who-owns-the-data.

However, notwithstanding the absence of any explicit designation of property rights, it is submitted that the PDPA as it is currently structured does not preclude or foreclose the adoption of property as *a* regulatory tool either at common law or by way of legislation. Indeed, we have already seen examples of judicial willingness to protect personal data as property against theft and conversion.[135] And while the Act was not intended to create property rights, it has nevertheless erected a structure that is conducive for such development by conferring rights of control (or exclusion) on data subjects, rendering the data in question a type of 'excludable' resource.[136] It is true that the rights of exclusion under the PDPA are qualified in material ways, but it is not necessary for a right of exclusion to be absolute in order to constitute a proprietary right. They can, as Smith had elucidated,[137] comprise a mix of exclusion and governance strategies so long as the former is dominant. Indeed, even real property does not confer absolute control, but is subject to state expropriation, adverse possession and nuisance laws.

Of course, the mere fact that a resource is excludable does not make it property. There must still be cogent reasons why the law should make a baseline allocation of a resource that places the burden on the non-owner to justify any encroachment on that resource. In a recent review, the Singapore Academy of Law's Law Reform Committee considered recommendations against the adoption of a property framework to protect personal data.[138] It cited, among other things, considerations that data is non-rivalrous, non-excludable, inalienable and expansible. It also identified policy reasons that militate against such development, namely that it would present greater barriers to beneficial data exploitation and unduly disrupt the existing legal framework. The following discussion addresses these concerns as it provides possible justifications for propertisation.

VI. Instituting a Proprietary Resource

Consumers' interests in data protection are popularly characterised as a form of privacy interest. Indeed, while the PDPA was not enacted to protect personal

[135] See above nn 34–41.

[136] Whilst rejecting property ownership as an appropriate legal framework for regulating personal data, the SAL LRC acknowledged that there are 'noticeable overlaps' between the key incidents of ownership (as identified by Tony Honoré) and the data subject's rights under the PDPA: see SAL LRC (n 132) [3.31].

[137] See above nn 85–92. Elsewhere, Smith (and Merrill) acknowledged that there exist 'intermediate rights' lying between contract and property: see T Merrill and H Smith, 'The Property/Contract Interface' (2001) 101 *Columbia Law Review* 773. These hybrid rights bear features of both contract and property. For a recent analysis of this idea in the Singaporean context, see H Tjio, 'Merrill and Smith's Intermediate Rights Lying between Contract and Property: Are Singapore Trusts and Secured Transactions Drifting away from English Law towards American Law?' [2019] *Singapore Journal of Legal Studies* 235.

[138] SAL LRC (n 132).

privacy per se, it was nevertheless designed on the assumption that consumers have vital interests in informational privacy that ought to be safeguarded.[139] Informational privacy is valued not as an end in itself, but as a means of securing fundamental values that 'underscore individuality and all that flows from a society that encourages individuality and creativity';[140] in other words, it is 'an extension of the protection of human autonomy and dignity'.[141] In Europe, a similar idea is expressed in the principle of self-determination that is currently the prevailing justification for data protection regimes.[142] Under the PDPA, the chief means by which to secure these foundational values are found in the obligation of consent and related measures.[143] The effect of these measures is to vest in a data subject primary and residual control over the collection, use and disclosure of information pertaining to himself or herself. Against this backdrop, recognising that the data subject 'owns' his or her personal data as a proprietary resource is congruent with both the rationale and structure of the Act. It affirms the primacy of his or her interests in informational privacy by conferring on him the highest level of control in relation to the access, use and disclosure of the resource.[144] Deployed in this way, property performs a mainly regulatory or protective rather than a market function, similar to the role of property in the context of criminal and constitutional law.[145]

The chief advantage of adopting a property-enhanced scheme is that it enables the data subject to exploit the *in rem* effects of the rights conferred by the Act. Explicit recognition that the protected rights constitute property interests would put third parties on notice of, and oblige them to respect, those interests. Thus, if someone should collect data in breach of the Act, the data subject would be able to sue not only the collector but also all who wrongfully obtain and use data from that source. In this way, data subjects are relieved of the burden of having to prove the precise role of each actor in data handling – a process that is usually opaque to data subjects.[146] Another significant benefit of propertisation is that it would make available property-based remedies for breaches of the Act. Section 32 of the PDPA currently provides a right of private action to a 'person who suffers *loss or damage* directly as a result of a contravention' of obligations of the Act.[147] Conceiving a

[139] *Re My Digital Lock Pte Ltd* [2018] SGPDPC 3 [33].

[140] G Wei, 'Milky Way and Adromeda: Privacy, Confidentiality and Freedom of Expression' (2006) 18 *Singapore Academy of Law Journal* 1 [23].

[141] Goh and Aw (n 103) [4.22]. See also Vera Bergelson, 'It's Personal But is it Mine?' (2003) 37 *UC Davis Law Review* 379, 429–32, discussing the 'personality theory' of property.

[142] See A Rouvroy and Y Poullet, 'The Right to Information Self-Determination and the Value of Self-Development: Reassessing the Importance of Privacy for Democracy' in S Gutwirth et al (eds), *Reinventing Data Protection?* (Springer, 2009) 51, 53.

[143] See the text accompanying nn 112–18 above.

[144] Bergelson (n 141) 428.

[145] N Purtova, *Property Rights in Personal Data: A European Perspective* (BOXPress BV, 2011) 83–84.

[146] ibid 242.

[147] Emphasis added. This right of private action relates to breaches of obligations under pts IV (collection, use and disclosure of personal data), V (access to and correction of personal data) and VI (care of personal data) of the PDPA.

data subject's rights of control as property would enlarge the concept of damage to include non-pecuniary losses such as those measured by user damage[148] or by analogy with the tort of conversion.[149] Designating ownership rights would also clarify who owns the *residual* interests in a resource[150] and thereby provide a 'baseline allocation' that assists in the analysis of novel questions arising from the application of, but not specifically addressed by, the Act. Finally, the rhetoric of 'property talk' will itself strengthen the protection of privacy by altering our legal and commercial culture.[151] Individuals who think of their data as property will come to see it not as mere information, but as a vital resource that they ought to control with vigilance. Property achieves this effect because it is 'ultimately of great practical and symbolic significance; and harnessed correctly it can transcend caricature and become once more a powerful agent of change'.[152]

Given that personal data is only 'excludable' by reason of the operation of the PDPA, its designation as a proprietary resource should logically also be effected by legislation and be confined to the application of the Act. On this approach, personal data would only constitute property *to the extent provided by the Act.* Confining the proprietary effects to the operation of the Act is also critical for overcoming the practical difficulties of identifying 'owners' of co-created data.[153] But even with this limited form of propertisation, one must contend with other difficult issues of both law and policy. One will have to ask, for instance, if an individual should be permitted to alienate personal data, what (if any) are the other circumstances in which a data subject's property interests would cease, and what would the nature of the interests of those lawfully in possession of such data be. The resolution of these issues will require more elaborate analysis and synthesis on another occasion, but some tentative thoughts are canvassed here.

On balance, it is likely that a property regime will not result in the constitution of personal data as a freely alienable resource. This is because, as observed, the PDPA currently envisages that a data subject would retain a measure of control in the data even after it has been lawfully 'acquired' by third parties. For example, section 16 of the Act allows a data subject to withdraw his or her consent for the collection, use and disclosure of his or her data. A counterparty who is notified

[148] As suggested in *Richard Lloyd v Google LLC* (n 26) [68], [69].

[149] Kohler and Palmer (n 19) 5.

[150] Absent any such designation, the residual rights would accrue to the data controllers; see the similar point made in respect of the GDPR in Duch-Brown et al (n 134) 17. See also the discussion in the text accompanying notes 167–72. For an example of a situation where the clarification of residual interests would assist data subjects, see C Chong, 'DoctorxDentist to Delist Doctors after clash with Singapore Medical Association' *Business Times* (10 November 2020), https://www.businesstimes.com.sg/garage/doctorxdentist-to-delist-doctors-after-clash-with-singapore-medical-association.

[151] L Lessig, 'Privacy as Property' (2002) 69 *Social Research* 247.

[152] P Kohler, 'The Death of Ownership and the Demise of Property' (2000) 53 *Current Legal Problems* 237, 258.

[153] See the text accompanying nn 66–70 above. This would also address the concern that data is expansible and too ill-defined to constitute property.

of such withdrawal will cease to be able to use the data collected.[154] In addition, section 18 of the Act limits the right to collect, use and disclose personal data for purposes that are appropriate as adjudged by a reasonable person, and only to the extent that the data subjects have been notified of the purposes. Clearly, the Act therefore does not envisage that data subjects would relinquish complete control of their personal data. That being the case, a property regime constructed on the back of the current legislative scheme will likely generate a *sui generis* type of property that is only partially alienable.[155] Consequently, data collectors do not acquire full 'title' to the data they collect, but their rights may be developed by analogy to those of lessees and licensees[156] or of bailees.[157]

It may be objected that property that is not freely alienable is not property at all. Writing with respect to confidential information, Aplin has observed that information is inherently inalienable because of its non-rivalrous nature, as there is nothing to stop a 'seller' from continuing to use the information in question after having 'sold' it to the 'buyer'.[158] This quality therefore militates against the application of property analysis to information. In a similar vein, Samuelson has argued that data subjects would likely prefer to have control over not just the initial transfer of data to data collectors, but also their subsequent transfers to third parties.[159] To retain such control would suggest that the data in question is not freely alienable, which is at odds with the very idea of property. A related objection is that propertisation of personal data is 'anathema' to the very conception of privacy as a fundamental civil right.[160] In this vein, Samuelson argues that it is 'morally obnoxious' to propertise personal data as a means of protecting privacy, for if 'information privacy is a civil liberty, it may make no more sense

[154] *Advisory Guidelines* (n 107) [12.53].

[155] Some would characterise a *sui generis* form of property that is not fully alienable as 'quasi-property'. Balganesh explains quasi-property as a legal category of property-like interests that arises in 'situations where the law attempts to simulate the functioning of property's exclusionary apparatus through a relational liability regime': see S Balganesh, 'Quasi-property: Like, But Not Quite Property' (2012) 160 *University of Pennsylvania Law Review* 1889, 1891. This means that the resource in question does not create a free-standing right of exclusion against the whole world, but its exclusionary signal is only triggered when two parties stand in a certain relationship with each other. Scholz has argued that privacy is a species of quasi-property; see LH Scholz, 'Privacy as Quasi-property' (2016) 101 *Iowa Law Review* 1113.

[156] On the analogy with leases and licences, see Purtova (n 145) 239–41.

[157] On the analogy with bailment, see Kohler and Palmer (n 19) 15–17.

[158] Aplin (n 23) 195–96. However, Aplin acknowledges that it is possible to contractually exclude the 'seller' from continuing to use the 'sold' information.

[159] P Samuelson, 'Privacy as Intellectual Property?' (2000) *Stanford Law Review* 1125, 1138. See also J Litman, 'Information Privacy/Information Property' (2000) 52 *Stanford Law Review* 1283, 1295–1301, where the author argues that the conception of personal data as freely alienable property is troubling because the opportunities for alienation (particularly on the World Wide Web) are ubiquitous. The routine and unthinking alienation of one's personal information would erode one's privacy interests. See also T Doyle, 'Privacy, Obfuscation, and Propertization' (2018) 44(3) *IFLA Journal* 229, 235–36.

[160] This objection underpins the European Union's unwillingness to frame and protect data subjects' interests as property rights; see Duch-Brown et al (n 134) 16.

to propertise personal data than to commodify voting rights'.[161] This criticism is similarly based on the conception of property as an absolutely alienable resource, so that propertisation is invariably seen to facilitate market exchange and promote commodification. In turn, commodification is objectionable because it undermines rather than protects privacy interests.

However, this chapter takes the position that absolute alienability is not a necessary feature of property. As Purtova points out, complete alienability is a myth because all forms of important property (including land, medicines and other scarce resources) are heavily regulated.[162] A building is no less a property even if it is inalienable by reason of the passage of law. Schwartz, too, argues that property may take the form of 'incomplete interests', of which copyright is an example.[163] He agrees that personal data should not be freely alienable, but would regard limitations on alienability to be proprietary restrictions that '[run] with the asset'.[164] These restrictions are therefore *erga omnes* in effect, shielding the data subjects' privacy interests even against third parties with whom they have had no direct dealings.[165]

Accepting that property need not be absolutely alienable also partially allays the fears concerning commodification, as restrictions on alienability underscore that the protective rather than the market exchange function of property is engaged in this context. Nevertheless, to the extent that a data subject could alienate part of his or her privacy interests, it has to be acknowledged that a property framework could conduce towards commodification. Yet that is not so much a criticism of a property-based approach than of the seemingly unalterable reality that personal data has *already* been commodified.[166] The explosion of commerce and social activities on digital platforms is testimony to the fact that there are undeniable social benefits in the trade-off of some personal information for greater convenience, cost savings, enlarged social space and increased access to services. Therefore, the question is not whether personal data should be commodified, but the extent to which the individual should have control over such trade-offs.

Rather than subverting privacy interests, propertisation restores control to consumers. There is a need to determine the ownership of personal data because failure to do so would 'effectively amount to the legitimisation of property rights "grabbed" by the Information Industry, rendering the individual defenceless in the face of corporate power eroding his/her autonomy, privacy and right to informational self-determination'.[167] The reason for this, Purtova explains, is that property

[161] Samuelson (n 159) 1143.
[162] Purtova (n 145) 84.
[163] Schwartz (n 78) 2092–2093. See also W Chik, ch 4 in this volume, for the suggestion that property analysis of personal data could be justified by analogy with copyrights.
[164] Schwartz (n 78) 2097.
[165] Jacob Victor, 'The EU General Data Protection Regulation: Towards a Property Regime for Protecting Data Privacy' (2013) 123 *Yale Law Journal* 513, 519.
[166] Bergelson (n 141) 431.
[167] N Purtova, 'The Illusion of Personal Data as No One's Property' (2015) 7 *Law, Innovation and Technology* 83, 84.

rights in a new resource is determined – in the absence of clear legal allocation – by the *ability to exclude others from the resource*.[168] Contrary to popular perception, valuable personal data generated in our current environment is in fact rivalrous and excludable. Such data is not:

> [M]erely individual pieces of information but an entire 'ecosystem', comprising interconnected but separate elements: (a) people themselves whose existence by itself generates personal data, (b) electronic platforms designed to 'capture' people by offering them unique electronic services and harvesting data of their users at the same time and (c) personal data not collected from people directly but inferred on the basis of personal data available earlier.[169]

Organisations that provide services on electronic platforms not only collect, harvest and analyse data of users, but are also able to exclude others from such information. Often, the personal data collected from users is excluded from users themselves because the users are not fully cognisant of what information is being collected and how they would be used. Such users are wont to consent to the use and collection of their personal data because they do not have any meaningful choice in declining services they perceive to be unique and valuable.[170] The same information is also excluded from other market players because the services of each business operator is typically unique.[171] Each operator is thus able to attract a distinct pool of users and capture data that cannot be replicated by competitors. Further, an operator can physically exclude or deny competitors access to the artefacts (eg, servers and storage devices) that host the data.[172] As such, the data harvested by the operators is typically rivalrous in nature. The de facto control they exercise is no less a form of property ownership. Unless this outcome is preferred as a matter of policy, assigning the relevant property right to the data subject is an important means by which to restore to him or her the control he or she expects to have in respect of his or her own personal information.

VII. Conclusion

Previously, personal data may simply have been private information that one would keep out of the public domain, but today it is a multi-dimensional resource that furthers the interests of an individual in the private, social and economic spheres. Indeed, it may be seen as an archetypical modern asset that transcends

[168] ibid 87–88. The author builds on the work of J Umbeck, *A Theory of Property Rights: With Application to the California Gold Rush* (Iowa State University Press, 1981).
[169] Purtova (n 167) 109.
[170] ibid 105–06.
[171] Although it is arguable that this capacity to exclude will be reduced with the introduction of data portability, see the text accompanying n 117 above.
[172] Purtova (n 167) 107–09.

conventional divisions between the private and public, the sacrosanct and the exploitable. The emergence of such assets challenges traditional legal conceptions and taxonomies in private law. It also raises novel tensions that have to be resolved, but not exclusively in the domain of private law. The characterisation of personal data as property within the context of the PDPA is an example of the continued relevance of private law techniques in areas that must, as a matter of necessity, be dominated by state regulation.

6

Transplanting the Concept of Digital Information Fiduciary?

MAN YIP*

I. Introduction

The importance of data in our increasingly digitalised world is old news. Equally stale is the realisation that too much protection may result in too little innovation and too much innovation may erode protection. Both objectives are good for societies and the people living in them. However, the staleness of the realisation does not make it any easier to find the correct balance. The question remains: how can we effectively regulate the use, collection and processing of personal data, especially in the light of rapid technological advancements?

This question is even more complex when posed in the context of Southeast Asia, where appetite and ambition for growth and developments are surging. Yet, Southeast Asia currently 'lacks the legal and technical infrastructure of developed states, such as the U.S. and EU members' to handle privacy challenges.[1] Against this background, two trends are hard to miss. In Southeast Asia, consumers' habits are changing: more and more people are interacting on social media, shopping online, booking transport and buying food through mobile apps, and watching movies online.[2] In a joint report released by Google, Temasek and Bain & Company in 2018, it is projected that the digital economy will continue to grow rapidly in the Southeast Asia region, soaring to US$240 billion by 2025.[3] Their 2019 report states

* This research is supported by the National Research Foundation, Singapore under its Emerging Areas Research Projects (EARP) Funding Initiative. Any opinions, findings and conclusions or recommendations expressed in this material are those of the author(s) and do not reflect the views of National Research Foundation, Singapore.

[1] www.asia.nikkei.com/Opinion/Data-regulation-opportunities-in-the-red-tape.

[2] See also 'Inside Thailand's Booming Social Media Sales Industry, Where Stars Can Make Millions within a Few Months' *South China Morning Post* (1 July 2019), www.scmp.com/news/asia/southeast-asia/article/3016727/inside-thailands-booming-social-media-sales-industry-where.

[3] 'e-Conomy SEA 2018: Southeast Asia's Internet Economy Hits an Inflection Point' *Think with Google* (November 2018), www.thinkwithgoogle.com/intl/en-apac/tools-resources/research-studies/e-conomy-sea-2018-southeast-asias-internet-economy-hits-inflection-point.

that the internet economies in Malaysia, Singapore, Thailand and the Philippines are growing by 20 per cent to 30 per cent annually, while Indonesia and Vietnam, on the other hand, are growing in excess of 40 per cent a year.[4] Indeed, in the extraordinary time of the COVID-19 pandemic, the demand for e-commerce has soared as various Southeast Asian nations come under various forms and degrees of lockdown.[5]

At the same time, around the world, data-driven global tech companies, such as Alibaba, Tencent, Facebook and Google, are increasingly coming under attack for their insufficient protection of users' personal data.[6] Today, data is no longer derived from simple online form-filling exercises, a format of data collection upon which data protection legislations promulgated in the past are based. More alarmingly, there is an acceleration of concentration of power over data in the hands of corporate giants.[7] In Southeast Asia, the concentration of influence in the hands of global tech giants is becoming increasingly obvious. For instance, the money that has been pumped into Indonesia's start-up scene comes largely from Alibaba, Tencent Holdings, Alphabet, and SoftBank Internet and Media Inc.[8]

Crucially, the COVID-19 pandemic has demonstrated to us that privacy and personal data protection are not simply about preventing the powerful from taking advantage of the ordinary man on the street. There is a need to balance privacy against other factors, such as public health. Citizens, businesses and governmental authorities must cooperate to enable a united and effective response. Attitudes towards privacy have also changed during the pandemic. In Singapore, for example, people are 'more willing to sacrifice some level of privacy' for safety considerations, but the type of surveillance technology and manner of use determines public acceptability.[9] Therefore, we need a legal framework that is flexible and capable of balancing protection against other equally relevant and important values, such as innovation and the public good.

This chapter is underlined by a mission to leave no stone unturned. It examines the utility of the concept of 'information fiduciary', most famously championed by American scholars such as Balkin and Zittrain, in providing or inspiring a new way of thinking about the effective protection of personal data and privacy. It examines how this innovative idea can be fully developed into a

[4] ibid.

[5] 'COVID-19 Whets Appetite for E-commerce in Southeast Asia, But Bottlenecks Remain' *S&P Global* (16 April 2020), www.spglobal.com/marketintelligence/en/news-insights/latest-news-headlines/covid-19-whets-appetite-for-e-commerce-in-southeast-asia-but-bottlenecks-remain-57985529.

[6] European Commission Press Release, 'Mergers: Commission Alleges Facebook Provided Misleading Information about WhatsApp Takeover' (Brussels, 20 December 2016), www.europa.eu/rapid/press-release_IP-16-4473_en.htm.

[7] See generally G Buttarelli, 'Strange Bedfellows: Data Protection, Privacy and Competition' (2017) 13 *Competition Law International* 21, 22–23.

[8] See n 1 above.

[9] TF Tay, 'Singaporeans Accept Some Privacy Loss in Covid-19 Battle But Surveillance Method Matters: IPS Study' *The Straits Times* (25 May 2020), www.straitstimes.com/singapore/singaporeans-accept-some-privacy-loss-in-covid-19-battle-but-surveillance-method-matters.

legal concept that is capable of application in Asian common law jurisdictions – Singapore and Malaysia – which have adopted the English doctrine of fiduciary law. This exercise consists of three assessments: what the gaps in existing solutions are (section II); whether this American idea has more virtues than shortcomings (section III); and whether this American idea may be transplanted to (or adapted for) Asian common law jurisdictions such as Singapore and Malaysia (section IV). The analysis proffered in this chapter is of course relevant to other common law jurisdictions. Further, it is hoped that this chapter paves the way for exploring whether the concept of 'information fiduciary' can inspire a new model of legislative intervention.

II. The Gap in Existing Solutions

In the domain of privacy/personal data protection, existing solutions lie in various areas of law, including contract law, tort law, the law of confidence and data protection/privacy legislation, as well as the deployment of technologies to ensure the protection of privacy. The discussion below provides a succinct summary of what these solutions seek to do and their inherent limitations. It will not cover emerging concepts such as the propertisation of data and data trust, as these are covered by other chapters in this volume.[10]

A. Contract Law

The core problems with contract law as a form of digital consumer data protection are captured by the Supreme Court of Canada's decision in *Douez v Facebook Inc.*[11] The case concerned the enforceability of a jurisdiction clause in Facebook's Terms of Use and its effect on the forum court's existence and exercise of jurisdiction. In short, Douez, a resident of British Columbia, proposed a class action in British Columbia against Facebook for using her personal data (name and likeness) without consent in their advertising product 'Sponsored Stories'. Facebook applied to stay the action on the basis that there is a jurisdiction clause mandating litigation to be brought exclusively in Northern Californian courts. We may put the conflict-of-laws issues to one side. In the 4-3 decision which dismissed the stay application, the majority reasoning, proceeding on two different lines, highlighted that the Terms of Use in the case were contracts of gross inequality in bargaining power. Indeed, Abella J (comprising the majority) concluded that the jurisdiction clause was unenforceable on contractual principles. She questioned

[10] For data trust, see C Reed, ch 3 in this volume. For the propertisation of data, see W Chik, ch 4 in this volume; and Lee, ch 5 in this volume.

[11] *Douez v Facebook Inc* 2017 SCC 33.

the quality of consumer consent within the online contracting context because it allowed no opportunity for renegotiation or adjustment of the terms and there was an 'automatic nature' to the commitments made.[12]

Indeed, Abella J's concerns apply equally in respect of contractual terms on the collection, use and transfer of consumer data. Studies have shown that the readership of terms and conditions for online consumer contracting is very low.[13] Nor is reading the full terms and conditions a practicable exercise.[14] The consumer may thus blindly or without consideration accept unfair or onerous terms on the collection, processing and use of his or her data.[15] Importantly, people frequently conduct transactions over their mobile phones, where the small size of the screen poses a significant challenge to readability (and readership) and therefore in obtaining meaningful consent. In fact, some consumers may not realise that a contract is being formed when they submit their personal data in exchange for what are frequently perceived as 'free' services.

A further limitation of the contractual regime is that it only governs the parties to the contract. In the context of the misuse of digital consumer data, the unauthorised transfer to third parties or processing by third parties would not be governed by the contract. Data subjects will have to look outside contract law for relief.

Of course, in the case of consumers, legislative standards provide important safeguards against unfair dealings, and contract law may be a platform through which legislative standards may be complied with. For example, consent as an authorisation mechanism for the collection, use and processing of personal data may be brought about through contract law. But consent as an authorisation mechanism for the purpose of personal data protection should not be conflated with contractual consent for the purpose of legal relation creation. The former is data subject-focused and in this sense unilateral; contractual consent is bilateral/multi-lateral. Further, the requirements for effective authorisation consent may not coincide with *consensus ad idem* for the purpose of contractual consent. For instance, data protection legislation may prescribe an opt-in only format of obtaining consent to ensure readership and conscious decision-making on the part of data subjects. Given these differences, whilst it may be practically convenient

[12] ibid [98]–[99].

[13] European Commission, 'Study on Consumers' Attitude towards Terms and Conditions (T&Cs): Final Report; (Brussels, 2016) 9 www.ec.europa.eu/consumers/consumer_evidence/behavioural_research/docs/terms_and_conditions_final_report_en.pdf; Yannis Bakos, Florencia Marotta-Wurgler and David R Trossen, 'Does Anyone Read the Fine Print? Consumer Attention to Standard-Form Contracts' (2014) 43 *Journal of Legal Studies* 1.

[14] According to a study by Cranor and McDonald, it would take 76 work days to read the privacy policies that an internet user would encounter in a year. See AC Madrigal, 'Reading the Privacy Policies You Encounter in a Year Would Take 76 Work Days' *The Atlantic* (1 March 2012), www.theatlantic.com/technology/archive/2012/03/reading-the-privacy-policies-you-encounter-in-a-year-would-take-76-work-days/253851.

[15] S Law, 'At the Crossroads of Consumer Protection, Data Protection and Private International Law: Some Remarks on *Verein fur Konsumenteninformation v Amazon EU*' (2017) 42 *European Law Review* 751, 765.

and strategic for authorisation consent to be sought together with agreement to contract formation, the two need not be contemporaneous if the collection or use of the consumer data is not necessary for the performance of the contract.[16]

B. Tort Law

Tort law may provide a more promising form of private law protection.[17] English law[18] recognises a more limited cause of action that rests on the foundation of the misuse of private information,[19] though the characterisation of this cause of action remains somewhat unclear. In the past, this claim for misuse of private information was shoehorned into breach of confidence, a cause of action that entailed two distinct strands: one to deal with cases of breach of privacy and the other to deal with cases concerning secret information. Victims of invasion of privacy would traditionally bring their claims under both heads. Over time, however, the claim for misuse of private information has been referred to as a tort.[20] For example, in *Vidal-Hall v Google Inc*, the English Court of Appeal decision characterised the claim as a tort for the purpose of service out of the jurisdiction.[21] English law remains influential in the common law world. For instance, in a recent Singapore decision, *My Digital Lock Pte Ltd*, the Commissioner of the Singapore Personal Data Protection Commission appeared to approve the English development of the tort of misuse of private information and considered that Singapore courts should be afforded an opportunity to consider and adopt the same approach.[22] Meanwhile, Malaysia has yet to recognise a right to privacy or a tort of invasion of privacy, although the claim has been invoked a number of times before Malaysian courts.[23]

If the tort of misuse of private information were to be adopted in the common law jurisdictions in Southeast Asia, such as Singapore and Malaysia, three points are of note. First, the English tort is presently underdeveloped. It is thought that the English tort would involve a two-element approach, as identified by Eady J in the case of *Mosley v News Group Newspapers*:

> If the first hurdle can be overcome, by demonstrating a *reasonable expectation of privacy* … the court is required to carry out the next step of *weighing the relevant*

[16] See EU General Data Protection Regulation (GDPR), art 6.1(b).

[17] See RL Rabin, 'Perspectives on Privacy, Data Security and Tort Law' (2017) 66 *DePaul Law Review* 313.

[18] English law does not presently recognise a general tort of invasion of privacy: *Wainwright v Home Office* [2004] 2 AC 406.

[19] This is generally traced back to Lord Nicholls' speech in *Campbell v MGN* [2004] 2 AC 457.

[20] See, eg, *McKennitt v Ash* [2008] QB 73 [8] (Buxton LJ); *Murray v Big Pictures (UK) Ltd* [2009] Ch 481 [24] (Sir Anthony Clarke MR); *Imerman v Tchenguiz* [2011] Fam 116 [65] (Lord Neuberger MR). *cf Douglas v Hello! Ltd (No 3)* [2006] QB 125 [96]–[97] (Lord Phillips).

[21] *Vidal-Hall v Google Inc* [2015] EWCA Civ 311.

[22] *My Digital Lock Pte Ltd* [2018] SGPDPC 3 [40].

[23] See, eg, *John Dadit v Bong Meng Chiat* [2015] 1 LNS 1465 [24].

> *competing … rights* [*of the parties*] in the light of an 'intense focus' upon the individual facts of the case. (Emphasis added)[24]

If the two-element approach is to be followed, Singapore and Malaysian courts would need to, first, work out what constitutes a 'reasonable expectation of privacy' and, second, the principles in guiding the courts' weighing of the relevant competing rights. It may be that local conditions and legislative frameworks would require a slightly different approach from English law.

Second, tort law is harm-focused and damage[25] would need to be proved in order to claim compensation. Exceptionally, exemplary damages would also be available. A harm-focused approach would mean that the tort is generally directed at 'mopping up the mess', as opposed to preventing the mess.[26]

Finally, the tort of misuse of private information is not coterminous with the protection afforded under the national forms of personal data protection legislation. The tort protects information that is meant to be *private*, which includes but is not limited to personal data,[27] whereas many national forms of data protection legislation protect against the unauthorised disclosure of *personal data*.[28]

C. Breach of Confidence

As mentioned, another avenue by which privacy is traditionally protected is through the law of confidence. However, 'confidential information' must be conceptually distinguished from 'private information'. As Lord Nicholls explained in *OBG v Allan*:

> As the law has developed breach of confidence, or misuse of confidential information, now covers two distinct causes of action, protecting two different interests: privacy and secret ('confidential') information. It is important to keep these two distinct. In some

[24] *Mosley v News Group Newspapers* [2008] EWHC 1777 (QB) [10].

[25] Damage need not be pecuniary: see *Mosley v News Group Newspapers* [2008] EWHC 1777 (QB) [216].

[26] Of course, injunctive relief offers the tort victim (or prospective tort victim) some degree of harm prevention. Prohibitory and mandatory injunctions, for instance, could reduce the extent of harm or prevent further harm being done. However, in the context of protection of private information, once the information has entered the public domain and loses its privacy, there is nothing left for the law to protect. See *Mosley* (n 24) [36]. A *quia timet* injunction, on the other hand, could prevent a tort that has yet to be committed. However, to succeed in obtaining a *quia timet* injunction, the plaintiff would have to demonstrate the existence of a threatened commission of the tort and imminent damage. It does not prevent the threat from arising in the first place. Moreover, in some cases, it may be that prospective tort victim is unaware of the pending unauthorised publication of private information. See PD Mora and A Savage, 'The Right to Privacy and Advance Notification' (2011) 22(8) *Entertainment Law Review* 233, 237.

[27] See, eg, *My Digital Lock Pte Ltd* (n 22) [38]: 'an intimate conversation within the confines of a taxicab may not contain any personal information. The right to prevent its publication lies with the common law right to prevent publication of private information, not with the PDPA.'

[28] For Singapore, see *My Digital Lock Pte Ltd* (n 22) [38]; for Malaysia, see the definition of 'personal data' under s 4 of the Personal Data Protection Act 2010 (Malaysia) (Act 709).

> cases information may qualify for protection both on grounds of privacy and confidentiality. In other instances information may be in the public domain, and not qualify for protection as confidential, and yet qualify for protection on the grounds of privacy. Privacy can be invaded by further publication of information or photographs already disclosed to the public. Conversely, and obviously, a trade secret may be protected as confidential information even though no question of personal privacy is involved.[29]

The establishment of a separate tort for the misuse of private information, as discussed above, would leave the law of confidence doctrinally more coherent, but also more restricted in its protection of privacy, as the equitable claim would only apply in respect of secret information.[30] Moreover, exemplary damages are not available for equitable claims.[31] The remedies for breach of confidence are equitable compensation and account of profits. As the law of confidence is relation-focused, it does not allow data subjects to sue parties who are involved in the breach of confidence, but are not themselves parties who owe the obligation of confidence.

D. Personal Data Protection Legislation

Designing a national data protection framework is a monumental task, as the law must balance between individual rights to privacy, the competing interests of economic growth and innovation, and other fundamental rights, such as human dignity and freedom of expression. In Southeast Asia, it is said that: 'The stakes are high for governments, which are counting on the digital economy to drive growth, and internet companies, which view Southeast Asia's social-media-loving population of 641 million as a key growth market.'[32]

It is therefore unsurprising that national forms of data protection legislation in Southeast Asia seek to strike a balance between data protection and promoting economic growth. For example, commenting on Indonesia's aim to enact a new law on personal data protection in 2020, Indonesia's Communications Minister Johnny G Plate said that the emphasis is not on fines, but on encouraging the proper and beneficial use of social media.[33] The Singapore legislation – the Personal Data Protection Act 2012 (hereinafter 'the Singapore PDPA') – has been described as a 'light touch regime'.[34] As the official website of the Singapore regulator describes, the statutory regime 'recognises both the rights of individuals to protect personal

[29] *OBG Ltd v Allan* [2008] 1 AC 1 (HL) [255].

[30] See generally T Aplin, 'The Relationship between Breach of Confidence and the Tort of Misuse of Private Information' (2007) 18 *King's Law Journal* 329.

[31] *Mosley* (n 24).

[32] E Davies and S Widianto, 'Indonesia Needs to Urgently Establish Data Protection Law: Minister' (16 November 2019), www.reuters.com/article/us-indonesia-communications/indonesia-needs-to-urgently-establish-data-protection-law-minister-idUSKBN1XQ0B8.

[33] ibid.

[34] HYF Lim, 'The Data Protection Paradigm for the Tort of Privacy in the Age of Big Data' (2015) 27 *Singapore Academy of Law Journal* 789, 816.

data, including rights of access and correction, and the needs of organisations to collect, use or disclose personal data for legitimate and reasonable purposes'.[35] A primary aim of introducing the Singapore legislation is to 'strengthen and entrench Singapore's competitiveness and position as a trusted, world-class hub for businesses'.[36] The Singapore legislation does not apply to governmental agencies, tribunals appointed by written law and specified statutory bodies (or their agents) in relation to their collection, use or disclosure of personal data.[37] Even more clearly, the Malaysian Personal Data Protection Act 2010 (hereinafter 'the Malaysian PDPA'), which came into force on 13 November 2013, only protects and regulates personal data that is used in respect of a commercial transaction.[38] The Malaysian legislation expressly excludes its application to federal and state governments.

Regardless of the statutory standards and approach, the more important point is that there is still a role for private law to enhance the protection of private information, even if the same conduct would very often constitute a breach of statutory duty.[39] First, save for explicit legislative exclusion, concurrent causes of action have always been allowed in the common law jurisdictions. Second, concurrent causes of action produce a stronger deterrent effect and are therefore more likely to lead to better human conduct in the long run. Third, regulators in some jurisdictions are also fearful of regulatory overkill and may refrain from responding to every new situation, without proper deliberation and consultation with the industry. Piecemeal solutions developed in the courtroom may be the fastest response in these novel situations. Fourth, private law solutions may provide for additional remedies, as regulations tend to focus on providing for administrative fines and/or compensation. Finally, private law protection is not coterminous with legislative protection. There is need and room to develop private law in meeting new challenges and providing redress to victims of bad behaviour that may not be covered under the personal data protection legislation.[40]

E. Integrating Technology as Part of the Solution

It has been argued that a strictly legal approach to privacy concerns is insufficient. Instead, a systematic approach that integrates both legal and technical tools for privacy protection would guarantee more robust, comprehensive and

[35] See www.pdpc.gov.sg/Legislation-and-Guidelines/Personal-Data-Protection-Act-Overview.

[36] See www.pdpc.gov.sg/Overview-of-PDPA/The-Legislation/Personal-Data-Protection-Act.

[37] Personal Data Protection Act 2012 (Singapore), s 4, read together with the definition of 'public agency' under s 2.

[38] For a commentary, see, eg, R Ong, 'Data Protection in Malaysia and Hong Kong: One Step Forward, Two Steps Back?' (2012) 28(4) *Computer Law & Security Review* 429. A public consultation on the review of the Malaysian legislation was undertaken in February 2020: www.pdp.gov.my/jpdpv2/assets/2020/02/Public-Consultation-Paper-on-Review-of-Act-709_V4.pdf.

[39] The Singapore PDPA allows for a civil claim to be brought based on a breach of statutory duty: PDPA, s 32.

[40] *My Digital Lock Pte Ltd* (n 22) [38].

consistent protection.[41] Indeed, one impact of data protection law is the emergence of technological tools and services (with artificial intelligence (AI) capabilities and encryption) to enhance and ensure data protection and security.[42]

Privacy-enhancing technologies may be viewed as a modest implementation of a systematic approach. 'Privacy by Design'[43] – a philosophy that has been adopted by a number of laws (including the General Data Protection Regulation (GDPR))[44] and incorporated into best practices guides[45] – is a more robust approach. It requires privacy to be directly built into the design and operation of technology, operations, systems, work processes, management structures, physical spaces and networked infrastructure.[46] The goal is to take pre-emptive action instead of 'locking the stable after the horse has bolted'.[47]

However, it is not clear whether a systematic approach can be successfully implemented. There are clear operationalisation challenges such as 'internal constraints, incentive misalignments, and broader normative challenges'.[48] Levin's case study of the implementation of 'Privacy by Design' in Ontario, Canada states that 'the principles of ["Privacy by Design"] offer little practical guidance to engineers'.[49] There is also concern that unfettered regulatory flexibility in respect of the application of 'Privacy by Design' based on the circumstances would lead to a watered-down version that would not bring about meaningful regulatory change.[50] Levin concludes that although 'Privacy by Design' may not succeed as an engineering solution, it 'is best realized as a rallying call for privacy, as a change and leadership tool that can be used internally in an organization but also externally by the regulator'.[51]

III. Fiduciary Law as Part of the Solution?

Before we examine the feasibility and value of imposing fiduciary obligations on digital businesses in this part of the common law world, let us first unpack the idea

[41] U Gasser, 'Recoding Privacy Law: Reflections on the Future Relationship among Law, Technology, and Privacy' (2016) 130 *Harvard Law Review Forum* 61.

[42] See n 1 above.

[43] See A Cavoukian, 'Privacy by Design: Origins, Meaning, and Prospects for Assuring Privacy and Trusts in the Information Era' in GOM Yee (ed), *Privacy Protection Measures and Technologies in Business Organization: Aspects and Standards* (IGI Global, 2011) 170.

[44] GDPR, art 25.

[45] See Personal Data Protection Commission (Singapore), 'Guide to Data Protection by Design for ICT Systems', https://www.pdpc.gov.sg/-/media/Files/PDPC/PDF-Files/Other-Guides/Guide-to-Data-Protection-by-Design-for-ICT-Systems-(310519).pdf?la=en.

[46] A Levin, 'Privacy by Design by Regulation: The Case Study of Ontario' (2018) 4 *Canadian Journal of Comparative and Contemporary Law* 1, 4.

[47] A Dix, 'Built-in Privacy: No Panacea, But a Necessary Condition for Effective Privacy Protection' (2010) 3(2) *Identity in the Information Society* 257.

[48] Gasser (n 41) 66.

[49] Levin (n 46) 34.

[50] ibid 38.

[51] ibid 42.

of 'information fiduciary' propounded by Balkin, Zittrain and other American scholars.

A. Unpacking the American Idea of an 'Information Fiduciary'

Different authors, writing during the different developmental stages of the digital economy, may present a slightly different picture of 'information fiduciary', but some core ideas may be extracted from the literature. In discussing the role and importance of a knowledge orientation in fiduciary relationships, Brooks says that the concept 'would incorporate both affirmative and negative duties':

> Fiduciaries, as we have seen, have not only duties of confidentiality and disclosure, but also duties to inquire, to inform, to speak with candor and other knowledge-based obligations and presumptions. The entire framework of knowledge in the fiduciary context would potentially apply to the information fiduciary. The difficult task would be to determine what makes one an information fiduciary as opposed to a mere possessor of information in one's own right. Knowing some otherwise private or personal information about another individual could not be sufficient to convert someone into a fiduciary. Only when someone possesses information pertinent to another while in a relation of trust or confidence with that other, could duties with respect to that knowledge arise, causing the information possessor to be treated as a fiduciary. In other words, the information must be connected to a relationship in an appropriate way.[52]

Brooks' depiction highlights that information fiduciaries do not owe merely duties of confidentiality and that fiduciary duties arise from the transfer and possession of information in a relationship of trust and confidence. The focus is directed at information as information, as opposed to information as property. As such, the conceptualisation is not based on the trust/property paradigm. It also neatly avoids the perplexing question of whether data is property.[53] Importantly, it would appear that fiduciary duties do not arise by reason of status, but by reason of the circumstances of the case. In other words, it would be a fact-based fiduciary relationship.

An even more developed concept of information fiduciary can be found in Balkin's writings. He explains his conceptualisation of the 'information fiduciary' as follows:

> An information fiduciary is a person or business who, because of their relationship with another, has taken on special duties with respect to the information they obtain in the course of the relationship. People and organizations that have fiduciary duties arising from the use and exchange of information are information fiduciaries whether

[52] RRW Brooks, 'Knowledge in Fiduciary Relations' in AS Gold and PB Miller (eds), *Philosophical Foundations of Fiduciary Law* (Oxford University Press, 2014) 240.

[53] See B Schermer, 'Privacy and Property: Do You Really Own Your Personal Data?' *Leiden Law Blog* (8 September 2015), www.leidenlawblog.nl/articles/privacy-and-property-do-you-really-own-your-personal-data.

> or not they also do other things in the client's behalf, like manage an estate or perform legal or medical services.[54]

As such, in Balkin's account, a trustee who receives sensitive information regarding his or her beneficiaries may be an information fiduciary, quite apart from his or her capacity as a custodian fiduciary. Balkin says that people tend to worry about their relationship to technologies and how they may control or displace them, but the correct way of perceiving technological developments is that 'technology is actually a way of exemplifying and constituting relationships of power between one set of human beings and another set of human beings'.[55] Behind the technologies are people, companies and governments. Whilst the data of more and more people is being collected and processed, the power to do so is concentrated in the hands of a small number of people.

Balkin further explains that the information fiduciaries of the digital age should owe different and fewer obligations compared to traditional professional fiduciaries such as doctors, lawyers and accountants, owing to three key differences between them.[56] First, deriving profits from personal data is the central plank of the business models of many online service companies and the monetisation helps to keep services free or low in cost. Second, unlike traditional fiduciaries, digital-age information fiduciaries (eg, Facebook and Instagram) have an interest in encouraging people to disclose as much information about themselves as possible because the data constitutes the constant stream of content for these companies. Third, Balkin says that people expect doctors and lawyers to act in their interests, but they do not have such high expectations for online service companies. He thus concludes that 'the central obligation' of digital information fiduciaries is that they cannot induce trust in their users for the purpose of obtaining the users' personal information and then use the information in ways that would amount to a betrayal of trust.[57]

Zittrain, on the other hand, suggests an opt-in model for the tech giants. He says that the duties 'could be light enough to the Facebooks of the world, and meaningful enough to their users, that those intermediaries could be induced to opt into them' through the government's offer of tax breaks or immunities from certain legal claims.[58] Zittrain's conceptualisation is to target clearly bad behaviour:

> Our information intermediaries can keep their sauces secret, inevitably advantaging some sources of content while disadvantaging others, while still agreeing that some ingredients are poison – and must be off the table.[59]

[54] JM Balkin, 'Information Fiduciaries and the First Amendment' (2016) 49 *UC Davis Law Review* 1183, 1209.

[55] JM Balkin, 'Free Speech in the Algorithmic Society: Big Data, Private Governance, and New School Speech Regulation' (2018) 51 *UC Davis Law Review* 1149, 1158.

[56] JM Balkin, '2016 Sidley Austin Distinguished Lecture on Big Data Law and Policy: The Three Laws of Robotics in the Age of Big Data' (2017) 78 *Ohio State Law Journal* 1217, 1229.

[57] ibid.

[58] J Zittrain, 'Engineering an Election' (2014) 127 *Harvard Law Review Forum* 335, 340.

[59] ibid 341.

As such, only predatory advertisements would be prohibited, but non-predatory, interest-based advertisements would not.[60]

B. The Merits and Shortcomings of the Concept of 'Information Fiduciary'

Gathering the different strands of thoughts highlighted above, in summary, the US concept of 'information fiduciary' orients focus on information transferred in the context of a relationship. It directs our attention to people who control the technologies, as opposed to the technologies themselves. Through the lens of 'information fiduciary', the problem is reframed as an abuse of trust based on informational asymmetry. At least for now, we need not be fearful of machine-led apocalypses (think Terminator's Skynet or Terminator: Dark Fate's Legion). A solution that does not harp on about the unknown sinister dangers of technologies will also supply us with a more neutral perspective in appraising technological advancements and innovation. Nor does the concept of 'information fiduciary' propose a solution that is focused on enhancing consumers/data subjects' autonomy. We know, from the discussion above, that such a choice-oriented solution has limited effect.

However, there are shortcomings with the concept of digital information fiduciary. Ohm has forcefully pointed out that the concept in execution is 'awfully vague and underdeveloped' as the core substantive obligations are not fully fleshed out.[61] He said that Balkin and Zittrain seem far more interested in identifying digital information fiduciaries, as opposed to what duties that status entails.[62] He also questioned the scope of application of the concept. He is of the view that Balkin and Zittrain would apply the digital information fiduciary designation to a small number of businesses as they appear to favour a 'relatively unregulated approach for most of the companies' under US law.[63]

More trenchant criticisms have been posed by Khan and Pozen.[64] They considered that the concept of 'information fiduciary' has moved the conversation on protection of privacy and personal information backward and strained the fiduciary doctrine. First, they point out that fiduciary obligations owed to the end-users are perpetually inconsistent with the tech companies' fiduciary obligations owed to their stockholders. The companies at which Balkin's concept of information fiduciary is targeted (eg, Facebook, Google, Twitter and Uber) are Delaware companies.

[60] J Zittrain, 'How to Exercise the Power You Didn't Ask for' *Harvard Business Review* (19 September 2018).

[61] P Ohm, 'Forthright Code' (2018) 56 *Houston Law Review* 471, 484.

[62] ibid.

[63] ibid.

[64] LM Khan and DE Pozen, 'A Skeptical View of Information Fiduciaries' (2019) 133 *Harvard Law Review Forum* 497.

Under Delaware law, officers and directors of a company must treat stockholder welfare as the only end, considering other interests only to the extent that doing so is rationally related to stockholder welfare.[65] In their view, Facebook and the like are companies which derive economic profits from behaviourally targeted advertising, a business model that is fundamentally incompatible with the imposition of fiduciary obligations.[66] The parallel with traditional fiduciaries such as doctors and lawyers is thus illusory. Second, they argue that that the parallel with traditional fiduciaries is further weakened by the fact that end-users and internet service providers stand in an 'unusually stark asymmetry of information', unlike doctor–patient and lawyer–client relationships.[67] Users of internet services are 'deeply ignorant' of these companies' operations.[68] Third, they say that deceptive, manipulative or abusive corporate practices – which Balkin's concept of 'information fiduciary' is supposed to target – are already being addressed by existing US laws.[69] It is not clear what the concept adds to the current protection. Fourth, they highlight that Balkin has not discussed the enforcement aspect of the fiduciary obligations or what remedies would be available.[70] Fifth, they argue that the concept paints a false image of these digital giants as 'fundamentally trustworthy actors who put their users' interests first'.[71] Sixth, they say that the concept of digital information fiduciary merely seeks to limit the dominance and power of tech giants over their users, but it fails to ask the more pertinent question as to whether these companies should enjoy such wide powers and market dominance to begin with.[72] Finally, given the list of problems identified, they conclude that the concept of 'information fiduciary' is likely to play only a supporting role in protecting privacy, as opposed to the prominent role which its proponents believe it should have. Ultimately, Khan and Pozen are inclined to think that a more structural reform is to target these tech giants' market dominance, as opposed to merely regulating their activities with a flexible, light touch.

C. The Difficulties of Legal Transplants

It would be foolish to dismiss the criticisms outlined above and go ahead with a legal transplant of the concept of information fiduciary. Four main problems stand out: digital companies' profit-driven business model and duties to their own shareholders are fundamentally at odds with the fiduciary doctrine of putting users'

[65] *Frederick Hsu Living Trust v ODN Holding Corp*, No. 12108-VCL 2017 WL 1437308 at 17 (Del Ch 24 April 2017).
[66] Khan and Pozen (n 64) 515.
[67] ibid 520.
[68] ibid.
[69] ibid 520–24
[70] ibid 524.
[71] ibid 534.
[72] ibid 524.

interests first; the vagueness of duties,[73] enforcement and remedies; the fiduciary doctrine has no role if the actor is fundamentally untrustworthy; and the role and impact of the concept, even if implemented, are unlikely to be massive.

Balkin responded to these criticisms in his latest article.[74] First, on the incompatibility between the fiduciary model and the digital companies' for-profit business model and their duties to maximise shareholder value, Balkin says that this criticism is 'misguided' because statutory law could simply provide that information fiduciary obligations trump a company's fiduciary duties to its shareholders.[75] Besides, the company's obligations to its shareholders 'assume that the corporation will attempt to comply with legal duties owed to those affected by the corporation's business practices, even if this reduces shareholder value'.[76] Second, as to the second criticism concerning the vagueness of the information fiduciary duties, Balkin clarifies that an information fiduciary owes three basic duties to the end-users: a duty of confidentiality, a duty of care and a duty of loyalty.[77] He stresses that these duties 'must run with the data', which means that third parties who share or use the data must also agree to take on information fiduciary obligations.[78] Third, on the irrelevance of the fiduciary doctrine to an untrustworthy actor, Balkin explains that the purpose of making these digital companies information fiduciaries is precisely to turn them into trustworthy stewards of personal data.[79] Finally, on the role and impact of the fiduciary model, he thinks that it has the potential to change business practices.

Whilst Balkin's responses to the criticisms are thought-provoking, not all of his arguments are relevant or equally compelling when applied to other jurisdictions seeking to adopt the fiduciary model of privacy protection. The remaining part of this chapter considers whether English law-inspired equitable jurisprudence (applied in common law jurisdictions such as Singapore and Malaysia) may accommodate the development of the concept of digital information fiduciary or a variant form of it. To this end, as the finer details of fiduciary principles may differ even between the common law jurisdictions, the analysis offered here will proceed on more generalised principles of fiduciary law. The discussion, in particular, addresses a principal conceptual hurdle: whether digital businesses owe fiduciary duties to their end-users. It also attempts to respond to the four main issues with the fiduciary model of regulation which were identified above.

[73] It should be pointed out that greater efforts have been made by other authors to flesh out the substantive content of the fiduciary obligations (see A Dobkin, 'Information Fiduciaries in Practice: Data Privacy and User Expectations' (2018) 33 *Berkeley Technology Law Journal* 1) and variant forms built on the concept of information fiduciary (N Richards and W Hartzog, 'Taking Trust Seriously in Privacy Law' (2016) *19 Stanford Technology Law Review* 431; Ohm (n 61)).

[74] JM Balkin, 'The Fiduciary Model of Privacy' (2020) 134 *Harvard Law Review Forum* 11.

[75] ibid 23.

[76] ibid.

[77] ibid 14 and 18.

[78] ibid 14, 17–18.

[79] ibid 26.

IV. An Equitable Conception of Digital 'Information Fiduciary' under Singapore and Malaysian Law?

As a starting point, what is clear and helpful is that the categories of fiduciary relationships are not closed.[80] It is also noteworthy that equity has 'a long-standard tradition of intervention in the activities of company directors, agents, trustees, solicitors and the like in the cause of exacting high standards of business and professional conduct'.[81] Accordingly, fiduciary law is well developed for setting high standards of conduct. However, why fiduciary duties arise, when they arise and what duties are uniquely fiduciary are questions that continue to stir debates.[82] Resolving these questions go beyond the scope of this chapter; instead, it shall consider the possibility of developing an equitable conception of 'information fiduciary' on two bases: first, on a generalised understanding of fiduciary law that is shaped by Harding's thesis on trust and fiduciary law;[83] and, second, following the suggestion in the US literature, to develop an equitable concept following a context-based understanding of fiduciary law by extrapolating from the doctor–patient relationship.

A. Harding's View of the Fiduciary Doctrine: Reliance on Discretion, Respect and Trust

i. *Summary of Harding's Propositions*

In his article entitled 'Trust and Fiduciary Law',[84] Harding offers four refreshing propositions. First, he identifies reliance on discretion as the common feature of all fiduciary relationships. Second, he argues that because every fiduciary relationship shares the common feature of one party's reliance on another's exercise of discretion, fiduciary relationships are likely to be characterised by 'thick' trust. According to him, the thickness of trust is assessed by three factors: '(i) the range of expected or anticipated choices at which it is directed; (ii) the importance of those choices to the person doing the trusting; and (iii) the content of beliefs that it is combined with'.[85]

Third, Harding points out that whilst trust and fiduciary relationships have a contingent connection, the former does not provide the moral justification for

[80] *English v Dedham Vale Properties Ltd* [1978] 1 WLR 93, 110.

[81] P Finn, *Fiduciary Obligations: 40th Anniversary Republication with Additional Essays* (Federation Press, 2016) 1.

[82] ibid (see generally).

[83] M Harding, 'Trust and Fiduciary Law' (2013) 33 *Oxford Journal of Legal Studies* 81.

[84] ibid.

[85] ibid 83. See examples to illustrate 'thin' and 'thick' trust: ibid 83–84.

the existence of the latter. Instead, he argues that the moral justification for the imposition of fiduciary duties lies in respect.[86] He illustrates his argument by reference to the (uncontroversial) fiduciary duty to avoid conflicts. In his words:

> In a fiduciary relationship, it is invariably the case that the fiduciary is given discretionary powers for the purpose of advancing the interests of her principal: this is the reliance on discretion that I described above, now viewed in light of its purpose. These discretionary powers create opportunities for the fiduciary, opportunities that may be used for the purpose of which they were made available, or that may be used selfishly to serve the fiduciary's own ends … in deciding what to make of an opportunity that is available to her only qua fiduciary, a fiduciary who deliberately subordinates her non-fiduciary duties to her own interests in her practical reasoning and who chooses accordingly has taken advantage of her principal in a way that violates the requirements of strong respect.[87]

Finally, Harding argues that the goal of fiduciary law is to enable 'people to form, maintain and develop relationships characterised by a cycle of trust and trustworthiness, relationships that are both instrumentally and intrinsically valuable'.[88] On this account of the goal of fiduciary law, the trust and trustworthiness in the relationship is likely to 'broaden and deepen over time'.[89] That trusting relationship is an intrinsically valuable good is easy to grasp – it 'may be considered a basic truth about moral life'.[90] Instrumentally, trusting relationships facilitates cooperation and enables a meaningful interpretation of such actions. In other words, fiduciary law performs a facilitative role as opposed to a coercive one. Most interestingly, in relation to this last proposal, Harding draws on law and economics scholarship to highlight that the 'distinctive strategy' of fiduciary law in guaranteeing conduct consistent with the requirements of trustworthiness is through setting general default rules.[91] This is in contradistinction to the alternative strategy of guaranteeing trustworthy conduct through specifically legally enforceable undertakings and specific systems for conduct monitoring. From law and economics analysis, as Harding points out, the 'general default rules' strategy as is characteristic of fiduciary law is more economically efficient than the alternative strategy of 'specifically contracted undertakings and monitoring systems', as it would be less costly to the parties.[92]

[86] ibid 90.
[87] ibid 94.
[88] ibid 96.
[89] ibid.
[90] ibid.
[91] ibid 98.
[92] In a similar vein, in respect of controlling company directors' conflicts of interest, Nolan has argued that adopting the 'general default rules' strategy – which is characteristic of the fiduciary law – is more efficient and practicable. See RC Nolan, 'The Legal Control of Directors' Conflicts of Interest in the United Kingdom: Non-executive Directors Following the Higgs Report' (2005) 6 *Theoretical Inquiries in Law* 413, 422–23.

ii. Reliance on Discretion in Data Collection, Use and Disclosure

Harding's analysis above is a rich resource from which to consider a tentative case for an equitable concept of 'information fiduciary'. First, reliance on discretion[93] may be used as a criterion to distinguish between mere information possessors who do not owe fiduciary duties and those who do. Indeed, reliance on discretion has been described as a core criterion to determine when fiduciary duties arise. In Paul Finn's terminology, this criterion is described as 'fiduciary powers'.[94] That one party is relying on the other to exercise discretion for his or her purposes may explain the oft-cited requirement of vulnerability and dependence.[95] Being put in a position to exercise discretion for another may also be interpreted as a voluntary undertaking to act for another's interests.[96] Accordingly, for the purpose of a traditional equitable construct, on the suggested generalised understanding, it is unnecessary to distinguish between trustee types of fiduciaries and non-trustee types of fiduciaries, and labelling the latter as being concerned with information sharing and safeguarding in the context of a relationship.

In the context of the collection of personal data by businesses, the mere act of collection and the consequent possession of the data does not turn the business into a fiduciary. Such conduct does not involve the exercise of discretion which is characterised by some degree of freedom in the making of a choice. In such a simple scenario, the core concern is with unauthorised collection, transfers and disclosure. The law of confidence, the tort law of misuse of private information (or analogous tort), the personal data protection legislation and contractual terms on privacy policy would be sufficient to provide the necessary protection. However, if the business (ie, the data controller) has some degree of discretion in respect of the use and disclosure of the data, fiduciary duties may arise as default general rules on how that discretion is to be exercised. In other words, the fiduciary relationship is fact-based as opposed to being status-based. In the case of consumers, for the reasons discussed above, it would be unrealistic to expect that a customer could rely on the contractarian model of protection. In fact, it is very likely that standard form contracts would stipulate highly generalised (or vague) terms of collection and use of the data principally because at the time of contracting, the business may not know clearly for what purpose the data may

[93] Following this criterion, it has been said that bare trustees – whose only duty is to hold the property for the beneficiary – do not owe fiduciary duties. See *Financial Management Inc v Associated Financial Planners Ltd* (2006) 367 WAC 70. See also PB Miller, 'The Fiduciary Relationship' in Gold and Miller (n 52) 77. *cf* R Flannigan, 'Bare Trustee – Fiduciary Obligation – Whether Bare Trustee Can Have Fiduciary Duty: *Financial Management Inc v Associated Financial Planners Ltd*' (2006–07) 26 *Estates, Trusts & Pensions Journal* 114.

[94] Finn (n 81) 3.

[95] *Hospital Products Pty Ltd v United States Surgical Corporation* (1984) 156 CLR 42,142 (Dawson J); *Lac Minerals Ltd v International Corona Resources Ltd* (1989) 61 DLR (4th) 14, 68–69 (Sopinka J). *cf* informational asymmetry, which may be another manifestation of vulnerability and dependence.

[96] *Bristol and West Building Society v Mothew* [1998] Ch 1, 18.

be used and what technological developments may facilitate that particular form of use.[97]

That there is discretion is insufficient for the imposition of fiduciary duties. Otherwise, all contracting parties who are conferred contractual discretions would find themselves owing fiduciary duties. In addition, the beneficiary must occupy a position in which he or she must rely on the fiduciary's exercise of discretion for his or her benefit. Harding, whose article was committed to illustrating the relationship between trust and fiduciary law, naturally could not delve into this point. In this connection, Paul Finn's analysis may be helpful:

> Where a person has his interests served by another, but has not himself agreed with that other the powers and duties to be exercised and discharged for his benefit, one finds reasons emerging for equity's intervention. If, in addition, he has not the general right to say how they are to be exercised and discharged for his benefit then the need for Equity's supervision becomes compelling. Here is the functionary who, within the limits of his powers and duties, is independent of, and not controlled by, the person for whose benefit he acts. In this independence, this freedom from immediate control, lies the final and decisive characteristic of the fiduciary office.
>
> …
>
> A person becomes a fiduciary through his independence in the position he occupies. If he serves a beneficiary who has not the general right to say how he wishes to be served then Equity steps in to ensure that the fiduciary does serve that beneficiary's interests. Though his position gives him autonomy Equity circumscribes that autonomy; it channels the direction of his activities.[98]

In the case of a trustee, the paradigmatic fiduciary, his or her duties and powers are derived from the trust deed, trust legislation and the general law, instead of a contract with the beneficiaries. The trustee thus owes fiduciary duties – which function to direct the trustee's activities – to the beneficiaries.

Turning to the context of a contract, if A is able to protect and advance his or her interests by agreement between themselves, Finn says that equitable intervention is unnecessary. However, in the case of a contract between a consumer and a digital business, the disparity in bargaining power between the parties would mean that the consumer is unable to make the necessary stipulations to protect or advance his or her own interests. In fact, the information asymmetry between the consumer and the online business in relation to the latter's technological capabilities for data processing would mean that the consumer could not, even if afforded the opportunity, adequately protect himself or herself through contract. Putting regulation to one side for now, there is one final difficulty to address: unlike trustees, directors, solicitors and agents who are appointed clearly

[97] There is a question of whether such a form of consent would satisfy the applicable data protection legislation. In the context where the GDPR applies, there is a question whether this form of drafting satisfies the conditions for consent under art 7.

[98] Finn (n 81) 13–14.

to serve and represent the beneficiaries, the same cannot be so straightforwardly said of the relationship between the online business and the consumer. The common law view of contract is that it concerns a self-regarding relationship – each contracting party is free to pursue his or her own interests.[99] However, that contract law facilitates self-interested pursuits does not mean that fiduciary law is incompatible with commercial exchange.[100] Indeed, it may be argued that fiduciary law supports commerce by ensuring certain standards that are necessary for fair commercial exchange would be complied with. Notably, in the context of our discussion, if we narrow our focus to only the protection of private information (including confidential information), general law and personal data protection legislations do impose obligations concerning privacy protection on the business. In this regard, a case may be made that the business is required by law to serve the privacy needs of the consumer and to exercise judgement and make decisions in a way that protects the consumers' privacy. In other words, other areas of law direct that such discretions are exercised for the consumer's benefit. A slightly different argument is that these businesses have a social responsibility arising from their power to protect the privacy of their consumers in the way in which they decide on how to use and whether to disclose the personal data collected. In the age of technological disruption and big data, a strong trusting relationship between an online business and its consumers is crucial for the functioning of certain social dealings as well as the progress of society. As Chamberlain points out, a traditional rationale of fiduciary obligations is to protect relationships that the society consider valuable.[101] This strand of argument may draw support from corporate social responsibility developments in the corporate world – businesses should not be driven by short-term profit; a long-term view of gaining consumers' trust and developing long-term relationships is in line with acting in the interests of the shareholders.

Proceeding on either line of argument, the undertaking to act in the consumer's interests in relation to privacy protection is not 'voluntary'. But this presents no real difficulty to finding that fiduciary duties arise because 'voluntariness' may not be present in all fiduciary relationships. For instance, in the context of an employee who is found to owe fiduciary duties by reason of the powers in his or her hands to affect the interests of the employer, it cannot be rightly said that he or she has *voluntarily* undertaken to act in the interests of the employer. In reality, the job scope of an employee is prescribed by the employer and the relevant powers might be conferred upon the employee after the signing of the employment contract. Further, in practical terms, on either line of argument, fiduciary regulation is introduced, as Balkin suggests,[102] to ensure accountable

[99] M Graziadei, 'Virtue and Utility' in Gold and Miller (n 52) 291.
[100] ibid 293.
[101] E Chamberlain, 'Revisiting Canada's Approach to Fiduciary Relationships', paper presented at the Seventh Biennial Conference on the Law of Obligations, Hong Kong, 15 July 2014.
[102] See discussion above at text accompanying n 79.

business practices in an age where a company's technological capabilities may increase exponentially, but which is usually not transparent (or even readily comprehensible) to the consumers.

iii. Interplay with Regulation

Thus far, our discussion has left data protection legislation out of the picture. If we bring it into the analysis, it becomes more complex. Introducing a private law solution at a time when regulation has already been put in place may prove to be tricky. Regulation may try to fill the entire void itself too rapidly and therefore inconsiderately, resulting in under-regulation or over-regulation. This is unlike a situation where private law solutions exist first to generate a body of case law to inform the direction of regulatory development.[103] As mentioned, regulatory approaches differ from jurisdiction to jurisdiction and may continue to evolve. For instance, the GDPR has opted for very specific rules and monitoring systems for personal data protection.[104] The costs of compliance for businesses are therefore very high. There are grave doubts as to whether companies affected are able to fully comply with the requirements. This leaves little room for discretion on the part of the business.[105] Equitable intervention is not particularly compelling and would in any event be very restricted in scope. By way of example, consent is an important basis for the lawful processing of data.[106] To ensure voluntary consent and readability, Article 7(2) prescribes that 'in the context of a written declaration which also concerns other matters, the request for consent shall be presented in a manner which is clearly distinguishable from other matters, in an intelligible and easily accessible form, using clear and plain language'. The requirements are very specific, with a focus on the form of seeking consent. However, it is not clear if they would achieve the purpose of obtaining meaningful consent, given the overload of consent transactions for online activities.

[103] For similar reasons, the English Law Commission decided not to intervene in the area of illegality and instead proposed that English courts should continue the trend of articulating underlying policy considerations so as to bring greater clarity to the law.

[104] In fact, the rules are overly prescriptive without being clear. On the data controller's obligation of 'data protection by design and by default', art 25 provides that: 'Taking into account the state of the art, the cost of implementation and nature, scope, context and purposes of processing as well as the risks of varying likelihood and severity for rights and freedoms of natural persons posed by the processing, the controller shall, both at the time of the determination of the means for processing and at the time of the processing itself, implement appropriate technical and organisational measures, such as pseudonymisation, which are designed to implement data-protection principles, such as data minimisation, in an effective manner and to integrate the necessary safeguards into the processing in order to meet the requirements of this Regulation and protect the rights of data subjects.' To know if one is GDPR-compliant, one may apply for the voluntary regime of certification (art 42), but it does not serve to shield the organisation from liability (art 42(4)).

[105] In Harding's terminology, the relationship does not entail a 'significant sphere of discretion': see Harding (n 83) 88.

[106] GDPR, art 6.

The Malaysian PDPA similarly adopts consent as the general basis for the collection, use, disclosure and processing of personal data.[107] The Malaysian legislation also requires that the data controller provides written notification to the data subject, amongst other information, of the purpose for which the personal data is collected and further processed, and the third parties to whom the data user discloses or may disclose the personal data.[108] The Malaysian PDPA is currently under review and the Personal Data Protection Commissioner has released a Public Consultation Paper[109] putting forward amendments that adopt some of the GDPR standards. For the purpose the present analysis, the question is whether legislative reform must necessarily take the GDPR route.[110]

By contrast, the Singapore Personal Data Protection Commission (hereinafter 'the Singapore PDPC') was recently reconsidering its regulatory approach and deliberating on introducing 'Notification of Purpose' as a basis for the collection, use and disclosure of personal data without the need to obtain express consent, but subject to the condition that it 'is not likely to have any adverse impact on the individual'.[111] The consideration of an alternative basis for the collection and use of personal data arises from the recognition that consent is not an effective authorisation mechanism from the perspective of self-determination[112] and that it is also economically inefficient. The notification of purpose basis for the collection, use and disclosure of personal data is now introduced into the PDPA in section 15A ('deemed consent by notification').[113] It has been explained that this new provision enables organisations to use the personal data of existing customers for new purposes by notifying the customers of the new purpose and giving them a reasonable period in which to opt out.[114] Section 15A uses the language of 'adverse effect' instead of 'adverse impact'. It is currently unclear as to what constitutes 'adverse effect'.[115] The PDPC's thinking appears to rely on safeguards – such as providing an opt-out to the data subjects[116] and requiring

[107] Malaysian PDPA, ss 6 and 8.

[108] ibid s 7(b) and (e).

[109] Public Consultation Paper No 01/2020: Review of Personal Data Protection Act 2010 (Act 709), www.pdp.gov.my/jpdpv2/assets/2020/02/Public-Consultation-Paper-on-Review-of-Act-709_V4.pdf.

[110] Adopting the GDPR standards may be a strategic move for jurisdictions where many of its businesses deal with data subjects in the EU, in view of the extraterritorial application of the GDPR (see GDPR, art 3(2)).

[111] www.pdpc.gov.sg/-/media/Files/PDPC/PDF-Files/Legislation-and-Guidelines/PDPC-Response-to-Feedback-for-Public-Consultation-on-Approaches-to-Managing-Personal-Data-in-the-Dig.pdf.

[112] An overload of consent transactions would result in 'consent fatigue' and 'consent desensitization'. See BW Shermer et al, 'The Crisis of Consent: How Stronger Legal Protection May Lead to Weaker Consent in Data Protection' (2014) 16 *Ethics and Information Technology* 171; M Yip, 'Personal Data Protection Act 2012: Understanding the Consent Obligation' (2017) *Personal Data Protection Digest* 266.

[113] This provision, together with other amendments to the PDPA, came into force on 1 February 2021.

[114] Opening Speech by Mr S Iswaran, Minister for Communications and Information, at the Second Reading of the Personal Data Protection (Amendment) Bill 2020 (2 November 2020) [40].

[115] Industry feedback raised the question as to whether the collection, use or disclosure of personal data for the purpose of marketing would constitute 'adverse impact'.

[116] PDPA, s 15A(2)(b) and (4)(b)(iii).

the organisation to assess the likelihood of adverse effect on the data subject, reduce the likelihood of adverse effect on him or her and mitigate the adverse effect on him or her[117] – to protect the data subject. However, these safeguards do not provide clarification as to what constitutes 'adverse effect', which determines whether an organisation may or may not collect, use or disclose personal data by notification of purpose.

Is there any room and value for introducing the 'default general rules' of fiduciary law? This would depend on the regulatory approach, especially how it would develop in the future. In the case of section 15A of the PDPA, the fiduciary duties may help to flesh out what 'adverse effect' means. For example, the business may not use the data for the purpose of generating unauthorised profits (the 'no-profit' rule). To retain these profits, the business must seek the informed consent of the consumer whose data it intends to use. As such, profitable advertising using consumers' data cannot be carried out merely on the basis that there has been 'notification of purpose'. Further, the business may not use the consumer's data in a way which would undermine the performance of its duties owed to the consumer (the 'no-conflict' rule). For instance, the company may not disclose the consumer's data to a third party or process the said data for the third party's use without the consumer's prior consent, based on its pre-existing obligations owed to a third party. Moving onwards to more controversial terrain, assuming that prescriptive fiduciary duties such as the duties of good faith and loyalty exist,[118] these duties could dictate that the use and disclosure of data on the basis of 'notification of purpose' is permitted where it would promote the performance of the duties owed to the consumer[119] or enhance the future experience of the consumer. The point is that general default rules supplied by the fiduciary law would obviate the requirement for very specific drafting of conditions and requirements.

If we turn to consider the GDPR, an important basis for the processing of data is 'consent'. In the context of jurisdictions that may not be inclined to fully follow the GDPR approach, the strategic regulatory approach of fiduciary law may provide some inspiration for a less restrictive/less extensive and cost-efficient regime. There are two ways in which fiduciary law may supply that inspiration. First, courts recognise that digital businesses may owe fiduciary duties to their consumers if they have discretion in terms of how to use the personal data collected, and fiduciary law works alongside a statutory regime that tolerates discretion. Second, this may be done by crafting and interpreting legislative standards based on or borrowing from the fiduciary rules. Such an approach allows for greater flexibility and may better cater to the need to balance between privacy protection and innovation facilitation.

[117] ibid s 15A(5).

[118] *Bristol and West Building Society v Mothew* (n 96) 18.

[119] For example, an understanding of the consumer's preferences may improve the services that are to be delivered to that particular consumer.

iv. Other Benefits

Viewing fiduciary law through Harding's lens, the imposition of fiduciary duties would provide the consumer with the assurance that he or she needs to rely on the business' exercise of discretion on how to use and whether to disclose his or her personal data. This is generally in line with the emerging trend of encouraging business accountability in data privacy practices, so as to foster consumer trust and confidence.[120] The instrumental value of fiduciary law is amplified in the context of the digital economy.

From the perspective of remedies, a fiduciary solution may afford stronger protection to consumers in respect of third-party participation in the breach, most notably through the doctrine of dishonest assistance. For breach of fiduciary obligations as well as accessory liability, equitable compensation, account of profits and proprietary relief could be available, provided that the qualifying conditions are satisfied.

B. Extrapolating from the Doctor–Patient Relationship

We now turn to consider the second route of developing an equitable concept of information fiduciary. This is, by comparison, the more difficult route. Two preliminary issues must first be dealt with before we can move on to analyse the possibility of constructing an information fiduciary by extrapolating from the doctor–patient relationship.[121] The first issue relates to the conceptual hurdle that doctors are not universally recognised as owing fiduciary duties across the common law world. In the famous English case of *Sidaway v Bethlem Royal Hospital Governors*, Lord Scarman said that 'there is no comparison to be made between the relationship of doctor and patient with that of solicitor and client, trustee and *cestui qui* trust or other relationships treated in equity as of a fiduciary character'.[122] However, scholars have argued that English courts should reconsider their stance for a number of reasons.[123] First, courts in other Commonwealth jurisdictions

[120] Under the GDPR, compliance certification under art 42 is arguably to help organisations build consumer trust. A similar regime has been established in Singapore by the regulator: Data Protection Trustmark Certification. See further E Denham, 'Transparency, Trust and Progressive Data Protection' (29 September 2016).

[121] Balkin acknowledges that there are key differences between doctors and lawyers on the one hand and digital businesses on the other. For example, the latter are in possession of computational power and AI capacities 'to make predictions and engage in forms of manipulation' that the former have never possessed. Also, digital companies such as Facebook do not perform the same kind of service as doctors and lawyers do. See Balkin (n 74) 15.

[122] *Sidaway v Bethlem Royal Hospital Governors* [1985] AC 871, 884. See also the first instance judgment of Popplewell J in *R v Mid-Glamorgan FHSA ex parte Martin* [1993] PIQR 426, 438, which concerned a patient's access to medical records.

[123] See, for example, P Bartlett, 'Doctors as Fiduciaries: Equitable Regulation to the Doctor–Patient Relationship' (1997) 5 *Medical Law Review* 193; S Ost, 'Breaching the Sexual Boundaries in the

have recognised, to varying degrees, that doctors owe fiduciary duties.[124] Second, reluctance on the part of English courts may be traced to their inclination to view fiduciary duties through the 'a paradigm of trusts of property'[125] or 'as a function of property law and equitable limitations on ownership'.[126] Third, the doctor–patient relationship is a fertile ground for opportunism (in respect of material or non-material interests) and/or conflicts, thus necessitating fiduciary regulation in specific applications.[127] Finally, the relationship of trust between doctors and patients is generally emphasised as one of the main reasons for equitable intervention. As such, English judicial reluctance to embracing doctors as fiduciaries in respect of certain aspects of their job scope is not entirely insurmountable. But it does mean that the doctor–patient relationship is not an entirely secured basis for innovation.

The second preliminary issue is whether we should extrapolate from the solicitor–client relationship. This is a well-established fiduciary relationship and similarly entails a professional acting on behalf of a party who shares confidential information in the course of the relationship. My answer to this question is rather straightforward. The doctor–patient relationship shares more critical similarities with the relationship between a business and a consumer. First, the client is in a stronger position than the patient or the consumer. As Bartlett astutely points out: 'Unless inconsistent with his or her duty to the court, the lawyer acts on the instructions of the client, even when the instructions do not reflect the lawyer's view of the client's best interest.'[128] Indeed, the client's control of the legal matter is particularly strong if the client is a wealthy and educated individual or a large corporate body. Second, the ways in which doctors may use information relating to the patient are similar to activities that may be undertaken by the online business, for example, using the patient's medical records to conduct research that may yield financial benefits or inducing patient consent for treatment for which the doctor receives undisclosed commissions. And Bartlett also reminds us that in modern society, medical professionals work 'in a world increasingly approximating business' and we must discard the rose-tinted view of the benevolent country doctor.[129] Finally, lawyers are considered fiduciaries by their status; doctors are, as argued by scholars, fiduciaries not by virtue of their representative capacity; rather, doctors owe limited fiduciary duties, on an ad hoc basis, in relation to part of their work scope or in certain circumstances. The model

Doctor–Patient Relationship: Should English Law Recognise Fiduciary Duties?' (2016) 24 *Medical Law Review* 206.

124 Australia: *Breen v Williams* (1996) 186 CLR 71 (no fiduciary duty to disclose medical records to patients); New Zealand: *Smith v Auckland Hospital Board* [1965] NZLR 191; Canada: *Norberg v Wynrib* [1992] 2 SCR 226; the US: *Moore v Regents of the University of California* (1990) 793 P 2d 479.

125 Bartlett (n 123) 198.

126 Ost (n 123) 223.

127 Scholars do not agree as to the proper context for equitable intervention.

128 Bartlett (n 123) 195.

129 Bartlett (n 123) 224.

of equitable intervention for the doctor–patient relationship (if accepted) is thus closer to the model of equitable intervention for the relationship of an online business and its consumers.

Having established that the doctor–patient relationship is not an inappropriate or implausible frame of reference, it is worth emphasising that scholarship advocating for the imposition of fiduciary duties on a doctor proceeds from the basis that English law should depart from a proprietary view of fiduciary law based on the trust paradigm. Following such a line of analysis could result in a fragmented rationalisation of fiduciary law based on functional characteristics. Such an approach calls into question the utility of generalised theories of fiduciary law. In respect of doctors, Bartlett said that: 'The contexts most likely to give rise to fiduciary issues between doctors and patients are based in either the use or availability of information about the patient, or issues surrounding pecuniary compensation of doctors.'[130] In respect of issues of information, Bartlett identified that there could be equitable obligations[131] in relation to disclosure of records, risks as well as facts that would be in the patient's interests to know (a wider obligation of candour).[132] Of course, it remains controversial as to whether fiduciaries owe a prescriptive duty of disclosure.[133] However, Bartlett's arguments are directed towards a refreshed look at fiduciary obligations arising in the doctor–patient relationship detached from the trust/proprietary perspective. As such, that not all fiduciaries owe a duty of disclosure (candour) does not defeat his point that a doctor may owe such a duty. In relation to issues of collateral profits (which a doctor receives from the medical industry itself), Bartlett said that this is an area appropriate for fiduciary regulation in view of the conflicts.

Bartlett helpfully distinguished the tort of negligence (which is a way to regulate professional standards) from fiduciary regulation. He argued that the tort of negligence is not concerned with intentional conduct, but fiduciary law deals with intentional conduct by a doctor that would harm the elements of trust and confidence inherent in the doctor–patient relationship.[134] Fiduciary duties do not only arise on the occurrence of some form of wrongdoing on the part of the doctor or damage to the patient.

[130] ibid 199.

[131] He excluded issues of confidentiality from his analysis.

[132] Bartlett cites the speech of Sir John Donaldson MR in *Naylor v Preston Health Authority* [1987] 1 WLR 958, 967.

[133] *Item Software (UK) Ltd v Fassihi* [2004] EWCA Civ 1244. Later cases generally confined *Item Software* to the context of directors: see, eg, *GHLM Trading Ltd v Maroo* [2012] EWHC 61 (Ch) [192]–[195]; *Stupples v Stupples & Co (High Wycombe) Ltd* [2012] EWHC 1226 (Ch) [59]. *cf ODL Securities Ltd v McGrath* [2013] EWHC 1865 (Comm). The reasoning in *Item Software* was also rejected in the Australian case of *P & V Industries v Porto* (2006) 14 VR 1, 24 ACLC 573, [2006] VSC 131, BC200601896. As for Singapore, the Singapore Court of Appeal has affirmed that an employee may owe the fiduciary duty of disclosure: see *Centre for Laser and Aesthetic Medicine Pte Ltd v GPK Clinic (Orchard) Pte Ltd* [2018] 1 SLR 180.

[134] Such elements are inherent in the doctor–patient relationship in the sense that these elements are necessary in order for the relationship to exist and produce the intended social benefits.

Transposed to the context of a consumer's relationship with an online business, other than commercial exploitation of consumer data for self-interests which may be reined in by the fiduciary principles of no conflict and no profit, should the business come under a duty of disclosure? More specifically, does the business have a duty to disclose data records[135] and to be forthright with all the relevant facts (for instance, in the event of a data breach that would result in an adverse impact on the data subject)? On one view, these duties are relevant and important for the proper functioning of the relationship, as confirmed by data protection regimes such as the GDPR, which has made provisions for the data subject's right of access[136] and the mandatory obligation of data breach notification.[137] Alternative prescription in equity may provide avenues to obtain different remedies since regulations are presently focused on administrative fines and compensation. The converse view is that regulatory prescription is sufficient and there is no obvious need for equitable intervention. This latter view may be strengthened on the basis of certainty: it is better to spell out clearly what needs to be disclosed as opposed to leaving it to the more general duty of disclosure founded in equity. However, an important advantage of allowing prescription of similar duties in equity is that equitable duties are articulated in more general terms. It could therefore cater for new situations presently unforeseen by regulators – what new risks/relevant facts would need to be disclosed to data subjects as technology continues to advance.

V. Conclusion

The analysis above has discussed two possible bases to introduce fiduciary duties on online businesses in their capacity as data controllers. Admittedly, neither route is free from problems. Doctrinal purists may even be dismayed by the stretching of the fiduciary doctrine in a way that would fundamentally undermine a single, principled explanation of the entire fiduciary terrain. Although the discussion is focused on developing a fiduciary model of personal data/privacy protection in Singapore and Malaysia, the arguments are of more general application to other common law jurisdictions. More critically, the discussion highlights a number of contemporary issues concerning the future of private law. First, it cannot be denied that modern society is increasingly being regulated by legislation. Traditional fiduciaries such as trustees, directors and lawyers are also regulated by statutes which curtail and, in some areas, even override fiduciary regulation. Is there any role for equitable intervention in new spaces that are created by modern living? Whilst

[135] In other words, from the perspective of the data subject, it relates to the right of access.
[136] GDPR, art 15.
[137] ibid art 34. Article 14(1) provides that: 'When the personal data breach is likely to result in a high risk to the rights and freedoms of natural persons, the controller shall communicate the personal data breach to the data subject without undue delay.'

there is a great need for certainty, predictability and doctrinal coherence, how do we balance that against the competing needs of innovation, flexibility and justice? The theme of reinvention also underlines other recent attempts to extend private law doctrines (or draw inspiration therefrom) to regulate the proper use of data, such as the propertisation of data and data trust.

Second, whilst the legislature and the courts insist that they each have their distinct functions and strengths, there is a need for a closer partnership in solving new problems. Chamberlain, in defence of the Canadian approach towards fiduciary obligations, describes the Supreme Court of Canada as simply being less timid than its counterparts elsewhere in the common law world, and has been willing to apply the spirit of fiduciary obligation in ways to perceived social needs.[138] Perhaps the North American jurisprudence not only teaches us what fiduciary law can do given some reinvention, but also what courts can do when society is faced with new challenges. Importantly, the flexibility that is inherent in equity can help to perform gap-filling in the law in two ways: first, it may fill gaps left by statutes and the common law; and, second, it can fill the gaps between statutory intervention. Equitable intervention in new instances of injustice that are not yet addressed by regulation may provide inspiration for regulatory reform. Judicial law-making is problem-solving through experience – showing what works and what does not. At an appropriate juncture, regulation may then take over to codify or improve upon the common law solutions.

Third, the spirit of fiduciary law or equity in general, characterised by default general standards, also shows us that contemporary problems need not always be resolved through 'hard and fast rules', specific monitoring and overly detailed prescription. Fiduciary standards may inspire regulatory standards and commercial best practices.

Postscript

The Singapore Academy of Law's Law Reform Committee published the 'Report on Civil Liability for Misuse of Private Information' in December 2020, which recommends the introduction of a new statutory tort of misuse of private information.

[138] Chamberlain (n 101).

PART II

AI, Technology and Private Law

7

Regulating Autonomous Vehicles

Liability Paradigms and Value Choices

CHEN SIYUAN*

I. Setting the Context

In technological terms, this decade hardly resembles the last: mass and private communications are now dominated by a small group of online social media platforms; spending currency is becoming entirely electronic and digital; unmanned and stabilised aerial imaging has become affordable and accessible, to name but a few prominent examples. A significant contributing factor to this change has been the unprecedented developments in creating systems that can function with minimal human intervention and process new datasets quickly to improve its decision-making abilities, although at the same time, concerns have been raised as to whether these technical complexities may obscure accountability when mistakes or malfunctions occur. The next decade may well see the widespread implementation of another application of such systems: self-driving vehicles or automated vehicles (AVs), which are supposed to help societies achieve greater transportation efficiencies, road safety for road users and overall economic productivity.[1]

On a theoretical level, it may seem that AVs do not represent a very big step forward from where we are, considering that some of their core technologies are already being used by human-operated cars today, such as sensors, GPS and image capture. There is also already some degree of automation technology that has been around for some time in certain cars, for instance, in the form of cruise

* This research is supported by the National Research Foundation, Singapore under its Emerging Areas Research Projects Funding Initiative. Any opinions, findings and conclusions, or recommendations expressed in this material are those of the author's and do not reflect the views of National Research Foundation, Singapore.

[1] See, for instance ZDNet, 'How AVs Could Save over 350k Lives in the US and Millions Worldwide' (1 February 2018), www.zdnet.com/article/how-autonomous-vehicles-could-save-over-350k-lives-in-the-us-and-millions-worldwide. To be clear, this article focuses on AVs that are to be used by individual consumers. See also SAL Law Reform Committee, *Report on the Attribution of Civil Liability for Accidents Involving Autonomous Cars* (2020).

control and self-parking. However, in practical, legal terms, one can imagine how the eventual complete removal of a human driver in the equation[2] changes everything for regulators, manufacturers and road users. This is especially so in the context of road traffic accidents that result in significant damage to property or persons – perhaps the most visceral fear of the public when it comes to mainstream acceptance of AVs being used for daily travel, which is now considered an inevitability.[3]

Specifically, when it comes to civil claims (in order to keep the analysis manageable, criminal claims will not be considered), existing laws that regulate road traffic accidents are universally predicated on the longstanding assumption that a human driver is behind the wheel, controlling all critical aspects of the vehicle's operation – this is so regardless of whether any attempt is made by the putative compensator to eventually locate fault on at least one driver (and, indeed, any other party).[4] Everyone knows the drill when an accident occurs – what evidence to preserve, who to contact and when to expect compensation.[5] But in the driverless context, absent a human driver as a starting point, one might think that if any fault is to be located, it could conceivably fall, albeit not in all instances, on the manufacturer of the AVs (or the manufacturer of its constituent parts, such as the software and hardware)[6] – this seems to be the most plausible conceptual framework to take things forward.

However, anyone with a basic appraisal of the technology powering AVs can immediately see how it might be challenging, especially evidentially, in practice to prove a breach of the standard of care if one builds a claim around negligence. For instance, how does one show that a decision made by the vehicle is traceable to a design decision? AVs constantly create and process a lot of data, and making sense of it by parsing through endless lines of code post-mortem (assuming access is even granted) would be neither expedient nor economical – and this is without even contemplating the post-mortem analysis being completely obscured by machine learning just yet.[7] The prospect of contributory negligence compounds the complexity of the fact-finding process. Even if the seemingly most viable alternative route of product liability is taken – quite apart from how this domain is not particularly well developed in many common law jurisdictions – notwithstanding a different conception of fault from negligence, there might just be similarly great

[2] See the classification system of the Society of Automotive Engineers.

[3] See generally 'Tesla's Latest Autopilot Death Looks Just Like a Prior Crash' *Wired* (16 May 2019), www.wired.com/story/teslas-latest-autopilot-death-looks-like-prior-crash.

[4] See also J Soh, 'Towards a Control-Centric Account of Tortious Liability for Automated Vehicles' (2021) 26 *Torts Law Journal* 221.

[5] See General Insurance Association, 'Dos and Don'ts Following an Accident' (2019), https://gia.org.sg/motor-insurance/22-premium-renewal-of-policy/349-dos-and-don-ts-following-an-accident.html.

[6] Other potential causes of the accident include other road users and third parties that have a role in ensuring that the AVs function properly.

[7] See generally L Alvarez Leon, 'Counter-mapping the Spaces of Autonomous Driving' (2019) 92 *Cartographic Perspectives* 10.

evidential difficulties in connecting the purported defect to the accident. In this light, would something less conventional, such as no-fault liability, be more appropriate, but implementable only with great attendant changes in societal attitudes? The purpose of this chapter is to answer these very questions. In so doing, it considers and compares the experience of four (Asia-Pacific) countries which are at different stages of their regulatory efforts regarding AVs involved in road traffic accidents.

The first country to be examined is Singapore, which, despite being touted as one of the leading jurisdictions to have promoted the testing of AVs in a variety of environments, still does not have any concrete regulatory or legal framework for the wider implementation of such technology. Further, much of what has been happening behind the (governmental) scenes has remained firmly behind the scenes. One assumes, then, that there is quiet confidence that the technology is stable and reliable, and presents no practical legal problem while testing gets ramped up. The second country is Australia, which appears to be heading in the direction of some degree of codification (of regulation), and there is also evidence aplenty that many efforts have been taken to engage and consult all relevant stakeholders thoroughly and publicly. This suggests, tentatively at least, that the prospect of meaningfully regulating autonomous vehicles is not an illusory one. The third country is New Zealand, which currently favours an expedient, lighter-touch, but clearly egalitarian approach that favours protecting potential victims over manufacturers and users with respect to the testing of AVs. However, it is unclear if the same approach would be taken once they move beyond the testing phase, but as it is, it would be a clear example of focusing on the practical (ensuring victims are compensated without questions) rather than the legally intricate. The fourth country is Japan, which is already a major player in the automobile industry, and AVs would represent an inevitable next step in its evolution. Though it has not settled on a regulatory framework, what sets it apart is that the law reform process has largely been driven by academic experts.

Yet, this comparative endeavour should not preclude us from looking beyond the Asia-Pacific. The UK, which already has what it considers to be pioneering legislation in place,[8] would form more than a useful marker for additional comparison, as would the European Union (EU), which has essentially endorsed an existing strict form of product liability as the way forward for much of the continent. As will be seen, it may well be down to what each society values the most when electing a liability paradigm to take things forward, rather than which liability framework is the most intricate or robust. At the same time, the expression and enforcement of these values would invariably be influenced by the relationship dynamics the government has with its people and the weight given to driverless transport being an inexorable feature of the future.

[8] The Automated and Electric Vehicles Act 2018.

II. Singapore: Still at a Regulatory Standstill with No Discernible Movements

Singapore's foray into AVs began a decade ago in 2010, but it was only in around 2014 that a proper blueprint on how the technology would be rolled out was introduced by the government.[9] Legislative or even regulatory change since then has been rather incremental. In 2017, Parliament amended the Road Traffic Act[10] to allow corporations to have trials with AV technology. At that point, the Singapore government's position on its general attitude towards regulation in this sphere was as follows:[11]

- The government wanted to adopt a balanced, light-touch regulatory stance that protected the safety of passengers and road users, but ensured that autonomous technologies could flourish.[12]
- Because autonomous technologies challenged the very notion of human responsibility that was at the core of Singapore's current road and criminal laws, developers of these technologies would be obligated to provide enough measures to ensure their safe operation on the roads.
- The traditional basis of claims for negligence might not work so well where there is no driver in control of a vehicle, but the courts might draw references from auto-pilot systems for airplanes and maritime vessels, and product liability law.
- Since issues of liability for AVs could be resolved through proof of fault and existing common law, all test AVs must log travel data to facilitate accident investigation and liability claims.
- AVs were expected to be able to operate on existing roads with minimal changes to existing road infrastructure.
- Questions regarding insurance, data sharing/intellectual property were still being studied by the authorities.

The amendments to the Road Traffic Act, which were passed without objection in that same year, stipulated the following requirements for self-driving cars that were approved by the government for trial on public roads:[13]

- A person cannot use or undertake any trial of AV technology on any road unless properly authorised to do so and with liability insurance in place.

[9] See Smart Nation Singapore, 'AVs' (2 May 2019), www.smartnation.sg/what-is-smart-nation/initiatives/Transport/autonomous-vehicles.

[10] (Cap 276, 2004 Rev Ed).

[11] See Singapore Parliamentary Debates, Official Report (7 February 2017) vol 94, 86–93.

[12] A similar attitude was espoused in Parliament when unmanned aerial vehicles (UAVs) became mainstream sometime in 2015, but the government has since effectively outlawed the consumer use of such technology through executive action. The use of personal mobility devices (PMDs) suffered a similar fate.

[13] Road Traffic (Amendment) Act 2017 (Bill 10 of 2017) cls 3, 6; Road Traffic (Autonomous Motor Vehicles) Rules 2017, ss 4, 7, 9, 14, 16–20.

The Land Transport Authority oversees the approval process and can require approved vehicles to undergo further tests.

- Any such person must ensure that the vehicle is functioning and maintained properly at all times.
- Any such person must ensure that the vehicle is installed with a data recorder capable of storing information when the vehicle is being used; this data must be in digital format and must include information such as date, time, location, speed, front- and rear-facing imaging, and must be kept for at least three years.
- Any such person has a duty to keep records and notify any incidents and accidents.
- The vehicle must have a failure alert system that allows the driver to take immediate manual control of the vehicle when a failure of the autonomous system or emergency is detected.
- Nobody is allowed to hinder or obstruct the carrying out of the use of autonomous motor vehicles.
- The violation of any of the above could result in substantial fines.

These amendments did not exactly reflect that light-touch approach as desired by the government, but they did leave many potential issues unaddressed, presumably to be revisited at a later time. But despite an increase in the number of tests that were approved, Singapore still does not have any new laws[14] for AVs that are used either outside trials or designated zones (such as fully autonomous shuttle buses plying the campus roads of a couple of universities as well as resorts)[15] and no timeframe on when such laws would materialise has been given either. The only meaningful point of reference remains the aforementioned amendments to the Road Traffic Act, which even with their limited treatment of self-driving cars clearly (but understandably) prioritise safety and accountability, and unmistakably reflect a highly cautious approach.[16] If there is anything more that is brewing on the regulatory or legislative front, there is no publicly available information on this yet.

If one were to surmise the reason for this impasse, Singapore, like many other jurisdictions, is waiting for major jurisdictions to produce substantial laws so that it can study them and weigh up the pros and cons before it makes its next move. This is understandable considering that the island city-state is extremely highly urbanised with a great density of roads and road users. Reforming the law in this context would require not only legal experts, but the input of the best computer scientists

[14] In 2019, Technical Reference 68 was released by Enterprise Singapore to provide technical guidance on automated driving, but dictated no legal rule or policy.

[15] See also 'Self-Driving Shuttle Bus Service on Sentosa from Next Week' *The Straits Times* (21 August 2019), www.straitstimes.com/singapore/transport/self-driving-shuttle-bus-service-on-sentosa-from-next-week. For those vehicles that are no longer used as part of a trial, one imagines that they would be governed by contractual arrangements with the Land Transport Authority of Singapore (LTA).

[16] Reference can also be made to Personal Data Protection Commission, 'A Proposed Model Artificial Intelligence Governance Framework' (January 2020), www.pdpc.gov.sg/-/media/files/pdpc/pdf-files/resource-for-organisation/ai/sgmodelaigovframework2.pdf.

and engineers too. In the meantime, consistent with its longstanding mandate to make decisions on the behest of its citizenry, wide-ranging road trials continue to be implemented even while a broader legal framework remains far from emerging. Since the trials can only take place after the government is extremely satisfied on safety standards and insurance coverage, they do not present undue risks.

However, in not adopting a proactive and pre-emptive approach towards regulation, the complication of assigning liability based on existing laws when a self-driving car is involved in a traffic accident is also obviated – the only self-driving cars that are permitted on the roads are those that have been approved, and presumably mandatory insurance is presented as a neat solution (or compromise) in those controlled circumstances. There is no need – yet – to rethink or reformulate road traffic laws or the laws on negligence, product liability or some form of strict liability. Have other jurisdictions done much more?

III. Australia: Years of Consultation Preceding the 2020 Legislative Agenda

Australia, like Singapore, has yet to pass any comprehensive laws or regulations concerning self-driving cars specifically (though the target set for this is 2021),[17] but what is markedly different is that its National Transport Commission (NTC), following several rounds of public discussions that began a few years ago, has issued a fairly substantial policy paper outlining possible regulatory approaches (as regards liability) that could be taken.[18] The NTC believes that the following should be reflected in whatever new set of laws is created for cars that are at least partially automated and used by private individuals:[19]

- An automated driving system (ADS)[20] must be properly approved by a safety assurance system[21] before it is allowed to perform dynamic

[17] NTC, 'Automated Vehicles in Australia' (1 July 2019), www.ntc.gov.au/roads/technology/automated-vehicles-in-australia.

[18] The main topics that were not part of the paper's terms of reference should also be noted: data recording, data sharing, privacy and criminal liability: see NTC, 'Changing Driving Laws to Support Automated Vehicles' (May 2018), www.ntc.gov.au/sites/default/files/assets/files/NTC%20Policy%20Paper%20-%20Changing%20driving%20laws%20to%20support%20automated%20vehicles.pdf. The data and privacy aspects were covered in NTC, 'Regulating Government Access to C-ITS and Automated Vehicle Data' (September 2018), www.ntc.gov.au/sites/default/files/assets/files/NTC%20Discussion%20Paper%20-%20Regulating%20government%20access%20to%20C-ITS%20and%20automated%20vehicle%20data.pdf.

[19] NTC, 'Changing Driving Laws to Support Automated Vehicles' (May 2018), www.ntc.gov.au/sites/default/files/assets/files/NTC%20Discussion%20Paper%20-%20Changing%20driving%20laws%20to%20support%20automated%20vehicles.pdf.

[20] This is the hardware and software that are collectively capable of performing the entire dynamic driving task on a sustained basis.

[21] This (entity) regulates the safety of an ADS will provide assurance that an ADS can safely perform the dynamic driving task. See also National Transport Commission, 'Safety Assurance for Automated

driving tasks.[22] The proposed criteria against which an ADS entity (ADSE)[23] is required to submit a statement of compliance include those relating to operational design domain,[24] human–machine interface, minimal risk condition,[25] system upgrades, cybersecurity, and education and training.

- The ADSE should be responsible for the actions of an ADS when it is engaged because an ADSE has the most control over the ADS; however, it should not be responsible for things it cannot control (such as non-dynamic driving tasks).
- If an ADS is operating at conditional automation, readiness-to-drive obligations should be imposed on the fallback-ready user[26] (but not a passenger) who must take over the driving task at the request of the ADS or where there is system failure; such a user must remain sufficiently vigilant, hold the appropriate licence, comply with general driver obligations and should not be permitted to engage in secondary activities.
- The safety risks of dedicated AVs[27] need to be mitigated through obligations on the ADSE.

As far as the appropriate insurance mechanism is concerned, Australia foresees two main issues absent law reform.[28] First, people injured or killed in an ADS crash may not have access to compensation under existing motor insurance schemes for human drivers. Second, existing motor insurance laws do not contemplate ADS-driven cars, require fault to be proven for compensation to be paid and are designed to cover situations caused by human error and not product faults. The options that Australia has put on the table are as follows:[29]

- To rely on the existing framework, although motor insurance may not provide coverage in certain situations. When that happens, injured parties may have to litigate under consumer law, contract law or tort law.
- To exclude injuries caused by ADS from existing motor insurance schemes.

Driving Systems' (November 2018), www.ntc.gov.au/sites/default/files/assets/files/NTC-decision-regulation-impact-statement-safety-assurance-for-automated-driving-systems.pdf.

[22] This refers to the operational and tactical functions required to operate the car in on-road traffic (steering, speed and so forth). This may be contrasted with strategic driving tasks, such as where and when to travel, and route selection.

[23] This may be the manufacturer or registered operator of the car.

[24] This refers to the specific conditions under which an ADS is designed to function.

[25] This refers to a condition to which the user or an ADS may bring the car to reduce the risk of a crash when the ADS reaches the limit of its operational design domain.

[26] This refers to human in the car with conditional automation who can operate it and who is receptive to requests from ADS to intervene and evident dynamic driving task performance-relevant system failures.

[27] This refers to a car that has no manual controls, which means the dynamic driving task is always performed by the ADS.

[28] NTC, 'Motor Accident Injury Insurance and Automated Vehicles' (October 2018), https://www.ntc.gov.au/sites/default/files/assets/files/NTC%20Discussion%20Paper%20-%20Motor%20Accident%20Injury%20Insurance%20and%20Automated%20Vehicles.pdf.

[29] ibid.

- To extend existing motor insurance coverage to include injuries caused by ADS, which appears to be the preferred option for now. This can be done by either shifting costs from manufacturers under product liability to vehicle operators and insurers under motor insurance schemes or creating a national reinsurance pool from compulsory contributions from all parties who could be responsible for an ADS malfunction.
- To create a purpose-built scheme for self-driving cars where premiums could be paid on a per vehicle basis. The scheme should preferably cover liabilities for injuries caused by both driver negligence and product failure, since fully automated systems might not be implemented just yet.
- To go the way of single insurer, which is to say that where an ADS causes an accident, the insurer would be able to pursue a claim against the manufacturer and the personal injury costs of ADS failures would be privately underwritten.

Like Singapore, Australia is clearly concerned about safety standards, accountability and compensation. But unlike Singapore, there is now at least a menu of options to choose from going forward. The NTC has also been proactive in its analyses and suggestions, despite the obvious complexities arising in this particular intersection of law and technology. The points it has highlighted for further research reflect what consumers might be most concerned about, which have tended to revolve around compensation or insurance coverage. The reform attempt is certainly forward-looking, though whether there would be an eventual legislative product would only be known a couple of years from now. The advantage of this approach is that the reform process is better immunised from changes in government – an executive entity is able to discharge its mandate without regard for that variable (as it should, some might argue). The ball is then placed in the legislature's court to give effect to the recommendations.

IV. New Zealand: One Scheme to Rule Them All

We turn now to Australia's neighbour, New Zealand. New Zealand's existing motor vehicle liability system is already unique in being one of the few no-fault liability systems in use around the world.[30] The Accident Compensation Corporation (ACC) is a government body that handles all claims for personal injuries, including injuries not caused by motor accidents.[31] Anyone, regardless of the circumstances leading to their personal injury, has coverage (this also means they essentially relinquish their right to sue the parties at fault). Funds for motor accident injury pay-outs come out from the ACC's Motor Vehicle Account. This account is funded

[30] See generally P Foley, 'New Zealand's World-Leading No-Fault Accident Compensation Scheme' (2008) 51(1) *Japan Medical Association Journal* 58.

[31] See generally ACC, 'What Your Levies Pay for' (December 2018), www.acc.co.nz/about-us/how-levies-work/what-your-levies-pay.

by levies on petrol as well as motor vehicle licensing fees. Seeking compensation is not meant to be a cumbersome process, and the longstanding status of the ACC implies that there is public buy-in into this method of fund creation.

No-fault liability systems are not driver- or party-centric, but accident- or event-centric. In light of this, New Zealand's Ministry of Transport (MOT) has stated in its published guidelines for the testing of self-driving cars that 'a particular advantage of testing AVs in New Zealand is that our legislation does not explicitly require a vehicle to have a driver present for it to be used on the road. So long as any testing is carried out safely, a truly driverless vehicle may be tested on public roads today'.[32] Consistent with this fairly laissez-faire approach, in 2019, the MOT published a brief five-step guide on an approved testing process: make contact with the Ministry; determine the vehicle and certification requirements; determine the licence class for the operator; submit a safety management plan; and apply for a trade plate.[33] The engagement with the government is bilateral, but facilitative (and clear).

Flowing from this, there is no apparent legal obstacle to testing self-driving cars, even fully autonomous ones, on New Zealand roads.[34] Approved users simply have to ensure that they do not impede traffic or reduce the efficiency of the network.[35] Should an accident occur, the injured parties may simply make claims, through their medical providers, from the ACC. The 'cost' of the injury is therefore spread amongst all road users who contribute to the ACC's Motor Vehicle Account, which gives it a more communitarian flavour when compared to insurance purchased on an individual-to-individual basis.

New Zealand, of course, is geographically very different from Singapore and even Australia in terms of population density and road design (and any road can be used for testing). From an economic standpoint, there remains a concerted effort on the part of the government to make New Zealand an attractive destination to run tests for self-driving cars, though the purported objective is to be an early reaper of AV benefits. But it remains unknown if the same approach to insurance and compensation would apply once New Zealand moves beyond the testing phase, though one would not be surprised if the same approach is indeed adopted, since one of the foreseeable difficulties of successfully litigating a claim in the context of driverless cars is proving what exactly went wrong. Perhaps in the formative years of the implementation of the technology where users of AVs are in a small minority, some adjustments will have to be made.

[32] Ministry of Transport, 'Testing AVs in New Zealand' (October 2016), www.transport.govt.nz/assets/Uploads/Our-Work/Images/T-Technology/69bb8d97ac/Testing-Autonomous-Vehicles-in-New-Zealand.pdf.

[33] ibid. A Customer Support Manager is also assigned to provide assistance and recommend approved testing processes.

[34] See also Ministry of Transport, 'Autonomous Vehicles in New Zealand' (December 2019), www.transport.govt.nz/multi-modal/technology/specific-transport-technologies/road-vehicle/autonomous-vehicles/autonomous-vehicles-in-new-zealand.

[35] Ministry of Transport (n 32).

V. Japan: Recourse to Academic Expertise

Japan is the fourth and final country in the Asia Pacific we will be considering here. As a civil law jurisdiction, it is unsurprising to see many codified rules that govern the use of cars. However, what this may sometimes also mean is that there may be a bias towards tweaking existing rules rather than creating a discrete regime to address a specific technological development. The motor traffic regime in one of the world's largest car manufacturers is governed by the following sources of law:

- The Japanese Civil Code (Act No 89 of 27 April 1896) (JCC).[36]
- The Products Liability Act (Act No 85 of 1 July 1994) (JPLA).[37]
- The Automobile Liability Security Act (Act No 97 of 29 July 1955) (JALSA).[38]
- The Road Traffic Act (Act No 105 of 25 June 1960) (JRTA).[39]
- The Road Transport Vehicles Act (Act No 185 of 1951) (JRTVA).[40]

Collectively, these laws enable three types of claims relevant to our analysis. First, Article 3 of the JPLA establishes strict product liability for manufacturers for any 'damages arising from the infringement of life, body, or property of others which is caused by the defect in the delivered product'. Article 2(3) of the JPLA then clarifies that 'manufacturer' refers to any person who 'manufactured, processed, or imported the product in the course of trade', as well as any person who, 'in light of the manner concerning the manufacturing, processing, importation or sales of the product, and other circumstances, holds himself/herself out as its substantial manufacturer'. This definition is wide enough to include primary car-makers and software developers.

Second, Article 709 of the JCC establishes potential tort liability for damages 'resulting in consequence' of any 'negligently infringed' rights or legally protected interests. Superficially at least, this would be comparable to the usual tort of negligence familiar to most common law jurisdictions. Article 3 of the JALSA then establishes that 'a person that puts an automobile into operational use for that person's own benefit is liable to compensate for damage arising from the operation of the automobile if this results in the death or bodily injury of another person'. This is unless 'the person and the driver' prove that they had exercised due care, the victim acted intentionally or negligently, and there was no 'defect in

[36] A translation is available online at Japan Ministry of Justice, 'Civil Code', www.moj.go.jp/content/000056024.pdf.

[37] A translation is available online at Japanese Law Translation, 'Product Liability Act', www.japaneselawtranslation.go.jp/law/detail/?id=86&vm=04&re=02.

[38] A translation is available online at Japanese Law Translation, 'Act on Securing Compensation for Automobile Accidents', www.japaneselawtranslation.go.jp/law/detail/?printID=&ft=2&re=02&dn=1&yo=%E8%87%AA%E5%8B%95%E8%BB%8A&ia=03&ph=&x=0&y=0&ky=&page=3&vm=02.

[39] A translation is available online at Japanese Law Translation, 'Road Traffic Act', www.japaneselawtranslation.go.jp/law/detail/?id=2962&vm=04&re=02.

[40] No translation appears to be available for this online.

automotive structure or function'. Article 3 thus reverses the burden of proof in the victim's favour. Article 4 of the JALSA clarifies that JALSA liability operates in parallel to JCC liability; Article 5 establishes a compulsory insurance scheme for motor vehicles.

It has been pointed out that the 'practical difficulty perpetrators face in substantiating all three of these exemption requirements effectively imposes no-fault liability on the perpetrator'.[41] Thus, it is usually sufficient for victims to show that the damage occurred due to the accident.[42] Further, it ought to be noted that the JALSA does not pin liability solely on the driver; rather, it is the 'person who puts an automobile into operational use' for his or her own benefit who is liable. Article 2(2) of the JALSA defines 'operation' to include using an automobile 'in keeping with the way that such a machine is used'.

A report chaired by Professor Ochiai analysed self-driving car liability from the viewpoint of the JALSA specifically, and its findings were adopted by the Japanese government in April 2018.[43] In a subsequent paper, it was explained that the group had considered the following three disjunctive liability mechanisms for the transition period where both AVs and conventional vehicles would share the road:[44]

- Leave the existing JALSA regime as is, such that the 'liability of the automobile operator can remain relevant even for Society of Automotive Engineers (SAE) Level 4 automobiles'.
- Complement the existing regime with 'a new mechanism that calls on automobile manufacturers and other related parties to pay a certain amount in advance as premiums for automobile liability insurance'.
- Complement the existing regime with 'a newly established legal concept of a "liability of the system provider" mechanism that assigns no-fault liability to automobile manufacturers and other related parties'.

The research group recommended the first proposal.[45] First, 'the legal interpretation of 'liability of the automobile operator' posed no problems even during the transition period'. Second, 'the existing system should not be drastically overhauled in the transition period'. Third, the other two proposals 'required the resolution of numerous issues to function smoothly'. Finally, other key countries were 'not moving toward legal system revisions that assign liability to automobile manufacturers and other related parties'.

Nonetheless, Professor Ochiai noted that under the status quo, operators and their insurers may have trouble seeking compensation from manufacturers where accidents could be attributed to ADS defects. The countermeasure proposed was

[41] S Ochiai, 'Civil Liability for Automated Driving Systems in Japan', *Japan's Insurance Market 2018*, https://www.toare.co.jp/english/img/knowledge/pdf/2018_insurance.pdf.
[42] ibid.
[43] ibid.
[44] ibid.
[45] ibid.

to require that event data recorders be installed in self-driving cars and for further feasibility studies on a cooperative framework that enables insurance companies to smoothly claim compensation from automobile manufacturers, as well as the establishment of institutions to investigate the causes of accidents during automated driving and the safety of automated driving systems.

Given that these recommendations have been adopted by the Japanese government, we can expect the Japanese liability regime to remain as stated in the JALSA above. Subsequent guidelines published by the government noted that JALSA liability would primarily fall upon vehicle owners as the relevant operators.[46] In terms of preventive regulations, Articles 72 and 73 of the JRTA provide specific measures that parties involved in accidents are to take. Amongst other things, the driver must 'immediately stop driving', 'aid injured persons', prevent road hazards and report details of the matter to the police. The implicit premise is that a human driver exists. Even if the article was to be read broadly to allow an ADS to take these measures, it would still be challenging and perhaps unrealistic to expect the ADS to perform them.

The JRTVA is the primary legislation detailing road traffic regulations in Japan.[47] The Japanese government recently approved amendments to the JRTA and the JRTVA in light of Japan's push towards facilitating the testing and deployment of AVs.[48] Specifically, planned amendments to the JRTA would make '[vehicles] that can handle routine driving without human input', or at least SAE Level 3 vehicles, legal on public roads.[49] Manufacturers will first have to demonstrate that the vehicles meet certain operational design domain criteria.[50] However, those behind the wheel may still be held responsible for 'criminal or civil liabilities for traffic accident[s]' caused by an AV, even though the driver operated the AV properly.[51]

Parallel amendments to the JRTVA were meant to introduce new safety standards and testing and servicing rules for self-driving systems.[52] These would add equipment necessary for self-driving, including cameras and radars to monitor

[46] No English translation of these guidelines is available online, but see 'Japan to Place Accident Liability on Self-Driving Car Owners' *Nikkei Asian Review* (31 March 2018), www.asia.nikkei.com/Economy/Japan-to-place-accident-liability-on-self-driving-car-owners. See also S Nishioka, 'Japanese Legal System Related to Automated Driving', in *Sompo Japan Nipponkoa Insurance Inc (2018), Laws and Insurance in Our Coming Automated-Driving Society*, available at https://www.sompo-japan.co.jp/~/media/SJNK/files/english/news/sjnk/2018/e_nikkei.pdf.

[47] No English translation appears to be available for this.

[48] 'AI, Autonomous Driving and the Question of Road Safety' *NHK World-Japan* (6 June 2019), www3.nhk.or.jp/nhkworld/en/news/backstories/572.

[49] 'Japan Revamps Laws to Put Self-Driving Cars on Roads' *Nikkei Asia* (9 March 2019), www.asia.nikkei.com/Politics/Japan-revamps-laws-to-put-self-driving-cars-on-roads.

[50] 'Japan Edges Closer towards Brave New World of Self-Driving Cars But Hard Questions Remain' *South China Morning Post* (5 January 2019), www.scmp.com/news/asia/east-asia/article/2180828/japan-edges-closer-towards-brave-new-world-self-driving-cars.

[51] D Matsuda, E Mears and Y Shimada, 'Legalisation of Self-Driving Vehicles in Japan: Progress Made But Obstacles Remain' (1 July 2019), www.mondaq.com/rail-road-cycling/819992/legalization-of-self-driving-vehicles-in-japan-progress-made-but-obstacles-remain.

[52] ibid.

surrounding traffic, to the scope of vehicle safety standards.[53] Moreover, 'government approval will be necessary for any wireless software updates'.[54] Private insurance to cover accidents caused by SAE Level 3 vehicles will be compulsory.[55]

All things considered, Japan's forward-looking stance on the regulation of AVs and liability can perhaps be explained by how it is a large car-manufacturing – and car-exporting – jurisdiction with a real need for AV technology. As a start at least, it is looking to see how autonomous technologies can solve domestic problems that might be more unique to it. For instance, according to policy documents, self-driving cars would be instrumental to, inter alia, ply mountainous routes in rural areas populated primarily by relatively aged Japanese citizens – and Japan's ageing population issues are well documented.[56] But, as mentioned above, the distinct characteristic of the law reform process has been the leadership from academia. The speed at which the recommendations were made and adopted is also noteworthy.

VI. The UK: Attempting to Spearhead a Regulatory Framework

Moving out of the Asia Pacific, we consider the UK, which, as mentioned above, has been one of the more prominent jurisdictions as far as states taking a stab at new legislation go. The Automated and Electric Vehicles Act 2018 (AEVA) is designed to 'compensate the victim quickly and efficiently. It is not intended to allocate final legal responsibility for the accident'.[57] It defines a self-driving vehicle as one that is 'operating in a mode in which it is not being controlled, and does not need to be monitored, by an individual'.[58] So long as a vehicle has been listed as capable of safely driving itself and the automated driving system is engaged, no human user would be considered a driver and would be responsible for the immediate driving task.[59] However, the current regulatory framework is

[53] Japan's Ministry of Economy, Trade and Industry, 'Japan's Initiative to Promote Autonomous Driving' (June 2019), http://mddb.apec.org/Documents/2019/AD/AD1/19_ad1_018.pdf.

[54] 'Japan Revamps Laws to Put Self-Driving Cars on Roads' *Nikkei Asian Review* (9 March 2019), www.asia.nikkei.com/Politics/Japan-revamps-laws-to-put-self-driving-cars-on-roads.

[55] ibid.

[56] Ministry of Land, Infrastructure, Transport and Tourism, 'White Paper on Land, Infrastructure, Transport and Tourism in Japan, 2017', (2018) 96–97, 356–58.

[57] Law Commission of England and Wales and Scottish Law Commission, 'Automated Vehicles: Summary of the Preliminary Consultation Paper' (November 2018), s3-eu-west-2.amazonaws.com/lawcom-prod-storage-11jsxou24uy7q/uploads/2018/11/6.5066_LC_AV_Final-summary_061118_WEB.pdf. 'AEVA' also happens to be the name of an up-and-coming component manufacturer for self-driving cars; the two should not be confused.

[58] AEVA, s 8(1). See also Law Commission of England and Wales and Scottish Law Commission, 'Automated Vehicles: Summary of the Analysis of Responses to the Preliminary Consultation Paper' (June 2019), s3-eu-west-2.amazonaws.com/lawcom-prod-storage-11jsxou24uy7q/uploads/2019/06/Summary-of-Automated-Vehicles-Analysis-of-Responses.pdf.

[59] Law Commission of England and Wales and Scottish Law Commission (n 57).

silent as to whether the user of the car should be permitted to engage in secondary activities, such as checking a mobile phone, when the self-driving car is driving itself.[60]

While it has been suggested that there needs to be an intermediate role known as a 'user-in-charge' who can either be inside or outside the vehicle when 'the vehicle leaves its operational design domain' – such users are to 'undertake secondary activities and would not be responsible for any driving offences' and 'would not be required to take over a moving vehicle at short notice to guarantee road safety' – this has yet to be reflected in the AEVA or related legislation.[61] Part of this is because it is envisaged that 'in some situations an effective intervention could prevent an accident … it may be justifiable to impose [liability] for an omission where life is endangered, the situation is urgent, or the defendant has a special capacity to intervene'.[62]

Where an accident is caused by a self-driving car driving itself on a road or other public place, and the car is insured at the time of the accident, the insurer is liable for any damage caused to any person as a result of the accident.[63] Once the insurer has settled a claim with the injured party, it may then reclaim damages from other parties liable for the accident, such as the car manufacturer or supplier through means such as consumer protection laws or the tort of negligence (these are otherwise known as 'secondary claims').[64] However, if the car is not insured at the time of the accident, the owner of the car is liable for the damage.[65] Matters of causation are expected to be resolved on a case-by-case basis.[66]

It should be noted that contributory negligence is contemplated in both scenarios mentioned in the preceding paragraph.[67] Essentially, if an accident was to any extent the fault of the injured party, in theory at least, the normal principles of contributory negligence will apply and compensation will be reduced to the extent the court thinks is just and equitable.[68] It should also be noted that damage in this

[60] Law Commission of England and Wales and Scottish Law Commission, 'Automated Vehicles: A Joint Preliminary Consultation Paper' (November 2018), s3-eu-west-2.amazonaws.com/lawcom-prod-storage-11jsxou24uy7q/uploads/2018/11/6.5066_LC_AV-Consultation-Paper-5-November_061118_WEB-1.pdf.

[61] Law Commission of England and Wales and Scottish Law Commission (n 57). To be clear, once the user-in-charge assumes control following a handover, he or she would assume the responsibilities of a driver.

[62] Law Commission of England and Wales and Scottish Law Commission (n 60). See also Law Commission of England and Wales and Scottish Law Commission (n 58).

[63] AEVA, s 2(1).

[64] ibid s 5. See also Law Commission of England and Wales and Scottish Law Commission (n 57).

[65] AEVA, s 2(2). To be clear, this only applies to vehicles exempt from normal insurance provisions, such as those owned by public bodies.

[66] Law Commission of England and Wales and Scottish Law Commission (n 57) para 6.6. See also Law Commission of England and Wales and Scottish Law Commission (n 60) para 6.47. The Law Reform Commission gave the following example: 'if another human driver crashes into the back of an automated vehicle, shunting it into the car in front … the automated vehicle is in the chain of causation, but not at fault. It is possible that the automated vehicle insurer might have to pay for the damage to the car in front, but would then be able to recoup this money from the insurer of the human driver at fault. Alternatively, a court might hold that the accident was not caused by the automated vehicle'.

[67] AEVA, s 3. See also Law Commission of England and Wales and Scottish Law Commission (n 58).

[68] Law Commission of England and Wales and Scottish Law Commission (n 57).

context means death or personal injury and any damage to property other than the self-driving car, goods carried for hire or reward in or on that car, or property in the custody or under the control of the driver.[69]

Overall, the liability regime of the AEVA has been described as being 'a radical new approach to motor insurance. Rather than requiring insurers to indemnify road users against their own existing liability, it creates a wholly new form of liability which arises directly on insurers'.[70] In other words, 'the driver's liability and the automated vehicle's liability must be insured under the same policy'; this 'prevents disputes about whether the driver or the automated driving system is to blame, which could delay or hinder access to compensation'.[71]

To illustrate the difference: under the pre-AEVA regime, the insurer would only be liable for accidents if and only if the driver was liable. Primary liability for drivers is established through negligence. Thus, if an automated driving system-driven vehicle was involved in an accident, the victim, who bears the burden of proof, must show some form of negligence on the driver's part (for instance, by failing to override the system after being prompted to do so).

Under the post-AEVA regime, there is no requirement for the victim to prove primary liability against the driver. Instead, whenever an ADS-driven vehicle is involved in an accident, the vehicle's insurer is held directly liable to the victim. This regime therefore comes close to being a no-fault regime,[72] subject to derogations such as contributory negligence as mentioned above – say, where the accident was wholly due to the user's negligence in allowing the car to begin driving itself when it was not appropriate to do so; ordinarily, if there was no such negligence, the AEVA allows the insured to claim for personal injury to himself or herself.[73] This difference is important because it could be unduly onerous to victims in terms of evidential proof. Proof aside, there may also be legal lacunae that prevent the victim from being able to show negligence.

Another derogation from a full no-fault regime is reflected in the fact that an insurance policy may exclude or limit the insurer's liability if the damage suffered by an insured person arising from an accident occurring is a direct result of either software alterations made by the insured person (or with the insured person's knowledge) that are prohibited under the law or a failure to install safety-critical software updates that the insured person knows (or ought reasonably to know) are safety-critical.[74]

Over the next few years, the Law Reform Commission will be seeking a series of wide-ranging consultations from stakeholders to ensure that a fine balance is struck between safety, responsibility and innovation.[75] Its mandate in its first report was confined to passenger transport and not goods deliveries

[69] AEVA, s 2(3).
[70] Law Commission of England and Wales and Scottish Law Commission (n 60).
[71] ibid para 6.17.
[72] ibid.
[73] AEVA, s 3(2).
[74] ibid s 4(1).
[75] Law Commission of England and Wales and Scottish Law Commission (n 60).

and platooning.[76] It did not consider data protection, privacy and cybersecurity issues at that point.[77]

VII. The EU: An Overarching Regional Framework Supplemented by Domestic Laws

What about developments on the wider continental front? Self-driving cars have been tested quite extensively in other European countries such as Germany and Sweden. The European Commission, which is effectively the executive cabinet of the EU, has recently conducted a review of the existing framework for liability concerning motor vehicles in the EU, which mainly comprises the Motor Insurance Directive (MID) and the Product Liability Directive (PLD).[78] Each EU Member State may also pass laws to supplement these directives. This may be referred to as municipal traffic liability rules, and states are given the discretion to tailor their liability and compensation regimes as they see fit.[79] Therefore, regional regulations seldom represent the full regulatory picture of any given EU Member State.

At any rate, in the aforementioned review, the MID was found to be appropriate to deal with self-driving cars without any amendments – the provisions on third-party insurance and the process for settling claims were found to be more or less adequate. Nevertheless, the EU Parliament is in the process of considering the establishment of an additional fund which would pay for losses not covered by liability insurance; in return for contributing to this fund, manufacturers, programmers, owners and drivers could see their liability being limited to a certain amount.[80]

As for the PLD, the EC would issue interpretive guidance clarifying certain aspects of the Directive in light of the developments brought about by self-driving cars.[81] For now, subject to future interpretive guidance or amendments, in an accident involving self-driving cars, the victim will be compensated by an insurer under the MID. The insurer can, in turn, take action against the relevant manufacturer under the PLD where there is a defect in the self-driving car.[82] A self-driving

[76] ibid.

[77] ibid.

[78] European Commission, 'On the Road to Automated Mobility: An EU Strategy for Mobility of the Future' (17 May 2018), ec.europa.eu/transport/sites/transport/files/3rd-mobility-pack/com20180283_en.pdf.

[79] European Parliament, 'A Common EU Approach to Liability Rules and Insurance for Connected and AVs' (February 2018), www.europarl.europa.eu/RegData/etudes/STUD/2018/615635/EPRS_STU(2018)615635_EN.pdf.

[80] European Parliament, 'Civil Law Rules on Robotics' (16 February 2017), www.europarl.europa.eu/sides/getDoc.do?pubRef=-//EP//NONSGML+TA+P8-TA-2017-0051+0+DOC+PDF+V0//EN. See also Gerhard Wagner, 'Robot Liability' SSRN (2018), www.papers.ssrn.com/sol3/papers.cfm?abstract_id=3198764.

[81] European Parliament (n 79). One example is the regulation of data recorders.

[82] European Commission (n 78).

car would be considered defective where it does not 'provide the safety which a person is entitled to expect', taking into account the presentation of the vehicle, the 'use to which it could reasonably be expected' to be put and the time when the vehicle was put into circulation.[83]

Liability under the PLD is probably best described as strict, though this is subject to certain exceptions, some of which are likely to be relevant to self-driving cars. The first is where it is 'probable that the defect which caused the damage did not exist at the time when the product was put into circulation by him or that this defect came into being afterwards'.[84] In the context of self-driving cars, this may apply in situations where there is a 'black box' situation – where it is unclear what exactly an accident can be attributed to – and could also potentially cover situations where the software of the self-driving car is tampered with, causing a defect. However, insofar as the consumer must show that the product was defective at the moment the car left the factory, this is technically challenging and also involves a normative judgment on the required safety standard for what is still considered nascent technology.[85]

The second exception is where 'the defect is due to compliance of the product with mandatory regulations issued by the public authorities'.[86] Presumably, this would apply, for example, where the authorities mandate the inclusion of certain software/firmware or updates, causing a defect. However, it is questionable whether software would constitute products under the existing European framework, a perennial question that has unnecessarily plagued international trade and transactions without firm resolution.[87] Relatedly, the PLD would not cover damage from other parties' interventions or the failure of, say, telecommunication networks.[88]

The third exception is where 'the state of scientific and technical knowledge at the time when he put the product into circulation was not such as to enable the existence of the defect to be discovered'.[89] Considering the speed at which the technology of self-driving cars is developing, this exception is likely to be of particular relevance in due course. What is expected to be problematic is that manufacturers would likely have a wide margin of possibilities to shift costs of scientifically unknown risks through compliance and development risks defences to the consumer.[90]

Finally, 'in the case of a manufacturer of a component, that the defect is attributable to the design of the product in which the component has been fitted or to the instructions given by the manufacturer of the product'.[91] This exception would

[83] Council Directive (EC) 85/374 on the approximation of the laws, regulations and administrative provisions of the Member States concerning liability for defective products [1985] OJ L210/29 (Product Liability Directive), art 6.
[84] ibid art 7(b).
[85] European Parliament (n 79).
[86] Product Liability Directive, art 7(d).
[87] European Parliament (n 79).
[88] ibid.
[89] Product Liability Directive, art 7(e).
[90] European Parliament (n 79).
[91] Product Liability Directive, art 7(f).

provide protection to manufacturers of components for self-driving cars, assuming attribution can be established – as can be imagined, this assumption should not be taken lightly.

Significantly, the PLD further provides for the defence of contributory negligence, that is, where 'the damage is caused both by a defect in the product and by the fault of the injured person or any person for whom the injured person is responsible', the liability of the producer may be reduced or disallowed.

It would be remiss not to mention that even outside of the context of the existing PLD, which as noted earlier only applies where there is a 'defect', it is likely that the defence of contributory negligence will be available in accidents involving self-driving cars. The European Parliament in a recent resolution has also indicated that 'once the parties bearing the ultimate responsibility have been identified, their liability should be proportional to the actual level of instructions given to the robot and of its degree of autonomy'.[92]

While we are still in the realm of the EU, it should be pointed out that Member States such as Germany have proposed municipal legislation requiring manufacturers to install black boxes in self-driving cars.[93] Victims of accidents involving self-driving cars have the right to access such black boxes, enabling them to prove fault on the part of the driver or the self-driving car itself.[94] Such legislation would be in line with the EU's General Data Protection Regulation 2016/679, which confers upon citizens a 'right to explanation' – a right to obtain an explanation of decisions reached through automated means.[95] It cannot be overemphasised that the existence of this right is critical, as without it, accountability is at the discretion of the authorities and derogations are more easily justifiable, and there is little to sustain the premise that such a right is an international norm outside the EU.

VIII. Appraising the Different Approaches, Value Choices and the Necessary Political Will

As can be seen from the survey above, there has been no one-size-fits-all solution to the problem of regulating self-driving cars both in terms of how existing laws should be tweaked or replaced and in terms of how the law reform process is shaped. Whereas the formation of public laws is almost necessarily driven by the state, it is less obvious for the formation of private laws. In criminal law, for instance, state coercion is used to deter and punish acts that are unequivocally undesirable for society. No one but the government is expected to fulfil that

[92] European Parliament (n 80). See also Wagner (n 80).

[93] 'Germany to Require "Black Box" in Autonomous Cars' *Reuters* (18 July 2016), www.reuters.com/article/us-germany-autos-idUSKCN0ZY1LT.

[94] Wagner (n 80).

[95] See especially Regulation (EU) 2016/679 of 27 April 2016 on the protection of natural persons with regard to the processing of personal data and on the free movement of such data, and repealing Directive 95/46/EC [2016] OJ L119/1, recital 71.

function. Something like self-driving cars, with a greater range of stakeholders and competing interests, present a different sort of regulatory burden. The technology, despite its promises of greater efficiencies and safety, is pending full-scale deployment. It is also technology that few states have dared venture beyond providing general regulatory frameworks as an interim measure.

In this section, we will look at some of the possible liability paradigms that lie ahead in the light of what has been surveyed above. In looking at these possibilities, we should also be mindful of the necessary (especially political) ingredients and value choices (such as whether to promote innovation or to prioritise protecting potential victims) when seeking to adopt any given approach. To keep things streamlined, we will focus on what Singapore might be able to do going forward. We already know that Singapore does not yet have any specific framework for self-driving cars when they get into road traffic accidents. What we do have are longstanding rules and principles on negligence when 'normal' cars get into road traffic accidents. Can we simply tweak those rules and principles for self-driving cars or does its ostensible amenability quickly morph into intractable problems?

A. Difficulties in Using the Existing Negligence Framework without Major Modifications

Though the laws of negligence may differ depending on the (common law) jurisdiction in question, the fairly universal requirements are those of a duty of care (foreseeability of harm), breach (standard of care) and recoverable damage.[96] Singapore is no exception in this respect. The first requirement of duty of care might not pose much of an issue even in the context of self-driving cars:

> For the manufacturers of AVs … it is factually foreseeable that, should manufacturers be at fault in their design or manufacture of the AV, the owner or user or other road users will suffer loss and very likely personal injury as well. The first stage of the legal proximity test will also be satisfied as there is a physical and causal closeness between the manufacturer and the AV user … there would appear to be no policy reasons that would serve to negate the liability of the AV manufacturer.[97]

But as regards the second requirement concerning breach (of the duty of care), a more nuanced approach is necessary in light of the existing technology behind self-driving cars:

> [F]or an AV manufacturer to meet the standard of taking reasonable care in developing a usable and safe AV, the AV must be able to drive and adequately detect and avoid all kinds of obstacles … the AV must have on-board multiple redundant overlapping

[96] H Lim, *Autonomous Vehicles and the Law: Technology, Algorithms and Ethics* (Edward Elgar, 2019) ch 3.

[97] ibid 22. One could, of course, argue that negligence only makes sense if there is a driver, given the traditional 'reasonable person' analysis in the context of traffic accidents.

> detection systems … and they must be appropriately positioned on the AV … sonar systems and ultrasonic sensors … are to be encouraged as they do complement the work of lidars and radars.[98]

However, the above mainly pertains to hardware or, in other words, a verifiable standard of care. Software presents a different level of challenge altogether and renders the question of breach even more complicated to resolve, a problem that will probably be exacerbated as we move up the scale of automation, data processing and machine learning:

> Hard-coding software is tedious and time-consuming but it must be done with due care and properly. A machine learning algorithm, although itself mathematically sound, is to a large extent heavily dependent on the data it has been trained on, which in turn raises issues concerning the quantity and quality of the datasets, the duration of the training and the parameters and input variables … It is inconceivable that any regulator would be able to hire enough highly specialised personnel skilled … to evaluate all of the algorithms used in an AV … All of the foregoing difficulties would be even more acute for a plaintiff.[99]

In other words, bearing in mind that in the general negligence context the standard of care is pegged to industry standards, proving software defects would be nowhere near as feasible as proving hardware defects for the consumer. The relevant evidence for the former, such as the programming codes, are usually accessible only by the manufacturer; these are also likely to be proprietary, protectible material that would not be subject to easy discovery or disclosure. Further, one manufacturer's self-driving car may react differently from that of other manufacturers in a particular situation because the respective computer systems are presented with different datasets and different quantities in these datasets, and use different algorithms in their decision-making.

One possible way to overcome these evidential hurdles would be the reliance on *res ipsa loquitur* – this doctrine allows the courts to infer negligence from the circumstances in which such an accident occurred insofar as the occurrence of the accident can be said to 'speak for itself'.[100] But while *res ipsa loquitur* has been applied in motor vehicle situations by courts around the world,[101] its successful invocation has been the great exception rather than the norm. In any case, it is unlikely that the self-driving car scenario would fulfil the elements required for the doctrine to operate. Three elements are conjunctively required: (a) the defendant must have been in control of the situation or thing which resulted in the accident; (b) the accident would not have happened, in the ordinary course of things, if proper care had been taken; and (c) the cause of the accident must be unknown.[102]

[98] ibid.

[99] ibid chs 4 and 5.

[100] See *Tan Siok Yee v Chong Voon Kee Ivan* [2005] SGHC 157 [49].

[101] See *Ooi Han Sun v Bee Hua Meng* [1991] 1 SLR(R) 922; *In re Toyota Motor Corp Unintended Acceleration Marketing, Sales Practices, and Products Liability Litigation* [2013] WL 5763178.

[102] *Grace Electrical Engineering Pte Ltd v Te Deum Engineering Pte Ltd* [2018] 1 SLR 76.

For self-driving cars, one imagines that elements (a) and (b) are likely to be difficult to establish.

Without being able to prove breach (whether concerning hardware or software issues), the question of recoverability does not even arise, and the claim will necessarily fail once we are talking about self-driving cars that are of SAE Level 3 automation and above. Negligence is thus afflicted with a fundamental problem from both the consumer and regulatory standpoints and, on this basis, another mode of liability has to be considered – unless the preference is to essentially leave self-driving cars unregulated, which is unlikely, no matter how pro-business Singapore might generally be.

B. The Product or Strict Liability May Not Work That Well Either

If not negligence, perhaps some version of product liability? But, as mentioned above, the concept of product liability has never quite taken off in many common law jurisdictions, even though it is fairly well established in some jurisdictions such as the US (and also civil law jurisdictions such as China).[103] A characterisation of the US approach to this concept has been expressed in the following terms:

> Courts in the US have generally used two tests to determine whether a product has a design defect … a product is defective if it is 'dangerous to an extent beyond that which would be contemplated by the ordinary consumer who purchases it' … [or, under the Restatement, if] the foreseeable risks of harm posed by the product could have been reduced or avoided by the adoption of a reasonable alternative design by the seller or other distributor, or a predecessor in the commercial chain of distribution, and the omission of the alternative design renders the product not reasonably safe.[104]

However, when either test is applied to the context of self-driving cars, there is considerable difficulty:

> If an AV can navigate one roundabout without problems but crashes at the next roundabout, and the plaintiff cannot access, or cannot comprehend the machine learning algorithms on the entire AV, how does one determine the question of 'extent'?
>
> … At the best of times, it will be extremely difficult to discern the design of any given algorithm as it will be, for example, impossible to check through all of the training datasets fed to the algorithms, let alone suggest an alternative design.[105]

[103] There are, of course, consumer protection laws, but generally the threshold for the consumer to successfully prove unfair practices is quite high.

[104] Lim (n 96) ch 5. See also K Sunghyo, 'Crashed Software: Assessing Product Liability for Software Defects in Automated Vehicles' (2018) 16 *Duke Law & Technology Review* 300.

[105] Lim (n 96) ch 5. To be clear, product liability in the context of motor vehicles is an established area of law in the US, where references to standards such as the Federal Motor Vehicle Safety Standards are common.

Indeed, just as it is for negligence, the challenge lies not so much in showing that there was a hardware issue, but that a problem exists with the software – even if, say, the (reasonable) consumer can show that he or she would not have done what the AV did in an incident. This quagmire for the consumer (and the regulator as well) is also seen in the European conception of product liability. Reference has already been made above to Council Directive (EC) 85/374; in the context of self-driving cars, the challenge of applying the directive has been stated in the following terms:

> [W]hat a person would be entitled to expect with respect to safety is a fairly general test and would appear to set the bar quite high for manufacturers of AVs to ensure that their vehicles are safe, do not contain programming bugs or security flaws and so on. This would be the safety level a person is entitled to expect from an AV and a competent driver in the driving task, and since many competent drivers never encounter accidents, the AV should also not encounter accidents …
>
> [However] if a producer can show that the state of scientific and technical knowledge at the time when the product was put into circulation was not able to detect the defect, then it can escape liability …
>
> [This would] swing the pendulum too far in favour of the manufacturer of AVs … It opens the door for manufacturers of AVs to simply assert that they were not able to check through the millions of training datasets they had fed their algorithms.[106]

Thus, while it might seemingly be less problematic for the consumer to make a claim under product liability rather than negligence, the process (of investigating and gathering evidence, not to mention hiring lawyers with the right skill sets and overcoming challenges relating to manufacturers being out of jurisdiction) is still an unduly long and costly one such as to render dispute resolution illusory. We also have to bear in mind that the evidential hurdles would only increase as self-driving cars become more and more automated for the reasons mentioned above.

C. No-Fault Regimes: An Acquired Taste?

How about no-fault liability regimes then? To be clear, no-fault liability regimes (for instance, the one that has been adopted in New Zealand) must be carefully distinguished from strict liability regimes. Although liability in the latter is strict, this merely means that taking reasonable care does not defeat liability (unlike in a negligence framework). The victim still needs to show some sort of fault on the tortfeasor-manufacturer's part by proving that the product is defective. As explained above, this may be easier for victims of AV accidents than under a negligence rule, but other difficulties may still persist. Further, the victim must show that the defect caused the accident.

[106] ibid.

So a no-fault liability regime is better understood as a 'no questions asked' regime where the victim gets compensation so long as any harm is suffered. The victim's primary burden is showing that the accident in fact occurred and that the accident, rather than any negligence or product defect, caused the harm suffered.[107] Thus, there is veritably no element of fault whatsoever considered. For this reason, no-fault liability is usually administered through a central fund (as in New Zealand's ACC).

As a no-fault liability regime is quite a deviation from traditional common law thinking, an entirely no-fault tort regime is rare in practice and currently it seems may only be found in New Zealand. It is therefore remarkable that numerous jurisdictions studied here have relied on or referenced the concept of no-fault liability in devising AV liability frameworks. As explained above, although Japan's 'operator liability' rules are negligence-based in form, the high burden it imposes on the operator to prove three stringent exemption requirements bring it close to no-fault liability in substance. Likewise, the UK has described the AEVA's 'insurer liability' regime as coming close to a no-fault liability system, though with important derogations to allow for contributory negligence and limitations of liability (more will be said about the UK below).[108]

The relative simplicity of a no-fault liability regime seems particularly attractive for addressing the conceptual problems that self-driving cars create. Put simply, the strategy encapsulated in a move to no-fault liability is this: the legal and evidential issues raised are formidable, and therefore we shall not require victims to prove them. We are cutting the Gordian Knot rather than trying to unravel it to ensure victim compensation. But insofar as there exists cogent reasons as to why the law has required those legal and evidential issues to be proven in the first place, completely abandoning them would invariably raise further questions. In the case of a manufacturer-funded no-fault liability scheme, for example, it may be asked why manufacturers should be made to pay for accidents even if they had taken all reasonable care to produce a non-defective AV.

Further, without a system for screening out irresponsible manufacturers from responsible manufacturers, a free-rider problem could emerge: if all manufacturers contribute to the fund regardless of how safe their technology is, there would be inefficiently low incentives for manufacturers to ensure the safety of their products. The burden would then fall on the government (or whoever else administering this no-fault regime) to investigate each case in order to police irresponsible manufacturers. The government may indeed be better placed to do this than the victim, but given the complex state of AV technology, intractable difficulties are likely to remain.

[107] As this regime has not yet been ported to the AV context, it is unclear what will happen if the evidence shows that it was, say, a software problem that solely caused the accident to begin with. Whether the New Zealand courts still treat the car accident as having caused the harm remains an open question.

[108] Some proposals in the US for manufacturer-funded public funds likewise reference elements of no-fault liability.

The primary question with a no-fault liability regime is, at root, about who should bear the formal incidence of contributions to the fund and whether this fund can be administered in a way that does not overly disincentivise precaution and safety. Other policy considerations may also be relevant, including how compulsory manufacturer contributions would be received by and enforced against manufacturers (who may be based in another country).[109] Neither is imposing a broad-based levy of the sort seen in New Zealand (petrol and vehicle registration levies) a perfect alternative. The question is why all road users (including those who do not use or own self-driving cars) should bear formal incidence for this fund (assuming this fund only extends to self-driving car accidents). All things considered, as is the case for product liability, for any given jurisdiction to move to a no-fault liability regime, even if it is just for AVs, it may involve significant transition costs. If it were attempted here, there might be some persuasiveness in pointing to communitarian values. Self-driving cars would not be the exclusive remit of persons who can afford cars. Self-driving technology would probably also be used for hired cars and public buses. A technology that has wide societal benefit could warrant a community-wide cost.

D. Other Options?

At any rate, it emerges from the preceding analyses that every liability framework considered involves legal and evidential difficulties as well as policy trade-offs. For most common law jurisdictions, negligence rules might be similar to existing frameworks and would involve the lowest transition costs. However, it also involves significant legal and evidential problems, particularly for victims, and this may greatly impede consumer confidence even before a product can be launched. Strict product liability mitigates this by obviating the need for victims to prove that manufacturers failed to take reasonable care, but victims may still find it difficult to show that a vehicle was defective unless we take a very broad definition of what a 'defect' is. No-fault liability makes things easiest for victims and is likely to virtually guarantee compensation in every case, but would represent a radical departure from our current system and would involve the largest transition costs in terms of shifting risk allocations and burdens, creating funding, policy and legal processes associated with regime change. There is also the question of fairness to potential tortfeasors (that is, manufacturers and operators) rather than victims.

Given our current negligence-based regime, perhaps the question is whether we can make certain modifications to the existing regime to import the desirable

[109] However, if a manufacturer's contributions are tied to a measure of the safety of that manufacturer's vehicles (for example, the number of accidents in which its vehicles have been involved or performance on certain safety tests), then this compulsory contribution could become in itself a screening device to identify safe manufacturers, since unsafe manufacturers would be less willing to contribute and would self-select themselves out by exiting Singapore.

features of product liability and no-fault liability while preserving the advantages of a negligence rule. In this light, we turn to consider the UK's recent statutory experiment. The UK may have been bold to put forth the AEVA (and appears to be the only major jurisdiction that has expounded on safety driver standards and responsibilities), but in my view there are a number of issues with the legislation that warrant serious consideration.

First, the AEVA does not address the underlying legal issues with AV accidents. It should be recalled that the statute's primary mechanism lies in deeming the vehicle's insurer primarily liable for accidents. The intention is for the insurer to then claim against whoever is 'responsible' for the collision. The question of establishing who is 'responsible', as well as questions of causation (see the terms 'cause', 'direct result of', 'resulting from' and 'arising out of', which under conventional statutory interpretation do not refer to the same things), are presumably left to the courts to decide on a case-by-case basis or, less charitably, for subsequent law review. As it is, numerous issues have been raised in academic literature in relation to the unsuitability of existing common law doctrines in both product liability and negligence to AVs. This approach does not, and indeed was not intended to, resolve these underlying legal questions; rather, its primary purpose is to allow for efficient and quick victim compensation.

Second, the UK explicitly refused to follow the SAE International's definitions, preferring instead to establish a register of AVs. While this allows flexibility in the class of vehicles to be regulated, it may also introduce additional uncertainty to an AV industry already familiar with the SAE definitions. Notably, in the US, the definitions of the National Highway Traffic Safety Administration (NHTSA) are more aligned with those of the SAE. The US is not the one who is anomalous in this respect.

Third, there may be legal conceptual problems raised by the AEVA's approach. Implicit in the statute is the recognition that AVs may drive themselves,[110] 'cause' accidents[111] and have 'fault' for certain 'behaviour'.[112] It remains to be seen how a doctrine like causation, which requires both causation in fact and law, may be applied to AVs. One might argue that the statute confers a limited form of legal personality to the vehicle such that it is capable of the above legal acts. Yet this does not seem intentional, particularly after the UK's proposal to confer 'electronic personality' to autonomous systems was vehemently opposed by industry experts and promptly shelved.

For the sake of completeness, it is of course possible to consider product liability not in terms of fault, but of strict liability broadly conceived. Because it is so challenging, a system of strict liability could be justified on the following bases. First, given the nature of programming codes and machine learning, it would be

[110] This is implied by the definition of an automated vehicle as a vehicle capable of driving itself.
[111] Section 2 is titled 'Liability of Insurers where accident caused by automated vehicle'.
[112] Section 6(3) establishes that contributory negligence should take effect 'as if the behaviour of the automated vehicle were the fault of the person made liable for the damage by section 2 of this Act'.

extremely onerous for regulators to verify the software of AVs and ensure that they are safe for use. Second, a system of strict liability would enhance consumer confidence in AV technology, and consumers, knowing that they would have smoother recourse to compensation in the event of an accident, would presumably be more encouraged to use self-driving cars (whether privately or as a ride-hailer). Third, the untested nature of AV technology means that there is greater inherent danger in its widespread use. Commentators have also analogised the self-driving car situation to the strict liability framework imposed on the aviation industry, even after safety records had improved and commercial aviation became prevalent.[113] In this respect, any argument that strict product liability may stifle innovation and make Singapore a less desirable ground for AV technology should duly countenance the fact that AV manufacturers are in a prime position to alleviate any possible risks and take necessary mitigating measures when developing their technology; it would also not be fanciful to suggest that they have the most incentive to avoid costs by ensuring that their hardware and software are performing properly.[114]

But notwithstanding these arguments regarding strict liability, there is no question that strict liability is always by default considered an extreme option, not least because of its impact on costs and insurance. At best, it could be conceived as a stopgap measure until the technology reaches a very steady state, a scenario complicated by the sliding scale of autonomy for self-driving cars in the foreseeable future. One imagines that in most cases, moving to a strict liability regime from existing negligence regimes could involve significant transition and transaction costs, even if the new regime were tailored specifically to apply to self-driving car accidents only (and even this approach has drawbacks). The same conundrum returns: while Singapore is the one place in which swift and decisive government action can occur almost immediately, there is still a desire to be seen as a first mover in this form of autonomous technology. Such an objective invariably requires a light regulatory touch in favour of the sellers and manufacturers.

In the final analysis, short of a complete reimagining of existing liability frameworks, countries thinking about introducing autonomous vehicles into the mainstream would have to find some way to get past second gear when it comes to the practical difficulties of using the current conceptual frameworks of liability. It may not always be wise for the law to fashion an intricate labyrinth of permutations to regulate what may become a key aspect of daily living. This is especially so if there are no theoretical legal constraints in putting the focus on victim compensation – only practical (financial) ones.

[113] See K Graham, 'Of Frightened Horses and AVs' (2012) 52 *Santa Clara Law Review* 1241.
[114] See also J Zipp, 'The Road Will Never Be the Same: A Reexamination of Tort Liability for AVs' (2016) 32(2) *Transportation Law Journal* 162.

8

Medical AI, Standard of Care in Negligence and Tort Law

GARY CHAN KOK YEW*

I. Introduction

The use of artificial intelligence (AI) extends across the broad spectrum of medical services: diagnoses, predictions of medical risks, treatment or surgery, the giving of medical information and advice, monitoring of patients and even hospital administration. It has been forecast that the global market for AI solutions in the healthcare sector will increase significantly from US$1 billion to more than US$34 billion by 2025.[1]

The more common usage of AI for hospitals and doctors in clinical practice thus far has been in medical diagnosis and the predictive analysis of diseases and health conditions. AI medical diagnosis is typically conducted through machine recognition of patterns from training data comprising information of the various diseases and symptoms, the medical records and data concerning the patient, and prior diagnoses. In supervised learning, data that has been labelled in advance is inputted into a machine learning algorithm to teach the computer to recognise, for example, a tumour. In contrast, in unsupervised learning, data is fed to a machine learning algorithm in order to find, for instance, a method to distinguish different body fluids from the inputted data.[2] Deep learning algorithms are currently used in radiography, mammography for breast cancer detection, magnetic resonance imaging (MRI) for brain tumours and for diagnosing neurological disorders, including Alzheimer's disease

* This research is supported by the National Research Foundation, Singapore under its Emerging Areas Research Projects (EARP) Funding Initiative. Any opinions, findings and conclusions or recommendations expressed in this material are those of the author and do not reflect the views of National Research Foundation, Singapore. The author thanks Benjamin Tham, former Research Associate, Centre for AI and Data Governance (CAIDG) at SMU, for his research assistance.

[1] Tractica, 'Artificial Intelligence for Healthcare Applications', www.tractica.omdia.com/research/artificial-intelligence-for-healthcare-applications.

[2] Daniel Hashimoto, Guy Rosman, Daniela Rus and Ozanan Meireles, 'Artificial Intelligence in Surgery: Promises and Perils' (2018) 268(1) *Annals of Surgery* 70.

AI predictive analysis is undertaken via big data analysis or data aggregated from the Internet of Things, sensors and/or medical equipment. Natural language processing may be employed in the analyses of electronic medical record (EMR) data comprising the doctors' personal notes and narrations of symptoms. AI has even been employed in end-of-life decision-making. At the Stanford Hospital, a mortality prediction (deep learning) tool was used to help palliative care professionals identify dying patients within a 3–12-month period and who were likely to benefit from palliative care services.[3]

Hospitals and healthcare systems have introduced Clinical Decision Support Systems (CDSS) platforms that are integrated with machine learning to assist with diagnostic decisions and to predict treatment outcomes. The CDSS analyses the EMR data fed by the clinicians, including test results from pathology laboratories, radiological departments, genetics departments and information stored in biobanks and databanks of genome sequences, and supplies diagnostic recommendations based on algorithms derived from rules informed by established clinical guidelines and published medical research reviews.[4] AI has been developed[5] in Singapore to aid in diagnosing symptoms caused by diabetic retinopathy[6] and to screen for glaucoma and age-related macular degeneration. It is also utilised to predict the risks of relapse for stroke patients through the use of computer vision and fluid dynamics to measure the speed of blood flow in arteries and veins.[7] During the COVID-19 pandemic, an AI tool called RadiLogic was used to detect abnormal chest X-rays for COVID screening in Singapore.[8] Experimental work on neural network classification based on medical datasets[9] has been carried out by researchers from Universiti Teknologi Malaysia.[10] Furthermore, machine

[3] Anand Avati et al, 'Improving Palliative Care with Deep Learning' (2018) 18(4) *BMC Medical Informatics and Decision Making*, https://doi.org/10.1186/s12911-018-0677-8.

[4] Tamra Lysaght, Hannah Yeefen Lim, Vicki Xafis and Kee Yuan Ngiam, 'AI-Assisted Decision Making in Healthcare: The Application of an Ethics Framework for Big Data in Health and Research' (2019) 11(3) *Asian Bioethics Review* 299, www.doi.org/10.1007/s41649-019-00096-0.

[5] The AI was developed by the Singapore National Eye Centre (SNEC), the Singapore Eye Research Institute (SERI) and the National University of Singapore (NUS) School of Computing.

[6] See Channel News Asia, 'In a World First, Singapore-Developed Artificial Intelligence System Detects 3 Major Eye Conditions' (14 December 2017), www.channelnewsasia.com/news/health/in-a-world-first-singapore-developed-artificial-intelligence-9498742.

[7] See Nurfilzah Rohaidi, 'In Singapore's Healthcare Revolution, AI is the Key', www.govinsider.asia/inclusive-gov/singapores-healthcare-revolution-ai-key.

[8] The AI was trained on data consisting of 1,000 anonymised abnormal chest X-rays from COVID-19 patients and 4,000 anonymised normal chest X-rays. See Shabana Begum, 'Coronavirus: AI Tool Developed to Detect Abnormal Chest X-rays Quickly' (3 September 2020), www.straitstimes.com/singapore/ai-tool-developed-to-detect-abnormal-chest-x-rays-quickly.

[9] This includes datasets for the following conditions: Hepatitis, Heart Disease, Pima Indian Diabetes, Wisconsin Prognostic Breast Cancer, Parkinson's disease, Echocardiogram, Liver Disorders, Laryngeal 1 and Acute Inflammations.

[10] Zahra Beheshti, Siti Mariyam Hj Shamsuddin, Ebrahim Beheshti and Siti Sophiayati Yuhaniz, 'Enhancement of Artificial Neural Network Learning Using Centripetal Accelerated Particle Swarm Optimization for Medical Diseases Diagnosis' (2014) 18 *Soft Computing* 2253, https://doi.org/10.1007/s00500-013-1198-0.

learning models have been built using breast cancer data from the University of Malaya Medical Centre in order to identify the important prognostic factors for breast cancer survival.[11]

The use of AI has the potential to significantly reduce the time spent by medical doctors in diagnosis. It is able to scan a wide range of data to diagnose diseases more quickly and with lower error rates. As a starting point, it appears to be more economically efficient to use AI for medical services. Nonetheless, significant work is involved in supplying the AI with data so that it can provide sufficiently accurate diagnoses or predictive analysis. The quality of the AI analysis depends on the size of data used. In this regard, the availability of EMRs through the National Electronic Health Record in Singapore should play an increasingly important role.

Even as medical AI has progressed apace, the possibility of errors arising from its use cannot be underestimated. Consider these scenarios. The AI fails to diagnose a tumour and the patient's health condition deteriorates without timely treatment, or the AI prescribes the wrong drug or surgical procedure, causing adverse health effects to the patient. Moreover, errors from medical AI based on large datasets affecting patients admitted to a hospital may be more widespread than those committed by an individual human doctor. To what extent should medical doctors and hospitals using medical AI be legally responsible under existing tort laws in Singapore and Malaysia? What is the standard of care we expect from doctors and hospitals when using AI to provide medical services? To what extent should doctors and hospitals understand, evaluate and rely on black box medicine? Furthermore, where doctors and hospitals are found *not* to be at fault in the use of medical AI, should we nonetheless pin tortious responsibility on them for harms caused to patients? There is currently no product liability legislation in Singapore and the product liability regime in Malaysia does not apply to medical services, but we will consider the applicability of the tort doctrines of vicarious liability and non-delegable duties to the use of medical AI.

This chapter only covers tort liabilities from the use of medical AI for the purpose of directly providing medical services to patients. Section II will focus on the common law tort rules on standard of care in Singapore and Malaysia, and how they may be *applied* or *adapted* for determining liability arising from the use of medical AI. The general standard of care and its two major legal tests will be discussed, followed by their applicability to specific issues: (i) the doctors' or hospitals' reliance on medical AI, designers and approving authorities; (ii) their omission to utilise medical AI; (iii) the impact of inaccuracies, bias and opacity of medical AI on standard of care; and (iv) the giving of medical advice based on AI output. In addition to the usual techniques of judicial reasoning such as the extension of existing legal rules by the use of analogical reasoning and incrementalism, the discussion will be

[11] Mogana Darshini Ganggayah, Nur Aishah Taib, Yip Cheng Har, Pietro Lio and Sarinder Kaur Dhillon, 'Predicting Factors for Survival of Breast Cancer Patients Using Machine Learning Techniques' (2019) 19 *BMC Medical Informatics and Decision Making* 48, https://doi.org/10.1186/s12911-019-0801-4.

framed by more general competing policy considerations impinging on tort liability such as efficiency, the promotion of technological innovations, the relevance of ethical guidelines applicable to the medical profession and patient welfare. Section III focuses on the question of whether the doctors and hospitals should be liable for errors arising from medical AI in the absence of fault on the basis of vicarious liability and non-delegable duties respectively. Section IV concludes.

II. Extending the Law of Medical Negligence in Singapore and Malaysia to Medical AI

Singapore's healthcare system has modernised at a rapid pace since independence. Its public sector comprising government-restructured hospitals and a number of large private hospitals provide secondary and tertiary hospital facilities offering specialist care and advanced medical diagnosis and treatment. Singapore serves as a hub for manufacturing operations of global pharmaceutical and medical technology companies partaking in biomedical research and development. With its modern healthcare system and facilities, Singapore undertook initiatives to boost medical tourism and foreign patient figures[12] two decades ago. However, in view of the public sector mission to ensure affordable healthcare, medical tourism is no longer promoted.[13]

Like Singapore, Malaysia delivers a mixed healthcare system from both the public and private sectors. There has been a noticeable shift from the government welfarist approach in healthcare to the commercialisation and corporatisation of medical services, and the growth of private hospitals and specialised clinics since the 1980s.[14] In Malaysia, private clinics and doctors outnumber those in the public sector and with a higher concentration in urban compared to rural areas.[15] Overall, in Malaysia, the scope of medical services has been comprehensive and delivered at a relatively low cost,[16] although it continues to face the challenge of increasing the number of medical staff in the public sector to deal with the patient load.[17]

[12] The Healthcare Services Working Group working jointly with the Singapore Tourism Board, the Economic Development Board and International Enterprise Singapore.

[13] Jeremy Lim, *Myth or Magic: The Singapore Healthcare System* (Select Publishing, 2013) 145.

[14] Chee Heng Leng and Simon Barraclough, 'The Transformation of Health Care in Malaysia' in *Health Care in Malaysia: The Dynamics of Provision, Financing and Access* (Routledge, 2007) 1.

[15] Huy Ming Lim, Sheamini Sivasampu, Ee Ming Khoo and Kamaliah Mohamad Noh, 'Chasm in Primary Care Provision in a Universal Healthcare System: Findings from a Nationally Representative Survey of Health Facilities in Malaysia' (2017) 12(2) *PLOS ONE*, https://doi.org/10.1371/journal.pone.0172229. The survey on primary care clinics was conducted from June 2011 to February 2012.

[16] See Safurah Jaafar et al, 'Malaysia Health System Review' (2013) 3(1) *Health Systems in Transition*, www.searo.who.int/entity/asia_pacific_observatory/publications/hits/hit_malaysia/en; see also Jenny Goh, 'Malaysia to Face a Nursing Shortage by 2020' *MIMS Today* (6 January 2017), www.today.mims.com/malaysia-to-face-a-nursing-shortage-by-2020 (on the shortage of nurses).

[17] 'Public of Private Hospitals? The Choice is Yours' *Borneo Post Online* (18 February 2011), www.theborneopost.com/2011/02/18/public-or-private-hospitals-the-choice-is-yours.

Notwithstanding the growing evidence that AI can outperform human doctors in diagnoses,[18] it is not immune from errors. One important issue is how we should deal with injuries suffered by patients due to medical AI. Aside from the tort system, one alternative is to set up a no-fault system in which patients may obtain payments for medical injuries sustained without having to prove the fault on the part of the doctor or hospital. Such a system enjoys the advantages of simplicity and low transaction costs for the parties involved. In contrast, Malaysian commentators have recognised the practical problems in the implementation of the tort system evidenced by potential inefficiencies, costs and delays in the litigation system.[19] This may be exacerbated by the costs of medical expert witnesses, the confrontational courtroom setting for disputing parties and the spectre of defensive medicine practised by doctors who are concerned with potential lawsuits.[20]

However, unlike the no-fault-system, the tort system can play an important role in allowing for the full extent of compensation of losses, setting fault-based standards for the medical profession[21] and ensuring its accountability. Disputing parties need not undergo a full-blown litigation, but may choose mediation to settle medical negligence disputes. The adversarial nature of litigation can be tempered by a shift to an inquisitorial approach to settling disputes.[22] Pre-action protocols for medical negligence cases in Singapore[23] have been instituted with a view to obtaining resolution of disputes without protracted litigation. In practice, medical doctors, who are covered by compulsory indemnity, do not have to pay compensation directly to patients. The availability of such indemnity does not mean that doctors are not deterred by medical negligence claims. Legal actions can affect the amount of insurance premiums payable and the doctors' reputations, not to mention the time and costs in defending the claims.

Notwithstanding the above pros and cons concerning the most appropriate system to deal with medical injuries, the tort system on medical negligence is firmly established in both Singapore and Malaysia. For this reason, its full potential and possible role in the regulation of the use of medical AI must be investigated, even as we explore alternative or supplementary regulatory tools.

[18] A Michael Froomkin, Ian Kerr and Joelle Pineau, 'When AIs Outperform Doctors: Confronting the Challenges of a Tort-Induced Over-Reliance on Machine Learning' (2019) 61(33) *Arizona Law Review* 33.

[19] Siti Naaishah Hambali and Solmaz Khodapanahandeh, 'Review of Medical Malpractice Issues in Malaysia under Tort Litigation System' (2014) 6(4) *Global Journal Health Science* 76; Puteri Nemie bt Jahn Kassim, 'Medical Negligence Litigation in Malaysia: Whither Should We Travel?' (2004) 33(1) *Journal of the Malaysian Bar* 14, 18.

[20] Paula Case, 'The Jaded Cliche of "Defensive Medical Practice": From Magically Convincing to Empirically (Un)Convincing?' (2020) 36(2) *Professional Negligence* 49.

[21] Puteri Nemie bt Jahn Kassim, 'Medical Negligence Litigation in Malaysia: Whither Should We Travel?' (2004) 33(1) *Journal of the Malaysian Bar* 14, 18.

[22] Sundaresh Menon, Chief Justice of the Supreme Court of Singapore, 'Evolving Paradigms for Medical Litigation in Singapore', speech to the Obstetrical and Gynaecological Society of Singapore (2014).

[23] Supreme Court Practice Directions, Appendix J (High Court Protocol for Medical Negligence Cases), which took effect from 2017; and State Courts Practice Directions 39 (Medical Negligence Claims), which took effect from 1 October 2018.

The issue of breach – a core aspect of medical negligence – is based on a number of factors: the foreseeability and probability of harm, the extent of harm, the costs of precautions to be undertaken, industrial practices and norms. This is to be balanced against the actual and potential benefits to be obtained from the innovation, such as the superior performance and speed of AI, as highlighted above. Though pegged to an objective standard of reasonableness, the standard of care when applied to technological innovations can fluctuate in tandem with the human expectations and understanding of and their evolving interactions with the technology.

The standard of care of a medical doctor is assessed based on his or her prevailing knowledge at the material time of the breach without the benefit of hindsight.[24] Hence, the doctor's standard should be judged by what he or she knows concerning the AI being utilised for medical services. If the AI was known to be functioning with great accuracy at the time of the breach, the doctor cannot be faulted for using the AI should it be discovered subsequently that the algorithm was insufficiently sophisticated to detect the patient condition and thereby resulted in a wrong diagnosis. Furthermore, we should not take account of subsequent media reports of mishaps or accidents relating to the use of medical AI or new scientific discoveries regarding the flaws, inaccuracies or weaknesses of the AI in order to show that the doctor was negligent.

Our main focus is on AI errors impinging on medical diagnosis, treatment and advice that result in a patient's injuries. This chapter adopts a judicial approach to resolving a medical negligence dispute focusing on legal principles, doctrines and policy considerations when applied to novel technology. We will first look at the legal standard of care expected of medical doctors when dealing with medical innovations such as AI before discussing specific scenarios and challenges posed by AI.

A. *Bolam*, *Bolitho* and the Standard of Care in the Use of Medical AI

In the event of conflicting expert evidence on the standard of care expected of medical doctors, two legal tests are applied to determine whether there has been any negligence in medical diagnosis and treatment. The *Bolam* test[25] – in stating that a doctor is not negligent if he or she has acted in accordance with a practice accepted by a responsible body of medical doctors – is deferential to the medical profession's views. In *Hunter v Hanley*, Lord President Clyde stated that '[i]n the realm of diagnosis and treatment, there is ample scope for genuine difference of opinion'.[26] When new AI is being developed for use in diagnosis and treatment,

[24] *Roe v Minister of Health* [1954] 2 QB 66.
[25] *Bolam v Friern Hospital Management Committee* [1957] 1 WLR 582, 587.
[26] *Hunter v Hanley* [1955] SLT 213, 217.

such differences in opinion on the scope of the use of medical AI and the doctor's negligence may arise. Thus, a mere mistake in diagnosis or treatment does not necessarily amount to negligence on the part of medical doctors. As the *Bolam* test considers the doctor's act or omission viewed by the medical profession at the time of the alleged breach, a finding of negligence 'reasoned through hindsight, hindsight bias and outcome bias from the plaintiff's adverse outcome' may be avoided.[27]

If the *Bolam* test is satisfied, the courts proceed to a second inquiry – the addendum in *Bolitho v City and Hackney Health Authority*[28] – which requires that the medical opinion be subject to the requirement of logic and the weighing up of comparative risks and benefits to reach a defensible conclusion. Hence, when there is 'genuine medical controversy', the courts should not prefer one medical opinion over another unless the medical opinion is illogical.[29] Essentially, in applying *Bolitho*, the court rather than the medical profession will decide on the standard of care required of the defendant. The Singapore Court of Appeal in *Khoo James v Gunapathy d/o Muniandy*[30] laid out a two-stage analysis based on the *Bolitho* addendum: (a) whether the expert had directed his or her mind to the comparative risks and benefits; and (b) whether the expert had arrived at a 'defensible' conclusion in relation to two factors: (i) whether the medical opinion was internally consistent on its face, and (ii) whether the opinion ignores or is contrary to known medical facts or advances in medical knowledge.

Let us assume that the patient claims that the doctor was negligent in using AI to diagnose the patient's condition. Given the requirement of an existing 'practice' of a responsible body of medical opinion, it would be difficult (though not impossible) to apply the *Bolam* test to a situation where the AI technology in question is at the cutting edge. In this sense, *Bolam* is generally inappropriate for assessing the use of AI innovations which have yet to be adopted (much less accepted as proper) by at least a respectable body of medical opinion. At the same time, this responsible body of opinion is not to be treated as merely a quantitative matter. A small but responsible body of medical opinion can qualify under the *Bolam* test.[31]

Even if *Bolam* is applicable, the *Bolitho* test demands an explanation by the defendant experts as to the logical basis for their opinion that the use of medical AI was acceptable. The opacity of medical AI may make it difficult for the experts to justify their opinions in considering the comparative benefits and potential risks from the use of medical AI. This will be further discussed below.[32]

[27] Jem Barton-Hanson and Renu Barton-Hanson, '*Bolam* with the Benefit of Hindsight' (2016) 56(4) *Medicine, Science and the Law* 275.

[28] *Bolitho v City and Hackney Health Authority* [1998] AC 232.

[29] *Noor Azlin bte Abdul Rahman v Changi General Hospital Pte Ltd and Others* [2019] 1 SLR 834 [65].

[30] *Khoo James v Gunapathy d/o Muniandy* [2002] 1 SLR(R) 1024 (hereinafter *Gunapathy*).

[31] *De Freitas v O'Brien and Connolly* [1995] 6 Med LR 108. The court held that 11 doctors specialising in spinal surgery out of more than 1,000 orthopaedic and neurosurgeons in the country constituted a responsible body of opinion.

[32] See section II.D below.

In addition, the *Bolitho* test demands internal consistency within the expert opinion and external coherence of the expert opinion with the state of existing medical knowledge. At present, it is not clear whether the state of and advances in medical knowledge would include knowledge of medical AI, as the latter is not normally regarded as within the domain expertise of doctors. But we should not discount the possibility that the use of medical AI would in the near future become so prevalent amongst doctors such that they would be expected to possess knowledge of certain types of medical AI as part of clinical practice.[33] Information of such medical AI may in future be commonly found in medical journals and literature which doctors may need to keep abreast of.

Though there may be difficulties in applying the *Bolam* and *Bolitho* tests directly to medical AI, the tort of medical negligence can nevertheless accommodate AI innovations. First, the mere fact that the doctor's use of medical AI deviates from existing medical practice does not in itself amount to negligence. Otherwise, it would not be feasible at all to introduce any medical innovations in clinical practice. Such a proposition was endorsed in *Rathanamalah d/o Shunmugam v Chia Kok Hoong*,[34] in which a novel surgical technique, or novel combination of surgical procedures,[35] was used by the doctor. The expert evidence indicated that the novel technique gave rise to a potential benefit, posed minimal risk and even had the potential to reduce the risk of injury. Furthermore, there was no evidence that no responsible body of medical opinion, logically held, would support such innovation,[36] and the doctor was found not to be negligent in using the innovative technique.

Gobinathan Devathasan v SMC[37] is a medical disciplinary case on the novel use of therapeutic ultrasound on a patient who was suffering from a neurological syndrome. Although *Gobinathan* is not a claim in negligence, its general thrust is aligned with *Rathanamalah*. The Singapore High Court held that where a medical doctor embarks on a novel treatment that is not generally accepted by the profession but which the doctor thinks is beneficial to the patient, the latter will have to show that the novel treatment poses no harm to the specific patient. This, according to the court, seeks to strike a balance between promoting innovation and progress and the particular patient's well-being.[38] There is no requirement for

[33] For example, at Yong Loo Lin School of Medicine at the National University of Singapore, medical students attended workshops on Health Informatics, and other workshops on AI and machine learning were being planned; see Dr Kenneth Ban, 'Health Informatics – Equipping Students with Skills for the Digital Age' (November 2019), www.medicine.nus.edu.sg/newsletters/issue-32/insights/health-informatics-equipping-students-with-skills-for-the-digital-age.

[34] *Rathanamalah d/o Shunmugam v Chia Kok Hoong* [2018] 4 SLR 159 [127] (Aedit Abdullah JC). *cf Hepworth v Kerr* [1995] 6 Med LR 139, where the defendant anaesthetist was negligent in experimenting with new hypotensive anaesthetic technique which exposed the patient to excessive risk.

[35] Foam sclerotherapy was used in combination with endovenous laser therapy to treat a patient diagnosed with venous eczema.

[36] *Rathanamalah* (n 34) [127].

[37] *Gobinathan Devathasan v SMC* [2010] 2 SLR 926.

[38] ibid [62].

the medical doctor to additionally prove that the novel treatment is beneficial to patients generally.

The above cases show that safety, the minimisation of harm and benefits are key, a position in line with section B6 (Untested Practices) of the SMC Ethical Code and Ethical Guidelines (ECEG 2016) that endorse the minimisation of harm principle: 'Patients expect doctors to offer only treatments or therapies that will benefit them while minimising harm.' The ECEG 2016 also states that doctors must treat patients only according to 'generally accepted methods, based on a balance of available evidence and accepted best practices'. This guideline extends to new medical devices. According to *Pang Ah San v SMC*,[39] a particular treatment is generally accepted where 'the potential benefits and risks of that treatment and the ability to control these are approaching a level of predictability that is acceptable to the medical community in general'. There are other situations where innovations may be utilised. Innovative therapy may be offered when conventional therapy is 'unhelpful and it is a desperate or dire situation'. Moreover, 'experimental and innovative treatment which is *therapy* administered in the best interests of the patient is permissible'.[40]

Thus, from the macro-policy perspective, medical innovation plays an important role in *ex ante* regulation whether through disciplinary actions or medical negligence claims. The Singapore High Court in *Pang Ah San* couched the issue in the disciplinary action as follows: 'How does the current regulatory regime balance the need to ensure the safety of patients without stifling innovation which might benefit patients?'[41] Such a sentiment was echoed by the Singapore Court of Appeal in *Hii Chii Kok v Ooi Peng Jin London Lucien*.[42] It had considered imposing a stricter standard as an alternative to the *Bolam* and *Bolitho* tests for assessing the standard of care of medical doctors in diagnosis and treatment, but rejected the idea due to the potential adverse impact on innovations:

> [R]eplacing the *Bolam* test and *Bolitho* addendum with a more demanding standard may encourage therapeutic and scientific conservatism, as doctors might be incentivised to cling to the most established and mainstream approaches regardless of their relative effectiveness. Such an undue focus on orthodoxy could well discourage innovation and unnecessarily prolong the lifespan of 'best practices' which, in truth, may be inferior to newer but less established competing practices.[43]

Second, the argument for applying the *Bolam* test to assess standard of care in diagnosis and treatment – that medical doctors with their medical expertise are better positioned to decide on the intricacies of diagnosis and treatment where genuine differences of opinion exist – is less persuasive when assessing the use of

[39] *Pang Ah San v SMC* [2014] 1 SLR 1094 [55], [56].
[40] ibid [61].
[41] ibid [2].
[42] *Hii Chii Kok v Ooi Peng Jin London Lucien* [2017] 2 SLR 492 (CA).
[43] ibid [82].

medical AI. This is because medical doctors, as it stands, do not necessarily have the requisite expertise in medical AI. In fact, they would likely require some training from software developers and designers or AI providers prior to the deployment of novel medical AI for their clinical practice. Again, as mentioned above, such a position can change over time as the use of medical AI becomes more prevalent.

Finally, we must remember that the *Bolam* and *Bolitho* tests do not constitute the whole of the reasonable doctor standard. The Singapore Court of Appeal in *Hii Chii Kok* had observed that the *Bolam* and *Bolitho* tests are merely heuristics to aid the courts in determining the standard of care of doctors. What is ultimately crucial is whether the doctor acted reasonably.[44] Applying this principle to medical AI, the main inquiry should be whether it would be reasonable for the doctor to use medical AI given a holistic assessment of the risks and benefits of the innovation without being confined exclusively to the medical expert opinions.

With respect to technological innovations generally, Henderson[45] argues that the negligence rule allows for the balancing of risks of technological innovations and likelihood with the costs of precaution. As mentioned above, the non-hindsight rule ensures that doctors would not be responsible for the effects of technological innovations which were not apparent at the time of the alleged breach of duty. The dangers of hindsight bias – that the new or increased knowledge and experience from the use of medical AI after the event should not be utilised to render the doctor liable for negligence – were specifically highlighted by the Singapore Court of Appeal in *Hii Chii Kok*.[46]

Admittedly, the negligence standard does not always give certainty in terms of judicial outcomes and is based on *ex post* regulation. Indeed, in view of the nature of the evolving technology and implementation of medical AI, some uncertainty is inevitable. Nonetheless, negligence principles and their application to medical AI can be refined over time based on the overarching objective standard that is capable of balancing competing considerations in a way that is sensitive to the contexts and the risks involved.

B. (Un)Reasonable Reliance on Medical AI and Related Parties

The medical doctor or hospital may seek to absolve themselves of liability on the basis that reasonable reliance was placed on the AI developers or the authority

[44] ibid [104].

[45] James A Henderson Jr, 'Tort vs Technology: Accommodating Disruptive Innovation' (2015) 47 *Arizona State Law Journal* 1145.

[46] *Hii Chii Kok* (n 42) [159], citing *Rosenberg v Percival* [2001] HCA 18 [68] and *Maloney v Commissioner for Railways* (1978) 18 ALR 147, 148. The court in *Rosenberg* noted that perfection or the use of increased knowledge or experience embraced in hindsight after the event should form no part of the components of what is reasonable in all the circumstances.

approving the use of AI. The use of medical AI in Singapore requires the approval of the Health Sciences Authority[47] under the category of 'medical devices' as stated in the Health Products Act.[48] For example, the developers of Selena+ (or Singapore Eye Lesion Analyser plus) – a deep learning system to analyse retinal photographs to detect diabetic eye diseases – had sought approval from the Health Sciences Authority (HSA).[49] The HSA has recently approved the use of an AI-powered software – Augmented Vascular Analysis (AVA) – as a class B device for the automated analysis and reporting of vascular ultrasound scans.[50]

Under the Health Products (Medical Devices) Regulations 2010, the two main criteria are the intended use of the medical device and the health risks posed to the end-user (ie, the patient). The medical devices are classified according to the risks involved.[51] Registration of the medical device will be allowed where the 'overall intended benefits to an end-user of the medical device outweigh the overall risks' and it is 'suitable for its intended purpose and that any risk associated with its use is minimised'.[52] The intended purpose also has to conform to the safety and performance requirements for the medical device.

To deal specifically with AI-driven medical devices, the HSA issued in December 2019 the *Regulatory Guidelines for Software Medical Devices – A Lifecycle Approach*. One section of the *Regulatory Guidelines* pertains to pre-market registration for Artificial Intelligence Medical Devices (AI-MD) as well as process controls and validations to monitor the learning and evolving performances of devices with continuous learning capabilities. Product registration entails the provision of various categories of information relating to the input data and features (such as the patient's historical records, diagnostic images and medication records), the training, validation and test datasets, the AI model selection, the device workflow (eg, whether it is human-in-the-loop) and so on.[53]

Assuming the medical AI is approved for use by the authorities, can the medical doctor or hospital justify their reliance on the AI developers and/or approving authorities? According to the Singapore case of *TV Media Pte Ltd v De Cruz Andrea Heidi*,[54] the defendant, an importer and distributor of slimming pills, could not absolve negligence liability by placing 'unquestioning reliance' on a health-approving authority with respect to certain pills that caused the plaintiff's injuries.

[47] The governing laws are the Health Products Act (Cap 122D, Rev Ed 2008) and the subsidiary legislation (Health Products (Medical Devices) Regulations 2010).

[48] Health Products Act (Cap 122D, Rev Ed 2008), sched 1.

[49] Timothy Goh, 'An AI for the Eye' *The Straits Times* (6 July 2019), https://www.straitstimes.com/singapore/health/an-ai-for-the-eye.

[50] Eileen Yu, 'Singapore Approves AI for Vascular Ultrasound Scans' (10 December 2019), www.zdnet.com/article/singapore-approves-ai-for-vascular-ultrasound-scans.

[51] See the Third Schedule.

[52] Health Products (Medical Devices) Regulations 2010, cl 25.

[53] See the US Food and Drug Administration (FDA)'s White Paper, 'Proposed Regulatory Framework for Modifications to Artificial Intelligence/Machine Learning (AI/ML)-Based Software as a Medical Device (SaMD)', www.fda.gov/media/122535/download.

[54] *TV Media Pte Ltd v De Cruz Andrea Heidi* [2004] 3 SLR(R) 543 [71].

In that case, there were suspicious circumstances arising from tests conducted on the pills. If this argument were to be used in the context of medical AI, the doctor would have to show that he or she had reasonably relied on the AI developers and/or approving authorities as opposed to placing mere unquestioning reliance. If the doctor were aware that certain aspects of the medical AI (such as the training data or its method of implementation) might enhance the risks of errors or bias, such reliance on the AI developers and/or approving authority would not be reasonable.

To determine the reasonableness or otherwise of reliance on medical AI which has been approved as a medical device, we should consider the authority's scope of approval, the review process before granting approvals and the knowledge of the medical doctor regarding such processes. The extent of the medical doctor's reasonable reliance on AI should also depend on whether the AI is employed either as a primary diagnostic or treatment tool or is merely used as an ancillary diagnostic or treatment tool to provide statistics or analysis to assist and/or complement the doctor in the treatment of the patient.

Useful analogies may also be drawn from existing law relating to the medical doctor's reliance on non-AI medical diagnostic or predictive tools. In the Singapore High Court decision of *Hii Chii Kok v Ooi Peng Jin London Lucien*,[55] the doctor's heavy reliance on the high positive predictive value of the patient's Gallium scan for a specific type of tumour was justified on the grounds that the Gallium scan was the most 'sensitive and advanced diagnostic tool' available for the detection of the tumour, the results of malignancy being based on 'the state of learning at that time' and that the 'index of suspicion' was raised due to the hotspots indicated by the patient's Gallium scan.[56] These grounds relating to the sensitivity and sophistication of the tool and the level of suspicion from observed symptoms based on medical knowledge at the relevant time are arguably valid considerations for assessing the reasonable use of medical AI.

C. (Un)Reasonable Omission to Utilise Medical AI

Would the medical doctor be liable to a patient who suffers injury as a result of the doctor's omission to use AI? AI may be able to detect patterns in the training data for the purpose of diagnosis which doctors are unable to find. Topol[57] refers to System 1 thinking for medical diagnosis, which is automatic, quick and intuitive using heuristics (or rules of thumb) rather than System 2 deliberative thinking, and that System 1 thinking is prone to cognitive biases in doctors. Moreover, doctors do not deal with as wide a range of patient data as an AI system with a large dataset. For example, it was reported that IBM Watson diagnosed a rare form

[55] *Hii Chii Kok v Ooi Peng Jin London Lucien* [2016] 2 SLR 544 (Chan Seng Onn J).
[56] ibid [162].
[57] Eric Topol, *Deep Medicine* (Basic Books, 2019) 43.

of leukaemia which was overlooked by the University of Tokyo treatment team.[58] Where AI is known to deliver more accurate diagnosis or treatment compared to human doctors, but the doctor refuses to use medical AI that was made available to him or her without any cost impediments, he or she is likely to be prima facie in breach for his or her own error in diagnosis which resulted in the patient's injury unless justified on other grounds (eg, lack of general practice for its use).

We can draw analogies from cases on the omission to use technology. The US court in *The TJ Hooper*[59] held that it was negligent for a tugboat not to have a working radio on board to receive up-to-date storm weather warnings. Most tugboats did not have any at that time, though the technology was readily available, relatively inexpensive and, if used consistently, would potentially prevent the accident in question. Justice Learned Hand in *The TJ Hooper* stated:

> In most cases reasonable prudence is in fact common prudence; but strictly speaking it is never its measure; a whole calling may have unduly lagged in the adoption of new and available devices. It never may set its own tests, however persuasive be its usages. Courts must in the end say what is required; there are precautions so imperative that even their universal disregard will not exclude their omission.[60]

Indeed, it is the court that will ultimately decide on reasonableness and legal liability. Nonetheless, the liability for the omission to use technology depends to a large extent on the existence of a general practice relating to its use. In *BNM v National University of Singapore*,[61] the university was found not to be liable for failing to provide automated external defibrillators at its swimming pool as the significance of having defibrillators at the pools had 'not yet coalesced into a general practice', even though there was 'an emerging acceptance' at that time.[62] Reference was also made to authoritative bodies which might be able to provide guidance on the prevailing standards.[63] Extrapolating from this principle, the omission to use medical AI may be unreasonable only when there is a general practice regarding its use. That said, such general practices and standards, though an important factor, are not determinative as they may be regarded as too lax. The overarching standard of reasonable care would still govern.

Another possible allegation might be that the doctor failed to discharge his or her duty of keeping abreast of medical developments and technology. Again, this duty is not absolute, but is based on reasonable care. The fact that a medical

[58] Bernie Monegain, 'IBM Watson Pinpoints Rare Form of Leukemia after Doctors Misdiagnosed Patient' *Healthcare IT News* (8 August 2016), www.healthcareitnews.com/news/ibm-watson-pinpoints-rare-form-leukemia-after-doctors-misdiagnosed-patient.
[59] *The TJ Hooper*, 60 F 2d 737 (2d Cir 1932).
[60] ibid 740.
[61] *BNM v National University of Singapore* [2014] 4 SLR 931 [54].
[62] *cf Thompson v Smiths Shipbuilders (North Shields) Ltd* [1984] QB 405. In this case, the court held that it was the defendant's responsibility to provide protective equipment when social awareness arose as to the dangers of deafness due to industrial noise.
[63] *BNM* (n 61) [54].

doctor was not aware of certain medical information in medical journals that was relevant for the diagnosis or treatment of a patient did not necessarily mean that he or she was negligent.[64] However, it is a different situation when an AI-driven knowledge interface such as Watson is made available to the doctor, and the doctor fails to consider the AI results derived from the AI's review of millions of patterns of a disease. It would call for an explanation from the doctor should the patient be diagnosed wrongly. Existing case law supports the position that a doctor may be adjudged negligent in failing to use assistive diagnostic tools to help him or her make more accurate diagnoses.[65] Considerations of relative costs and utility of the medical AI would also be relevant here. As diagnostic AIs improve over time and become more affordable and commonly used, there would likely be increased 'legal' pressure on doctors and hospitals to make use of them in medical diagnosis.[66]

A more controversial situation may arise where the doctor uses medical AI diagnostics, but decides to override the decision made by the AI. Where the medical AI is known or generally accepted to be reliable, and the practice of using that medical AI for the provision of specified medical services has been generally accepted as proper, it is argued that the defendant doctor would have to provide concrete justifications for his or her decision (such as the potential risks of inaccuracy or bias) if and when he or she wishes to override the decisions from the medical AI output.

D. Inaccuracy, Bias, the Opacity of Medical AI and the Standard of Care

The problem of potential bias and inaccuracies from AI are well documented. This can sometimes occur when the AI operates from logical processes based on the inputs fed into the system without the benefit of human intuition and common sense. Machine learning has, for instance, wrongly predicted that patients with both pneumonia and asthma are in better condition than those with pneumonia only and that such patients should be discharged, even though they are in fact of higher risk. The wrong predictions arose because the patients with a history of asthma were directly taken to the intensive care unit, which meant their files rarely appeared in the 'requires further care' data category; as a result, the algorithm classified them as low risk.[67]

Bias or errors can also arise from flawed or badly designed algorithms, or where the training data fed into the AI system may not be sufficiently comprehensive

[64] *Crawford v Charing Cross Hospital*, *The Times*, 8 December 1953; *Dwan v Farquhar* [1988] 1 Qd R 234.

[65] *Bergen v Sturgeon General Hospital* (1984) 38 CCLT 155; *Smith v Salford HA* [1994] 5 Med LR 321.

[66] Froomkin, Kerr and Pineau (n 18).

[67] Kate Crawford and Ryan Calo, 'There is a Blind Spot in AI Research' (2016) 538 *Nature* 311, www.nature.com/news/there-is-a-blind-spot-in-ai-research-1.20805.

or representative of the population. For example, where there is a significantly disproportionate number of images of lesions on dark skins made available in the training data, the output may manifest biases against darker-skinned individuals. Moreover, there could be a mismatch between the training and operational data which requires adaptation to new patient contexts.[68] Despite the greater efficiency and speed of AI generally in medical diagnosis, AI may in fact perform worse than human doctors in these specific scenarios.

It is argued that legal liability under the tort of negligence should depend on the doctors' and hospitals' level of control over the training data or algorithms, their extent of knowledge of possible inaccuracies or biases, their ability or otherwise to take steps to modify or remove the data or bias, and the extent to which the AI can explain the outputs or process.

It should be noted that not all harms from biased medical AI are relevant in pinning legal liability on doctors and hospitals. For example, biased training data may generate outputs that wrongly predict health conditions of certain disadvantaged groups and, as a result, doctors do not provide the proper treatment for members of those disadvantaged groups. But it is not always easy to prove that the patient in question is a member of the disadvantaged classes who had in fact suffered the damage arising from the doctor's negligence in relying on medical AI.

In litigation proceedings, the doctors may be put on the stand to explain his or her decision for the diagnosis or treatment in connection with the AI output. Currently, the machines learn based on the recognition of patterns from the training data. They are adept at finding correlations. However, learning machines may not have the capability to provide *causal* explanations to questions such as 'What if I had acted/omitted?' or the retrospective 'What if I had acted differently?' based on counterfactual analysis. That causal reasoning in machines may form part of the drive towards strong AI[69] is a matter of consideration for the future. If the AI cannot explain its decisions in human-interpretable terms, what can be reasonably expected of the doctor in terms of giving an explanation?

Price[70] suggests that even though healthcare providers would find it difficult to evaluate the substantive accuracy and reliability of opaque medical AI, they should nonetheless exercise due care to evaluate the procedural quality of the AI (eg, by examining the expertise of the developer and performing independent external validation). Hence, based on Price's proposal, the subject matter of the standard of care shifts from exercising care in respect of the patient's diagnosis and treatment to exercising care in scrutinising AI quality. With regard to the use of algorithms in AI models generally, other procedural measures include the reproducibility of

[68] Robert Challen et al, 'Artificial Intelligence, Bias and Clinical Safety' (2019) 28 *BMJ Quality Safety* 231.

[69] Judea Pearl, 'Theoretical Impediments to Machine Learning with Seven Sparks from the Causal Revolution' (January 2018), www.arxiv.org/pdf/1801.04016.pdf.

[70] W Nicholson Price, 'Medical Malpractice and Black-Box Medicine' in Glenn Cohen, Holly Lynch, Effy Vaynea and Urs Gasser (eds), *Big Data, Health Law, and Bioethics* (Cambridge University Press, 2018).

results using the same AI model, the traceability of the AI's decisions and the datasets, and the auditability of algorithms by internal or external assessors.[71] The need for procedural validation may depend on the assessment of risks by the clinics and hospitals involved in the use of medical AI as part of their quality assurance obligations. This also relates to the point highlighted above on assessing the hospital's or doctor's reasonable reliance on the approving authorities and developers when assessing their standard of care in the use of medical AI for patient care.

In addition, the explainability of AI does not exist in a vacuum, but should be balanced against other values (such as the accuracy of outputs, the consistency of performance, and the nature and extent of the risks involved) when assessing the standard of care of doctors and hospitals.[72] Where the AI system is known to produce accurate results (eg, 99 per cent accuracy in diagnosing particular illnesses) and consistency in observable effects for sustained periods, but the outcomes cannot be explained, should doctors and hospitals use such medical AI? After all, not all medical outcomes are supported by underlying theoretical or causal explanations. For example, the scientific explanation as to why electroconvulsive therapy can treat severe depression and other mental disorders remains elusive, though it is widely used with the informed consent of patients.[73] In the medical domain, the pathophysiological disease is often uncertain and clinical practice is largely based on accumulated experience, empirical and clinical findings as opposed to explanations underlying a universal causal system.[74]

It is thus suggested that medical AI without such causal explanations may be used with the patient's informed consent,[75] subject to certain caveats. First, its accuracy rate for diagnosis should be superior to that of human doctors. Second, we would need to enquire if its accuracy can be verified by reference to independent evidence (such as the positive responses of the patients to treatment based on the AI diagnosis). If so, such AI diagnosis should be relied upon in the short term if there are significant health benefits for patients and provided the risks of relying on the AI are not grave. The explainability of the AI should remain a medium- to long-term target, but may arguably be sacrificed in the short term, provided there is clear independent evidence of the superiority of AI diagnosis and its accuracy.

[71] Personal Data Protection Commission, 'A Proposed Model Artificial Intelligence Governance Framework' (January 2020), www.pdpc.gov.sg/-/media/files/pdpc/pdf-files/resource-for-organisation/ai/sgmodelaigovframework2.pdf, paras 3.25 ff.

[72] Phillip Hacker, Ralf Krestel, Stefan Grundmann and Felix Naumann, 'Explainable AI under Contract and Tort Law: Legal Incentives and Technical Challenges' (2020) *Artificial Intelligence and Law*, www.doi.org/10.1007/s10506-020-09260-6.

[73] Neuroimaging studies have revealed anticonvulsant effects (decreased blood flow and decreased metabolism) in the frontal lobes, and neurotrophic effects (increased perfusion and metabolism and increased volume of the hippocampus) in the medial temporal lobes: see Christopher C. Abbott et al, 'A Review of Longitudinal Electroconvulsive Therapy: Neuroimaging Investigations' (2015) 27(1) *Journal of Geriatric Psychiatry and* Neurology 33, www./doi.org/10.1177/0891988713516542.

[74] Alex John London, 'Artificial Intelligence and Black-Box Medical Decisions: Accuracy versus Explainability' (2019) 49(1) *Hastings Centre Report* 15, 17, www.doi.org/10.1002/hast.973.

[75] See section II.E below.

E. Medical Advice Based on AI Output

The giving of medical advice directly by medical AI without human doctors in the loop may become a reality in the future. The task requires the AI to understand patients' subjective preferences and values, which may be challenging for medical AI at this current stage of development. At present, the more plausible scenario is one where the human doctor gives medical advice to the patient based on the medical AI outputs that the doctor has had an opportunity to review. Should doctors disclose to the patient the roles and risks of emerging technology such as medical AI in the giving of medical advice? Should they reveal information concerning the risks of inaccuracy and bias in the medical AI used for diagnosis, prediction of risks or treatment? For instance, AI-assisted CDSS can predict, in real time, the patient's chance of survival to discharge and their ability to recover.[76] If there is a significant risk that the AI predictive analysis might be inaccurate due to the lack of representative training data at the relevant time, should such risks be disclosed to the patient when giving medical advice?

In Singapore, the Parliament has recently passed amendments to the Civil Law Act[77] concerning the standard of care expected of medical practitioners when giving medical advice. In essence, the new section 37 stipulates that the standard of care for medical advice is based on 'peer professional opinion' in line with the *Bolam* (deference to a respectable body of medical opinion) and *Bolitho* (logic) tests.[78] Such peer professional opinion must require the medical practitioner to give to the patient: (i) information which the patient would reasonably require to make an 'informed decision about whether to undergo treatment or follow a medical advice'; and (ii) information that the medical practitioner 'knows or ought reasonably to know is material to the patient' for the purpose of making such informed decision.[79] The materiality of information would be assessed based on any specific queries or concerns raised by the patient to the treatment or medical advice which has been *either* expressly communicated by the patient to the medical doctor *or*, in the absence of express communications, which would be apparent to the medical doctor from the patient's medical records to which the doctor has reasonable access and ought reasonably to review.[80] Furthermore, the peer professional opinion must support the non-provision of the abovementioned information to the patient only where there is reasonable justification (for example, in cases of an emergency life-saving situation and where the patient waives his or her right to the information).[81] The reasonable patient perspective and the justifications for the non-provision of information are similar to those enunciated

[76] Lysaght et al(n 4) 309.
[77] Civil Law (Amendment) Bill No 33/2020. At the time of writing, the law has yet to take effect.
[78] Civil Law Act, s 37(1).
[79] ibid s 37(2)(a).
[80] ibid s 37(3).
[81] ibid s 37(2)(b) and the illustrations.

in the Court of Appeal decision in *Hii Chii Kok*,[82] which had in turn adapted the UK Supreme Court's approach in *Montgomery v Lanarkshire Health Board*.[83] Hence, insofar as medical advice is concerned, the *Hii Chii Kok* approach has been substantially integrated within the general framework of the *Bolam* and *Bolitho* tests.

With respect to information that the patient would consider relevant and material, the court in *Hii Chii Kok* had referred to factors such as the likelihood of the risk as well as the severity of the consequences.[84] Relevant information would include the benefits and likely side-effects or risks from a recommended treatment, and also the advantages and disadvantages of alternative procedures and of non-treatment[85] – and with respect to diagnosis, the degree of certainty of a diagnosis, the reasons for the lack of certainty and 'whether more could be done to clarify the uncertainty'.[86]

In comparison, the Malaysian common law position is encapsulated in *Foo Fio Na v Dr Soo Fook Mun*.[87] Insofar as medical advice is concerned, the Malaysian Federal Court favoured the Australian test in *Rogers v Whitaker*[88] that the courts should 'adjudicate on what is the appropriate standard of care after giving weight to the paramount consideration that a person is entitled to make his own decisions about his life'[89] instead of the *Bolam* test. It has in two subsequent cases[90] affirmed that the principle in *Foo Fio Na* applied only to medical advice and not diagnosis and treatment. Further, as observed by the Malaysian Federal Court in *Dr Hari Krishnan v Megat Noor Ishak bin Megat Ibrahim*,[91] the doctor's obligation to explain the risks to which a reasonable patient would attach significance extended beyond giving general precautions of risks of the operation in the consent form signed by the patient. For diagnosis and treatment, on the other hand, *Bolam* and *Bolitho* will continue to apply to determine the standard of care with respect to medical diagnosis and treatment.[92]

Applying this to medical AI, the first point to highlight is that just as doctors do not have to share with patients the equipment, methods, prior training and medical treatises they rely on in coming to a decision on diagnoses or treatment,

[82] *Hii Chii Kok* (n 42) [132].
[83] [2015] UKSC 11; [2015] 1 AC 1430.
[84] *Hii Chii Kok* (n 42) [140].
[85] ibid [142], [146].
[86] ibid [143].
[87] *Foo Fio Na v Dr Soo Fook Mun* [2007] 1 MLJ 593.
[88] *Rogers v Whitaker* [1992] 175 CLR 479.
[89] Cited in *Foo Fio Na* (n 87) [47].
[90] *Zulhasnimar bt Hasan Basri and Another v Dr KuppuVelumani P and Others* [2017] 5 MLJ 438; *Dr Hari Krishnan v Megat Noor Ishak bin Megat Ibrahim* [2018] 3 MLJ 281.
[91] *Dr Hari Krishnan* (n 90) [73], [74].
[92] But note the Malaysian Court of Appeal decision in *Ahmad Zubir bin Zahid (Suing by Himself and as the Administrator of the Estate of Fatimah bt Samat, Deceased) v Datuk Dr Zainal Abidin Abdul Hamid and Others* [2019] 5 MLJ 95, which continues to cite *Foo Fio Na* (which adopted the *Rogers v Whittaker* approach, but rejected *Montgomery* without explaining the differences, if any, between *Rogers* and *Montgomery*).

there is no general obligation for doctors or hospitals to disclose the use of medical AI. There does not appear to be any violation of patient autonomy here. Prima facie, the equipment, methods, training and medical treatises per se relied upon by the doctor do not relate to the risks to which a reasonable patient would attach significance under Malaysian law. In Singapore, the obligation arises only with respect to information given by the medical doctor that, in the peer professional opinion, the patient would reasonably require in order to make an informed decision and information that is material to the patient about whether to undergo the treatment or follow the medical advice. Material information in this regard would likely include, as mentioned in *Hii Chii Kok*, uncertainties in the diagnosis, the risks and benefits of the treatment, complications and options.[93] Though these factors are not specifically provided for in the Singapore statutory amendments, they are consistent with the scope of the materiality of information pertaining to the patient's decision as to whether to undergo treatment or follow medical advice stated in section 37.

If the medical AI comes up with a diagnosis of the patient's skin lesions that are quite rare based on training data (images of such lesions), would the doctor have to disclose the inadequacies of the training data? Commenting on the use of a particular scan by the doctor for diagnosis in *Hii Chii Kok*, the patient alleged that the defendants had failed to inform him that the Gallium PET/CT scan 'was a newly introduced scan and had only been used in 20 patients and particularly only in 5 instances' to diagnose the disease. The Singapore Court of Appeal said that it was not necessary to disclose such specific information,[94] but that a reasonable patient would wish to know 'the limitations of the Gallium scan, and, in particular, that there was a possibility that the scan results could have identified false positives – not the specific number of times the scan had previously been used'.[95] Extrapolating to medical AI, the material limitations if any of the medical AI used for diagnosis and the potential unreliability of the outcomes generated (from inadequate training data) would arguably be relevant and material information for disclosure.

Where the proposed treatment via medical AI is experimental or novel, should the doctor be obliged to disclose such information? In *Gunapathy*, the technique of laser radiosurgery known as 'XKnife'[96] used by the defendant doctor was experimental at the relevant time.[97] The Singapore Court of Appeal, applying the *Bolam*

[93] *Hii Chii Kok* (n 42) [138]–[146].

[94] *cf Johnson v Kokemoor* 545 NW 2d 495, 498 (Wis 1996), where the court held that information concerning a physician's relative inexperience in performing a particular procedure and his risk statistics compared to other physicians was relevant to the patient's informed consent.

[95] *Hii Chii Kok* (n 42) [186].

[96] ibid [32]. This 'XKnife' procedure was described by the Singapore Court of Appeal as involving 'high-energy X-ray photon beams artificially generated by a linear accelerator, delivered in a single high dose of irradiation to the desired area of the brain. The beams are directed through a collimator, which concentrates and guides each x ray beam in the required direction'.

[97] *Gunapathy* (n 30) [39]. The treatment of neurocytomas by radiosurgery at that time was largely uncharted territory.

and *Bolitho* tests to medical advice without the benefit of the 'material' risks test viewed from the patient's perspective, did not consider the omission to disclose the experimental nature of the technique to be relevant for assessing the neurosurgeon's standard of care.[98] Based on the current statutory position in Singapore and *Foo Fio Na* in Malaysia for medical advice, it could be argued that the experimental nature of the technique would be 'material' to the patient where it is linked to the risks of laser radiosurgery to treat a brain tumour based on the facts in *Gunapathy*. Following this line of reasoning, the risks of medical AI options that have potential adverse effects on the health conditions of the patient would be material to the patient and should therefore be disclosed unless the risks or the potential harms are *de minimis*.

Where the doctor's advice is reliant on medical AI-driven diagnosis or treatment, information concerning the potentially biased or inaccurate AI outputs or training data and the opacity of AI might be relevant to a reasonable patient. This is provided that the use of medical AI would materially increase the risks of errors or uncertainties in diagnosis or treatment or the likelihood of complications. Not all cases of unexplainable medical AI warrant disclosure. Where the medical AI has been reliable in generating accurate outputs based on available external validation processes and there is no evidence of foreseeable risks of errors that can adversely affect the patient, there should not, as a general principle, be any obligation to disclose the non-explainable feature. However, the obligation is ultimately dependent on the context at the relevant time (eg, the extent of usage of the AI and the patient's knowledge thereof).[99] The patient has the burden to show that the information is, according to peer professional opinion, material to the decision as to whether to undergo the treatment or to follow medical advice in Singapore or, in the case of Malaysia, the information is that which a reasonable patient would attach significance. In any event, when doctors are obliged to disclose the risks from medical AI, they are also entitled to share the methods they have used (eg, external and institutional validation of AI quality and processes) to mitigate the AI-related risks and uncertainties insofar as information regarding such methods is relevant to the particular patient's health conditions.

Whilst medical AI-related information *can* be relevant, doctors must also guard against the practice of bombarding the patient with excessive technical details (such as those relating to the AI functioning and models) – a warning sounded by the Singapore Court of Appeal in *Hii Chii Kok*[100] – as that would adversely affect doctor–patient communications and would defeat the raison d'etre of informed consent.

[98] ibid [123]–[131]. The doctors only informed the patient of a five per cent risk of complications as a result of the XKnife procedure, such as brain swelling and brain damage.

[99] Glenn Cohen, 'Informed Consent and Medical Artificial Intelligence: What to Tell the Patient?' (2020) 108 *Georgetown Law Journal* 1425, 1451.

[100] *Hii Chii Kok* (n 42) [143].

III. Alternative Basis for Tortious Liability? Assessing Vicarious Liability, the Independent Contractor Defence and Non-delegable Duties

From the discussion above, the standard of care principles under the tort of negligence are sufficiently adaptable for assessing the liability of hospitals and medical doctors based on fault in the use of medical AI. They are capable of balancing the competing considerations of efficiency and innovations, and the professional and ethical responsibilities of the medical profession with compensatory justice for injured patients, even if there are aspects that are still to be ironed out. That said, we should also consider the liability issue from another angle. Should doctors and hospitals be ever liable in tort for the use of medical AI when there is no proof of negligence? Are there good grounds under existing tort law for making them strictly liable for errors in medical AI?

Strict liability for the tortious acts of another apply to owners of chattels who lent them to others, resulting in injuries suffered by third parties,[101] the principal for the acts of agents based on authority (whether actual or ostensible), and to persons for harms caused by ultra-hazardous activities.[102] On a prima facie level, it seems natural to consider strict liability regimes in respect of medical clinics and hospitals. Such enterprises are in a better position to insure themselves against claims by patients for medical injuries and also have deeper pockets. Organisations, especially large hospitals, have the resources to implement quality assurance programmes relating to the deployment of medical AI. As there is no strict liability (legislative) regime in Singapore pertaining to products,[103] and the product liability regime under Part X of the Consumer Protection Act 1999 in Malaysia does not extend to 'products' used in the provision of medical services,[104] this section will instead focus on whether clinics and hospitals may be strictly liable in tort in respect of the use of medical AI with reference to the existing common law doctrines of vicarious liability and non-delegable duties. From the ensuing discussion, it will be apparent that these existing doctrines are not directly applicable to determine the legal liabilities of medical doctors and hospitals in utilising medical AI. Nonetheless, the analysis below will help us explore the relevance of strict liability doctrines to medical AI and their limits.

[101] *Morgans v Launchbury* [1973] AC 127.

[102] *Biffa Waste Services Ltd v Maschinenfabrik Ernst Hese GmbH* [2009] QB 725 [78].

[103] This is on the assumption that medical AI can qualify as products under the putative product liability system, which is not necessarily the case.

[104] The term 'product' under the statute refers to goods that are primarily purchased, used or consumed for personal, domestic or household purposes: see s 66 read with s 3 of the Consumer Protection Act. Moreover, s 2(2) of the statute specifically excludes healthcare services provided by healthcare professionals or healthcare facilities from its scope. See also Anisah Che Ngah, Sakina Shaik Ahmad Yusoff and Rahmah Ismail, 'Product Liability in Malaysia' in Helmut Koziol et al (eds), *Product Liability: Fundamental Questions in a Comparative Perspective* (De Gruyter, 2017) 120–46.

A. Vicarious Liability

Under existing law, the defendant may be vicariously liable for the tortious acts of the tortfeasor committed in the course of employment to the extent that it is fair and just to impose liability on the defendant.[105] Applied to the clinical setting, this means that the hospital or clinic may be legally responsible for the tortious acts of its employees even if there is no proof of any fault on their part.[106] Can the medical AI be regarded as an autonomous agent which performs a task on behalf of the clinic or hospital and be treated as an employee or akin to an employee? There are three obstacles to applying the doctrine of vicarious liability to medical AI. First, the employer's vicarious (secondary) liability can only arise where the employee is himself or herself liable under tort law. If the AI is not a legal person, it cannot be subject to tortious liability. The vicarious liability doctrine is therefore not applicable to render the hospital or doctor liable for the use of medical AI. Even if the fully autonomous AI can be regarded as a legal person,[107] there is the additional issue of whether there is any practical advantage in commencing a lawsuit against the AI for its errors since it has no assets to compensate the victim.

Second, the requirement of the existence of an employment relationship[108] between the defendant and the tortfeasor or a relationship akin to employment is far from straightforward. The hospital/doctor–AI relationship is, strictly speaking, *not* an employment relationship. But can it be argued as being akin to an employment relationship? Applying to medical AI, we observe a continuum of expertise and level of autonomy in the decision-making of AI systems. Where the medical AI applies machine learning based on the labelled data fed into the AI and carries out instructions to perform specific medical tasks, it is arguable that the relationship between the human doctor/hospitals and the AI is analogous to one of employment. The position should not change even if it is generally accepted that the medical AI can outperform human doctors in those specific tasks. Employees sometimes possess greater expertise than their employers in specific tasks. The expertise of the employee does not in itself automatically exclude him or her from being regarded as an employee for the purpose of vicarious liability.[109]

Other factors to consider would be whether: (a) the medical AI is integrated into the work processes of the clinic and hospital's provisioning of medical services; (b) control is exercised by the hospital and clinic over the data fed into the AI system and the labelling of data; and (c) there are review processes for the adoption

[105] *Skandinaviska Enskilda Banken AB (Publ), Singapore Branch v Asia Pacific Breweries (Singapore) Pte Ltd* [2011] 3 SLR 540.

[106] *Gold v Essex County Council* [1942] 2 KB 293; *Cassidy v Ministry of Health* [1951] 2 KB 343; *Dr Hari Krishnan* (n 90) [111].

[107] See Belinda Bennett and Angela Daly, 'Recognising Rights for Robots: Can We? Will We? Should We?' (2020) 12(2) *Law, Innovation and Technology* 60.

[108] Such an employment relationship is based on certain indicia, including control, integration into organisation, personal investment and contract terms.

[109] *Gold v Essex County Council* [1942] 2 KB 293, 305 (McKinnon LJ) and 313 (Goddard LJ).

of AI output that will form the bases for the ultimate decisions to be made by the clinic or hospital vis-a-vis their patients.

Third, we need to ascertain whether the medical AI, even assuming that it can be treated as being akin to an employee, has committed a tort (eg, negligence). In this regard, we need to answer the earlier question concerning the legal standard of care we expect from the medical AI itself. Abbott[110] suggests that if the computer is safer than humans, the new standard of care should be the reasonable computer standard based on the 'industry customary, average, safest technology'.[111] But we may legitimately question why safety should necessarily prevail over other considerations such as efficiency or accuracy. More specifically for medical AI, Chung and Zink[112] argue, on the premise that medical AI should be given a unique legal status akin to personhood, that the expected standard under medical malpractice may be analogised to that of a 'medical resident' (or similar to a medical houseman in Singapore and Malaysia). However, this standard overlooks the fact that the AI may be capable of outperforming the experienced human doctor (not to mention the medical resident) in diagnoses. Apart from the fact that the appropriate standard for medical AI itself is open to debate, such standards may be moving targets, given the fast-evolving changes and improvements in technology.

B. Independent Contractor Defence and Non-delegable Duties of Hospitals and Doctors with Respect to Medical AI

Where the hospitals and medical doctors using the medical AI will not be in a position to understand or exercise any meaningful control over the method of interpreting the data collated and processed by unsupervised machine learning, and the AI is capable of making its own rules as to how to diagnose or treat patients, medical AI may be treated as analogous to an independent contractor. In effect, the medical AI functions like a 'second doctor'. In that future scenario where the medical AI functions autonomously without any human doctors in the loop, the hospital or medical doctors should not, as a general rule, be liable for the wrongs committed by the medical AI. This is based on the independent contractor defence that one should not be responsible for the harms caused by his or her independent contractors. Additionally, it might be argued that where the hospital or medical doctor is not proved to be negligent (as discussed in the previous section) for the use of medical AI, it would be ironic to make him or her *indirectly* liable for the acts or omissions of the AI designer or software provider over whom he or

[110] Ryan Abbott, 'The Reasonable Computer: Disrupting the Paradigm of Tort Liability' (2018) 36(1) *George Washington Law Review* 1.

[111] ibid 41.

[112] Jason Chung and Amanda Zink, 'Hey Watson: Can I Sue You for Malpractice? Examining the Liability of Artificial Intelligence in Medicine' (2018) 11(2) *Asia Pacific Journal of Health Law & Ethics* 51.

she has no control.[113] The one possible exception to this is the doctrine of non-delegable duties that may be imposed on hospitals and medical doctors, which we will now examine.

The doctrine of non-delegable duties is distinct from vicarious liability in that the former focuses on the relationship between the defendant and the claimant rather than the defendant and the tortfeasor. The commercial reasons underpinning vicarious liability (such as employers having deeper pockets and being able to shoulder risks since they reap the benefits of the enterprise) are irrelevant to non-delegable duties as stated by the Malaysian Federal Court in *Dr Kok Choong Seng and Sunway Medical Centre Berhad v Soo Cheng Lin*.[114] A hospital and doctor may owe non-delegable duties to a patient under their care, supervision or control[115] and remain liable despite the fact that they have delegated an integral function relating to the care of the patient to an independent contractor.

Under the two-stage test in Singapore, the claimant would have to show that his or her case either: (a) fell into one of the established or recognised categories of non-delegable duties (one of which includes the hospital with regard to patients under its care);[116] or (b) possessed all of the five defining features outlined by Lord Sumption JSC in the UK Supreme Court decision of *Woodland v Swimming Teachers Association and Others*.[117] These include the vulnerability and dependence of the claimant on the defendant, the assumption of a positive duty to protect the claimant and the delegation of an integral aspect of the assumed positive duty. The ultimate decision as to whether to impose non-delegable duties on particular defendants depends on questions of fairness, justice and reasonableness.[118] The Malaysian court in *Dr Kok Choong Seng*[119] adopted a similar legal approach to Singapore to non-delegable duties with respect to hospitals.

The *Woodland* features have been specifically applied in both Singapore and Malaysia. One important feature concerns the evidence underlying the existence of an antecedent relationship and scope of a positive assumption of responsibility by the doctor or hospital towards the patient under their care and custody.[120] In *Dr Kok Choong Seng*,[121] for instance, the hospital had not assumed any positive

[113] Daniel Schönberger, 'Artificial Intelligence in Healthcare: A Critical Analysis of the Legal and Ethical Implications' (2019) 27(2) *International Journal of Law and Information Technology* 171.

[114] *Dr Kok Choong Seng and Sunway Medical Centre Berhad v Soo Cheng Lin* [2018] 1 MLJ 685 [65].

[115] *Hii Chii Kok v Ooi Peng Jin London Lucien* (n 55) [70]; *Cassidy v Ministry of Health* [1951] 2 KB 343; *cf Farraj v King's Healthcare NHS Trust* [2010] 1 WLR (CA) 2139, where no non-delegable duty was imposed on the hospital as the patient was not in the hospital's custody or care.

[116] *Ng Huat Seng v Munib Mohammad Madni* [2017] 2 SLR 1074 [100], citing *Cassidy v Ministry of Health* [1951] 2 KB 343.

[117] *Woodland v Swimming Teachers Association and Others* [2013] 3 WLR 1227.

[118] For a criticism of the *Woodland* factors and the uncertainties generated, see Paula Giliker, 'Non-delegable Duties and Institutional Liability for the Negligence of Hospital Staff: Fair, Just and Reasonable?' (2017) 33(2) *Professional Negligence* 109.

[119] *Dr Kok Choong Seng* (n 114) [40].

[120] *Dr Kok Choong Seng* (n 114); *Dr Hari Krishnan* (n 90).

[121] *Dr Kok Choong Seng* (n 114) [66]. See also *Kee Boon Suan and Others v Adventist Hospital & Clinical Services (M) and Others and Other Appeals* [2018] 5 MLJ 321 [55].

duty to the patient as the latter reasonably expected the operation to be conducted by the medical doctor, regardless of where the operation may take place, and the hospital's role was to merely provide the relevant facilities required for the patient's admission and operation. Furthermore, as indicated in the Singapore High Court decision of *Hii Chii Kok*, the doctor or hospital may, according to the evidence adduced, be held to assume responsibility for an aspect of medical services (eg, diagnosis), but not another (eg, post-operative care).[122]

Enter medical AI. At present, in order to establish liability for breach of non-delegable duties, the patient will have to show that the AI developers and/or designers, as independent contractors, have acted without reasonable care in the development or design of medical AI, which resulted in the patient's injuries. To the extent that AI developers and designers are aware of the AI systemic responses to tasks, they should take reasonable steps to modify the algorithms to prevent anticipated harms.[123] If it is shown that the designed algorithms react to and learn from the environment and training data in unpredictable ways, the AI providers and designers may be absolved from negligence due to the lack of foreseeability of risks and expected harm.[124] It also depends on the extent to which the developer or designer knows or ought to know of the contexts in which the medical AI is put to use. As a first principle, it would be unfair to 'assign blame to the designer of a component whose work was far-removed in both time and geographic location from the completion and operation of the AI system'.[125]

In a future scenario, where the medical AI is completely autonomous and independent in its functioning, and the hospital or doctor does not have any control or review powers over the AI's decisions in pattern detections and predictive analysis, the medical AI may be analogised to an independent contractor. If so, the hospitals may in future choose to outsource certain functions (eg, diagnosis) to the AI system as an independent contractor and only take on the responsibility to administer treatment and give medical advice to patients. However, if the human doctor remains in the loop for diagnosis, the medical AI should not be treated as an independent contractor in respect of the diagnosis.[126]

There are at least two challenges to applying non-delegable duties to medical AI, even assuming that medical AI can be regarded in law as an independent contractor. First, based on the current technology, the AI system may not be capable of

[122] *Hii Chii Kok v Ooi Peng Jin London Lucien* (n 55) (HC) [74] (Chan Seng Onn J).

[123] Helen Smith and Kit Fotheringham, 'Artificial Intelligence in Clinical Decision-Making: Rethinking Liability' (2020) 20(2) *Medical Law International* 1, 13.

[124] Constantine Simon (ed), *Applying Ethical Principles for Artificial Intelligence in Regulatory Reform* (Singapore Academy of Law, Law Reform Committee, Sub-committee on Robotics and Artificial Intelligence, 2020) para 2.14.

[125] Matthew Scherer, 'Regulating Artificial Intelligence Systems: Risks, Challenges, Competencies, and Strategies' (2016) 29(2) *Harvard Journal of Law & Technology* 353, 372.

[126] The AI system is currently also not 'independent' in terms of the capacity to conduct a business on its own account. Hence, it cannot be treated as a legal person capable of owning assets, or suing and being sued on its own account.

taking over the responsibility for the patient's care as mentioned in *Woodland*. There is no evidence so far that AI has the ability similar to human doctors to understand and evaluate patients' preferences and values, and to communicate advice in a manner that is understandable to the patient. This means that the human doctor may have to be in the loop to make the ultimate decisions to advise the patient under the doctor or the hospital's care, custody and supervision.

Second, to find the hospital or medical doctor liable for breach of a non-delegable duty to the patient, it must be shown that the AI system had performed its task without reasonable care. Similar to the case for vicarious liability, there is therefore a need to determine the appropriate legal standard of care expected of the medical AI. We have already discussed in section II above the difficulties in selecting the criteria for determining the standard in the face of the evolving AI technology.

IV. Conclusion

Tort law needs to keep abreast of the developments in medical AI in the healthcare sector. Analogies may be drawn from existing common law case precedents generally as a starting point for application to medical AI. These legal rules and principles, together with public policy, as applied to the contexts in Singapore and Malaysia should have further resonance in the wider common law world as it starts getting to grips with the emerging AI technology in the delivery of healthcare services.

The robustness of a legal doctrine may be subject to stress tests in novel cases. Given the intrinsic nature and historical evolution of the doctrine of negligence beginning with *Donoghue v Stevenson*,[127] it is certainly not anathema to but is capable of embracing future changes. A tentative argument may be made that the standard of care principles in the common law tort of negligence provide a fault-based framework that is sufficiently flexible to accommodate the use of AI innovations in healthcare and to deal with the challenges posed as the technology continues to develop. The process of determining the appropriate standard of care allows for a judicious balance amongst the competing considerations: the efficiency and benefits generated by medical AI, encouraging the adoption of AI innovations by doctors and hospitals, granting injured patients compensation for the harms that have been caused by the negligence of the doctors or hospitals if they can prove fault, and taking into account the ethical responsibilities of the medical profession and patient well-being.

[127] *Donoghue v Stevenson* [1932] UKHL 100.

9

Contractual Consent in the Age of Machine Learning

GOH YIHAN*

I. Introduction

Machine learning has now enabled sophisticated algorithms to function like a human employee with a task to achieve rather than being a mere tool.[1] In the area of commerce, this has in turn given rise to algorithmic contracts, which are contracts where one or more parties use an algorithm to determine whether to be bound or how to be bound, and what the terms of the contract are.[2] This technological change goes to the heart of autonomous human choice.[3] The user, voluntarily and willingly, removes himself or herself from the decision-making process. He or she still chooses which algorithm to employ and may set at least part of the decision parameters. But other choices then follow automatically. Further, due to developments in deep learning, a process by which the algorithm's decision parameters are continuously updated and refined based on data analysis, the user might have no information about which parameters underlie the algorithm's choice or how much weight is given to each parameter. Alternatively, the user might not have the capacity or the permission to exercise effective control over the algorithm's choices.[4]

These technological developments raise important issues of contractual consent. Traditionally, in theory at least, a party is only taken to have assented to being contractually bound if he or she knows the precise term to which is binding.

* This research is supported by the National Research Foundation, Singapore under its Emerging Areas Research Projects (EARP) Funding Initiative. Any opinions, findings and conclusions or recommendations expressed in this material are those of the author and do not reflect the views of National Research Foundation, Singapore. The author would like to thank Gary Chan, Soh Kian Peng and Yip Man for all their helpful comments, and would also like to especially thank Soh Kian Peng for his excellent copyediting. All errors remain the author's.

[1] LH Scholz, 'Algorithmic Contracts' (2017) 20 *Stanford Technology Law Review* 128, 133.

[2] ibid 133.

[3] MS Gal, 'Algorithmic Challenges to Autonomous Choice' (2018) 25 *Michigan Technology Law Review* 59, 66.

[4] ibid 63.

However, the rise of algorithmic contracts in practice threatens to upend this foundational theoretical understanding. Indeed, as will become clear in our discussion below, the crucial difference between an algorithm and a person determining terms is that a computer rather than a conscious human being is implementing the rules.[5] When a human makes a choice, ordinary principles of liability and agency clearly link the acts of the human to the company he or she works for. However, the same may not be possible when algorithms are involved. Indeed, the more complicated the algorithm, the more limited the ability of a human to anticipate its output.

This chapter considers how contract law should react to the very practical phenomenon of algorithmic contracts through a consideration of the underlying theory and real-world considerations. The discussion is broken down into four subsequent sections. Section II will discuss the underlying technology behind algorithmic contracts. This will provide the necessary background against which to discuss the legal problems that follow. Section IIII will consider contractual consent in the realm of contract formation so as to provide a foundational overview of how consent should be dealt with in the light of algorithmic contracts. Section IV will examine contractual consent as it is applied to the doctrine of mistake. This serves to build on the foundational discussion in relation to contract formation. Section V concludes by considering whether the existing law of contract needs to adapt its approach towards contractual consent to remain relevant in the age of algorithms.

II. The Technology behind Algorithmic Contracts

At the very outset, given the hype around so-called 'smart contracts', it must be said that while algorithmic contracts can be smart contracts, they need not be. Indeed, this chapter is *not* about the issues raised by smart contracts, which are quite separate from those discussed here. At its simplest, a smart contract is an agreement whose performance is automated.[6] Indeed, according to Nick Szabo, one of the pioneers in the analysis of automated self-performing agreements, a smart contract is a computerised transaction algorithm, which performs the terms of the contract.[7] Thus defined, algorithmic contracts which are self-performing amount to smart contracts. However, it is possible that the algorithm only concludes the contract, but does not perform it, in which case the resulting contract is not a smart contract. In any event, whether an algorithmic contract is a smart contract

[5] Scholz (n 1) 134–35.

[6] A Savelyev, 'Contract Law 2.0: "Smart" Contracts as the Beginning of the End of Classic Contract Law' (2017) 26 *Information & Communications Technology Law* 116, 120.

[7] N Szabo, 'Smart Contracts' (1994), www.fon.hum.uva.nl/rob/Courses/InformationInSpeech/CDROM/Literature/LOTwinterschool2006/szabo.best.vwh.net/smart.contracts.html (accessed 7 November 2020).

should not affect the legal analysis below. It simply ought to be stressed that, given the debate surrounding 'smart contracts', the present case is not directly about the legal enforceability of such contracts.

A. What is an Algorithm?

Leaving behind 'smart contracts' then, in order to understand the technological background behind algorithmic contracts,[8] it is apposite to consider the character of an algorithm. Simply put, an algorithm is a process or set of rules to be followed in calculations or other problem-solving operations, especially by a computer. Algorithms execute these rules on the basis of data inputs. The decisional parameters and rules for weighting them can be set by the algorithm's designer.[9] Advanced algorithms employ machine learning, in which the algorithm self-adjusts based on its own analyses of data previously encountered, partially freeing the algorithm from predefined preferences.

In this sense, algorithms have much to offer – indeed, as Gal writes, particularly in terms of speed, lower transaction costs and efficiency in decision-making, thereby enabling the user to enjoy lower-cost and higher-quality products.[10] Furthermore, artificial intelligence coupled with the analysis of big data enable algorithms to make more complex choices. Computer scientists predict that as more data about human actions and choices is accumulated and analysed, algorithms may know us better than ourselves.[11] However, it is precisely these advantages that raise important questions about how the law should analyse a user's choice and intention in contracts reached by such algorithms.

B. Algorithms and Decisional Parameters

In order to understand how the law should ascertain the user's choice and intention in algorithmic contracts, we need to delve more deeply into the algorithm's design and technological capabilities. At the outset, it is important to dispel a commonly held myth: the algorithm *itself* cannot 'know' or 'intend' anything. This is because algorithms are simply a series of mathematical equations and nothing more than that. As such, it would be wrong to speak of algorithms taking over the decision-making process because they possess human agency themselves.

More precisely, two aspects of algorithmic *design* affect the user's choice: the decision parameters employed by the algorithm and the level of choice which

[8] Gal (n 3) 66.
[9] ibid) 65.
[10] ibid 61.
[11] ibid.

remains at the hands of the user.[12] Indeed, in the context of analysing algorithmic assistants, Gal identifies various categories of decision parameters used by algorithms, with growing effects on users' autonomous choice.

i. Decision Parameters Used by Algorithms

The first aspect is the decision parameters used by the algorithm. The ability to ascertain the decision parameters used by algorithms presupposes that the algorithm can be deciphered. Indeed, algorithms can be clear box, where inner components or logic are decipherable by humans, or black box, where the logic of the algorithm is functionally opaque.[13] Where the algorithm is black box, it will be a question of evidence whether its true nature can be ascertained. But assuming that the decision parameters used by the algorithm are known, we can then break down the algorithms broadly into three design types.

The first type of algorithm can be described as 'deterministic'. In fact, these algorithms form the vast majority of all algorithms. Here, the user sets the exact decisional parameters to be used by the algorithm as well as the weight to be given to each one.[14] The algorithm then chooses among the options it detects according to these preferences. Gal terms these algorithms 'Stated Preferences Algorithms'.[15] Ooi in turn terms these algorithms as 'passive' contract forming mechanisms.[16] In his view, passive contract-forming mechanisms do no more than act as a communication device, relaying the representations of the user without altering it in any way.

Here, the algorithm simply serves as the automated and efficient long arm of the user. The algorithm has no discretion of its own; its behaviour in response to a particular universe of possible user input is exhaustively specified by the explicit rules that the algorithm is programmed to apply.[17] While the algorithms may make choices about contractual terms, these tend to be rather limited in scope.[18] Thus, the user's and algorithm's choices completely overlap, but the algorithm enables a more *efficient* execution of the decision. A contract that is formed as a result of such an algorithm may be broadly said to be the result of the user's voluntary and deliberate decision to employ a certain algorithm and to allow it to make decisions for him or her. Therefore, once that algorithm is set in motion by the user, it acts as the user's long arm.[19]

[12] ibid 66.
[13] Scholz (n 1) 135.
[14] Gal (n 3) 61.
[15] ibid 66.
[16] V Ooi, 'Contracts Formed by Software: An Approach from the Law of Mistake', *Journal of Business Law* (forthcoming), www.papers.ssrn.com/sol3/papers.cfm?abstract_id=3322308, 3.
[17] S Chopra and L White, 'Artificial Agents and the Contracting Problem: A Solution via an Agency Analysis' (2009) 2 *University of Illinois Journal of Law, Technology & Policy* 363, 368.
[18] ibid.
[19] Gal (n 3) 97. See also Scholz (n 1) 165.

In contrast to deterministic algorithms, there are 'non-deterministic' algorithms. In this type of algorithm, the algorithm does not apply to decisional parameters which are wholly based on the user's stated or chosen preferences;[20] rather, the algorithm generates a simulation which attempts to mimic and predict user preferences. Ooi terms such algorithms 'active' contract-forming mechanisms.[21] Rather than simply relaying the user's representation in a 'passive' manner, these algorithms are able to decide the terms and conditions of the contracts in ways that the user may not be able to predict specifically. In this sense, such algorithms are non-deterministic.[22]

We can refer to two examples to illustrate the use of such algorithms in commercial settings, which can include consumer contracts. First, in the context of daily interaction with consumers in the commercial sphere, data points are collected from numerous sources to make such predictions. Rapidly advancing techniques of data science such as pattern recognition and machine learning, when used in a particular fashion, are combined with traditional tools such as statistics to mine valuable information from the data. The data analysis serves as the basis for the creation of user profiles, which generally act like a 'digital shadow', attempting to mimic users' preferences. These enable the algorithm to not only identify but also predict a user's future preferences. The algorithm may even identify preferences that the user is unaware of.[23] In this sense, data scientists argue that algorithms can teach us things we do not know about ourselves.[24]

Second, consider the example of an algorithm that calculates the credit limit to assign to a credit card application, referencing factors such as credit history, income, assets and so forth.[25] The rules that such an algorithm applies are embodied in the algorithm's programming. In that sense, the algorithm has no discretion. However, for risk-assessment algorithms that employ more sophisticated decision-making mechanisms using online learning algorithms, there may be no strictly binary rules which determine the outcome; rather, it is the combination of relevant factors, and the relative weights the system accords them, that determines the outcome.[26] While conceptually, such algorithms are still rule-bound, it could be said from the point of view of explaining the algorithm's conduct that it is 'exercising discretion' as to how much credit to extend.[27] This is thus the sense that such algorithms are non-deterministic. This may correspond to what some

[20] Gal (n 3) 67.
[21] Ooi (n 16) 4.
[22] V Kothari, 'Difference between Deterministic and Non-deterministic Algorithms' *GeeksforGeeks* (11 September 2018), www.geeksforgeeks.org/difference-between-deterministic-and-non-deterministic-algorithms.
[23] Gal (n 3) 68.
[24] N Thompson, 'When Tech Knows You Better than You Know Yourself' *Wired* (4 April 2018), www.wired.com/story/artificial-intelligence-yuval-noah-harari-tristan-harris.
[25] Chopra and White (n 17) 369.
[26] ibid 369.
[27] ibid 370.

have termed 'probabilistic computing'. This is computing that is neither deterministic nor autonomous, but is based on a probability that something is the correct answer.[28]

Finally, the last type of algorithm has not become reality yet, but it may have the largest effect on choice. These algorithms make choices for the user which are assumed to be best for him or her overall, even when they clash with his or her immediate preferences.[29] Such algorithms may purposely give more weight to long-term preferences over short-term ones, and to rational preferences over immediate and emotionally driven ones. This may correspond to what some have termed 'truly autonomous' computing, although it must be noted that, even in deterministic systems, there is some measure of autonomy inasmuch as the algorithm makes decisions without direct human intervention, albeit with a preprogrammed outcome.

What then can we make of these three types of algorithms? One important point to note is that in real life, software does not usually just contain a single algorithm; rather, almost every form of real software will contain some components that are purely deterministic and non-deterministic, leaving out the so-called truly autonomous algorithms for the moment. As such, while it is helpful to conceptualise what algorithms are doing by way of neat divisions, this may not always be possible, especially when we have algorithms interacting with one another in the real world.

ii. Level of Control Over the Decision

Apart from the decision parameter used by the algorithm, the second dimension which affects users' choice is the level of control over the decision which remains in the user's hands once the algorithm is employed – as Gal calls it, the so-called 'human-in-the-loop', regardless of what type of algorithm we are concerned about.[30]

At one extreme, all potential options are presented to the user, such as Google Search. However, even in this case, the choice architecture, such as which options are presented first, may still affect the user's choice. At the other end of the spectrum, the algorithm automatically identifies a need, searches for the optimal solution and executes the transaction. The user provides what Gal terms 'second-order consent', waiving his or her right to choose directly or even to approve the choice made on his or her behalf.[31] The self-executing quality of these autonomous

[28] 'Singapore Court's Cryptocurrency Decision: Implications for Cryptocurrency Trading, Smart Contracts and AI' *Norton Rose Fulbright* (September 2019), www.nortonrosefulbright.com/en/knowledge/publications/6a118f69/singapore-courts-cryptocurrency-decision-implications-for-trading-smart-contracts-and-ai.

[29] Gal (n 3) 69.

[30] ibid 69.

[31] ibid 70.

algorithms limits the need for human intervention beyond the employment of the algorithm and the provision of the initial data parameters. For example, in high-frequency trading, it is not realistic for the algorithm to return the choices to the trader in a manner similar to Google Search results. Thus, the level of control exercised by the user corresponds to Gal's explanation of 'second-order consent'.

So far, we have seen how the underlying technology discussed above, particularly the decision parameters used by the algorithms and the user's level of control over the decision, may affect the practical issue of contractual consent. In the following section, we will discuss these practical facts with reference to the underlying theoretical legal questions for consideration. In doing so, we will use two paradigm examples of contractual doctrines that illustrate contractual consent: the law of formation and the law of mistake, which builds on the discussion on the law of formation.

III. Questions of Contractual Consent in the Law of Formation

A. The Theoretical Considerations in Formation

Both offer and acceptance constitute the traditional theoretical starting points in the formation of a contract under the common law.[32] For example, the Singapore courts have affirmed the objective principle. For example, in the Court of Appeal decision of *Bakery Mart Pte Ltd (in Receivership) v Sincere Watch Ltd*,[33] Chao Hick Tin JA, who delivered the judgment of the court, reaffirmed the basic principle that:

> Where negotiations are protracted the court is entitled to look at all the circumstances and apply an objective test to determine whether the parties had reached an agreement as far as the essential terms are concerned, or whether the parties intended to reserve their rights pending a formal agreement.[34]

Therefore, in order for a promise to come into being, someone must propose the *content* of the promise and *communicate* this to *another party*, for it is nonsensical to speak of someone making a promise to oneself.

How then should these trite principles of formation apply to contracts made by computer systems operating via algorithms? Writing in 1996, Allen and Widdison pointed out that if the use of computer technology is restricted to providing a

[32] This also includes implied contracts: see the Singapore Court of Appeal decision of *Cooperatieve Centrale Raiffeisen-Boerenleenbank BA (Trading as Rabobank International), Singapore Branch v Motorola Electronics Pte Ltd* [2011] 2 SLR 63 [46], [50].

[33] *Bakery Mart Pte Ltd (in Receivership) v Sincere Watch Ltd* [2003] 3 SLR(R) 462.

[34] ibid [22].

medium for communications between human trading partners in the context of electronic trading, then it is probable that significant legal implications will arise only in 'adjectival' domains such as evidence and the security and authentication of documents.[35] By contrast, in that scenario, the substantive law can be expected to follow a relatively orderly progression in which the courts will simply continue to elaborate on established precedents, such as those concerning contracting by means of instantaneous and non-instantaneous electronic communications.[36]

However, if the role of the computer evolves from that of a passive cypher to that of an active participant in the trading process, the legal situation changes significantly. The use of computer technology to make contracts for humans is now reality. As we have seen above, technology has developed that enables individuals to use electronic agents to arrange exchanges without direct human intervention.[37] Bellia Jr raises the example of a consumer releasing an algorithm[38] into cyberspace with instructions to purchase a good within a range of specified prices and other terms. The seller, for its part, uses an algorithm instructed to sell certain goods within a specified range of prices and other terms to the highest bidders. These algorithms, after interacting with each other to find the best deal, arrange the sale of the good.[39]

Thus, in order to answer how contractual consent is affected by the use of algorithms in contracting, we need to return to three basic tenets of contractual consent in theory: assent, intent and content of choice.

i. Assent

As is traditionally known, assent is a major cornerstone of the law of contract: objectively manifested agreement to contractual terms is a critical element of a contract.[40] How does the fact that a decision is reached by an algorithm affect the meeting of minds? Arguably, the contract is the result of the user's voluntary and deliberate decision to employ a certain algorithm and to allow it to make decisions for him or her. Thus, one answer is that once the algorithm is set in motion by the user, it acts as the user's long arm.[41]

However, this assumption may be problematic when applied to certain types of algorithms. This is particularly the case with regard to non-deterministic and truly autonomous algorithms, which have the ability to learn, thereby divorcing critical aspects of decision-making in contractual agreements from conscious

[35] T Allen and R Widdison, 'Can Computers Make Contracts?' (1996) 9 *Harvard Journal of Law & Technology* 25.

[36] ibid.

[37] AJ Bellia Jr, 'Contracting with Electronic Agents' (2001) 50 *Emory Law Journal* 1047.

[38] ibid 1051–52.

[39] ibid.

[40] RE Barnett, 'A Consent Theory of Contract' (1986) 86 *Columbia Law Review* 269, 319.

[41] Scholz (n 1) 165.

determination by any individual.[42] Indeed, the user may not be aware of all the possible choices that can be made by the algorithm, let alone keep track of all the parameters that the algorithm considers on his or her behalf.[43] This knowledge gap is entirely a result of the algorithm's comparative advantage in being able to consider a breadth of data that no human could, and it can sometimes predict the user's future choices better than the user himself or herself.

Moreover, in some cases, the user may not care about the actual choice made by the algorithm, so long as it makes a choice.[44] In such cases, algorithms stretch the requirement of assent too much, far beyond the intents and capacities of the algorithms' authorising entities.[45] The manifested intent to use an algorithm to set contractual terms is not the same as an objective assent to the actual contract the algorithm reaches. Indeed, the more vague the instructions given to the algorithm, the less the instructions can be said to reflect the level of objectively manifested assent necessary to ground a contractual promise. In other words, the user's assent to be bound may not be made at a sufficient level of specificity which is necessary to form an enforceable contract.[46]

ii. Intent

Related to the question of assent, consider the situation where the algorithm engages in autonomous decision-making, which is one step removed from the user, but is initiated by him or her. This raises issues relating to the user's mental state, ranging from recklessness, through negligence and intent, to specific intent.

The issue of a mental state or knowledge is especially relevant in the case of machine-learning algorithms, which are designed to achieve a given goal. They can do so by independently determining the means to reach that goal, through self-learning and the reactions to its actions. In such cases, the decision is not the fruit of explicit human design, but the outcome of evolution, self-learning and independent machine execution.[47] Yadav notes that proof of the required mental state in such situations, unless strict liability is imposed, is not simple.[48]

Similarly, Gal suggests that where the user is demonstrably aware of the potential for harm, the fact that a sophisticated system containing an autonomous algorithm performed the actual harmful act should not prevent establishing a mental state.[49] This fixes the state of knowledge at the point of employing the algorithm, even if what 'employing' the algorithm means can differ in cases.

[42] ibid 132.
[43] ibid 132.
[44] Gal (n 3) 97.
[45] Scholz (n 1) 132–33.
[46] ibid 155.
[47] Gal (n 3) 99.
[48] Y Yadav, 'The Failure of Liability in Modern Markets' (2016) 102 *Virginia Law Review* 1031, 1034.
[49] Gal (n 3) 99–100.

iii. Content of Choice

Finally, the nature of the algorithms used affects the act of choice: the user chooses to employ the algorithm, and the algorithm then makes choices, which can be autonomously made, for the user. To complicate matters, the choice of an algorithm might be made by an algorithm which compares algorithms that make final decisions, which, in turn, might be chosen by an algorithm which compares among comparison algorithms. The user may be even further removed from his or her final choice.[50]

Algorithms can also affect the content of the decision made on behalf of the user.[51] In this regard, the user may be unaware of the algorithm's effects on choice due, among other things, to the limited transparency of the algorithm's 'black box' quality. A user who is unaware of the algorithm's limitations would likely not be aware of the choices he or she has foregone. Indeed, as algorithms become more complicated, even their designers might not completely understand the algorithm's decisional parameters.[52] Thus, not only is the act of choice affected by autonomous choice algorithms, but so too is the content of the choice.

B. How should Consent be Ascertained in Practice in Algorithmic Contracts?

Following from the theoretical considerations above, the next question is how we ascertain an agreement in this situation. It is useful to divide up our discussion along the decision parameters used by algorithms referred to earlier.

i. Deterministic Algorithms

In this situation, the question is whether a person who willingly uses an algorithm to arrange transactions based on a broad set of instructions (for example, price) should be bound to arrangements made thereby. The algorithms can be deterministic, but the user may not know *which* deterministic outcome will eventually ensue, where there are several choices for the algorithm to deterministically select.

Allen and Widdison consider what follows when a computer is programmed not only to negotiate details such as the price and quantity, but also to decide whether to make or accept an offer without reference to any human trader.[53] Such relationships have been characterised by repeat ordering of pre-defined commodities through 'interchange agreements'. However, as we have seen, technological innovation now allows computer algorithms to seek out trading

[50] ibid 70.
[51] ibid.
[52] ibid 74.
[53] Allen and Widdison (n 35) 28.

partners in circumstances where human traders have no direct knowledge or contact with their trading partners. These human traders will therefore have little or no detailed knowledge of, or input into, the terms of the transactions in question.[54] Allen and Widdison ask a similar question – if agreement is manifested by a meeting of minds, can it be meaningfully said that there is a meeting of the parties' minds where both parties use algorithms to contract?[55]

a. The Legal Difficulty of Finding Agreement

The legal difficulty of finding agreement in this case is illustrated by Bellia Jr, who suggests that this first depends on whether the user has sufficiently manifested assent.[56] Writing in the context of American law, Bellia Jr suggests that a promise is not the commitment that the promisor subjectively intends, but the intention that the promisee objectively perceives. This is also the case in Singapore law. The use of an algorithm would seem to be properly characterised as an act or conduct. Indeed, if a contract exists, it must be justified by reference to acts that preceded or coincided with its formation.[57]

On this premise, Bellia Jr suggests that the conduct of releasing an algorithm to negotiate a deal for the purchase of a good or service does not manifest assent in the same way that the conduct would normally do.[58] In the case of the algorithm, neither party is aware of the other's manifestation until after their respective algorithms arrange the transaction. The question is whether conduct may manifest assent when neither party is aware of the other's conduct until *after* the contractual obligation arises – if it arises at all. Thus, *before* the algorithms arrange the contract, there is not the same basis upon which to ask whether either party has reason to know that the other party assents, as compared to when at least one party is known to the other.[59]

It is true that persons using algorithms have reason to know that other unknown persons may be using electronic agents capable of arranging transactions with theirs. However, what persons using algorithms do not know or have specific reason to know is whether unknown persons assent to perform an arrangement thus made.[60] There may be no basis upon which to know the assent of the other until after the existence of a legal obligation, if indeed the exchange is enforceable. Insofar as a promise must be communicated to another person, a contract, if one exists, precedes the making of the promise.[61] While the user can find out the

[54] ibid 28.
[55] ibid 31.
[56] Bellia Jr (n 37) 1049.
[57] ibid 1053.
[58] ibid 1054.
[59] ibid 1055.
[60] ibid.
[61] ibid 1056.

price that the seller is willing to accept, it is the enforceable sale that is conveyed to the user, not the seller's manifestation of assent to sell the item. The question is then whether the arranged exchange is itself a contract, which, if a promise must precede a contract, it is not, since at the time that the exchange is arranged, neither party is aware that the other has made a commitment.[62]

b. Possible Practical Solutions

The computer as a mere tool: The first practical solution to this legal difficulty of finding agreement is to treat the computer as a mere tool. While an autonomous computer differs from other machines because it can engage in complex interactions with the environment around it without human intervention, the law can choose to ignore its autonomy and treat it as no more than a passive adjunct or extension of the relevant human trader.[63] Accordingly, all intentions manifested by, or embodied within, the machine would be regarded as the intentions of the controller. It follows that all transactions entered into by the computer would be treated as transactions entered into by the human trader.[64]

According to Allen and Widdison, this approach carries with it several advantages. Apart from the fact that it would not involve any change to existing doctrine, it also allocates the risk of mistakes to the person who chose to involve the machine in the trading process in the first place.[65] It may be further argued that it puts the risk of unpredicted obligations on the person best able to control them – those who program and control the computer. It gives that person a strong incentive to ensure that the computer is properly programmed and policed.[66]

However, this approach has been criticised as creating an unsatisfactory legal fiction by which an algorithm is treated as a mere tool of communication of the user.[67] In many realistic settings, the user cannot be said to have a pre-existing 'intention' in respect of a *particular* contract which is communicated to another party by the algorithm. Indeed, this arguably remains true even for deterministic or passive algorithms, because at the point of communication, the user is not aware of the *exact* information being communicated and to whom.[68]

Recognition that parties may assent in advance: A second solution would be for the law to recognise assent given in advance. Indeed, in other words, may parties assent in advance? May the parties, as offerors, assent in advance to the anticipated assent of the other?[69]

[62] ibid.
[63] Allen and Widdison (n 35) 46.
[64] ibid.
[65] ibid.
[66] ibid.
[67] Chopra and White (n 17) 371.
[68] *cf* Ooi (n 16) 5.
[69] Bellia Jr (n 37) 1057.

Allen and Widdison suggest that the requirement of intention can be relaxed to make room for a 'generalised and indirect intention to be bound by computer-generated agreements'.[70] Another way to frame this approach is that the parties can express a prior intention to be bound by all contracts within a certain class or type entered into via their algorithms, rather than a specific contract.[71]

Ooi notes that this extended assent approach is a logical extension that is necessary to enable the common law to keep pace with technological developments.[72] Indeed, the common law already recognises the validity of a general offer made to the world at large in unilateral contracts.[73] Such contracts occur on a daily basis when someone purchases a drink from a vending machine or buys a parking ticket from an automatic ticketing machine. As Ooi points out, unless he or she is constantly monitoring the machine, the owner or operator of the vending machine would not be aware of the specific drink purchased by a customer in a specific transaction.[74] By placing these machines in operation and relying on them, the owners or operators are inferred to have evinced a general intention to be bound by all the different permutations or transactions their machines can handle.[75]

Thus, according to Ooi, recognising a general intention to be bound by a class of contracts is not wholly without precedent.[76] It has long been recognised and applied by the courts in analysing unilateral contracts. Extending this concept to a limited class of contracts formed by deterministic algorithms would be an incremental development rather than a radical and unprecedented change in the law of contract.[77]

However, this characterisation raises the problem of cross-offers, which the law holds not to result in a contract. Under this principle, a contract would no more result from crossing offers to buy and sell something at a price to be fixed by the algorithm than it would from crossing offers to buy and sell something at a price to be fixed by a third party.[78] The use of an algorithm to buy something is akin to making an offer to buy on terms to be fixed by the algorithm. The use of an algorithm to sell something is akin to making an offer to sell on terms to be fixed by algorithm.[79] That the offer is made with open terms is not the problem if all the parties mutually manifest assent to an agreement. The problem here is that neither party's assent to uncertain terms is made with reference to the other party's assent to uncertain terms.[80] The solution to this is for the law to recognise that both parties may expressly assent with reference to the anticipated but unknown assent of the other.[81]

[70] Allen and Widdison (n 35) 43–44.
[71] Ooi (n 16) 14.
[72] ibid 15.
[73] *Carlill v Carbolic Smoke Ball Company* [1893] 1 QB 256.
[74] Ooi (n 16) 15.
[75] ibid.
[76] ibid.
[77] ibid. However, Ooi would extend this approach to even 'active' contract forming mechanisms.
[78] Bellia Jr (n 37) 1058.
[79] ibid.
[80] ibid.
[81] ibid.

In sum, theoretical modifications will need to be made to existing contract law to accommodate the practical formation of contracts made by deterministic algorithms. Specifically, there would be a need to decide that human intention need not underlie the making of an offer or an acceptance, at least as far as computer-generated agreements are concerned.[82] In other words, the law would hold that the human trader's generalised and indirect intention to be bound by computer-generated agreements is sufficient to render the agreements legally binding. This would extend the accepted principle that a person who signs a contract without reading it is nonetheless bound by its terms. It is difficult to construct any intention relating to the specific terms of the agreement and the fact that an agreement is made is sufficient.[83]

Thus, when applied to computer-generated contracts, it might be said that if a person can be bound by signing an unread contract, it would seem reasonable to say that by making the algorithm available, the human operator would be bound by the agreements it generates. As Atiyah has said, the truth is that a party is bound not so much because of what he or she intends, but because of what he or she does. He or she is liable because of what he or she does for the good reason that other parties are likely to rely upon what he or she does in ways which are reasonable and even necessary by the standards of our society.[84] In both situations, there is a realisation that the relevant acts are likely to result in an agreement on which there will be reliance, and hence there is a sound basis for treating the agreement as a legally binding contract.[85]

Thus, insofar as deterministic algorithms are concerned, it might be said that contracts made by such algorithms can be considered to have been formed on the basis that the user of the algorithm assented in advance to the *particular* contract formed. This is the case even though the user does not actually know how the algorithm will choose from the myriad of options open to it, deterministic as the outcome to *each* of those options might be. In short, by using the algorithm, the user is taken to have assented to each and every particular contract that can be formed by following through the deterministic algorithms.

ii. Non-deterministic Algorithms

a. Unrealistic to Apply 'Mere Tools or Extended Assent' Approach

As we have seen above, one solution to the problem of algorithmic contracting is to treat the algorithms as mere tools or as mere means of communication.[86] While

[82] Allen and Widdison (n 35) 44.
[83] ibid.
[84] P Atiyah, *Essays on Contract*, 2nd edn (Oxford University Press, 1990) 22.
[85] Allen and Widdison (n 35) 44.
[86] S Chopra and L White, 'Artificial Agents: Philosophical and Legal Perspectives' (2007), http://www.sci.brooklyn.cuny.edu/~schopra/ChopraWhiteChapter1.pdf, 60.

this can make some sense in the case of deterministic algorithms, this is not realistic when applied to non-deterministic algorithms. Ooi notes that the 'mere tools' solution is immediately exposed as an unrealistic fiction once we consider software used in an 'active' manner.[87] As the role of the human user is limited to stipulating the rules or objectives that guide the algorithm in the process of contracting, it is clearly at odds with reality to suggest that the 'active' software was a mere tool of communication.[88] Ultimately, as the autonomy, social ability and proactivity of algorithms increases, it will be less realistic to approach them as mere tools of their operators and as mere means of communication.

Yet another solution is the extended assent approach discussed above. However, while it may be possible to say that the user assents to an outcome that he or she envisaged, but did not know would specifically be implemented, it may be a stretch to say the user assents to an outcome that he or she did not know. This would be the case when non-deterministic algorithms are used. Even if the user can set the parameters for the way in which the algorithm decides, unlike a deterministic algorithm, the end result may be one which the user did not know. As such, even the extended assent approach does not apply to non-deterministic or probabilistic algorithms.

b. Agency Principles

Separately, it has been suggested that the most cogent reason for adopting the agency law approach to algorithms in the context of contracting is to allow the law to distinguish in a principled way between those contracts entered into by an algorithm that should bind the principal and those that should not.[89] Ooi notes that the agency approach recognises the 'active' nature of algorithms used in contract formation.[90]

When approaching the notion of electronic agents that are 'autonomous', lawyers are immediately tempted to draw a parallel with the theory of agency. After all, computers only replace what human agents are normally doing. According to Fischer, the comparison seems obvious:

> When computers are given the capacity to communicate with each other based upon pre-programmed instructions, and when they possess the physical capability to execute agreements on shipments of goods without any human awareness or input into the agreements beyond the original programming of the computer's instructions, these computers serve the same function as similarly instructed human agents of a party and thus should be treated under the law identically to those human agents.[91]

[87] Ooi (n 16) 7.
[88] ibid 7.
[89] Chopra and White (n 17) 393.
[90] Ooi (n 16) 6.
[91] JP Fischer, 'Computers as Agents: A Proposed Approach to Revised UCC Article 2' (1997) 72 *Indiana Law Journal* 545, 570.

Scholz, who thinks that algorithms can *never* be regarded as mere tools of the human user, similarly suggests that algorithms can be regarded as constructive agents for the purpose of contract formation.[92] According to her, agency law makes it possible to impute knowledge and intent to principals who are not directly involved in tasks, including forming contracts. Principals can authorise their agents formally, by implication or by ratification. In agency law, the principal is usually liable for the mistakes the agent makes because the principal assumed such a risk by opting to use an agent in the first place.

Kerr likewise argues that deeming an algorithm to be an agent for the purpose of computerised contracting would not be far-fetched. After all, it is a well-established principle in the law of agency that one need not have the capacity to contract for oneself in order to be competent to contract as an agent.[93] The rationale for this appears to be that the agent is a mere instrument and that it is the principal who bears the risk of inadequate representation.[94]

Thus, more specifically, Kerr argues that if a user consents to using an algorithm to form contracts, the algorithm has actual authority to contract on behalf of the user.[95] There is no need for the agent to have agreed to or to have knowledge of the conferring of knowledge at all.[96] Alternatively, Kerr also argues that if a user makes it appear that an algorithm is acting on the user's behalf to form contracts, then the algorithm has apparent authority to contract on behalf of the user.[97]

Ultimately, the agency approach appears to be an attractive solution in relation to non-deterministic algorithms because to some extent, it reflects the reality that the user of such algorithms delegates part of the decision-making process to the algorithm, resulting in a loss of *some* control over the process of contract formation.[98] Further, much like how a principal defines the scope of authority of his or her agent, the user sets the parameters of operation for the algorithm to carry out his or her wishes. This is very much the essence of an agency relationship.[99]

To be sure, there are some commentators who object to the use of the agency analysis. Gal points out that even in agency law, the principal cannot be assumed to know any action taken by the agent, and much would depend on the level of knowledge required.[100] However, this objection can be addressed by restricting the agency analysis to a situation where the principal can indeed be assumed to know the broad outcome of the algorithmic use. Thus, as an illustration, the

[92] Scholz (n 1) 132.
[93] IR Kerr, 'Spirits in the Material World: Intelligent Agents as Intermediaries in Electronic Commerce' (1999) 22 *Dalhousie Law Journal* 190, 240.
[94] ibid.
[95] ibid 243.
[96] ibid 241.
[97] ibid 243.
[98] Ooi (n 16) 7.
[99] ibid 7.
[100] Gal (n 3) 98.

law of agency distinguishes between express and implied authority. In an example garnered from a textbook, a producer may ask its agent to sell its products within a stipulated price range.[101] The express authority conferred upon the agent by the principal is therefore the type of product, as well as the acceptable price range. However, during the actual sale of the product, the agent may encounter practical issues relating to the time and place of delivery. Even though these were not expressly provided for, the law of agency treats the principal as bound by the agent's decisions in these matters on the basis that the agent had implied authority with regard to them. Thus, as has been said, the principal, by authorising the agent to act for him or her in a particular way, simultaneously assents to the agent to do all other actions that are necessary and incidental to the principal's express instructions.[102] Transposed to the situation of algorithmic use discussed above, the principal, having consented to the broad outcome, would at the same time have also consented to any 'necessary and incidental' actions that are necessary to give effect to the principal's expectations that the broad outcomes are realised.

Bellia Jr makes a more fundamental objection: algorithms cannot consent to act as a user's agent.[103] He argues that consent is important because it justifies the legal obligations assumed by both parties to an agency relationship, even if bots may be programmed to obey and act loyally. Thus, if agency principles are to apply to algorithms, the law must dispense with the consent of the 'agent'.[104] However, this objection may be easily met by dispensing with such consent, which would not make much sense when applied to algorithms to begin with. Indeed, this is consistent with the view, under the traditional law of agency, that an act is authorised even though neither the agent nor the relevant third party was told of the principal's assent.[105] The rationale behind this view is that it ensures that a transaction will be binding on the principal and third party where the principal has assented to the agent acting on the principal's behalf, and the agent has in fact done so, but was unaware of the principal's assent (and thus could not have consented in the first place).[106] Thus, Tan suggests that it would be overly technical to say that the purported transaction between the principal and the third party is not enforceable simply because the agent was not specifically informed of the principal's assent and thus could not in turn consent.[107] This is especially so when no unfairness is caused to any party. Considering Bellia Jr's argument that the agent's consent is required, one may therefore ask *why* such consent is needed

[101] T Cheng Han, *The Law of Agency*, 2nd edn (Academy Publishing, 2017) 44.
[102] ibid 45.
[103] Bellia Jr (n 37) 1060.
[104] ibid.
[105] P Watts (ed), *Bowstead and Reynolds on Agency*, 20th edn (Sweet & Maxwell, 2014) paras 1-006 and 2-033.
[106] Cheng Han (n 101) 36.
[107] ibid.

in the first place. As we have seen, that consent is needed to avoid prejudice to the agent itself, especially since the agent may be owed certain responsibilities by the principal. However, where such prejudice is absent, the arguments in favour of consent by the agent similarly dissipate. This applies with even stronger reason in relation to algorithms which, being non-living entities, cannot possibly suffer any prejudice. It would therefore make little sense to insist on their 'consent'. Indeed, to paraphrase Tan, it would be 'overly technical' to insist on the algorithmic agent's 'consent' when not only does the law of agency not require consent of an agent in every instance, but also that such insistence serves no substantive reason in the situation being considered.

Bellia Jr also points out that since agency law presupposes the freedom of autonomous beings, it does not govern the relationship between a principal and a mere mechanical tool or instrument.[108] Instead, it governs the relationship between a principal and a person in whose discretion and understanding the principal places his or her trust. That is why when a person performs for another a task involving no exercise of human discretion or judgement, the law does not deem that person to be an agent.[109] Thus, according to Bellia Jr, when a person is not capable of exercising judgement and understanding, that person cannot be an agent; the same should apply to algorithms.[110] However, this argument can be addressed on two fronts. First, even human agents, in a sense, exercise limited discretion in the execution of the principal's authority because they are bound by a discernible range of conduct informed by human experience. Thus, what may at first sight be seen as an exercise of pure discretion may actually be a decision constrained by the principal's express and implied authority, or one that is informed by industry norms and customs. In other words, the agent's decisions are pre-determined to some extent. Similarly, even where a deterministic algorithm is used, the decision it 'makes', while pre-determined, can be likened to how a human agent makes its decision. Further, even if we disregard the argument just made and insist that the human agent does in fact exercise pure discretion, it is also possible to argue that the algorithm does actually exercise some kind of 'discretion'. Such discretion is exercised by the algorithm in that the human principal does not know *exactly* which of the pre-determined outcomes would be executed. Moreover, in 'deciding' which of those pre-determined outcomes to execute, the algorithm may take into account a range of factors that a human cannot otherwise comprehend or process in as quick a time. Thus, it may be too technical to regard an algorithm as not exercising any 'discretion' simply because all the outcomes were preprogrammed. Second, as opposed to a deterministic algorithm, where a non-deterministic algorithm is concerned, it exercises autonomous judgement and therefore the agency analysis is applicable.

[108] Bellia Jr (n 37) 1063.
[109] ibid.
[110] ibid.

c. The Practical Application of Agency Principles

Having considered as unpersuasive the theoretical objections against applying agency principles to analyse algorithms making decisions, it remains for us to consider *how*, in practical terms, agency principles should be so applied to algorithms. In this regard, Ooi suggests that in the context of algorithmic contracts, the relationship of agency can arise as it does normally.[111] This relationship arises from the authority conferred by the principal to the agent and comes in three forms, namely: (a) actual express authority, which arises through express words of consent from the principal to the agent that the agent is to act on his or her behalf;[112] (b) actual implied authority, which arises through implied consent inferred from the words or conduct of the principal;[113] and (c) apparent authority, which arises when the principal has made representations to the third party that the alleged agent was acting under his or her authority.[114]

As we have seen above, it is not objectionable to analyse the human principal as 'authorising' the algorithmic agent, even though: (a) the principal does not know the *precise* outcome from the use of the algorithm; (b) the algorithm cannot consent to being an agent; and (c) the algorithm is in fact executing pre-determined outcomes and hence cannot be said to exercise any degree of discretion. Thus, if we accept that these objections are not persuasive, then the application of the agency analysis must *necessarily* entail the reference to the doctrine of *authority*, which is the very premise of the law of agency. In practical terms, the doctrine of authority is of key importance in delimiting the field of the principal's contractual liability: if entering a given contract is within an agent's actual or apparent authority, then the agent's principal is bound, even if he or she had no knowledge of the particular contract referred to and even if the agent exercises its discretion in a way that is different from how the principal would have exercised that discretion.[115] But if the contract is outside the agent's actual or apparent authority, then the principal is not bound by the contract.[116]

iii. Autonomous Algorithms

So far, we have dealt with the issue of contract formation in relation to deterministic and non-deterministic algorithms. But what happens if the algorithms are even more autonomous? A sufficiently advanced artificial intelligence, so-called artificial general intelligence (AGI), will not need to operate through agents. While AGI

[111] Ooi (n 16) 7.
[112] *Hely-Hutchinson v Brayhead Ltd* [1968] 1 QB 549.
[113] ibid.
[114] *First Energy UK Ltd v Hungarian International Bank* [1993] 2 Lloyd's Rep 194.
[115] S Chopra and L White, 'Artificial Agents and the Contracting Problem: A Solution via an Agency Analysis' (2009) 2 *University of Illinois Journal of Law, Technology & Policy* 363, 393.
[116] ibid.

does not yet exist, it is likely to become a reality in the future.[117] Given that AGI is still in its infancy, this discussion will be kept deliberately brief.

a. The Legal Difficulty of Finding Agreement

In the context of investing AGI with the capacity to contract, contract law itself will face few problems in recognising AGI as a contracting party if AGI has the cognitive machinery with which to engage in contract relationships with humans.[118] AGI will need to interact with human parties and value contractual prices in a way that is compatible with the principles inherent in contract law. Indeed, the general law has had no real difficulties recognising entities with no cognition as legal entities. One prominent (though not perfect) example is indeed the law's recognition of companies as an artificial person, even though companies do not have cognition. In sum, while AGI may be in the distant future for now, it will be more practical to align their cognition to contract law and the values it represents than to change contract law and the humans who invented it.[119]

b. Vicarious Liability

From the standpoint of vicarious liability, there is no reason why truly autonomous algorithms might not in appropriate situations be considered 'independent contractors'.[120] This would insulate the human principal from liability. This might be the case where intelligent machines employed to displace human activities on occasion bring about idiosyncratic legal outcomes which vary from those which would have resulted had the transaction been accomplished by a human. The relation then to contractual consent is that this affects whether the human can be said to be a responsible actor in the entire contracting endeavour.

c. Legal Personality

A more far-fetched idea, which need not concern us unduly for the purposes of this chapter, is to confer legal personality on truly autonomous algorithms.[121] This would raise a host of difficult ethical and policy issues. However, if algorithms, empowered by AGI, become capable of exercising judgement and understanding, there may come the day when legal personality is conferred upon them to contract on their own behalf.

[117] J Linarelli, 'Artificial General Intelligence and Contract' (2019) 24 *Uniform Law Review* 330, 331.
[118] ibid 347.
[119] ibid.
[120] LE Wein, 'Responsibility of Intelligent Artifacts: Toward an Automation Jurisprudence' (1992) 6 *Harvard Journal of Law & Technology* 103, 115.
[121] ibid 10.

IV. Questions of Contractual Consent in the Law of Unilateral Mistake

A. The Relationship between Mistake and Formation

Having considered how the law of contractual formation should deal with algorithmic contracts, the law of mistake offers a *practical application* of those foundational principles in a defined doctrine in the law of contract. In this regard, the doctrine of mistake in the law of contract deals with two different situations. In the first, there is some mistake or misunderstanding in the communications between the parties which prevents there being an effective agreement or at least that there is no agreement on the apparently stated terms.[122] This first category of mistake, which is generally referred to as 'mistake as to the terms or identity', includes 'mutual mistake', where each party is mistaken as to the terms intended by the other, and 'unilateral mistake', where only one of the parties is mistaken in relation to the terms of the contract or the identity of the other party.[123]

In the second situation, the parties are agreed as to the terms of the contract, but have entered into it under a shared and fundamental misapprehension of the facts or the law. This category of mistake is generally referred to as 'common' mistake, as both parties must have contracted under the same misapprehension.[124] Yet another way of categorising the two situations discussed above is to distinguish between mistakes as to the terms of the contract and mistakes as to the facts about the contract. This is because unilateral and mutual mistakes are relevant only if the mistake is over the terms (or the identity of one party), while common mistake is concerned with mistakes about the facts.[125]

It is arguable that in the cases where there is a mistake as to the terms of the contract or as to the identity of one of the parties, the legal analysis really involves the application of general principles of formation and interpretation.[126] This is due to the following reasons. First, no contract can be formed if there is no correspondence between the offer and the acceptance or if the agreement is not sufficiently certain. The starting point here is whether the parties have reached an agreement that there is a contract between them on the same terms, so that subjectively they are agreed on the same thing. If so, there will be a contract on the agreed terms.

However, if one party claims that he or she did not intend a contract at all, or did not intend to contract on the terms which the other party claims were agreed, then the question is whether there is a contract. The intention of the parties is generally to be construed objectively.[127] Yet, it may happen that one party accepts

[122] HG Beale (ed), *Chitty on Contracts*, vol 1, 33rd edn (Sweet & Maxwell, 2018) 343.
[123] ibid.
[124] ibid 344.
[125] ibid.
[126] ibid 349.
[127] ibid 349–50.

a promise knowing that the terms stated by the other differed from what the other party intended. In such circumstances, the mistake may prevent the party's acceptance being effective at face value: either the contract will be on the terms the other party actually intended or, possibly, the 'mistake' will render the contract void.[128] In this way, the objective test is designed to protect the plaintiff who in fact reasonably relies on what he or she believes the other party is agreeing to, and if he or she had formed no view one way or the other as to what the defendant intended, he or she does not merit that protection.[129]

Second, where the parties are genuinely at cross-purposes as to the subject matter of the contract, the result may be that there is no offer and acceptance of the same terms because neither party can show that the other party should reasonably have understood his or her version.[130] Alternatively, the terms of the offer and acceptance may be so ambiguous that it is not possible to point to one or the other of the interpretations as the more probable, and the court must therefore hold that no contract exists.[131]

Thus, in sum, how the doctrine of mistake should apply to contracts made by computerised trading systems depends on the resolution of the more fundamental issue of how contracts are formed in the first place, which was discussed above.

B. The Singapore Approach Towards Mistake in Algorithmic Contracts

Having established that the law of mistake is very much connected with the law of formation, it is worthwhile now to consider the Singapore courts' approach towards mistake in algorithmic contracts. Indeed, interesting issues of how mistake should apply in such a situation were considered by the Singapore Court of Appeal in *Quoine Pte Ltd v B2C2 Ltd*.[132] In that case, B2C2, a market maker trading on Quoine's currency platform, had sold Ethereum (ETH) in exchange for Bitcoins (BTC) to other margin traders at the rate of 10 BTC for 1 ETH. This was approximately 250 times the (then) prevailing price of ETH. These anomalous trades were traceable to a technical glitch in Quoine's trading software that caused it to stop placing orders on the platform. The abnormally thin order book triggered a margin call and forced the sale of the counterparties' currency holdings. It also prompted B2C2's trading software to generate orders at the 'deep price' of 10 BTC for 1 ETH. A further design flaw in the system led to the matching of the other margin traders' orders with those of B2C2, resulting in the anomalous trades. Upon discovering

[128] ibid 350.
[129] *Maple Leaf Macro Volatility Master Fund v Rouvroy* [2009] EWHC 257 (Comm) [228].
[130] Beale (n 122) 352.
[131] ibid.
[132] *Quoine Pte Ltd v B2C2 Ltd* [2020] 2 SLR 20.

the errors, Quoine unilaterally cancelled the trades and reversed the transactions. B2C2 then sued Quoine for breach of contract and breach of trust.[133]

More specifically, the relevant contracts were entered into pursuant to deterministic algorithmic programmes that had acted *exactly* as they had been programmed to act. B2C2 had through its algorithm placed sell orders for ETH on Quoine's platform at prices of 9.99999 BTC and 10 BTC to 1 ETH. As for the counterparties, orders had been placed on behalf of them to buy ETH at the best available price on the platform. These two orders matched and resulted in the relevant contracts, albeit at a price that was highly advantageous to B2C2. Yet, it is important to note that the terms of the resulting contract were entirely within the parameters that the respective algorithms were programmed to execute. Thus, as the majority stated, 'it is not clear what mistake can be said to have affected the formation of the contracts'.[134] The mistake, if it existed at all, was in the way in which Quoine's platform had operated due to Quoine's failure to update several critical operating systems, which eventually led to the relevant contracts. This, as the majority put it, 'might conceivably be seen as a mistake as to the premise on which the buy orders were placed, but it can in no way be said to be a mistake as to the terms on which the contracts could or would be formed'.[135]

Thus, the case could be resolved on the simple basis that there was no operative mistake to begin with. However, the court took the opportunity to consider some of the interesting issues as to how the law of mistake should react to the phenomenon of algorithmic contracts. First, Sundaresh Menon CJ for the majority of the Singapore Court of Appeal in *Quoine Pte Ltd v B2C2 Ltd*[136] confirmed the requirement of actual knowledge in order to invoke unilateral mistake as to the terms at common law.[137] Menon CJ further held that actual knowledge is concerned with the subjective knowledge of the non-mistaken party. It must therefore be shown that the non-mistaken party actually knew of the relevant fact. However, consistent with the analysis above, the means by which the subjective knowledge of the non-mistaken party is ascertained may include considerations of the matter from an objective perspective.

Second, generally, the time at which to assess whether the non-mistaken party had the requisite actual knowledge of the mistake is at the point of contract formation. However, the facts of *Quoine Pte Ltd v B2C2 Ltd* required a reconsideration of this general approach.[138] As will be recalled, the contracts in that case

[133] Interestingly, Thorley J also held that Quoine held the cryptoassets credited to B2C2's account on trust for B2C2 and acted in breach of trust when it wrongly reversed the trades. This assumed, controversially, that the cryptoassets constituted 'property' that could be the subject of a trust. This holding was reversed on appeal; however, the court did not rule on whether cryptoassets constituted property. See ibid [144]–[149].

[134] ibid [114].

[135] ibid.

[136] ibid [89].

[137] ibid.

[138] ibid.

were entered into by deterministic algorithms. These algorithms, while bound by what the programmer has programmed them to do, could enter into a range of (pre-determined) possibilities at the point of contract formation. Thus, it would be artificial to assess the contracting parties' state of knowledge at the point of formation because, having left the algorithms to determine the specific terms in the contract, the parties did not have any knowledge or direct personal involvement in the formation of the contract.[139]

As such, Menon CJ, writing for the majority of the Court of Appeal in *Quoine Pte Ltd v B2C2 Ltd*,[140] held that the correct approach is to assess the programmer's state of knowledge from the time of programming to when the relevant contract was formed. In the first place, it is the programmer who sets the parameters which the algorithm is bound by. Thus, it is realistic to assess the programmer's state of knowledge to see if he or she actually knew of a mistake or sought to take advantage of it.

In addition, Menon CJ justified the relevance of assessing the programmer's knowledge from the point of programming, since that is when the programmer's knowledge is most concretised. However, the enquiry cannot end there as there may be situations where a programmer or the person running the algorithm who did not contemplate the relevant mistake at the point of programming came to learn of it subsequently *before* the contract had been formed, and yet allowed the algorithm to continue running, thereby intending to take advantage of the mistake. In such a case, it would be wrong to ignore the subsequent acquisition of knowledge. This is why it is appropriate to have regard to the state of knowledge up to the time of the contract.[141]

Finally, in contrast to the uncertainty elsewhere, it is clear that there is a doctrine of unilateral mistake in equity in Singapore. Indeed, following the court's previous decision in *Chwee Kin Keong v Digilandmall.com Pte Ltd*,[142] Menon CJ explained that the Singapore courts have an equitable jurisdiction with regard to unilateral mistake. The rationale behind this equitable jurisdiction is to 'assist [the court] in achieving the ends of justice in appropriate cases'.[143] As such, according to Menon CJ,[144] there are two requirements that must be met before the equitable jurisdiction can be invoked: first, it must be shown that the non-mistaken party had constructive knowledge of the mistaken party's mistake; and, second, that it was unconscionable for the non-mistaken party to insist on the performance of the contract because it had engaged in some unconscionable conduct or sharp practice in relation to that mistake.[145] In addition, the mistake must be one as to

[139] ibid [98].
[140] ibid [89].
[141] ibid [99].
[142] *Chwee Kin Keong v Digilandmall.com Pte Ltd* [2005] 1 SLR(R) 502.
[143] *Quoine Pte Ltd v B2C2 Ltd* (n 132) [89].
[144] ibid.
[145] ibid.

the fundamental term of the contract. There is some uncertainty as to whether the mistake can extend beyond a mistake as to a term of the contract.[146]

This brief coverage of the Singapore courts' approach towards the law of mistake in the realm of algorithmic contracts illustrates that the law as it traditionally stands can be quite successfully adapted to disputes involving new technology. It also illustrates that contractual theory, as translated into practice, need not undergo a complete overhaul.

V. Conclusion

Thus far, we have seen the various issues brought about by algorithmic contracts in the realm of contractual assent, which can affect the law of formation and the law of mistake. We have also seen that these issues can, generally speaking, be dealt with quite adequately by the current law, albeit with a bit of adaptation. Given the clarity of the common law and the need for flexibility, it may be that there is no need to enact legislation to guide the development of the law. However, it may be useful for practical guidance to be given, such as consultation papers that can help seed debate which will ultimately be useful to the courts as they develop the law in the face of new technologies.

Ultimately, whichever legal solution is adopted, it should be recognised that there are clear practical benefits that follow from making computer-generated agreements binding in law.[147] First, as is already the case, treating computer-generated agreements as contracts would make them assignable for value. If there is a secondary market in futures contracts for the particular commodity in question, the computer-generated agreements should be tradeable on the secondary market. This requires such contracts to have the same legal status as other agreements. Second, computer trading is a fact regardless of the legal treatment of computer-generated agreements. This, by itself, is a sign that doing business through computer-generated contracts is more efficient than doing it through other media. The law should follow commercial practice and uphold such agreements.[148]

In the end, how the law does it can be debated, but it has been suggested above that different legal analyses can be used depending on the type of algorithm used. This may have an impact on how the law of contract reacts to finding contractual consent in the age of machine learning.

[146] ibid [91].
[147] Allen and Widdison (n 35) 50.
[148] ibid 51.

10

Digital Assets

Balancing Liquidity with Other Considerations

GAL ACRICH, KATIA LITVAK, ON DVORI,
OPHIR SAMUELOV AND DOV GREENBAUM*

I. Introduction

Digital assets have become increasingly popular over the past few decades and the law has been unable to keep pace with them. Even the term itself lacks a clear legal and even colloquial definition as there are many valuable and invaluable assets that can fall under its rubric.

While much has been written on cryptocurrency and its regulation,[1] less has been discussed about other digital areas. Notably, given the wide spectrum of digital assets, each asset ought to be regulated independently, if at all. Although this is a growing area of research, both practical and theoretical, there are few supportive cases and primary sources. This is also an evolving area, with constant new attempts at rule-making. Finally, it is an expansive area, where a full treatment for even a single jurisdiction is far beyond the scope of this chapter. Nevertheless, we will endeavour to convey some practical and timely considerations within the space constraints.

This chapter will look at four different types of digital assets. The first are digital currencies. Distinct from cryptocurrencies, these are most often used in video games. Most have no real-world value beyond the gaming platforms for which they were created. However, their continued expansion outside of games and into the real world make their regulation increasingly relevant.

* Zvi Meitar Institute for Legal Implications of Emerging Technologies, IDC Herzliya. This research is supported by the National Research Foundation, Singapore under its Emerging Areas Research Projects (EARP) Funding Initiative. Any opinions, findings and conclusions or recommendations expressed in this material are those of the authors and do not reflect the views of National Research Foundation, Singapore.

[1] D Greenbaum, 'What Bitcoin Needs is a Few Good Regulations' *Wall Street Journal* (14 December 2017), www.wsj.com/articles/what-bitcoin-needs-is-a-few-good-regulations-1513294030.

The second type is also related to video games. These refer to those facsimiles of real-world assets that are acquired through labour and effort in the various virtual environments. Often these assets do not yet have actual financial value, but they may hold significant sentimental value and will thus raise considerations when passed intestate.

The third type is emails and personal files. As described below, courts struggle between the idea of comparing these assets to their metaphorical physical equivalents and the reality that while the heirs may have access to physical documents, the platforms that host digital documents might not grant the heirs access. This tightrope distinction has to find the balance between ownership of the amorphous intellectual property locked away on a platform, and the ownership of the physical things that the deceased leaves behind. The heirs might own the intellectual property per se, but the platforms may be obligated by other laws (eg, privacy and computer fraud laws) to prevent the heirs from accessing that intellectual property.

The fourth type relates to the online persona, specifically on social media. In rare examples, this persona may hold substantial value, especially if the holder is an influencer.[2] Particularly in these cases, code is often law and the terms of service associated with the social media platforms may regulate the ability to transfer ownership of these assets, both through sales or through inheritance.

Finally, we will cover the area of tokens (ie crypto tokens or cryptoassets), which is probably the most legally mature area of this sector. Tokens are a subset of cryptocurrency in that they facilitate transactions, but they do not always function as money per se – some are more like assets: utility tokens are akin to coupons that are traded for services or products; security tokens are more like stocks and securities; and payment tokens are what most typically associate with cryptocurrencies – they are digital currencies to facilitate transactions. They comprise coins like NFTs (Nonfungable Tokens) and Altcoins, ie, alternatives to Bitcoin.[3] Some tokens are hybrids.

The discussion will highlight the key attributes of the different types of digital assets and the specific legal issues that arise with respect to each type of digital asset, with a focus on the issues of ownership, inheritance and privacy. This chapter will also note how artificial intelligence (AI) is playing an increasing role in these digital developments, especially in the commodification and monetisation of digital assets.

We aim to discuss not only the many different types of digital assets and their considerations vis-a-vis ownership and inheritance, but also their important privacy implications. Like other special classes of data, such as health or genomics,[4]

[2] Y Zhang, Y Lin, and KH Goh, 'Impact of Online Influencer Endorsement on Product Sales: Quantifying Value of Online Influencer' *Pacific Asia Conference on Information Systems* (2018), https://core.ac.uk/download/pdf/301375963.pdf.

[3] J Frankenfield, 'Crypto Tokens' *Investopedia* (30 June 2020), https://www.investopedia.com/terms/c/crypto-token.asp.

[4] D Greenbaum, A Sboner, XJ Mu and M Gerstein, 'Genomics and Privacy: Implications of the New Reality of Closed Data for the Field' (2011) 7(12) *PLOS Computational Biology*. See also D Greenbaum, J Du and M Gerstein, 'Genomic Anonymity: Have We Already Lost it?' (2008) 8(10) *American Journal of Bioethics* 71. See also D Greenbaum, 'Genomic Data Disclosure: Time to Reassess the

digital assets, more so than other property, can raise problematic privacy considerations as they reflect their owners' online activities, their proclivities, orientations, preferences and desires – this is especially the case with social media data. These privacy considerations, or at least the lip service paid to these concerns, are often at the heart of litigation in the area of access to social media digital assets. And, often at the crux of many considerations with regard to the inheritance of digital assets or access to digital assets post-mortem are the privacy concerns of the now-deceased owner.

The discussion is mostly focused on US law. This is for practical reasons. First, the US is leading much of the legal and regulatory innovation in this space, albeit not the only jurisdiction that is considering this area.[5] As such, it is valuable to examine how the US rules and regulations can provide guidance to other jurisdictions.

Second, with many of the relevant stakeholders headquartered in the US, they often choose US jurisdictions as their forum of choice (also known as governing law, forum selection or submission to jurisdiction contract clauses) for any relevant civil matters, as might be detailed in their extensive terms of service (TOS). Where these forums are often chosen, US courts have upheld choice of forum clauses,[6] as have other countries like Israel[7] and Singapore.[8] US courts have even upheld arbitration clauses (which are similar in design to forum selection clauses)[9] against a minor.[10] The upholding of forum selection clauses is an important component of international trade.[11] Thus, even a social media user

Realities' (2013) 13(5) *American Journal of Bioethics* 47; D Greenbaum, A Harmanci and M Gerstein, 'Proposed Social and Technological Solutions to Issues of Data Privacy in Personal Genomics' (2014) *IIEEE International Symposium on Ethics in Science, Technology and Engineering* 1–4.

[5] R Genders and A Steen, 'Financial and Estate Planning in the Age of Digital Assets: A Challenge for Advisers and Administrators' (2017) 3(1) *Financial Planning Research Journal* 75.

[6] *We are the People Inc v Facebook* 19-CV-8871 (2020) (noting that forum selection clauses 'are prima facie valid and should be enforced unless enforcement is shown by the resisting party to be "unreasonable" under the circumstances'); *Sunrise Medical HHG, Inc v Health Focus of NY*, 278 F App'x 80, 81 (2d Cir 2008) (quoting *M/S Bremen v Zapata Off-Shore Co*, 407 US 1, 10 (1972)); *Atlantic Marine Construction Co v US District Court for Western District of Texas*, 571 US 49 (2013)).

[7] See 'Israeli Court Refuses to Enforce Forum Selection Clause in Online Foreign Exchange Agreement: What's Next?', www.sherby.co.il/blog/2017/02/14/israeli-court-refuses-to-enforce-forum-selection-clause-in-online-foreign-exchange-agreement-whats-next (noting that in general, 'Israeli courts are deferential to forum selection clauses in international commerce.').

[8] See www.singaporelawwatch.sg/About-Singapore-Law/Overview/ch-06-the-conflict-of-laws, citing *Vinmar Overseas (Singapore) Pte Ltd v PTT International Trading Pte Ltd* [2018] 2 SLR 1271, which states that: 'Exclusive jurisdiction clauses play an important role in international commercial contracts.' See also *Shanghai Turbo Enterprises Ltd v Liu Ming* [2019] 1 SLR 779, regarding the threshold in non-exclusive jurisdiction clauses.

[9] *Scherk v Alberto-Culver Co*, 417 US 506 (1974), 519, where the court held that: 'An agreement to arbitrate before a specified tribunal is, in effect, a specialized kind of forum-selection clause that posits not only the situs of suit but also the procedure to be used in resolving the dispute.'

[10] *Heidbreder v Epic Games, Inc*, No 19-348 (EDNC, 3 February 2020)).

[11] *The Bremen v Zapata Off-Shore Co*, 407 US 1 (1972), 9, where the court held that: 'The expansion of American business and industry will hardly be encouraged if, not-withstanding solemn contracts, we insist on a parochial concept that all disputes must be resolved under our laws and in our courts … We

in Asia or a video-game player in Europe may be subject to US laws if and when there is arbitration or litigation. For example, Facebook's forum selection clause chooses the Northern District of California, as does Twitter.[12]

Third, when assessing practical applications of digital assets for clients, especially tax implications, attorneys should keep in mind that the US collects taxes from all citizens, regardless of where they physically reside, or other citizenships.

II. The Timeliness of the Topic

There is an increasing interest in digital assets and, as such, a greater interest in legal oversight. For example, during the recent COVID-19 pandemic, investors saw cryptocurrencies as alternatives to government-backed currencies. Digital assets are also an increasingly common method of sheltering assets from tax authorities. Some may believe that when the pandemic is over and government largesse is reconsidered, there might suddenly be increases in taxes.[13]

In the case of digital assets, some, like cryptocurrencies, may seem like a good place to park your money during times of extreme volatility in the same way that investors often turn to gold. However, they also often attract significant government oversight due to their (suspected) rampant use in the criminal underworld; the borderless nature of emerging digital assets makes it difficult for governments to regulate and tax even legitimate uses. One group, the OECD/G20 Inclusive Framework, is working to develop rules to regulate the movement of digital assets.[14]

In other instances, the COVID-19 pandemic and related governmental measures have driven huge swaths of the population into isolation and quarantine. Concurrently, video games have seen a surge in popularity soaring to almost $11 billion in US sales during the first quarter of 2020. Analysts see this growth as related to the 'comfort and connection' that video games bring to a growing community of millions during a challenging time like the COVID-19 crisis.[15]

Simply playing the games can generate digital assets. Items can also be bought, sold or traded within gameplay. Even the gameplay itself is often monetised via

cannot have trade and commerce in world markets and international waters exclusively on our terms, governed by our laws, and resolved in our courts.'

[12] *Brittain v Twitter, Inc*, No 19-cv-00114-YGR (ND Cal, 15 March 2019).

[13] C Taylor, 'Coronavirus Crisis Could See Wealth Taxes Implemented around the World, Economist Claims' *CNBC* (22 May 2020), www.cnbc.com/2020/05/11/coronavirus-wealth-taxes-may-be-rolled-out-globally-economist-says.html.

[14] S Doherty and AS Verghese, 'In the Digital Era, Tax, Trade and Competition Rules Need an Upgrade' *World Economic Forum* (11 October 2019), www.weforum.org/agenda/2019/10/digital-tax-trade-business-consumption-e-commerce.

[15] D Lazarus, 'Column: Video Games are Thriving amid COVID-19 – and Experts Say That's a Good Thing' *Los Angeles Times* (16 June 2020), www.latimes.com/business/story/2020-06-16/column-coronavirus-video-games.

advertising revenue when the games are viewed by the general public, for example, on YouTube and Twitch.[16]

Games are not the only way in which people are finding human interaction during the pandemic. Many are looking to social media as both a source of companionship as well as a source of information. The data collected by internet platforms is increasingly viewed as a digital asset, as are many social media accounts, particularly those that have reached an influencer status where they can monetise their fame through product placements and the like.[17]

III. The Different Types of Digital Assets and their Legal Considerations

Generally, these sorts of assets range from cryptocurrencies, which have been discussed widely,[18] to other virtual currencies that are increasingly popular in the multi-billion-dollar video-game market, to blockchain-based tokens such as NFTs, to the even less tangible digital persona associated with social media, and everything in between, including algorithmic-driven transactions and electronic records.

We will review a number of these below, including virtual currencies, video-game assets, emails and personal digital files, crypto tokens and social media accounts.

A. Virtual Currencies

Legal issues related to Bitcoin have been reviewed extensively;[19] however, much less has been written on other virtual currencies, especially those that are employed in video games.[20] These are particularly unique assets, in that the video

[16] This is a convoluted area of copyright law; see, eg, N Robinson, 'From Arcades to Online: Updating Copyright to Accommodate Video Game Streaming' (2018) 20 *North Carolina Journal of Law & Technology* 286.

[17] A Arora et al, 'Measuring Social Media Influencer Index-Insights from Facebook, Twitter and Instagram' (2019) 49 *Journal of Retailing and Consumer Services* 86. See also SV Jin, A Muqaddum and E Ryu, 'Instafamous and Social Media Influencer Marketing' (2019) 37(5) *Marketing Intelligence & Planning* 567.

[18] Congressman D Schwikert et al, 'Letter to CP Rettig, Commissioner Internal Revenue Service' (29 July 2020), www.schweikert.house.gov/sites/schweikert.house.gov/files/Final%20Proof%20of%20Stake%20IRS%20Letter%207.29.20.pdf. See also A Shome, 'US Crypto Users Receive Fresh IRS Notices' *Finance Magnates* (26 August 2020), www.financemagnates.com/cryptocurrency/news/us-crypto-users-receive-fresh-irs-notices. The question of 'crypto investment' is also explicitly mentioned in the draft Form 1040.

[19] See n 1 above. See also Congressional Research Service, 'Cryptocurrency: The Economics of Money and Selected Policy Issues' (9 April 2020), www.fas.org/sgp/crs/misc/R45427.pdf.

[20] See, eg, A Moiseienko and K Izenman, 'Gaming the System: Money Laundering through Online Games' *RUSI Newsbrief* (11 October 2019), www.rusi.org/publication/rusi-newsbrief/gaming-system-money-laundering-through-online-games.

game producers often claim them to have no real value outside the game itself. Yet, legal concerns arise when players or criminals find ways to extract real-world value from these otherwise fake currencies.

The US Internal Revenue Service (IRS) had expressed interest in these types of currencies, even listing V-Bucks, the currency of the popular video game *Fortnite*, as an example of taxable assets, although this was later retracted.[21]

Roblox, another popular video game, was also targeted by the IRS and, like *Fortnite*, it has a currency that can be traded through both legitimate and illegal channels back into fiat currency. Users who are at least 13 years old (*Roblox* doesn't require age verification) can cash out 'Robux' for US dollars through the game itself,[22] which provides myriad opportunities to generate in-game wealth.

In another instance, the Nintendo game *Animal Crossing: New Horizons*, a mundane but relaxing, drama-free online environment, has seen a tremendous rise in popularity during the COVID-19 pandemic.[23] Many are seeking to literally cash in on this gaming phenomenon and they do so in the open, on popular platforms like eBay, by selling 'bells' and 'Nook Miles Tickets' (virtual currencies of the *Animal Crossing* universe) for hard cash.[24]

These efforts are disconcerting for Nintendo. If a market becomes established and these virtual bells gain real-world value, the bells and the game itself may become regulated by the US Treasury's Financial Crimes Enforcement Network (FinCEN), if these currencies are found to fall under the Department of the Treasury's definition of convertible virtual currencies (CVC) a substitute for real currency, or has an equivalent value in real currency, like Bitcoin.[25]

FinCEN has anti-money laundering (AML) regulations for the use of CVCs.[26] If Nintendo allows or facilitates bells to be traded for the equivalent of real currency, bells could potentially be legally defined as a CVC and become regulated by FinCEN. If this is the case, then Nintendo may become a money transmitter

[21] See www.irs.gov/businesses/small-businesses-self-employed/virtual-currencies.

[22] A Versprille, 'Gamers Rich in Virtual Cash Freed from IRS Reporting Worry (1)' *Bloomberg News* (13 February 2020), https://news.bloombergtax.com/daily-tax-report/irs-pulls-wording-subjecting-gamers-to-virtual-currency-question.

[23] H Sparks, 'Inside the Cult of "Animal Crossing"' *New York Post* (12 May 2020), www.nypost.com/2020/05/12/inside-the-cult-of-animal-crossing.

[24] T Geigner, 'Tales from the Quarantine: People are Selling "Animal Crossing" Bells for Real Cash after Layoffs' *Techdirt* (8 May 2020), www.techdirt.com/articles/20200507/11080044454/tales-quarantine-people-are-selling-animal-crossing-bells-real-cash-after-layoffs.shtml; D Greenbaum, 'How Covid-19 Might Create an Onerous Economy inside Video Games' *CTECH by Calcalist* (15 May 2020), www.calcalistech.com/ctech/articles/0,7340,L-3822874,00.html.

[25] JG Gatto, 'What Game Companies Need to Know about FinCEN's Updated Guidance on Virtual Currency' *National Law Review* (10 May 2019), www.natlawreview.com/article/what-game-companies-need-to-know-about-fincen-s-updated-guidance-virtual-currency.

[26] 'Application of FinCEN's Regulations to Certain Business Models Involving Convertible Virtual Currencies' *FIN-2019-G001* (9 May 2019), www.fincen.gov/resources/statutes-regulations/guidance/application-fincens-regulations-certain-business-models.

under FinCEN regulations and subject to AML oversight. In addition to federal oversight, states are also keen on licensing businesses that trade CVCs.[27]

Fortunately, for Nintendo, currently as per the Financial Action Task Force (FATF), a global money laundering and terrorist financing watchdog, *Animal Crossing* bells might not yet be considered CVCs as they cannot yet be easily converted into fiat currency. However, 'it is possible that an unofficial, secondary black market may arise that provides an opportunity to exchange the "nonconvertible" virtual currency for fiat currency or another virtual currency'. In these cases, the development 'of a robust secondary black market in a particular "nonconvertible" virtual currency may, as a practical matter, effectively transform it into a convertible virtual currency'.[28]

The US Department of the Treasury is particularly concerned with the CVC black market, as there is a growing use of CVCs not only in money laundering, but also in drug trafficking, terrorist financing, weapons of mass destruction proliferation and financing, organised crime, human trafficking and corruption in general.

This is a real fear as online gaming can become a haven for money launderers and other criminal enterprises seeking to exploit their current lack of oversight and the pandemic.[29] The multi-billion-dollar free-to-play online video game *Fortnite* is reportedly becoming a money-laundering safe harbour where accounts are created and local digital currencies are purchased illicitly. Eventually, these accounts are sold on eBay or the dark web in return for clean untraceable money.[30]

The mounting regulatory concern over increasing criminal activities can create problems for games that have marketplaces where tokens can be purchased with real money (for example, for premium content), as is the case with many emerging video games. Valve Corp, a major stakeholder in the video-game market, recently changed the way in-game purchases can be traded in its *Counter Strike: Global Offensive* game, reportedly because of these fears.[31]

This increasing focus on CVCs, especially those originating in online games, would create real problems for all game developers if the currencies in their games were to reach even unintended CVC status.

[27] MS Sackheim and NA Howell, *The Virtual Currency Regulation Review*, 2nd edn (2019), www.sidley.com/-/media/publications/united-states--the-virtual-currency-regulation-review--edition-2.pdf?la=en

[28] FATF, 'Virtual Currencies – Key Definitions and Potential AML/CFT Risks' (June 2014), www.fatf-gafi.org/media/fatf/documents/reports/Virtual-currency-key-definitions-and-potential-aml-cft-risks.pdf.

[29] FinCEN Advisory on Cybercrime and Cyber-Enabled Crime Exploiting the Coronavirus Disease 2019 (COVID-19) Pandemic (30 July 2020), www.fincen.gov/sites/default/files/advisory/2020-07-30/FinCEN%20Advisory%20Covid%20Cybercrime%20508%20FINAL.pdf.

[30] US Treasury Department., 'National Strategy for Combating Terrorist and Other Illicit Financing' (2020), www.home.treasury.gov/system/files/136/National-Strategy-to-Counter-Illicit-Financev2.pdf.

[31] AE Bigart and ER Minsberg, 'Regulatory Risks of in-Game and in App Virtual Currency' *Venable* (22 May 2017), www.venable.com/insights/publications/2017/05/regulatory-risks-of-ingame-and-inapp-virtual-curre.

In an effort to combat money laundering, some have suggested that various jurisdictions enforce transparency requirements on gamers, including identifying information such as time zones, login information, duration of play, type of device used, and the serial and other identifying numbers of that device, ie, personally identifiable video game information (PIVGI).[32] In some instances, this information can be augmented with more identifying billing information.

B. Other Gaming-Related Assets

Not everything valuable in video games is convertible into a CVC, yet it might still have actual value,[33] if not sentimental value. These assets can potentially be bought, stolen, inherited, taken away or otherwise manipulated. In these cases, the terms and conditions of various games may control and limit what owners can and cannot do with aspects of the game that they may have laboured over.

Notably, China recently passed a law in May 2020 relating to the inheritance of video game virtual assets and items, although the mechanics of this are not yet clear.[34] In general, there is not much information as to how these issues will be dealt with in China. In fact, until 2020 the law had not changed much to accommodate virtual property. In this context, it is worth mentioning the recently legislated Article 127 of China's General Principles of the Civil Law, which states that: 'If other laws particularly provide for the protection of data and online virtual assets, such provisions shall prevail.'[35] Under the previous laws, Chinese internet platforms allowed users to enjoy virtual properties without full ownership.[36] These non-negotiable TOS often ended up in courts giving inconsistent rulings, given the lack of clear guidance from the law.[37]

In one particular case, a son made efforts to show that the law provided for the inheritance to another type of digital asset (albeit unrelated to video games) – a phone number with all of its associated network of contact numbers, a potentially especially valuable asset in an increasingly cashless society. According to reports, none of the major telecommunication companies had any provisions in their TOS relating to this, although they had contemplated the post-mortem transfer of money left on the phone-based account.[38]

[32] C Witbracht, 'Level up: Video Games and AML' *ACAMS Today* (19 December 2019), www.acamstoday.org/level-up-video-games-and-aml.

[33] N Jurgenson, 'The IRL Fetish' *The New Inquiry* (28 June 2012), www.thenewinquiry.com/the-irl-fetish.

[34] H Chen, 'China's Civil Code Allows in-Game Virtual Items to Be Inherited' *Pandaily* (22 May 2020), www.pandaily.com/chinas-civil-code-allows-in-game-virtual-items-to-be-inherited.

[35] General Provisions of the Civil Law of the People's Republic of China, art 127, www.npc.gov.cn/englishnpc/lawsoftheprc/202001/c983fc8d3782438fa775a9d67d6e82d8.shtml.

[36] ibid.

[37] ibid.

[38] L Fen, 'Dead Man's Phone Numbers Spark Virtual Inheritance Debate' *Sixth Tone* (24 May 2018), www.sixthtone.com/news/1002346/dead-mans-phone-numbers-spark-virtual-inheritance-

This will become a growing concern as more and more valuable items are created for the virtual world. For example, without their catwalks and fashion weeks during the COVID-19 pandemic, top fashion houses like Valentino and Marc Jacobs have turned to online platforms like video games to showcase their designs. Virtual versions of their fashion are often even freely available for a user's avatar in a game.[39]

Similarly, the Metropolitan Museum of Art in New York and the Los Angeles Getty Museum are allowing users to decorate their virtual *Animal Crossing* homes with art from their famous collections.[40] Some interior design companies are even offering their services online for *Animal Crossing* players who want to upgrade their virtual homes.[41]

The misappropriation of this potentially valuable virtual inventory in video games has been dealt with by law enforcement. For example, in South Korea, there has been a longstanding police unit dedicated to virtual crimes within video games.[42] While it is not clear how most regulatory bodies in most jurisdictions would deal with these types of misappropriation,[43] virtual crimes are still relatively rare. In some instances, games may have glitches that allow users to easily (and legally?) misappropriate other players' inventories.[44] In one case, the Federal Bureau of Investigation (FBI) was brought in when gamers found an exploitable software bug. The two defendants were charged with a misdemeanour, but nothing much amounted to what in the end was a victimless crime, as the game producer gave the victims their items back.[45]

In other instances, games may provide players with inventory through what are known as loot boxes. Instead of spending time in gameplay collecting items,

debate: 'Since his father was a businessman, Liu [the son] thought that gaining access to his contacts would be important for maintaining the family's business relationships. But getting the phone numbers transferred to Liu required more effort than he anticipated, because his father could not be present for the process – as telecom companies generally require for such transfers.'

[39] J Fingas, 'Top Fashion Houses are Showing Their Latest Styles in "Animal Crossing"' *Engadget* (10 May 2020), www.engadget.com/animal-crossing-fashion-houses-231541432.html?guccounter=1&guce_referrer=aHR0cHM6Ly93d3cuY2FsY2FsaXN0ZWNoLmNvbS9jdGVjaC9hcnRpY2xlcy8wLDczNDAsTC0zODIyODc0LDAwLmh0bWw&guce_referrer_sig=AQAAAJGjkV1G32nVeXHU0R6e-RxLSMx5f2ez2VI1kQBR6nsw3UkwZcvubiQiGh0S-gKH-ozTlCycgBJHytJi7e5L5v1By6HJEnsmkJN-6lY_ZXYG2lhR5d46BPxZTc8ZZHzH4ltuT_LwL5IG7j3srFq_VnB-xy-SdFjsxCFH1_obuBLtW.

[40] 'Own a Van Gogh … in Animal Crossing, with the Met's New Share Tool' *The Met Museum* (27 April 2020), www.metmuseum.org/blogs/collection-insights/2020/animal-crossing-new-horizons-qr-code.

[41] See, eg, www.olivias.com/pages/become-a-virtual-interior-design-consultant-in-animal-crossing-new-horizons.

[42] M Ward, 'Does Virtual Crime Need Real Justice?' *BBC News* (29 September 2003), www.news.bbc.co.uk/2/hi/technology/3138456.stm.

[43] O Herzfeld, 'What is the Legal Status of Virtual Goods?' *Forbes* (4 December 2012), www.forbes.com/sites/oliverherzfeld/2012/12/04/what-is-the-legal-status-of-virtual-goods/#4c8d6524108a.

[44] P Tassi, 'Watch One Guy Steal 500+ "Fallout 76" Players' Gear in an Exploit That's Destroyed the Game' *Forbes* (24 December 2019), www.forbes.com/sites/paultassi/2019/12/24/watch-one-guy-steal-500-fallout-76-players-gear-in-an-exploit-thats-destroyed-the-game/#b0d5f8f49d2a.

[45] T Geigner, '2 Teen Diablo Players were Charged, Got Probation for "Stealing" Virtual Items That were Replaced' *Techdirt* (27 May 2015), www.techdirt.com/articles/20150520/10195431065/2-teen-diablo-players-were-charged-got-probation-stealing-virtual-items-that-were-replaced.shtml.

players can be gifted these items through the game. Although these loot boxes have little if any actual value, many jurisdictions, including Belgium and the Netherlands, have sought to regulate them like gambling, while other jurisdictions are concerned that while not gambling per se, because the pay-out is virtual, these loot boxes could become a gateway drug to more problematic gambling.[46] In the US, various states have proposed legislation to regulate loot boxes. In addition, there has been at least one proposal from a US senator for a federal law, but no laws have yet been passed.[47]

C. Emails and Personal Files

Not all hard-to-value assets are related to video-game play; some assets hold at least sentimental if not outright value and may be especially pertinent with regard to inheritance. In addition, in many cases, the content from these assets are controlled or protected by one or more federal laws relating to intellectual property, user privacy or both.

User privacy is further complicated post-mortem where it is not universally accepted. For example, depending on the US state, the next of kin may or may not control the right of publicity that the deceased enjoyed while alive. Generally, however, as per the Restatement (Second) Torts, there is no post-mortem privacy-related tort.[48]

One particularly problematic area of digital assets is emails and their associated files. Under US federal laws, any original and creative writing by the deceased that is fixed in a tangible medium is automatically protected under copyright law, the bar of originality and creativity being especially minimal. In essence, most emails with any original text are likely to be protected by US copyright law. As a form of intellectual property, that property passes to the inheritors of the deceased. This law comes into direct conflict with the TOS of many email providers, which allow them to delete the files upon death, as well as in conflict with the privacy of the deceased, who may not want his or her inheritors to have access to his or her personal files.

This becomes especially complicated with courts seeking to draw parallels between physical letters and emails, wherein the physical letters belong to the

[46] E Chansky and E Okerberg, 'Loot Box or Pandora's Box? Regulation of Treasure Chests in Video Games' *National Law Review* (8 August 2019), www.natlawreview.com/article/loot-box-or-pandora-s-box-regulation-treasure-chests-video-games-0.

[47] S Millar and T Marshal, 'FTC Staff Perspective Paper Offers Key Takeaways on Loot Box Workshop' *National Law Review* (20 August 2020), www.natlawreview.com/article/ftc-staff-perspective-paper-offers-key-takeaways-loot-box-workshop.

[48] JL Simmons and MD Means, 'Split Personality: Constructing a Coherent Right of Publicity Statute' (2018) 10(5) *Landslide*, www.americanbar.org/groups/intellectual_property_law/publications/landslide/2017-18/may-june/split-personality.

next of kin, regardless of their content, and digital files that are essentially just their content. One way to circumvent this issue is to expand the nature of the parallel between the physical letters and the next of kin. How can this be done? Arguably, while the emails and letters belong to the family of the deceased, the locked letterbox or password-protected email account that holds the copyrighted letters in question does not. In the case of email, the deceased has contracted with the owner of the password-protected emails box via the TOS of the platform to not allow third parties to access the site. Thus, while the letters may belong to the next of kin, they have no right to demand access to the box holding them, barring explicit instructions by the deceased.

In the US, there have been only a handful of cases where email platforms withheld access to emails on account of the privacy of the deceased. Yahoo! has been sued on a handful of occasions due in part to its No Right of Survivorship and Non-transferability clause for the email accounts that it hosts. In the case of *In re Ellsworth*,[49] a probate court in Michigan ordered the online platform to release the emails of deceased US Marine Justin Ellsworth to his father, who the court found was the next of kin with regard to what it decided was property.

In *Ajemaian v Yahoo!*,[50] co-administrators of their brother's estate sued in the Probate and Family Court, seeking their brother's emails after he was killed suddenly in a car accident. The lower court, based in part upon the Federal Stored Communications Act (SCA),[51] had denied access. The SCA was enacted by Congress in 1986 'to update and clarify Federal privacy protections and standards in light of dramatic changes in new computer and telecommunications technologies … to protect the privacy of users of electronic communications by criminalizing the unauthorized access of the contents'.[52]

While not ordering Yahoo! specifically to turn over the emails, an appellate court remanded the case back to the lower court for a factual determination and ruled that 'the personal representatives may provide lawful consent on the decedent's behalf to the release of the contents of the Yahoo e-mail account'. In a later ruling, the court also found 'that the SCA does not prohibit such disclosure. Rather, it permits Yahoo to divulge the contents of the e-mail account where, as here, the personal representatives lawfully consent to disclosure on the decedent's behalf'.[53]

In contrast to Yahoo!, Google and Microsoft, two other popular email providers have less onerous requirements vis-a-vis turning over emails to users' next of kin.

[49] *In re Ellsworth* (No 2005-296, 651-DE, Mich Prob Ct 2005).
[50] *Ajemian v Yahoo!, Inc*, 83 Mass App Ct 565, 987 NE 2d 604 (App Ct 2013).
[51] 18 USC ss 2701 et seq.
[52] *Ajemian v Yahoo!, Inc*, 478 Mass. 169, 84 NE 3d 766, 171 (2017).
[53] ibid.

D. Social Media Accounts

Consider, for example, the Instagram account of social media influencers.[54] Kylie Jenner is a member of the Kardashian family – with a reach of over 100 million fans. Accounts like hers are hugely valuable marketing tools and Jenner is reportedly paid over $1.25 million for each sponsored post on her account.[55]

The contents of Jenner's posts are regulated. The US Federal Trade Commission (FTC) – officially vested with the responsibility to regulate misleading and deceptive advertising under the 1938 Wheeler-Lea Act – has promulgated guidelines and provided guidance,[56] although with little enforcement.[57] However, the inheritance or otherwise transmittal of Jenner's branded account is less controlled or understood.

Social media accounts, especially of influencers, could potentially be something that can be bought, sold or inherited, like a medical practice of a trusted retiring physician. Alternatively, it might not be. It could be innately tied to the individual account holder, both in spirit and by law. Notably, while most types of property can be assigned, it is not necessarily the case that all contractual rights are assignable or transferable, especially those rights associated with social media accounts.

To appreciate how tied a social media account is to an individual, consider that the sum total of one's social media presence can be reportedly used to create an online bot that closely mimics the personality of a deceased individual.[58] Depending on the jurisdiction and who develops the bot, such an action may violate any privacy[59] or publicity rights[60] that the deceased retains.

In addition to sales, the legal status of a conveyance of social media accounts comes up most often in issues of inheritance. As with many other aspects of digital legacies, or e-legacies, social media accounts can confound standard inheritance

[54] See 'Instagram Influencer Marketing is a $1.7 Billion Dollar Industry' *MediaKix* (7 March 2019), www.mediakix.com/blog/instagram-influencer-marketing-industry-size-how-big//#gs.8o8ist.

[55] M Hanbury, 'The 35 Celebrities and Athletes Who Make the Most Money per Instagram Post, Ranked' *Business Insider* (23 July 2019), www.businessinsider.com/kylie-jenner-ariana-grande-beyonce-instagrams-biggest-earners-2019-2019-7.

[56] See: 'FTC Staff Reminds Influencers and Brands to Clearly Disclose Relationship' *Federal Trade Commission* (19 April 2017), www.ftc.gov/news-events/press-releases/2017/04/ftc-staff-reminds-influencers-brands-clearly-disclose. See also L Fair, 'Three FTC Actions of Interest to Influencers' *Federal Trade Commission* (7 September 2017), www.ftc.gov/news-events/blogs/business-blog/2017/09/three-ftc-actions-interest-influencers.

[57] See '93% of Top Celebrity Social Media Endorsements Violate FTC Guidelines' *MediaKix*, www.mediakix.com/blog/celebrity-social-media-endorsements-violate-ftc-instagram/#gs.8o68dq.

[58] T Knowles and M Bridge, 'Death Bots Will Let Loved Ones Speak from the Grave' *Sunday Times* (21 September 2019), www.thetimes.co.uk/article/death-bots-will-let-loved-ones-speak-from-the-grave-x5lwrmv3g.

[59] E Harbinja, 'Post-mortem Privacy 2.0: Theory, Law, and Technology' (2017) 31(1) *International Review of Law, Computers & Technology* 26.

[60] See, eg, California Code, Civil Code – CIV s 3344.1, which recognises the right of publicity of the deceased.

laws: social media accounts are hosted by online platforms that generally claim some rights over these accounts via licences spelled out in their TOS.[61] These additional parties can confuse the division of assets or the assessing post-mortem ownership of the assets.

Inheritance of social media accounts (especially intestate) can be particularly problematic. If the deceased does not provide for post-mortem control over his or her accounts, then social media platforms might prevent access to those accounts, especially as they claim to often represent the privacy and security concerns of the deceased. Thus, social media accounts may be under the control – and perhaps even the ownership – of their respective online platforms, like Google, Facebook and Twitter, and not the heirs.

Moreover, unlike most properties passed on by will or intestacy, digital files and accounts not stored on actual physical infrastructures (such as hard drives, memory sticks or other physical media that are under the actual physical care and ownership of the deceased); rather, they are often squirrelled away in the amorphous cloud and they may not even be recognised as part of the inheritable estate in some jurisdictions.

And it is not only ownership that is legally confusing. With many social media accounts actively surviving the passing of their operators,[62] there is an increasing need for stewardship of social media accounts and their ongoing digital presence after death, especially if friends, fans and family return to those accounts to pay their respects or remember the deceased. In the past, such stewardship obligations would be limited to famous personalities and celebrities with clearly valuable personas. Now that anyone can claim their 15 minutes of fame online, many more estates could need long-term stewardship commitments.

[61] For example: Facebook's TOS spell out: 'Permission to use content that you create and share: Some content that you share or upload, such as photos or videos, may be protected by intellectual property laws. You own the intellectual property rights … *However, to provide our services, we need you to give us some legal permissions (known as a "license") to use this content … Specifically, when you share, post or upload content that is covered by intellectual property rights on or in connection with our Products, you grant us a non-exclusive, transferable, sub-licensable, royalty-free and worldwide license* to host, use, distribute, modify, run, copy, publicly perform or display, translate and create derivative works of your content (consistent with your privacy and application settings)' (emphasis added) See www.facebook.com/terms.php. Twitter's TOS spell out: 'You retain your rights to any Content you submit, post or display on or through the Services. What's yours is yours – you own your Content (and your incorporated audio, photos and videos are considered part of the Content). By submitting, posting or displaying Content on or through the Services, *you grant us a worldwide, non-exclusive, royalty-free license* (with the right to sublicense) to use, copy, reproduce, process, adapt, modify, publish, transmit, display and distribute such Content in any and all media or distribution methods now known or later developed (for clarity, these rights include, for example, curating, transforming, and translating). This license authorizes us to make your Content available to the rest of the world and to let others do the same' (emphasis added) See www.twitter.com/en/tos. Instagram's TOS spell out: 'Permissions You Give to Us. As part of our agreement, you also give us permissions that we need to provide the Service. *We do not claim ownership of your content, but you grant us a license to use it.* Nothing is changing about your rights in your content. We do not claim ownership of your content that you post on or through the Service' (emphasis added). See www.help.instagram.com/478745558852511

[62] CJ Öhman and D Watson, 'Are the Dead Taking over Facebook? A Big Data Approach to the Future of Death Online' (2019) 6(1) *Big Data & Society*, https://doi.org/10.1177/2053951719842540.

It is not always clear as to who should be legally responsible for this stewardship. This can be especially difficult in the US, where state laws guide many of the questions regarding the estate and federal intellectual property rights often dictate what happens to creative works as per copyright law.

Again, this is an area that has increased in complexity as society becomes increasingly digital. While in the past, only a small portion of the population created creative works, social media has turned many into creators, especially in platforms like Twitch for gamers, YouTube for almost anybody, and massive online multi-player games like *Roblox* and *Minecraft* where users are given the tools to create anything and everything.[63]

Further muddying the issue of stewardship, until recently, although some jurisdictions like France allow the deceased to decide many of these issues of post-mortem ownership and stewardship while they are still alive and some like Canada allow the executor to access digital assets regardless of the deceased's lack of instructions,[64] most, like the UK, do not have any set of particular rules, leaving the untangling of these digital assets for the courts to work out.[65]

To deal with this growing uncertainty, 47 US states and territories, most recently Pennsylvania,[66] have enacted some form of the Revised Uniform Fiduciary Access to Digital Assets Act (RUFADAA). This Act, while seeking to include digital assets like cryptocurrencies and digital files within the deceased's estate, nevertheless limits an executor's access to many digital properties that reside on online platforms when the deceased fails to provide how these assets will be distributed after his or her death.[67]

Succinctly, under the RUFADAA, the deceased is given the choice to prescribe how his or her digital assets will be dealt with. If the deceased does not provide that information, then the TOS will apply. Finally, next of kin can be granted access to some aspects of the digital assets, to the extent that the access granted does not contravene federal privacy laws. Given that most will not provide direction for some if not all of their digital assets post-mortem, typically the law ends up reverting control of digital assets to whatever entity has been granted it, as per the often very rigid and one-sided TOS for each online digital platform.

[63] M Gault, 'Thousands of People are Building a 1:1 Recreation of Earth in "Minecraft"' *Vice* (2 April 2020), https://www.vice.com/en/article/n7jykw/thousands-of-people-are-building-a-11-recreation-of-earth-in-minecraft.

[64] Revised Uniform Fiduciary Access to Digital Assets Act. See, eg, E Lynch, 'Legal Implications Triggered by an Internet User's Death: Reconciling Legislative and Online Contract Approaches in Canada' (2020) 29(1) *Dalhousie Journal of Legal Studies* 135.

[65] U Bacchi, 'Lack of Rules Leaves Experts Puzzled about Data Ownership after Death' *Reuters* (14 February 2019), www.reuters.com/article/us-britain-dataprotection-privacy-analys-idUSKCN1Q304F.

[66] T Pepper, 'Pennsylvania Adopts the Revised Uniform Fiduciary Access to Digital Assets Act' *JD Supra* (13 August 2020), www.jdsupra.com/legalnews/pennsylvania-adopts-the-revised-uniform-67466.

[67] Fiduciary Access to Digital Assets Act. Revised (2015). See s 7, 'disclosure of content of electronic communications of deceased user', which limits disclosure only to cases where 'a deceased user consented or a court directs disclosure of the contents of electronic communications of the user'; www.uniformlaws.org/committees/community-home?CommunityKey=f7237fc4-74c2-4728-81c6-b39a91ecdf22.

This can make for particularly problematic disagreements between next of kin and online services. Digital platforms typically have commercial interests in the decedents' accounts as well as concerns related to legal liabilities arising from the disclosure of personal data; as such, they will likely strongly align with general privacy interests and may actually represent the unspoken wishes of the dead. This is in contrast to the possibly competing stewardship wishes of the deceased themselves and the deceased's loved ones, which often come with an emotional or sentimental attachment.

There have been a number of cases, often between bereaved loved ones and Facebook, regarding access to the accounts of the recently departed.[68] Perhaps as a result of these lawsuits, Facebook has set up a system that allows users to specify what should happen to their accounts after they die.

Unfortunately, a recent study found that most online services do not have specific rules for succession outlined in their TOS. However, some of the larger platforms do. Google, for example, has an Inactive Account Manager that is designed to provide control over an account after the primary account holder has become inactive.[69]

In other instances, online accounts are simply terminated at death. For example, the TOS of Apple's iCloud state that 'unless otherwise required by law, you agree that your account is non-transferable and that any rights to your Apple ID or content within your account terminate upon your death … all content within your account will be deleted'.[70]

As per Instagram's terms of use, a user of the platform is not allowed to 'impersonate others or provide inaccurate information' or 'attempt to buy, sell, or transfer any aspect of your account'. This would seem to imply that the relationship between Instagram and the account holder is personal and cannot be transferred, even upon the latter's death.

Snapchat, on the other hand, states that 'you will not buy, sell, rent, or lease access to your Snapchat account, Snaps, a Snapchat username, or a friend link without our written permission'.[71]

While these and other TOS often allow some limited form of commemoration of a loved one after death on the platform themselves, they do not necessarily

[68] See, eg, *In re Facebook, Inc*, 923 F Supp 2d 1204 (ND Cal 2012). See also A Lisicka, 'Are Parents Entitled to Access the Facebook Account of a Deceased Child?' *newtech.law* (13 October 2017), www.newtech.law/en/are-parents-entitled-access-the-facebook-account-of-a-deceased-child. See also L Boyle, 'Grieving Parents Battle Facebook for Access to 15-Year-Old Son's Profile after He Committed Suicide' *Daily Mail* (19 February 2013), www.dailymail.co.uk/news/article-2280800/Facebook-bans-parents-accessing-sons-profile-committed-suicide.html. See also EA Epstein, 'Family Fights to Access Son's Facebook Account after His Suicide to Finally Gain Closure over Tragic Death' *Daily Mail* (2 June 2012), www.dailymail.co.uk/news/article-2153548/Family-fights-access-sons-Facebook-Gmail-accounts-suicide.html.

[69] Google Account Help Center, www.support.google.com/accounts/answer/3036546?hl=en.

[70] Welcome to iCloud, www.apple.com/legal/internet-services/icloud/en/terms.html.

[71] Snap Inc TOS (if you live in the US), effective 30 October 2019, www.snap.com/en-US/terms.

provide guidance as to how to deal with the more lucrative issue of control over valuable accounts. However, just because it violates TOS does not mean that users are not doing it anyway and many Instagram accounts, for example, are openly sold on the platform of its parent company, Facebook.[72]

It is not just online accounts that are implicated. In many jurisdictions, including New York, the right of publicity or privacy does not extend after death. In these jurisdictions, anyone can essentially use the likeness of a dead celebrity – also known as a 'deleb'[73] – including employing information that is culled from the deleb's publicly available social media presence. The technologically inclined can even create a 3D AI hologram of a likeness that has fallen into the public domain post death. For example, in 2018, Las Vegas-based company Base Hologram announced a licensed holographic tour by British singer-songwriter Amy Winehouse, who died in 2011. The tour was subsequently put on hold due to 'unique sensitivities'.[74]

E. Potentially High-Value Digital Assets: Tokens

Like the original blockchain that was created together with the initial cryptocoin the Bitcoin, Ethereum is a decentralised blockchain system that is programmed to allow the transaction of value. The Ethereum Blockchain is similarly based on miners and consensus mechanisms that allow for the finality of the payment.[75]

However, Ethereum added the smart contract invented by Nick Sabo in 1994.[76] Besides the automation, control and convenience, the implementation of smart contracts turns a peer-to-peer transaction into a fully established multi-transactional model that allows the community to plan and determine the costs and financial arrangements in advance, increasing efficiency between economic parties, and effectively duplicating the fiat world of cash and liquidity in the cryptocurrency world.[77]

Another revolutionary innovation of the Ethereum Blockchain is the enabling of different coin applications, allowing users to create a low-level form of

[72] E Grillo, 'For Sale: Instagram Account, Lightly Used' *Vox* (1 February 2019), www.vox.com/the-goods/2019/2/1/18204370/instagram-accounts-black-market-buy-sell.

[73] EW Kahn and PIB Lee, '"Delebs" and Postmortem Right of Publicity' (2016) 8(3) *Landslide*, www.americanbar.org/groups/intellectual_property_law/publications/landslide/2015-16/january-february/delebs_and_postmortem_right_publicity.

[74] L Snapes, 'Amy Winehouse Hologram Tour Postponed Due to "Unique Sensitivities"' *The Guardian* (22 February 2019), www.theguardian.com/music/2019/feb/22/amy-winehouse-hologram-tour-postponed.

[75] See www.ethereum.org.

[76] A Kosba et al, 'Hawk: The Blockchain Model of Cryptography and Privacy-Preserving Smart Contracts' (2016) *IEEE Symposium on Security and Privacy* 839.

[77] C Catalini and JS Gans, 'Some Simple Economics of the Blockchain' (2020) 63(7) *Communications of the ACM* 80.

cryptocurrency, also known as a token, on top of their blockchain protocol layer.[78] Ethereum is designed to allow the trade of different types of tokens that represent different types of economic activities all running on top of the Ethereum protocol layer and subject to its rules.[79]

When Ethereum launched at 2016, it became the first Initial Coin Offering (ICO)-funded venture. It issued its cryptocoin, Ether, to early adopters for a cheap price. The ICO is a dramatic hybridisation of an initial public offering (IPO) and crowdfunding: in order to fund the venture`s real activity, the company sells lower-level cryptocoins – the tokens – and enables the use and interchange of them through the Ethereum system.

The investors who buy the tokens believe that in addition to the growth of the company itself, the associated token value will similarly provide a large return to the investment; the investment decision is based solely on the belief of the investors.[80]

After their first successful ICO, the Ethereum Blockchain became an ICO hub for new and emerging ventures for technologies associated with the cryptocurrency and blockchain worlds, and even beyond. Through the decentralised platform and the accessible open-source code, Ethereum allows the easy creation of tokens. The ICO model allows many start-ups to gain capital with no attachment to the traditional fundraising models like venture capital angels or banks.

A token is the outcome of the ICO process that is based on the Ethereum protocol. In preparation for an ICO, the company presents a white paper declaring the company`s ambitions and business models, as well as its particular blockchain protocol. The token in this case is often more of a coupon-like asset than a fully encrypted currency like the Bitcoin or Ether, akin to an expression of a right that the owner of it holds rather than an intrinsic value asset.[81]

Following the emergence of this phenomenal fundraising ability, governments have attempted to regulate it, with varying levels of success.[82] Notably, while there can be enormous sums of money involved, many ICO markets are not secured at all. Some attempts include the US Securities and Exchange Commission (SEC), which released official government instructions in 2017 that tried to distinguish the different kind of tokens.[83]

[78] J Rohr and A Wright, 'Blockchain-Based Token Sales, Initial Coin Offerings, and the Democratization of Public Capital Markets (2019) 70(2) *Hastings Law Journal* 463.

[79] See A Rosic, 'What is an Ethereum Token: The Ultimate Beginner's Guide' *Blockgeeks*, www.blockgeeks.com/guides/ethereum-token.

[80] See J Batiz-Benet, J Clayburgh and M Santori, 'The SAFT Project: Toward a Compliant Token Sale Framework' *Cooley* (2 October 2017), www.saftproject.com/static/SAFT-Project-Whitepaper.pdf.

[81] See 'Cryptographic Assets and Related Transactions: Accounting Considerations under IFRS' *PricewaterhouseCoopers* (December 2019) 2, www.pwc.com/gx/en/audit-services/ifrs/publications/ifrs-16/cryptographic-assets-related-transactions-accounting-considerations-ifrs-pwc-in-depth.pdf.

[82] WA Kaal, 'Initial Coin Offerings: The Top 25 Jurisdictions and Their Comparative Regulatory Responses' (2018) *CodeX Stanford Journal of Blockchain Law & Policy*.

[83] Securities and Exchange Commission, Release No 81207: Report of Investigation Pursuant to Section 21(a) of the Securities Exchange Act of 1934: The DAO, 25 July 2017, www.sec.gov/litigation/investreport/34-81207.pdf. See also 15 USC s 77e.

There are three main categories of tokens: utility tokens (UTs), security tokens (STs) and currency tokens (CTs). The issuer decides which model to use when he or she releases his or her white paper to the potential investors. Depending on the token, there may be different levels of government oversight, depending on the jurisdiction.

UTs express the value of an actual utility product that the company offers. They grant the investor the right to convert the token into the product or service that the associated company is selling. The value of this token can be related to the actual product's value, which is decided by supply and demand of the product in the free market. As many jurisdictions still have little to no regulation for UTs, most of the ICO-issued companies use this definition to avoid jurisdictional problems and government interference.[84] UTs often have inflated value at the time of the ICO; ultimately, in most cases, the token loses all value.

STs are most similar to stock or other security assets that are typically transferred through a stock market. However, in contrast to standard stocks, STs do not allocate any profits or voting rights in the company. The return and value of this asset relies primarily on the valuation of the company.

This hybrid model of CTs is both an investment and a currency. These tokens were created with the express interest in avoiding SEC laws. As such, the hybrid definition includes both options in it, utilities being earned from the cheap acquisition of the token and future earnings that will follow after the sale of it in what resembles the stock market.

The complicated legal issues relating to tokens – much of which has yet to be resolved in most jurisdictions, especially their regulation and taxation – will be discussed in section V.

IV. Artificial Intelligence: Digital Asset Management and the Monetisation of Digital Assets

Conventional wisdom has it that in the information age, each successive year sees more information created than all years prior combined. This big data represents various data types from text and figures to images, movies and multimedia – essentially, anything and everything. As we each increasingly create more data that can fall within the shifting definition of digital assets, there has been recent growth in the development of AI digital asset management (DAM) systems.[85]

[84] AF McMahon III and TA Puthoff, '"Utility Tokens" and Securities Law: What Companies Need to Know before Attempting an ICO' *Taft Law Bulletins* (7 February 2019), www.taftlaw.com/news-events/law-bulletins/utility-tokens-and-securities-law-what-companies-need-to-know-before-attempting-an-ico.

[85] E Segal, 'Understanding AI-Based Digital Asset Management' *IBM Developer* (6 September 2020), www.developer.ibm.com/recipes/tutorials/understanding-aibased-digital-asset-management.

These systems employ AI to upload, identify, tag, sift and curate the increasing amount of content created. Although large businesses are a key consumer of these DAMs, as we each increasingly create more data, AI DAMs will become a necessity for those with large digital estates. In particular, AI is especially adept at identifying media content for these DAMs.[86]

DAMs are also increasingly valuable in searching the internet to confirm that no one is misappropriating the digital assets of the living or the deceased. Here, AI can seek out not only exact similarities online, but also those assets that have been altered to hide their illegal sourcing. AI can also provide for the automated licensing of digital assets without requiring the input of the asset owner or creator. For example, smart contracts (eg, self-executing code that has legal weight) can provide a portal for owners of digital assets to extract rents quickly and efficiently. The less onerous the interaction with the consumer, the more likely an owner of digital assets will be able to digitally monetise those assets.

In addition to the use of AI to catalogue and keep track of digital assets, it is also finding its place as a valuable tool in extracting value from everyday digital data. It has been famously said that when an online service is free, you are the product. Large companies like Google, Facebook and Twitter monetise the data that they collect from your everyday interactions with the platforms. They also collect data from various sources, including sensors in your wearable devices, in your vehicles, in your home and in your smartphone, even from your everyday interactions on the internet.

Companies are emerging to help individuals find value in their everyday activities, turning random data into valuable digital assets that can be sold to various digital platforms or exchanged for services and discounts. Employing edge AI technology – ie, the computation and analysis happens locally and not on the cloud or outside of one's control – these companies collect and compile data from all relevant sources, then encrypt it locally and finally send a semi-anonymous stream of data to those companies that value the data. For example, an insurance company may be able to infinitely discriminate in its pricing by collecting sufficient data from your vehicle to obtain a much better understanding and appreciation of how you drive and how you treat your vehicle.

Effectively, these companies turn random data streams from various platforms into valuable digital assets that can be monetised. Given that these digital assets have value, the law should provide rules and regulations with regard to their sale, trade, appropriation and passage intestate.

Privacy and security are also key. Consider, for example, Kneron, an AI company that has developed a KNEO platform that:

> [U]ses blockchain technology to secure your private data and convert them into digital assets you can manage. Exchange it for discounts on services or sell it to corporations,

[86] ibid.

> your data back in your hands … You can delete, keep it private, or choose to exchange to retail brands for discounts or sell it to advertisers for market value on the KNEO digital asset marketplace. The choice, the control, and your data are yours.[87]

This sort of service raises legal concerns vis-a-vis the ownership of these digital assets. Most jurisdictions do not provide intellectual property protection to factual information. For example, in the US, the Supreme Court in *Feist* ruled that factual information is not protectable simply because it was compiled.[88] Even the European database protection regime provides only thin protection for collected facts.[89]

However, companies like Kneron do not simply collect data – they compile and curate the data, creating non-intuitive new sets of data that, while related to the factual data, are the result of AI algorithmic operations. This sort of data may or may not be considered protectable under various data protection and ownership regimes. It has yet to be determined.

Moreover, even if the data is protectable, it is not clear whether a company that employs AI to analyse, curate and aggregate your data is the owner.[90] We have discussed this elsewhere both with regard to US and Singapore law, and thus this falls beyond the scope of this chapter.[91]

V. Tokens, ICOs and Specific Legal Issues

In practice, beyond the personal considerations associated with digital assets, tokens, more so than most other digital assets, also create practical concerns for their issuing bodies, ie, the corporations that are seeking to raise capital via ICOs. Initially employed by a number of blockchain-related start-ups, the ICO quickly became a tool to raise capital without all the concomitant rules, regulations and compliance obligations of other standard forms of raising capital, including the IPO of stock.

Regulatory bodies worldwide eventually reacted and responded to this new form of business by announcing, suggesting and, even in a handful of cases, implementing new regulations to regulate ICOs. Most jurisdictions have yet to codify

[87] See www.kneron.com/technology/KNEO.

[88] *Feist Publications, Inc v Rural Telephone Service Co*, 499 US 340, 111 S Ct 1282, 113 L Ed 2d 358 (1991).

[89] See, eg, the European Commission's most recent analysis of the scope of protection: www.ec.europa.eu/digital-single-market/en/protection-databases.

[90] D Greenbaum, 'On Big Data, Patent Law, and Global Warming' *CTECH by Calcalist* (13 December 2019), www.calcalistech.com/ctech/articles/0,7340,L-3775695,00.html.

[91] T Dadia et al, 'Can AI Find its Place within the Broad Ambit of Copyright Law?' (2020) *Berkeley Journal of Entertainment and Sports Law* (forthcoming). See also D Greenbaum, 'Makeup Artists Can Teach an AI a Thing or Two about Protecting its Copyright' *CTECH by Calcalist* (19 June 2020), www.calcalistech.com/ctech/articles/0,7340,L-3834214,00.html.

any final rules in this area, which makes it a somewhat treacherous environment for many companies. For some, the lack of regulation is an incentive to operate, but for most it is not.

Below we discuss some of the confusing aspects of the ICO vis-a-vis taxation and accounting. This is not meant to be comprehensive, but it should provide some appreciation of the confusion surrounding the implementation of ICOs.

A. Accounting Definitions from the Investors' Point of View: Tokens as Assets

As per the Conceptual Framework for Financial Reporting devised for the International Accounting Standards Board by the International Financial Reporting Standards (IFRS) Foundation, an asset is 'a resource controlled by the entity as a result of past events and from which future economic benefits are expected to flow to the entity'.[92] In order to recognise an asset in its financial statements, a company must meet four cumulative conditions. First, it must show that the resource is exclusively controlled by the company. While there is no explicit definition of the term 'control' within the conceptual framework, each transaction must be examined according to its economic nature and not necessarily its legal structure.

When an investor firm chooses to invest in an ICO, it assumes all the risks involved in the investment. Accordingly, the tokens that the investor receives in consideration for its investment are under its full control – the decision whether to hold them for future use or to trade them in the secondary trading markets is granted to it exclusively – and therefore all the benefits embodied in the token are under its control.

Second, the asset must be derived from a past event. The past event in the case of ICOs is the actual investment and the receipt of the token. This condition is fulfilled and can be easily verified via the indelible blockchain.

Third, in order for an asset to be recognised, it must be possible to measure it reliably. An investment in an ICO can be measured in two ways. First, the investment can be measured on a cost basis. Second, the tokens have an active market that update the value of the coins and tokens after each and every transaction, and so the tokens have a quoted market price at any given moment.

The last condition that must be met in order to recognise an asset is the expectation to generate future economic benefits, ie, the potential to contribute directly or indirectly to the flow of cash and cash equivalents to the entity.[93] Today, the conceptual framework defines an 'expectation' according to a probability threshold of 50 per cent.

[92] International Financial Reporting Standards Foundation, 'Conceptual Framework' (8 January 2017).

[93] ibid.

It seems as if the existing IFRS Conceptual Framework can be stretched far enough to include ICO tokens under the definition of 'assets'; however, the real question is which type of asset is at hand.

Accounting defines three types of assets: tangible assets, intangible assets and financial assets. While tokens are unlikely to be considered cash as they are not backed by any government and are often not yet subject to regulation, they could be considered an asset as their value is measurable in accordance with IFRS 13. However, tokens arguably lack the ability to award investors with a contractual right to receive or exchange cash, thus questioning that assessment. The prevailing view is that they are intangible assets; that is, identifiable, controlled by an entity and would be expected to generate economic benefits for the entity in the future.

As this is the widest definition of assets currently existing in the IFRS, many entities find it simpler to slide ICO tokens into their financial reports as such intangible assets. In our opinion, it is inefficient to attempt to squeeze ICO tokens into existing accounting standard definitions and it seems that it is time for regulators to accept tokens as the new unique assets that they are, thus creating a new specialised way for them to be accounted for in financial statements.

B. Taxation

Tokens can be considered as currencies, property or securities, and each of these is taxed differently. There is no clear guidance regarding the tax treatment of the different kinds of ICO tokens. While security tokens can be taxed as capital gains and be monitored by the US SEC, gains from UTs and CTs can be taxed as ordinary gains.

Different taxation classifications might affect the success and frequency of use of each kind of token. Tax classification will not only be affected by the intentions and claims of the issuers regarding the token; for taxation purposes, it will be decided by the nature of the token and its real use.

i. ICO Tokens as Currency

In theory, the acquisition of an ICO token can be regarded as a foreign exchange for tax purposes, the same as exchanging US dollars with euros. Other jurisdictions see it an acquisition of a security or an asset, and tax at a capital gains rate.

However, according to US law, any foreign currency gain or loss, including this ICO token, will be treated as ordinary income or loss.[94] A foreign currency exchange gain or loss is the gain or loss realised due to the change in exchange rates between the acquiring date and the date of disposition. Treating tokens as foreign currencies will benefit investors because the tax report for ordinary

[94] 26 USC s 988.

income is probably the simplest of all options. Tax on income is reported on a periodic basis as opposed to other tax methods that require a report for each and every transaction.

ii. ICO Tokens as Property

In March 2014, the IRS issued Notice 2014–21, *Virtual Currency Guidance*.[95] The notice clarifies how existing tax rules will apply to transactions that involve the use of these kinds of currencies: 'Virtual currency that has an equivalent value in real currency, or that acts as a substitute for a real currency, is referred to as "convertible" virtual currency.'

Bitcoin is clearly a convertible virtual currency. It can be digitally traded between users and can be purchased for, or exchanged into, US dollars, Euros and other real or virtual currencies. Although most ICO tokens can be bought only in exchange for virtual currencies (like Bitcoin and Ether), they can still fit the broad definition of convertible virtual currencies. Almost every token has an equivalent value in Bitcoin, which is (as seen above) a convertible virtual currency, meaning that every token as an equivalent value in real currency through an exchange from token to Bitcoin and from Bitcoin to real currency.

According to the IRS notice, virtual currencies are categorised as property for gain and loss calculations. This means that users of virtual currencies must keep track of the gains and losses of every virtual currency transaction according to the IRS regulations. Each and every case of buying or selling of tokens should be reported as a single different transaction that has to be reported. The categorisation of virtual currency as property places costs on the users and creates obstacles to compliance. It seems that for now, tokens will not be considered as virtual currencies because it is indicated in the notice that: 'No inference should be drawn with respect to virtual currencies described in this notice.'

In summary, a token bought for investment purposes will be considered a capital asset and will be taxed appropriately. On the other hand, if someone buys tokens as an investment vehicle and is planning simply to trade them, it will not be considered as capital, but probably as ordinary income.

iii. ICO Tokens as Securities

Although regarding tokens as securities or stocks has no tax consequences for the issuer, it might affect the holders. Security tokens that grant the holder voting rights or some kind of ownership will be subject to the SEC regulation just like ordinary stocks in an IPO. Gains are taxed as capital gains. Many tokens are meant to be exchanged back and forth between the company and customers.

[95] IRS Notice 2014-21.

If tokens will be regarded as stocks, the selling of tokens back to the company that issued them can be considered as dividend income according to US law under section 302(b)(1) of the Internal Revenue Code.[96]

It is not clear how the IRS will deal with this issue in the case of tokens, where the issuing company will always be willing to buy back its stocks (tokens).[97] In addition, while all capital gains of individuals and companies are taxable, only losses that are not sales of personal sales are deductible. That means that if a private holder loses money from an ICO transaction, these losses cannot be deducted from his or her other capital earnings in the future.

C. Taxation Reflections

The main aspect that differentiates ICO tokens from cryptocurrency 'coins' such as Bitcoin and Ether is their ability to encompass a specific functionality rather than a simple exchange value.[98] This functionality is completely structured by the developer and issuer of the token, which may award it an array of different qualities. While STs usually behave similarly to financial instruments such as stocks and bonds, UTs are often designed in a way that allows them to interact with the product that the issuers plan on developing.

Many tax authorities, although making decisions regarding the taxation of ICOs, have left many things open to interpretation and have not created certainty among the public for entrepreneurs and investors alike. In our opinion, creating certainty regarding taxation issues is one of the most important things in the field of taxation in general and in cryptocurrency issues in particular.

A country which is able to establish, in the near future, certainty in tax issues regarding coin offering-based companies, will attract many players in that field. The countries that succeed in giving certainty to entrepreneurs and investors can expect to attract many cryptocurrency entrepreneurs to register their companies in their territory.

As part of the taxation policy, it is necessary to determine not only the taxation methods, but also the reporting methods. On the issue of timing and taxation, we believe that there should be a distinction between different types of tokens and the nature of their use. At a conceptual level, security tokens should be treated as an asset and be taxed according to capital gains tax. In this case, a report should be made for any transaction (purchase or sale) of the token (asset), whether it is being made in the primary or the secondary market.

[96] Internal Revenue Code 26 US §302(b)(1), Distributions in redemption of stock.

[97] DJ Shakow, 'The Tax Treatment of Tokens: What Does it Betoken?' (2017) *Penn Law: Legal Scholarship Repository*, https://scholarship.law.upenn.edu/faculty_scholarship/1942.

[98] R Massey and L Pawczuk, 'Initial Coin Offering: A New Paradigm' *Deloitte US*, www2.deloitte.com/us/en/pages/consulting/articles/initial-coin-offering-a-new-paradigm.html.

In our opinion, a security currency that gives its owners certain rights in the target company correlates with the definition of an asset and is very similar to shares or any other financial assets. In contrast, as we see it, UTs should be treated as a regular buying or selling transaction, just like the purchase or sale of any goods or services.

A token that provides its owner with a right for a certain product or service or a discount is equivalent to having any other membership, for example, Amazon Prime. Just as there is no obligation for companies that sell memberships to report each and every transaction as it occurs, the same should apply to UTs. In a case in which a certain token grants both rights in the company and rights for products, the rights in the company should play the dominant part of the currency and the method of taxation, and the timing of the reporting should be identical to that used in STs.

For the purposes of taxation, we do not see any importance in relation to the question of whether the purchase was made by fiat currencies or through other digital currencies. In our opinion, when a currency was purchased, especially in an initial offering, this purchase has an economic tangible value, according to which taxes should be collected. The topic of taxation of the purchase of cryptotokens with other digital currencies raises other questions, such as evaluating the value of the cryptographic currency at the time of purchase, due to the volatility of these currencies and the absence of an official index, but these questions will need to be left for another time.

Nevertheless, tax certainty is not sufficient. In order to attract companies to incorporate in a specific country and in order to continue developing the blockchain field, countries will have to make attractive taxation incentives. A relatively low tax rate on income from tokens, whether in the initial offering or in the secondary market, and whether it is a security or utility token will attract entrepreneurs. A low tax rate will encourage companies and entrepreneurs to establish themselves in the country and to invest their resources. Although a low tax rate leads to a loss of potential economic profit for every dollar earned in the economy, it might well increase the amount of money invested.[99] With a proper tax policy, not only will countries not lose money on taxation, but they can also earn more money in addition to technological development, job creation and the promotion of the country's economy.

D. International Regulation

In the race to regulate or ban ICOs, states have been mostly acting independently, establishing their own set of rules and approaches. However, we believe that the basis of the most appropriate regulatory model for such global and boundaryless

[99] Disposable income and investments which are affected by taxes.

technology would be the establishment of an international treaty. The international treaty could be established under an existing organ or through the establishment of a special international body that would focus solely on the regulation and activity of blockchains. There are various benefits to the approach of forming an international basis to the model, which would eventually lead to each state's self-regulation. First, the technology by its nature crosses national boundaries. The activity of ICOs is inherently global – the investors could be from any country in the world, while the ICO could be operating from another country. In this way, an enabling environment will be created, giving confidence for both investors and ICOs.

Second, an international treaty would establish the common recognition of the activity of ICOs, which would also diminish the negative perception that often surrounds cryptocurrencies generally and ICOs in particular. Further, it would establish commonly accepted definitions to crucial aspects of ICOs – for example, the definition and classification of tokens. A similar initiative has been already announced by 22 European countries that have signed a declaration on the establishment of the European Blockchain Partnership, which would be a tool to exchange experiences and expertise in the regulatory and technical fields of blockchain-related activities.[100]

The states that aim to attract as many ICO companies and activity to operate from their territory as possible would be forced to follow and act in accordance with the treaty, and they would be bound by the same standards as all other countries, which would possibly result in them losing much of their attractiveness and advantage over other states. Hence, an international treaty could prove to be less effective for the case of ICOs and blockchain technology unless states find other ways to distinguish themselves – for example, in terms of efficiency and speed of regulatory approval. Also, as with any international treaty, it involves a process of adaptation to and an examination of the compatibility of the treaty with the internal existing laws of a state, and the implementation process could be long and gruelling. This is undesirable; as has been mentioned above, a fast adoption of regulation would ensure greater ICO activity.

E. Self-Regulation

The mechanism of ICOs raises many concerns among states and their authorities. The ability of the technology to be unfettered by a physical location, the lack of dependence on traditional banking and the relative ease of transactions and anonymity under the protection of digital wallets and the internet expose countries

[100] See 'European Countries Join Blockchain Partnership' (10 April 2018), www.ec.europa.eu/digital-single-market/en/news/european-countries-join-blockchain-partnership.

and investors to relatively high risks. The blockchain-based technology enables the transfer of funds from one side of the world to the other, albeit with traces and documentation of the deal in the ledger, but with a real difficulty in tracking and authenticating the identity of the parties to the transaction. The anonymity, which is provided by the internet in general and digital wallets in particular, is a source of great concern regarding the capacity to misuse the blockchain-based technology platform for illegal purposes. Each of these characteristics makes it relatively easy to exploit the technology and increases the need for the supervision and enforcement of the transactions carried out through it.

The US can enact laws and enforce them whether through existing or new regulatory bodies. But a question arises: can supervision and regulation by the state be effective and efficient?

While a state can enforce and oversee transactions directly through its various authorities, ultimately such a practice is neither effective nor desirable. One state authority will not be capable of covering the entire range of situations associated with tokens. While the protection of investors is the duty and designation of the SEC, the IRS is responsible for taxes, and other bodies are responsible for monitoring money laundering and any support given to terrorist organisations. Dealing with the difficulties that are generated by this technology requires the work and cooperation of various authorities.

Ultimately, market forces will provide the optimal regulation. Whether or not regulatory bodies will be established, market forces will eventually lead to accepted practices. The ICO hype has already subsided from its peak and investors are unlikely to continue to rush to invest. Due to the high risk of ICOs, investors will force companies to present more ripe products before they invest. A similar trend is seen in the field of equity crowdfunding, where investors now demand more than simply nice presentations. Still, the market will take time to adjust itself without any guidance; only an integration between a well-orchestrated self-regulating market and market forces regulation will suffice.

VI. Conclusions

In this chapter we have reviewed numerous legal considerations relating to digital assets, with a focus on the US.

Digital assets are amorphous and hard to pin down, if not simply to describe, without extensive regulations. However, as is the case with all innovation, too much regulation or the wrong regulation will hamper and harm the properties that we are trying to promote.

In the area of public law, it behoves regulators in these areas to carefully choreograph regulation such that it is: (i) not too pre-emptive; (ii) not focused on soon to be defunct technology; (iii) not overly restrictive so as to push this easily transported technology abroad; and (iv) not overly permissive such that the judiciary does not know what to do with the technology. Overall, this is a tall order for our regulators, but one that can be facilitated through the inclusion of the many stakeholders in the regulation process.

In the area of private law, the aforementioned RUFADAA is a useful combination of private contracting between parties and overarching government rules. It provides a hierarchy of rules to be followed in cases of inheritance in terms of outlining how to deal with digital assets. In the likelihood that legal instructions are not left by the deceased, the digital platforms are allowed to contract with individuals as to what should happen after their death, including, importantly, through providing tools that both highlight the need to make decisions before death and providing rules in the event that no decisions have been made.

There is a simple solution that is applicable in nearly all the jurisdictions, even those that have not implemented a RUFADDAA-like law, and addresses many of the concerns raised in this chapter, especially in the case of inheritance. To this end, given the ongoing uncertainty in the law, the best advice for attorneys would be to have their clients plan ahead, leave specific instructions regarding how digital assets should be divided and keep files on usernames and passwords that would allow an inheritor to interact with the platform without necessitating any overt discussions with the platform regarding the transference of ownership.[101] Employing this advice will help attorneys deal with their clients' digital assets in light of the current law, or lack thereof.

In the end, both the public and governments should be educated as to both the value and the inherent complexity of digital assets. Importantly, as mentioned in this chapter, many digital platforms are emerging that raise serious legal concerns. The law is consistently slow to catch up to these advancements in technology. Hopefully this chapter will serve at least to help the necessary regulatory bodies catch up.

[101] See, eg, P Tan and S Lek, 'Digital Assets and Legacy Planning in Singapore' *Fortis Law Corporation* (14 August 2019), www.fortislaw.com.sg/publications/digital-assets-and-legacy-planning-in-singapore.

11

Blockchain in Land Administration?

Overlooked Details in Translating Theory into Practice

ALVIN W-L SEE*

I. Introduction

There is an important correlation between the quality of a country's land administration and its economic prosperity. A good land administration which ensures a sufficient degree of security in land rights will naturally attract the trust and confidence of its users. This will in turn encourage land dealings, be it sale and purchase, investment in land development or offering of land as collateral to raise capital to pursue a broad range of business activities. The final example, according to economist Hernando de Soto, is an important element in any successful capitalist economy.[1] His thesis posits that many underdeveloped nations fail in their attempts to replicate the success of a capitalist economy, despite adopting the same economic model, because of their inability to turn resources into capital. As he explains:

> The poor inhabitants of these nations – the overwhelming majority – do have things, but they lack the process to represent their property and create capital. They have houses but not titles; crops but not deeds; businesses but not statutes of incorporation. It is the unavailability of these essential representations that explains why people who have adapted every other Western invention, from the paper clip to the nuclear reactor, have not been able to produce sufficient capital to make their domestic capitalism work.[2]

* I am grateful to Chris Reed, Gary Chan and Man Yip for their helpful comments on the earlier drafts of this chapter. I also thank my research assistants, Su Jin Chandran and Pesdy Tay, for their able research assistance. All errors are my own. This research is supported by the National Research Foundation, Singapore under its Emerging Areas Research Projects (EARP) Funding Initiative. Any opinions, findings and conclusions or recommendations expressed in this material are those of the author(s) and do not reflect the views of National Research Foundation, Singapore.

[1] H de Soto, *The Mystery of Capital* (Black Swan, 2001).

[2] ibid 7.

Among the mentioned classes of assets, land undoubtedly carries special significance. Even as the global economy undergoes rapid digital transformation, the importance of land has not diminished, owing to its permanence and physical connection to human existence. However, to maximise the economic potential of land, it is crucial that the legal relationship between persons and land be defined with a sufficient degree of certainty and transparency. To meaningfully say that a person owns something, his or her right in relation to that thing must have 'some degree of permanence or stability'.[3]

Any land that is, or might be, saddled with ownership disputes is unlikely to play any significant role in capital generation. In many developing economies, this problem tends to be systemic owing to the primitive laws of land ownership upon which the land administration is built.[4] This results in significant obstacles – time, effort and cost – to discovering who owns what. The problem is often also aggravated by external factors, such as corruption and personnel incompetence, which tend to be more difficult to resolve. The intuitive response is to substitute the deficient system with one that avoids these problems altogether. In many jurisdictions with troubled land administrations, where inefficiency and corruption are major contributors to the insecurity of land rights, an increasingly mooted solution is to build a land register on the blockchain. As the blockchain technology promotes transparency and finality in records, the hope is that this will translate into clear and secure land rights. In other words, the solution to the problem lies in a revolutionary way of managing data on land ownership. Unsurprisingly, de Soto has been a major proponent of this solution and is notable for his involvement in the pilot project in the Republic of Georgia.

However, translating theory into practice is often easier said than done. Despite the numerous trials that have been carried out around the world, the results have been far less pronounced compared to the initial excitement they have generated. The technical details of these projects have also been obscured by the hype surrounding the revolutionary changes that the new technology is expected to bring about. The blockchain technology first gained mainstream popularity in the context of cryptocurrencies. In that context, it provides a platform for payment transactions to occur without the need for a trusted intermediary such as a financial establishment. If this idea is directly transplanted into the context of land administration, one would expect the omission of the central land registry, which is a known point of failure in many poor land administrations. However, although most of the existing pilot projects are government-backed, it is difficult to imagine any government being willing to give up control over land administration. Unfortunately, the existing reports have mostly been ambiguous on this point. In general, there are more questions than answers about what the blockchain solution truly entails.[5]

[3] *National Provincial Bank Ltd v Ainsworth* [1965] AC 1175, 1248.

[4] For an overview of the situation in Southeast Asia, see L Hsu, P Koh and M Yip, 'Improving Connectivity between ASEAN's Legal Systems to Address Commercial Issues' (March 2018) 83–101.

[5] On the importance of distinguishing the different ways in which the blockchain technology can be employed in land administration, see G von Wangenheim, 'Blockchain-Based Land Registers: A Law-and-Economics Perspective' in A Lehavi and R Levine-Schnur (eds), *Disruptive Technology, Legal Innovation, and the Future of Real Estate* (Springer, 2020) 103.

The goal of this chapter is to fill in the often overlooked details in the attempt to translate theory into practice. Section II briefly explains the essential features of the blockchain technology, as well as its variants and trade-offs, all of which will help us understand what the technology can do and what it cannot do. Section III identifies the prerequisite to a successful implementation of blockchain technology in land administration, namely a conclusive record of land ownership. Section IV stresses the importance of determining whether the technology is compatible with the system of property law that the jurisdiction in question is currently adopting or intends to adopt. The blockchain is designed to maintain indelible records, whereas most existing property systems allow, on various grounds, rectification of land records. Where two incompatible systems meet, implementation becomes impossible until a clear choice is made. Finally, section V observes that the desirability of the blockchain solution, and how success is to be measured, will necessarily differ from country to country, depending on the specific problem encountered in each jurisdiction. In discussing the three criteria – prerequisite, compatibility and motivation – this chapter draws mainly on the experience of India, but with comparative references to Georgia and Singapore. This chapter also alludes to the danger of the blockchain hype overshadowing other technologies, such as artificial intelligence, that might be employed to solve specific problems, whether in lieu of the blockchain technology or in facilitating its adoption.

II. Introducing Blockchains

The blockchain, most popularly associated with cryptocurrencies such as Bitcoin and Ethereum, may be broadly described as a distributed ledger which is replicated and stored across the computers of participating users (*nodes*).[6] The blockchain is made up of blocks containing transaction information. New blocks are continuously added by *miners* and all blocks are cryptographically linked. The nodes running the same software are preprogrammed to validate only the addition of blocks that meet certain requirements. As the blockchain is not managed by any central authority, there is no single point of failure.

At the heart of this system is a cryptographic puzzle known as the *hash* function, which converts information within a particular block (input) into a unique string of 64 characters (output). As the output for any given input is always fixed, the unique output, also known as hash, may be seen as the digital fingerprint of each block. For the Bitcoin blockchain, this process is made more complex by the requirement that all blocks must have hash values that begin with a certain number of zeros. This sets the foundation for the *proof of work* system which brings miners

[6] S Nakamoto, 'Bitcoin: A Peer-to-Peer Electronic Cash System' (31 October 2008), www.bitcoin.org/bitcoin.pdf; V Buterin, 'Ethereum White Paper: A Next Generation Smart Contract & Decentralized Application Platform' (November 2013), www.blockchainlab.com/pdf/Ethereum_white_paper-a_next_generation_smart_contract_and_decentralized_application_platform-vitalik-buterin.pdf.

into the picture. Competing *miners* invest computational power to find a compatible hash of a new block. This time- and energy-consuming process involves altering certain arbitrary digits (*nonce*) within the block to produce a compatible hash. The miner who succeeds earns the right to add the block to the blockchain and is rewarded with a predetermined number of Bitcoins. The miner is regarded as having performed sufficient work, thereby satisfying the proof-of-work requirement. The nodes are preprogrammed to validate the addition of this block. In the rare event that multiple miners solve the puzzle at the same time, the competition continues and will be resolved by the system rule that the longest chain prevails.

These rules set the foundation for the immutability of the blockchain. When a new block is added to the blockchain, it will contain the hash of the earlier block. As the same applies to every block, all the blocks are, in a sense, cryptographically linked. If the transaction information within any block is tampered with, its hash value will change and the link with the subsequent block(s) will be broken. The nodes will reject this corrupt block. The only way to maintain the link is to recalculate new hashes for all subsequent blocks. Figure 11.1 below provides a simple illustration.

Figure 11.1 Multiple chains

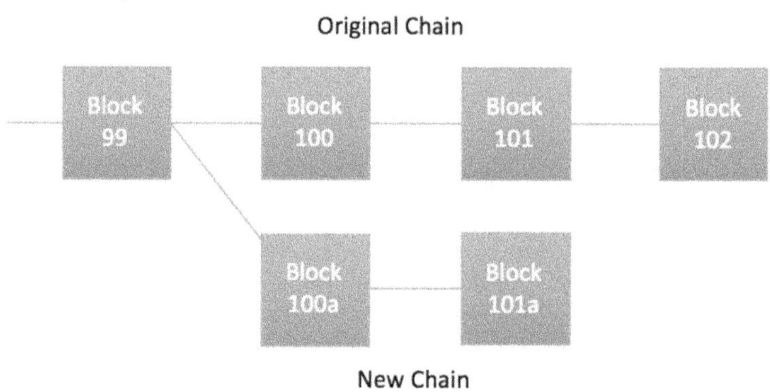

Suppose the blockchain is currently at Block 101. A group of corrupt miners decide to modify the transaction information in Block 100, leading to the creation of Block 100a. The two blocks are different in content (however slightly) and hence their hashes will differ. As Block 101 contains the hash of Block 100, not Block 100a, the latter will be rejected by the nodes. The only way to win the approval of the nodes is for the chain building upon Block 100a to overtake the original chain in length. This will require the corrupt miners to calculate the hash for Block 100a and for all subsequent blocks adding to the new chain. However, this would usually be an unworthy endeavour for two reasons. First, most miners will continue adding to the original chain as only the longest and recognised chain will yield mining rewards. Second, as the process of finding a compatible hash requires about the same amount of computational power, the new chain will almost never catch up with the original chain. One exception is where the corrupt miners have more than half of the total computational power to perform what is known as a *51% Attack*. Given sufficient time, the new chain will eventually surpass the original chain in length and become the recognised chain. However, this will be rare as the majority of miners will be participating according to the pre-agreed rules.

In short, the public blockchain is designed to be practically immutable as this is crucial in facilitating open and anonymous participation without a trusted intermediary. In contrast, a private (or permissioned) blockchain is a very different creature and is often used to serve particular institutional needs. As participation will usually be based on permission, the identity of the users will be known. In such a case, the proof-of-work system can be dispensed with. Validation of new blocks is instead performed by a trusted party, such as the host institution itself, based on any pre-agreed rules. The private blockchain may even be freely configured to allow the host institution to modify information in existing blocks. This may be achieved in a number of ways.[7] Suppose an erroneous transaction is recorded in Block 100. As the sole validator, the host institution may ignore Block 100 and validate a new Block 100a which excludes the erroneous transaction. This will result in a *fork* and the blockchain will now have two separate chains. However, the host institution will continue adding only to the new chain.[8] The original chain, which contains Block 100, simply fades into irrelevance. However, this solution might be cumbersome in practice if the erroneous transaction is found in a much earlier block. Suppose the blockchain is currently at its 1000th block, but the erroneous transaction to be undone is found in Block 100. This is illustrated in Figure 11.2 below.

Figure 11.2 Rebuilding the chain

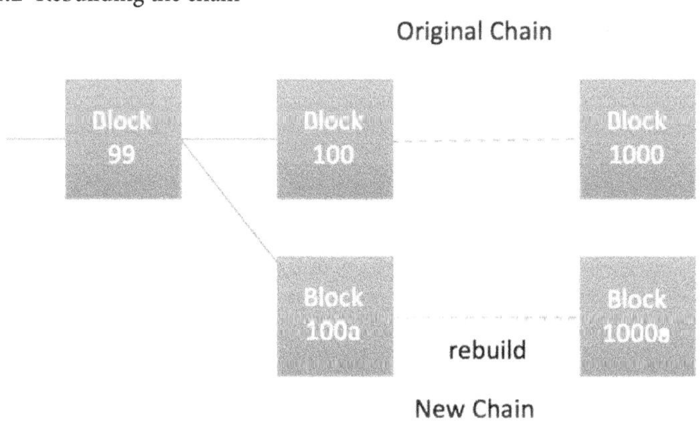

[7] G Greenspan, 'The Blockchain Immutability Myth' *CoinDesk* (9 May 2017), www.coindesk.com/blockchain-immutability-myth.

[8] In the case of public blockchains, there is no way of ensuring that everyone participates only in the new chain.

In such a case, implementing a fork would entail the creation of a new Block 100a which excludes the erroneous transaction and also the making of relevant amendments to subsequent blocks so as to maintain the cryptographic links. Even for unaffected blocks, new hashes have to be generated to ensure that they are cryptographically linked to the new Block 100a (and not Block 100). This process of rebuilding all subsequent blocks will inevitably be time-consuming. Certainly, as the technology develops, more convenient solutions can be found. One possibility is to equip the blockchain with a *chameleon hash* function, which will allow 'designated authorities to edit, rewrite or remove previous blocks of information without breaking the chain'.[9] The cryptographic link is maintained as the designated authority can use a *private key* to generate a hash for Block 100a which is identical to the hash of Block 100. As this maintains the cryptographic link between Block 100a and Block 101, there is no need to rebuild all subsequent blocks by recalculating their hashes. In other words, the original chain is preserved. For the sake of transparency, it is even possible to configure the system to leave an inerasable *scar* on Block 100a to show that a modification has been made. Although the system is not tamper-proof (immutable), it is tamper-evident.

From this basic comparison of public and private blockchains, it is easy to see how they serve different purposes. A public blockchain facilitates transactions between strangers without the need for a trusted intermediary, hence the emphasis on immutability. In contrast, a private blockchain maintained by an institution trades immutability for control. This reflects the fundamental difference between a trustless system and a trust-based system. The point of the comparison is to stress the importance of identifying the specific blockchain variant when proposing any kind of solution. Numerous reports that tout the benefits of the blockchain technology in reforming land administrations are ambiguous in this respect. If the blockchain is mentioned without any specificity, we can expect most uninformed readers to turn their minds to the public blockchain, not only due to its common association with cryptocurrencies but also because the idea of blockchain immutability resonates with the goal of achieving conclusive land titling. If the true intention is for the land register to be centrally managed and editable by an official institution, then any suggestion that the land records are more immutable than they already are is clearly misleading. Clarity is crucial to facilitate meaningful discussion and avoid talking at cross purposes.

Despite advancements in the blockchain technology and the revolutionary changes that it is expected to introduce, its impact on land administration has not been as widespread and successful as some might have hoped. As the discussion in section III below will show, the implementation process is often far from straightforward, as evidenced by the many stalled attempts at introducing

[9] 'Editing the Uneditable Blockchain: Why Distributed Ledger Technology Must Adapt to an Imperfect World' *Accenture* (September 2016), www.accenture.com/t00010101T000000__w__/es-es/_acnmedia/PDF-33/Accenture-Editing-Uneditable-Blockchain.pdf.

blockchain-based land registers. In identifying whether the blockchain technology, and which variant, may be used to improve a particular land administration, it is important to first identify the problem(s) with the existing system. Very often, the hype surrounding the topic obscures the complexity of the problems, which come in different forms and sizes, and overestimates the ability of the blockchain to provide a solution.

III. Conclusive Record of Land Ownership as a Prerequisite to Successful Implementation

Many countries with troubled land administrations turn to the blockchain technology in the hope of finding a complete solution. Focusing on Asia, the experience of India deserves a closer study. Despite the country's positive economic outlook owing to its booming manufacturing and technology sectors, its antiquated land administration has proven to be the weak link resulting in many missed opportunities.[10] The latest World Bank report on the ease of doing business ranked India 63rd overall and 154th on the ease of registering property.[11] The quality of land administrations in Mumbai and Delhi, the two largest cities, failed to achieve passing grades.[12] Unsurprisingly, the possibility of reforming its land administration with a blockchain technology has been variously mooted.[13] Several state governments have initiated pilot projects to explore the use of the blockchain technology for recording land titles and transactions.[14] Most of these states announced optimistic timeframes for the creation of proofs of concepts to actual implementation. However, at present, most of these projects remain vague on details and, with the exception of Andhra Pradesh, there have been no reports of successful implementation. Evidently, the blockchain technology has not been the panacea that many hoped it would be. The broad observation is that these setbacks are closely tied to India's existing struggle to improve the quality of its land records with the goal of implementing conclusive land titling. In short, having land records of sufficient quality is a prerequisite to harnessing the benefits of the blockchain technology.

[10] World Bank, *India: Land Policies for Growth and Poverty Reduction* (Oxford University Press, 2007).

[11] World Bank, 'Doing Business 2020', www.doingbusiness.org/en/data/exploreeconomies/India.

[12] Out of a total score of 30, Mumbai scored 14 and Delhi scored 8: World Bank Group, *Doing Business 2020: Economy Profile of India* (2019) 40–55.

[13] M Bal, 'Securing Property Rights in India through Distributed Ledger Technology' (2017) 105 *ORF Occasional Paper*, www.orfonline.org/research/securing-property-rights-india-through-distributed-ledger-technology; V Thakur et al, 'Land Records on Blockchain for Implementation of Land Titling in India' (2019) 52 *International Journal of Information Management* 101940.

[14] Andhra Pradesh (2017), Rajasthan (2018), Haryana (2018), Uttar Pradesh (2018), Telangana (2018) and Maharashtra (2019).

Land disputes form a significant proportion of civil litigations in India.[15] Although compulsory land acquisition by the government has been the flashpoint insofar as reported cases are concerned, the problem that affects the greater population is the poor land administration. A 2001 McKinsey report observed that unclear land ownership has been a major inhibiter of India's economic growth:

> Most land parcels in India – 90 per cent by one estimate – are subject to legal disputes over their ownership. The problem might take Indian courts a century to resolve at their current rate of progress. Being unclear about who owns what makes it immensely difficult to buy land for retail and housing developments. Indian developers also have trouble raising finance since they cannot offer land to which they do not have a clear title as collateral for loans. As a result, most new housing developments are constructed either on land already owned by the developers, or by the few insiders who know how to speed up the bureaucratic title-clearing process.[16]

There is little evidence that much has changed two decades on. The blame has mostly been directed at ill-maintained land records. The problem is multi-faceted and spans both legal and practical dimensions.[17] On paper, most common types of land dealings are invalid unless made by a registered instrument.[18] However, title acquisition continues to be governed by the principles of common law, which is underscored by the *nemo dat* rule.[19] For a person to acquire good title, the transferor must have a good title to give. This places the onus on a transferee, especially a purchaser, to inspect past transactions to ensure that there is no defect in the earlier chain of transfers. The objective of making registration a formality is to place transactions on the public record for ease of inspection. However, this objective has been hampered by the prevalence of unregistered dealings. On the ground, the most commonly encountered difficulty in the attempt to formalise land dealings is the cumbersome and time-consuming processes, often involving multiple government departments. This in turn creates opportunities for corruption, which adds to the cost of formal land dealings. According to one study, nearly 40 per cent of survey respondents have had to pay bribes to an officer of the registration department to facilitate the registration of documents.[20] Unsurprisingly, many transactions are conducted informally to avoid the process altogether.

[15] 'Access to Justice Survey 2015-16' *Daksh* (2016), www.dakshindia.org/wp-content/uploads/2016/05/Daksh-access-to-justice-survey.pdf; R Chandran, 'Court Battles Underline Complexity of India's Myriad Land Laws' *Reuters* (10 July 2019), www.reuters.com/article/us-india-landrights-lawmaking/court-battles-underline-complexity-of-indias-myriad-land-laws-idUSKCN1U501P.

[16] McKinsey Global Institute, *India: The Growth Imperative* (2001) 4, www.mckinsey.com/featured-insights/india/growth-imperative-for-india.

[17] World Bank (n 10).

[18] Transfer of Property Act 1882: gratuitous transfer (gift) (s 123), sale where the value exceeds 100 rupees (s 54), a mortgage securing a debt exceeding 100 rupees (s 59) and a lease for any term exceeding one year (s 107). See also ss 17 and 49 of the Registration Act 1908.

[19] *Nemo dat quod non habet* (no one can give what they do not have).

[20] Transparency International India, *India Corruption Study 2005* (Transparency International India, 2005) 44.

Once gaps appear in the land records, there will be serious knock-on effects given the derivative nature of title acquisition. If a transfer from A to B is invalid for non-registration, then any purported transfer from B to C will equally be invalid even if registered, for B cannot give what he or she does not own. In light of the prevalence of unregistered dealings, a strict application of the law would result in an unwanted chilling effect on the land market. This would be especially unfortunate where the broken link occurred a long time ago. Using the same example, the risk of C acquiring no title from B remains even if the unregistered dealing between A and B occurred several decades earlier. In the attempt to resolve this problem, in 1929, the Indian Parliament introduced the doctrine of part performance as a gap-filling device.[21] In short, if a sale is signed in writing and the transferee has taken possession of the land, then the transferor is prevented from relying on the non-registration of the instrument to say that no title had passed to the transferee.[22] In this situation, if title passes from A to B by virtue of the doctrine of part performance, B will now be in a position to pass the same to C. However, although this exception mends gaps in the title chain, it is not difficult to imagine how it might have further contributed to the prevalence of unregistered dealings, as people now realised that registration is no longer crucial in title acquisition.

Responding to these problems, in the late 1980s, the Indian government launched a national effort to modernise its land administration. The first crucial step was to migrate existing land records into the digital domain. This started with the Computerisation of Land Records (CLR) project in 1988. There was nothing then to suggest that the existing law was to be altered in any way. The significant step was taken only three decades later, in 2008, with the introduction of the National Land Records Modernization Programme (NLRMP).[23] The goal was:

> [T]o develop a modern, comprehensive and transparent land records management system in the country with the aim to implement the conclusive land-titling system with title guarantee, which will be based on four basic principles, i.e., (i) a single window to handle land records (including the maintenance and updating of textual records, maps, survey and settlement operations and registration of immovable property), (ii) the mirror principle, which refers to the fact that cadastral records mirror the ground reality, (iii) the curtain principle which indicates that the record of title is a true depiction of the ownership status, mutation is automated and automatic following registration and the reference to past records is not necessary, and (iv) title insurance, which guarantees the title for its correctness and indemnifies the title holder against loss arising on account of any defect therein.[24]

[21] Transfer of Property Act 1882, s 53A.

[22] See AK Srivastava and B Kishna, 'Nature of Right under Section 53A of the Transfer of Property Act 1882' (1973) 15 *Journal of the Indian Law Institute* 608.

[23] Department of Land Resources, Ministry of Rural Development, *The National Land Records Modernization Programme (NLRMP) Guidelines, Technical Manuals and MIS 2008–09* (2008).

[24] ibid 8.

Clearly the intention was to pave the way for adopting a system of title by registration such as the Torrens system.[25] To facilitate the intended transition, the central government prepared the Land Titling Bill 2011 as a model law for the consideration of implementing states. In 2016, the NLRMP was reformulated as the Digital India Land Records Modernization Programme (DILRMP) with revised guidelines for its implementation.[26] The original goal of the programme remained unchanged.

The overall progress of this national programme is difficult to assess as its implementation has been a state-level affair. However, the official website provides up-to-date details of its progress on several components, such as 'Computerisation of land records', 'Digitalisation of maps' and 'Survey and resurvey'.[27] As of 1 January 2020, the only states to have recorded progress exceeding 75 per cent on all components are Gujarat and Tripura. India's below-average performance in the World Bank's *Registering Property* index is also an indication that the DILRMP has yet to produce the desired outcome.

Figure 11.3 World Bank, *Registering Property* index 2007–20

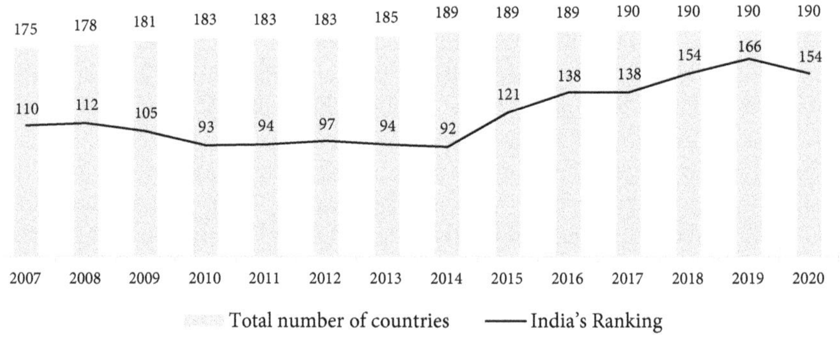

Interestingly, Rajasthan, the first Indian state to have enacted legislation towards implementing conclusive land titling, has less than 25 per cent of its land surveyed and maps digitalised.[28] Two years after the enactment of this legislation, Rajasthan announced its plans to employ the blockchain technology in its land administration. However, at the time of writing, there have been no reports of successful implementation.

[25] R Sinha, 'Moving Towards Clear Land Titles in India: Potential Benefits, A Road-Map, and Remaining Challenges' in K Deininger et al, *Innovations in Land Rights Recognition, Administration, and Governance* (World Bank, 2010) 14–19.

[26] Digital India Land Records Modernization Programme (DILRMP), 'Guidelines, Technical Manuals and MIS 2018–19', Department of Land Resources, Ministry of Rural Development (2018).

[27] See www.dilrmp.gov.in.

[28] Rajasthan Urban Land (Certificate of Titles) Act 2016. In theory, the migration need not occur all at once. The old and new systems can operate side by side until the migration is complete. Under English law, for example, there are separate sets of laws for registered and unregistered land.

What the existing data does not tell us is how close each Indian state is to meeting the basic requirement of transitioning to a system of land titles registration. This qualitative question is more than simply about enacting the relevant laws or digitalising existing land records. In order for the Torrens system to operate, both *textual* and *spatial* records must be of sufficient quality and adequately linked. At the very least, one must be able to tell from the land register *who* owns *what*. The proposed blockchain-based land register demands the same, but with the added requirement that the records be fully digitalised.[29]

There is little evidence to suggest that India is close to meeting these requirements, even in states that boast a high degree of computerisation of their land registries.[30] The challenges are well known. Insofar as textual records are concerned, this is far from simply a matter of digitalising the existing Record of Rights maintained by the Revenue Department. As revenue collection has traditionally been tied to agricultural land, there is no equivalent record for urban land, which has to be created from scratch.[31] Even for existing records, they are merely presumptive, not conclusive, proofs of ownership. As explained earlier, there are likely to be significant gaps due to the prevalence of unregistered dealings. Even for land records that appear to be complete, certain types of defects such as fraud are difficult to discover. As for spatial records, many of the old maps are not suitable for digitalisation either because they are in poor physical condition or are insufficiently accurate. Map accuracy is also closely linked to land survey, which aims to identify the boundaries of each parcel of land. Unfortunately, land surveys have traditionally been met with resistance – vocal and physical – owing to the public distrust of government officials. This has greatly reduced the political attractiveness of pushing for comprehensive surveys. As the official data shows, the vast majority of Indian states have had less than a quarter of their lands surveyed. These uncertainties contribute to long-drawn-out land disputes which impede the process of populating the new land register with conclusive titles. Against this background, it should come as little surprise that most of India's attempts to introduce blockchain-based land registers have not truly gotten off the ground.

Interestingly, the success story of the Republic of Georgia also illustrates the importance of quality land records.[32] In April 2016, the National Agency of Public Registry (NAPR) announced its partnership with Bitfury Group and economist Hernando de Soto for the design and piloting of a blockchain land-titling project. Merely one year later, 100,000 land titles had been recorded on a public blockchain.[33]

[29] The Torrens system can operate using paper records, as illustrated by its initial implementation in South Australia in 1858.

[30] World Bank (n 10).

[31] This is supported by the data on the highly urbanised city of Delhi: ibid 54–55.

[32] M Weiss and E Corsi, 'Bitfury: Blockchain for Government' (2018) *Harvard Business School Case 9 818 031*; D Allessie, M Sobolewski and L Vaccari, 'Blockchain for Digital Government' (European Commission, 2019), https://joinup.ec.europa.eu/sites/default/files/document/2019-04/JRC115049%20blockchain%20for%20digital%20government.pdf, 18–21.

[33] V Smerkis, 'Georgia Records 100,000 Land Titles on Bitcoin Blockchain: BitFury', *Cointelegraph* (20 April 2017), www.cointelegraph.com/news/georgia-records-100000-land-titles-on-bitcoin-blockchain-bitfury.

By 2018, the number rose to over 1.5 million land titles.[34] The successful implementation has been attributed to the existence of high-quality data:

> Without accurate data, the power of a Blockchain-based solution for a land registry would have been greatly limited, as poor-quality information posted on the Blockchain would make third-party verification of land titles difficult … This speaks to an important truth of Blockchain-based solutions for governments: while the technology can ensure the security and immutability of information, it cannot be a substitute for the institutional infrastructure that is essential for ensuring the quality of data.[35]

The groundwork that has proven to be so crucial was laid in 2004, when political reforms led to the establishment of the NAPR and the electronic database of land records. Since the necessary infrastructure and content were already of high quality, the project did not involve creating a new land register from scratch; instead, a blockchain-based timestamping layer was added on top of the existing electronic land register.

However, aside from illustrating the importance of quality land records, the comparison between India and Georgia is not truly meaningful. The land titling project in Georgia started on a more stable footing. As a post-Soviet state, most (if not all) land in Georgia was originally state-owned. Only from 1992 onwards, a year after Georgia's separation from the collapsed Soviet Union, were plans put in place to increase private ownership of land. In other words, Georgia's land titling project started with a clean slate, whereas India first had to address existing problems. India's challenge, to put it broadly, is to identify ways to wipe the slate clean and begin afresh.

One Indian state, Andhra Pradesh, achieved this in an unconventional manner, thus paving the way for its implementation of a blockchain-based land register. Merely months after the announcement of the project in late 2017, 100,000 titles were reported to have been recorded on a blockchain. However, the important background story started in 2014, when Andhra Pradesh was divided into two states: Andhra Pradesh and Telangana. The existing capital, Hyderabad, was allocated to Telangana, but would be shared with Andhra Pradesh for up to 10 years. In that same year, Andhra Pradesh decided to construct a new state capital – Amaravati – from scratch. To acquire the necessary land, the state government resorted to land pooling instead of the conventional compulsory acquisition.[36] Under this voluntary scheme, rural landowners (mostly farmers) were persuaded to surrender their land in exchange for smaller but developed plots when the

[34] Bitfury: Exonum, 'Improving the Security of a Government Land Registry', https://exonum.com/story-georgia.

[35] Q Shang and A Price, 'A Blockchain-Based Land Titling Project in the Republic of Georgia' (2019) 12 *Innovations: Technology, Governance, Globalizations* 72, 77–78. See also JM Graglia and C Mellon, 'Blockchain and Property in 2018: At the End of the Beginning', paper presented at the 2018 World Bank Conference on Land and Poverty (2018) 10–15.

[36] RR Ravi and S Mahadevan, 'Pooling Land for Development of Andhra Pradesh' (2018) 13 *Urban Solutions* 72, www.clc.gov.sg/docs/default-source/urban-solutions/urb-sol-iss-13-pdfs/10_case_study-amaravati-land-pooling-scheme.pdf.

proposed city is fully constructed. Within a few months, the government successfully acquired over 33,000 acres of land, thus allowing land titling to start afresh. The newly subdivided plots were then recorded, with all the necessary textual and spatial details, on a blockchain. Insofar as land reform is concerned, this is undeniably a breakthrough. But the success story was short-lived. Following a change of the state government in 2019, existing construction plans were cancelled on the ground of impracticality. As this sent land prices in Amaravati crashing, the technical success of the blockchain project has since been overshadowed by protests from farmers who had subscribed to the land pooling scheme.

Yet, for our present purposes, it is important to ask, putting aside the unforeseen politically triggered circumstances, whether the initial success in Amaravati can be replicated in other parts of India and beyond. Unlike compulsory acquisition, land pooling is more cost-effective and less intrusive on private land rights. However, its acceptance will depend on the government's ability to command public confidence. Following the failure of the Amaravati project, the public is expected to be more cautious, especially in times of political uncertainty. Even ignoring this, it is doubtful whether such a scheme would be sufficiently attractive in urban areas, where land is often already developed, more densely populated and subject to existing disputes.

This brings us back to the drawing board. Perhaps a different emerging technology, artificial intelligence (AI), might offer some hope. While it is true that records under the old system is merely presumptive of ownership, the probability of the presumption being accurate (ie, unchallenged) would likely differ for different parcels of land. A predictive system may be used to identify parcels of land with low(er) risk of ownership dispute to be transferred over to the new system. In Croatia, a company called Terra Adriatica pioneered an AI-driven platform to overcome the problem of unclean land titles. Potential claimants will provide the necessary data and the platform will 'connect tens of millions of historical, unstructured and disparate data records to provide clarity'.[37] The company applies legal process automation to assist its legal team in establishing clear title for its customers with the goal of selling the land. The entire process will be funded by investors who bear the risk, but with the expectation of earning a profit from the eventual land sales. Insofar as spatial data is concerned, it has been suggested that an imagery-based machine learning model, fed with images collected from satellites, planes and drones, may be used to determine land boundaries in lieu of traditional land surveys.[38] Whether these AI-driven initiatives are truly as effective as they claim remains to be seen, but they are possible solutions that should be explored alongside the blockchain technology.

[37] https://terraadriatica.hr/en/technology.

[38] Y Panfil, C Mellon, T Robustelli and T Fella, 'Machine Learning and Property Rights' (2019) *New America*, https://www.newamerica.org/future-property-rights/reports/proprightstech-primers/machine-learning-and-property-rights.

IV. The Compatibility Issue

Even if a jurisdiction has met the prerequisite for adopting the blockchain technology, it is nonetheless crucial to determine if the technology is compatible with its applicable laws. India's intention to harness the benefits of the blockchain technology appears to be aligned with its national plan to move away from the common law system of derivative title acquisition towards a system of conclusive land titling. Every system of property law functions to protect title. However, title security may be viewed from two opposite ends.[39] Consider a classic example where X, impersonating A, fraudulently executed a transfer in favour of a purchaser, B. X then absconds with the purchase money, leaving A and B, who are both innocent, to compete over ownership of the land. The common law system favours A because B derives no good title without A's consent. This is a system of static title security which protects an existing landowner. The public blockchain, if viewed as a property system with immutability at its core, favours B because the record of B as the landowner is conclusive of B's ownership, even though A did not consent to the transfer. This is a system of dynamic title security which favours whoever appears on the land register to be the owner. To be sure, there is no universally correct answer as to how the dispute between A and B is to be resolved. However, most existing systems of property law attempt to find a balance between the two opposite extremes.

At first sight, the Torrens system, which is similarly a system of dynamic title security, seems to be a good fit with the blockchain technology.[40] Just as how a transaction recorded on the blockchain is immutable, a Torrens title, which derives its validity from registration itself, is prima facie indefeasible. However, the appearance of compatibility quickly diminishes once it is recognised that the principle of indefeasibility is not absolute but subject to exceptions. Even as originally conceived in South Australia, fraud by the transferee renders the registered title defeasible.[41] Fraud has been the core exception in every other Torrens legislation. Unsurprisingly, India's Land Titling Bill 2011 similarly provides for defeasibility of a registered title 'in the case of fraud'.[42] Moreover, fraud is susceptible to broad and narrow definitions.[43] Given the inverse relationship between the principle of

[39] R Demogue, 'Security' in A Fouilleé, J Charmont, L Duguit and R Demogue (eds), FW Scott and JP Chamberlain (trans), *Modern French Legal Philosophy* (Boston Book Co, 1916) ch 13; P O'Connor, 'Registration of Invalid Dispositions: Who Gets the Property' in E Cooke (ed), *Modern Studies in Property Law* (Hart Publishing, 2005) 45; KFK Low and E Mik, 'Pause the Blockchain Legal Revolution' (2019) 69 *International & Comparative Law Quarterly* 135, 153–55.

[40] EM Petsinis, 'A Land Transfer Registration Revolution? Exploring the Opportunities and Limitations for Implementing the Blockchain in Electronic Land Transfer Transactions in Australia' (2018) 27 *Australian Property Law Journal* 65; *cf* L Griggs, R Thomas, R Low and J Scheibner, 'Blockchains, Trust and Land Administration: The Return of Historical Provenance' (2017) 6 *Property Law Review* 179; R Thomas and C Huang, 'Blockchain, the Borg Collective and Digitalisation of Land Registries' [2017] *The Conveyancer and Property Lawyer* 14;

[41] Real Property Act 1858 (South Australia).

[42] Land Titling Bill, s 37(2) (India).

[43] See, for example, the disagreement in *Bahr v Nicolay (No 2)* (1988) 164 CLR 604 (Australia) on whether fraud is confined to fraud in obtaining registration (narrow meaning) or also includes

indefeasibility and the fraud exception, a broad definition of fraud will lead to a greater number of cases where a registered title can be successfully challenged.

As the Torrens system became more widely adopted throughout Australia and beyond, opposing views and approaches to the principle of indefeasibility started to emerge. As Whalan observed:

> No other part of Torrens system law has created such diversity of judicial and academic opinion as that concerned with indefeasibility and the effect of registration under the Torrens Act. The principal reason is that this is the point at which the doctrines of the general law and the Torrens statutes meet most forcefully; from earliest times it has proved to be a flash-point.[44]

For the present purposes, it is sufficient to list just a couple of prominent examples. The first is the disagreement about whether a donee, ie, a person who receives title without paying for it, should be afforded the same protection as a purchaser. Even within Australia, the position differs, with four states answering in the affirmative[45] and two in the negative.[46] Interestingly, although Singapore's Torrens legislation was modelled after that of New South Wales, its drafter preferred the contrary position that a donee is not similarly protected[47] for the reason that the Torrens system is 'predominantly a purchaser's system'.[48] The second disagreement relates to whether a registered title can be defeated only on the basis of an exception that has been expressly provided for in the legislation. Referring again to India's Land Titling Bill 2011, the only express exception is fraud. Does this mean that a registered title cannot be defeated on the basis of other vitiating factors such as mistake, duress and unconscionability? While there has been judicial recognition that some of these claims should be allowed,[49] the extent to which non-statutory exceptions should be recognised has been a matter of considerable debate.[50]

As these examples illustrate, even within the Torrens system, there are choices to be made, and these choices would impact the extent to which registered titles are (in)defeasible. Having said that, the divergent approaches share a common goal: to

subsequent unconscionability (broad meaning): Wilson and Toohey JJ preferred the narrow meaning (at 636–37) while Mason CJ and Dawson J preferred the broad meaning (at 615–16). In Singapore, the broad meaning was impliedly preferred in *United Overseas Bank Ltd v Bebe bte Mohammad* [2006] 4 SLR(R) 884 (Singapore) [73], [76].

[44] DJ Whalan, *The Torrens System in Australia* (Law Book Company, 1982) 297.

[45] New South Wales, Northern Territory, Queensland and Western Australia.

[46] South Australia and Victoria.

[47] Land Titles Act, s 46(3).

[48] J Baalman, *The Singapore Torrens System: Being a Commentary on the Land Titles Ordinance 1956 of the State of Singapore* (Singapore: Government Printer, 1961) 86.

[49] *Bahr v Nicolay (No 2)* (1988) 164 CLR 604 (Australia); *Frazer v Walker* [1967] 1 AC 569 (Privy Council); *Oh Hiam v Tham Kong* [1980] 2 MLJ 159 (Privy Council). *cf United Overseas Bank Ltd* (n 43).

[50] See generally KFK Low, 'The Nature of Torrens Indefeasibility: Understanding the Limits of "Personal Equities"' (2009) 33 *Melbourne University Law Review* 205; HW Tang, 'Beyond the Torrens Mirror: A Framework of the in Personam Exception to Indefeasibility' (2008) 32 *Melbourne University Law Review* 672; LB Moses and B Edgeworth, 'Taking it Personally: Ebb and Flow in the Torrens System's in Personam Exception to Indefeasibility' (2013) 35 *Sydney Law Review* 107; R Havelock, 'Reconciling Equitable Claims with Torrens Title' (2019) 41 *Sydney Law Review* 455.

find an appropriate balance while operating broadly on the principle of dynamic title security. If the public blockchain is immutable by design, then it is difficult to imagine how limitations to the principle of indefeasibility can be accommodated. A property system building upon the public blockchain is essentially a Torrens system on steroids.[51] In fact, if the immutability were truly absolute, even a transfer procured through theft or fraud would be irreversible. Such an outcome is likely to undermine the original goal of the blockchain solution, which is to restore public confidence in the system.

This issue, which has been put to the test in the context of cryptocurrency theft, serves to illustrate more generally the difficulties that can be encountered in using the blockchain technology. On 17 June 2016, an anonymous person exploited an error in the Ethereum code to steal some US$50 million worth of Ether from a venture fund. Opinions diverged as to what an appropriate response would be. On the one hand, according to the blockchain purists, immutability is not merely a technical design but also an ideology. They take the view that any attempt to unwind the problematic transaction, even in the name of righteous intervention, should be refrained from, as it would undermine the integrity of the blockchain design. On the other hand, there is the intuitive response that the thief should not be allowed to keep the ill-gotten gains. Eventually, the disagreement resulted in the permanent split of the Ethereum blockchain into two separate blockchains: Ethereum Classic (ETC) and Ethereum (ETH). In the ETC blockchain, the theft was left undisturbed, whereas the same transaction was reversed in the ETH blockchain by a *hard-fork*, specifically by the introduction of a software update endorsed by 89 per cent of Ether holders.

While the hard-fork appeared to have produced a fair outcome, it is not without its problems. First, as the solution depends on a collective response, there is no guarantee that it will be employed in every case involving theft or fraud. The 2016 incident was high profile not only in terms of value but also because of its significant impact on the reputation of Ethereum's smart contract platform. Isolated incidents of theft or fraud are unlikely to attract sufficient attention to push for a hard-fork. Such inconsistent treatment of substantively similar cases is contrary to the principle of legal certainty. Second, the *hard-fork* is an overly blunt solution. While the victims of the 2016 Ether theft were presumably satisfied with the outcome, it is not difficult to imagine that some other innocent persons might have been aggrieved for having their legitimate transactions undone, which might have led to further complications. The basic design of the public blockchain does not lend itself easily to case-by-case solutions. Third, there is no way of ensuring that the compromised blockchain goes away. At the time of writing, the ETC blockchain continues to be mined and transacted on. While cryptocurrency splits are rather common, a split of a blockchain-based land register is simply unacceptable as there cannot be two land registers which identify different owners for the same

[51] KFK Low and EGS Teo, 'Bitcoins and Other Cryptocurrencies as Property?' (2017) 9 *Law, Innovation and Technology* 235, 240.

physical asset. Insofar as competing ownership claims to land are concerned, there can only be one winner.

Assuming that hard-fork is a bad idea, other solutions have to be explored. According to ETC's developers, blockchain immutability does not preclude traditional legal recourse:

> So, code is law on the blockchain. All executions are final, all transactions are immutable. For everything else, there is a time-tested way to adjudicate legal disputes and carry out the administration of justice. It's called legal system.[52]

If the real-world identity of the Ether thief were known, the victims could bring legal proceedings which would culminate in a court order directing either a retransfer of the stolen Ether or, if the Ether has been spent, payment of an equivalent sum of money.[53] However, the process of recovering land has traditionally been different due to the existence of a central land registry. In Singapore, for example, the court would direct the land registry, which manages the land register, to rectify the relevant record so that title in the land is restored to its rightful owner (A). As the order is not directed at the wrongful party (B), it is irrelevant that B is uncooperative or has absconded. This would be impossible in the case of a blockchain-based land register since no person, even if a centralised land registry continues to exist, has an overriding power to modify land records. The law would have to be amended so that a successful claim against B can be enforced in other ways.

Assuming that rectification of the land register is impossible, there are three alternative solutions if the law is minded to give A a remedy. First, the court may order B to retransfer the land to A. This would not be a rectification of the blockchain, but an altogether new transaction, ie, a new transfer from B to A. This solution would be the closest, in terms of outcome, to rectification. Second, the court may order B to pay A monetary compensation equivalent to the value of the land. This would not involve any movement of title on the land records. However, this solution falls short in cases where monetary compensation is inadequate – for example, where A has sentimental attachment to the land. Third, if the earlier solutions are ineffective, either because B refuses to comply or cannot be located, A may be compensated from an assurance fund.[54] However, in addition to the possibility of monetary compensation being inadequate, the fact that B gets to retain title to the land is hardly a satisfactory outcome. Even if B simply holds on to the land without deriving any benefit from it, the land is excluded from the real estate market, which goes against the economic motivation of the blockchain technology. Moreover, if the number of such cases is high, this will inevitably drive up transaction cost as the source of the assurance fund is a levy imposed on every registered transaction.

[52] Arvicco, 'Code is Law and the Quest for Justice' *Ethereum Classic Blog* (9 September 2016), www.ethereumclassic.org/blog/2016-09-09-code-is-law.

[53] This is a title-based proprietary claim: *Armstrong GmbH v Winnington Networks Ltd* [2012] 3 WLR 835.

[54] Almost every Torrens jurisdiction has an assurance fund to compensate landowners for certain types of losses arising from the operation of the Torrens system. The only known jurisdiction to have departed from the norm is Malaysia.

The public blockchain prioritises immutability at the expense of other important aspects of a property system. However, a good property system goes beyond the maintenance of land records to providing a dispute resolution framework that is fair and balanced in the treatment of innocent parties. The strength of any system is truly tested not when things proceed as intended, but when things go wrong. As the existing Torrens jurisdictions have been continuously fine-tuned towards achieving a satisfactory balance, it is difficult to imagine that any of these would be abandoned in favour of a system of absolute indefeasibility. Matters are quite different if one is referring to a private blockchain, which can be freely configured to suit the needs of an existing system.[55] There is no fundamental change to the existing property system; the blockchain merely enhances the transparency of the electronic land register. As the land registry remains the trusted intermediary, there is no role for miners, thus omitting the need for the proof-of-work system which is what makes the blockchain immutable.

Given the fundamental differences between public and private blockchains, it is important to be absolutely clear, when announcing any plans to modernise an existing land administration with the blockchain technology, on how precisely it is to be done and which variant of the blockchain is to be employed. Although the private blockchain is clearly more flexible, the choice may ultimately turn on the specific problem that a particular reform is intended to address. It is not entirely inconceivable that a public blockchain might have greater appeal to certain troubled land administrations where the administrators command low levels of public trust and confidence. As the next section will illustrate, the motivation for adopting the blockchain solution is likely to differ from jurisdiction to jurisdiction.

V. Motivations for Taking the Leap

In recommending the use of the blockchain technology in land administrations, it is important to be clear about the problem that is intended to be addressed. This is to ensure that there is no mismatch between a problem and its proposed solution. As the experience of India has shown, the problem of messy land records is not something that the blockchain technology is able to solve. However, we may ask the following question: assuming that the prerequisites for implementation have been met, what precisely does India seek to achieve with the blockchain technology? What we know for certain is that digitalisation of land records alone did not significantly improve the existing system. In one survey, about 56 per cent of the respondents considered the quality of service to be poor, and in this respect there was no perceivable difference between states that have computerised land records

[55] On the introduction of 'legal impurities' into the blockchain technology, see C Reed, UM Sathyanarayan, SH Ruan and J Collins, 'Beyond BitCoin: Legal Impurities and Off-Chain Assets' (2018) 26 *International Journal of Law & Information Technology* 160.

and those that do not.[56] Possible reasons for this are corruption among registry officers[57] and the unlawful tampering of land records.[58] Although the system has been significantly computerised, it continues to be operated by human officials who are susceptible to wrongdoing. The problem, broadly stated, is that the system commands low levels of public trust and confidence.

Against this backdrop, it is easy to see how the blockchain technology might provide a solution to the problem. The migration to a trustless system will directly address the lack of trust. This is obviously attractive to the general populace who are eager to avoid bureaucratic corruption, whether actual or perceived. From the government's perspective, although such a reform would restore public confidence in the system, it would come at the expense of control, which no reasonable government will forgo. Unsurprisingly, on a careful reading of the news reports, nothing suggests that the role of the traditional land registry will be dispensed with. But if the blockchain-based land register continues to be managed by a central land registry, then clearly it is not decentralised as a public blockchain would be. This hints at a private blockchain instead. Indeed, as a co-founder of Ethereum observed:

> The consortium or company running a private blockchain can easily, if desired, change the rules of a blockchain, revert transactions, modify balances, etc. In some cases, eg, national land registries, this functionality is necessary; there is no way a system would be allowed to exist where Dread Pirate Roberts can have legal ownership rights over a plainly visible piece of land, and so an attempt to create a government-uncontrollable land registry would in practice quickly devolve into one that is not recognized by the government itself.[59]

While the decision to use a private blockchain is understandable, the importance of clear communication cannot be stressed enough. Not infrequently, news reports and even government authorities continue to claim that the blockchain will make land records tamper-proof (or immutable).[60] However, that is to conflate public and private blockchains. Private blockchains are tamper-evident, not tamper-proof, and the extent of its transparency may also differ depending on how it is configured. As one commentator remarked about the Amaravati blockchain project:

> That the Andhra Pradesh government is using a private blockchain complicates things further. The public can view information but not directly monitor whether any illicit changes have been made to their records. They have to go through the usual red tape to get those answers. The system may not be susceptible to hacking, but authorities could

[56] Transparency International India (n 20) 40–43.

[57] ibid 44.

[58] 'Andhra Government to Adopt Blockchain Tech to End Land Record Tampering' *New Indian Express* (15 December 2019), www.newindianexpress.com/states/andhra-pradesh/2019/dec/15/andhra-government-to-adopt-blockchain-tech-to-end-land-record-tampering-2076359.html.

[59] V Buterin, 'On Public and Private Blockchains' (6 August 2015), www.ethereum.github.io/blog/2015/08/07/on-public-and-private-blockchains/.

[60] 'Andhra Government to Adopt Blockchain Tech to End Land Record Tampering' (n 58).

> deliberately enter wrong information or refuse to reveal instances of fraud even if they are logged.[61]

Instead of promoting the immutability of land records, which is technically untrue, authorities should pay more attention to educating the public on the pitfalls of a public blockchain and improving the transparency of the private blockchain. As explained earlier, in approaching the issue of title security, it is important to look at the broader picture instead of focusing on only a single aspect. None of the existing property systems comes close to subscribing to the concept of absolute immutability. Although the various systems may differ in some ways, they share the goal of finding a fair balance in the treatment of competing innocent parties. The flexibility of the private blockchain allows the trade-offs in existing property systems to be maintained. The value of the private blockchain, despite being editable, is that tampering with information can be easily discovered owing to the cryptographic link between blocks. However, the system is truly transparent only if the blockchain, and not just the land records, is open for public scrutiny. The system may also be configured such that any editing of the blockchain is traceable to a specific account so that the wrongdoer can be held accountable. In comparison to the immutability of land records, transparency in the system is arguably no less important in the effort to restore public trust and confidence in the system.

In this regard, the pilot project in Georgia may be a source of inspiration as it was similarly aimed at addressing a deep-rooted blemish on the history of Georgia's land administration.[62] In the 1990s, there were reports of the government unilaterally terminating land rights and rogue officials altering land records for their own benefit.[63] The establishment of the NAPR and the electronic land registry under its management have significantly improved the situation. However, even these have not fully mitigated the public distrust, as the complained infringements are technically still possible, even though the system has gone fully electronic. The use of the blockchain technology was aimed at solving this problem. However, as in the case of India, the majority of the reports have been ambiguous about which kind of blockchain was being used. The official message was that: 'It is impossible to delete, alter, rewrite or illegally manipulate the data stored in Blockchain.'[64] This hints at a public blockchain. Indeed, according to the developer Bitfury, the hashes of digital certificates of title are added to the Bitcoin blockchain. What this achieves is that 'information about a property title could not be altered, and that any attempted

[61] A Bhattacharya, 'Blockchain is Helping Build a New Indian City, But There's No Cure for Corruption' *Quartz India* (18 July 2018), www.qz.com/india/1325423/indias-andhra-state-is-using-blockchain-to-build-capital-amaravati.

[62] Weiss and Corsi (n 32).

[63] L Rolfes Jr and M Grout, *Assessment of Citizens' Property Rights in Georgia* (Landesa Rural Development Institute, September 2013).

[64] P Ugrekhelidze and E Grigolia, 'Using Blockchain in Georgia', paper presented at the Annual World Bank Conference on Land and Poverty (22 March 2017).

tampering would be equivalent to tampering with the Bitcoin Blockchain (making it publicly visible to everyone on the Bitcoin network)'.[65]

However, the very idea of a central registry promoting the use of a public blockchain, a decentralised ledger, ought to have raised some eyebrows. As it turns out, while the hype is built around the use of the Bitcoin blockchain, the bulk of the actions occur on a private blockchain managed by the NAPR. The land records are first placed on the private blockchain. The cryptographic hashes of such records are then published on the public blockchain.[66] If a record on the private blockchain is altered – for example, the identity of the landowner of BitAcre is changed from *A* to *B* – the *hash* of that particular record will also change. By cross-checking the relevant *hashes* on both the private and public blockchains, any alteration of the private blockchain will be easily discoverable. In this manner, the public blockchain serves as an immutable master record for cross-checking. The focus is on transparency, not immutability. The additional advantage of this solution is that the existing legal framework underlying the land administration is unaffected, which means that it is applicable whether one is dealing with a traditional deeds system or a modern system of title by registration.[67]

Finally, we turn to the case of Singapore. Unlike India and Georgia, Singapore did not have a history of troubled land administration. The Torrens system, modelled after that of New South Wales, was introduced in 1956.[68] Following independence in 1965, the government was confronted with the urgent need to develop its public infrastructure. As land ownership was concentrated in the hands of a few wealthy individuals, the government turned to compulsory acquisition as a means of wealth redistribution.[69] The acquired land were brought within the land registration system, thereby hastening the conversion of unregistered land to registered land. Through a series of conversion initiatives,[70] the outcome is that today, over 99.9 per cent of land in Singapore are registered in a centralised land register managed by the Land Titles Registry.[71] The Singapore Land Titles Registry is no stranger to technological innovations. The digitalisation of land records allowed the introduction of a platform for electronic land title searches in 1995. Since 2003, documents of land dealings can be lodged electronically. This e-lodgment system is equipped with built-in verification function to minimise data entry errors by conveyancing lawyers. In 2016, the Paperless Title Scheme was introduced to phase out the use of physical title certificates in mortgage transactions to reduce incidents of mortgage fraud. Another notable aspect of Singapore's conveyancing

[65] Bitfury: Exonum (n 34).

[66] Graglia and Mellon (n 35) 33–34.

[67] Von Wangenheim (n 5) 111.

[68] Land Titles Ordinance (No 21 of 1956).

[69] B Chew, V Hoong, LK Tay and M Vellasamy, 'Compulsory Acquisition of Land in Singapore: A Fair Regime?' (2010) 22 *Singapore Academy of Law Journal* 166.

[70] See HW Tang and KFK Low, *Tan Sook Yee's Principles of Singapore Land Law*, 4th edn (LexisNexis, 2019) ch 13.

[71] The less than 0.1 per cent of land that is unregistered was because the owners could not be identified.

system is that conveyancing lawyer(s) are required to certify the correctness of the information in the documents of dealing.[72]

As a whole, Singapore's land administration commands strong public confidence. The integrity of the Land Titles Registry has never been called into question on the basis of fraud or corruption by its officials. This is unsurprising given the nation's strong stance against corruption since its founding days. According to the *Corruption Perception Index*, Singapore was the third least-corrupt country in 2019[73] and it has never fallen outside the top 10 since the inception of the index in 1995.[74] In the unlikely event of an administrative error causing a loss of land ownership, the assurance fund managed by the Land Titles Registry, which is currently in the excess of $37 million,[75] can be utilised for compensation.[76] Aside from the trusted Land Titles Registry, the land administration is also supported by a strong legal system and judiciary, which ensure that the Torrens system is continuously fine-tuned with the goal of resolving land disputes in a fair manner.[77] This is equally, if not more, important in instilling trust and confidence in the system generally, which will in turn encourage more land dealings.

Figure 11.4 Transparency International, 'Corruption Perception Index' 1995–2019

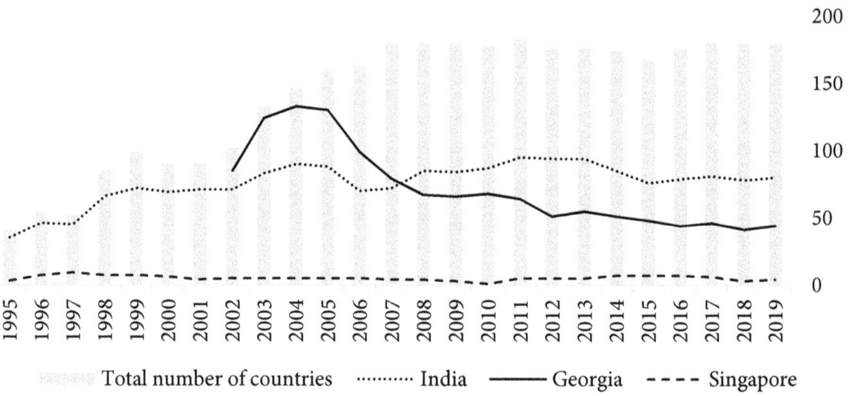

Against this background, it is easy to see why in Singapore, absolute immutability does not have the same appeal as it has in India and Georgia. As Singapore's land administration commands a high level of public trust and confidence, it makes

[72] Land Titles Act, s 59.

[73] Transparency International, 'Corruption Perception Index 2019', www.transparency.org/cpi2019.

[74] www.transparency.org/research/cpi/overview.

[75] Singapore Land Authority, *Annual Report 2019/20*, https://www-sla-gov-sg-admin.cwp.sg/qql/slot/u143/Newsroom/Annual-Reports/SLA%20Annual%20Report%2020192020.pdf.

[76] There has only been one reported case of administrative error resulting in compensation from the assurance fund: *United Overseas Bank Ltd* (n 43).

[77] See generally Tang and Low (n 70) chs 14 and 15; A See, M Yip and YH Goh, *Property and Trust Law in Singapore* (Kluwer Law International, 2018) chs 4 and 5; WJM Ricquier, *Land Law*, 5th edn (LexisNexis, 2017) ch 8.

little sense to abandon the trusted Land Titles Registry in favour of an entirely trustless system.[78] Moreover, as explained earlier, the absolute immutability of a public blockchain is incompatible with the Torrens system in relation to both substantive and remedial aspects. Although a private blockchain avoids these difficulties, there must be compelling reasons for its adoption, especially when it will likely involve significant technical adjustments to the existing operating system. Often, the cost of the transition outweighs the anticipated benefit.[79]

At present, the blockchain technology has been used mainly as a political tool, by drawing on its ideological underpinning, to restore trust and confidence in troubled land administrations. The experience of Georgia suggests that the blockchain technology also improves workflow and reduces transaction time. According to the World Bank reports, the average time for effecting a transfer of property in Singapore is 4.5 days,[80] whereas the same process in Georgia takes only one day.[81] However, it is unclear from these reports whether the difference of 3.5 days is attributable solely to the blockchain technology applied in Georgia or to something else. If efficiency of the conveyancing process is the true concern, then one would expect to look beyond the blockchain technology to other more obvious ways of enhancing workflow. In this regard, advancements in the field of AI offer exciting possibilities. As is now clear, human involvement in the processes has always been the weak link.[82] When an AI-driven facial or image recognition technology is capable of validating an identity and document, this will not only reduce human errors but will also potentially prevent fraud. If this is the kind of technology that we should be considering, then it is important to say so plainly without obscuring them with the blockchain hype.

VI. Conclusion

Despite the optimism about how the blockchain technology will revolutionise land administrations around the world, its real-world impact has clearly been far less pronounced than the hype it has generated. For a solution that is allegedly revolutionary, it is only appropriate that it is put to the test in truly difficult cases. As the experience of India has shown, the unfortunate reality is that many countries

[78] M Basu, 'Exclusive: AI Takes over Singapore's Property Estate' *GovInsider* (8 March 2017), www.govinsider.asia/digital-gov/ai-takes-over-singapores-property-estate.

[79] Von Wangenheim (n 5).

[80] World Bank Group, *Doing Business 2020: Economy Profile of Singapore* (2019) 22.

[81] World Bank Group, *Doing Business 2020: Economy Profile of Georgia* (2019) 23.

[82] Even in Singapore, where the legal profession is held to a high standard with stringent regulations, there have been reported instances of conveyancing lawyers failing to properly verify the identity of the clients they were acting for. See, eg, 'Lawyer Fined for Falsely Certifying Property Documents in S$2.3m Housing Loan Cashback Scam' *Channel NewsAsia* (10 June 2020), https://www.channelnewsasia.com/news/singapore/lutfi-law-corporation-maybank-housing-loan-cashback-scam-12823570.

which show the most interest in the blockchain technology are also often the least prepared to harness its benefits. The transition would require quality land records to be created from scratch, a process in which the blockchain technology offers no assistance. Even if this prerequisite for implementation has been met, it is not immediately obvious that the absolute immutability of land records is a desirable feature for any property system. The removal of the power to rectify land records from a central land registry would limit the available legal recourse when things go wrong. If the preservation of a central land authority along with its power to rectify land records is considered desirable, then one has to turn to the private blockchain, which can be freely configured to meet specific needs. Unlike a public blockchain, a private blockchain is not immutable, but retains sufficient transparency to prevent unlawful tampering with records.

The problem with the existing popular literature is the tendency to overgeneralise and exaggerate the merits of the blockchain solution. The lack of specificity inevitably leads to a mismatch between problems and solutions. In the context of land administration, discussion on how advancements in the field of AI may solve some of the problems that the blockchain technology is not able to resolve is unfortunately sparse. A number of possibilities identified in this chapter are worth exploring. Certainly, new challenges are expected to arise with the use of any AI solution, such as addressing systemic biases and regulating data use.

Ultimately, in recommending any kind of technological solution to fix or enhance a land administration, it is important to avoid speaking at cross-purposes. It is crucial that the different stakeholders engage in an interdisciplinary dialogue with the goal of finding a balance between problem-solving, harnessing the benefits of new technologies and preserving the intricacies of the existing property law. In the present context, this will require not only technical knowledge of what the different technologies have to offer, but also an understanding of the law, the conveyancing practices and the internal processes of the land registry of the jurisdiction in question. While there is likely to be no perfect solution, any proposed solution that fails to account for the different perspectives is unlikely to be satisfactory.

INDEX

A

Algorithmic contracts
- contractual consent
  - how to ascertain agreement in practice 208–18
  - law of unilateral mistake 219–23
  - theoretical considerations in law of contract formation 205–8
  - 'theory meets practice' 223
- decisional parameters of algorithms
  - 'knowing' and 'intending' 201–2
  - level of control over decisions 204–5
  - three design types 202–4
- defined 200–1
- impact of technological developments 199
- overview 12, 14, 200
- 'smart contracts' distinguished 200
- underlying character of algorithms 201

Artificial intelligence (AI)
- evolving role 4
- governance and strategic frameworks 71–2
- growing importance 1
- impact of technological change in SE Asia 117–18
- implications for data subjects 73
- improved efficiency and speed of analysis 3
- influence on development of private law 17–19
- insidious nature and effects 72–3
- management of personal data 69–70
- meaning and scope
  - absence of consistent definition 72
  - EU law 2–3
  - human-AI interface 3–4
  - as a means to achieving goals 3
  - simulation of human traits 3
- medical AI *see* **Medical AI**
- promotion of innovation and other competing interests 19–20
- shared relationship with data generation 22
- usefulness of property rights in personal data and deployment of AI
  - effects on use of AI in relation to personal data 87–9
  - strengthening rights of data subjects and control over personal data 82–7

Assets *see* **digital assets**

Australia
- autonomous vehicles
  - insurance 153–4
  - menu of options going forward 154
  - policy paper by NTC 152–3
- consumer trust 7
- pseudonymisation of data 7
- Torrens system of land ownership 267

Autonomous vehicles
- Australia
  - insurance 153–4
  - menu of options going forward 154
  - policy paper by NTC 152–3
- comparative overview 149
- development of new systems 147
- difficulties of existing negligence framework 165–7
- difficulties of proving breach (standard of care) 148–9
- EU law
  - contributory negligence 164
  - EC review 162
  - insurance and claims settlement 162
  - interpretive guidance 162–3
  - liability under PLD 163–4
  - municipal legislation 164
- inadequacies of strict and product liability 167–8
- influence on development of private law 17
- Japan
  - academic report on JALSA 157–8
  - amendments to primary legislation 158–9
  - forward-looking stance 159
  - modification of existing rules 156–7
- New Zealand
  - approved users 155
  - no-fault liability 155

possible need for future adjustments 155
role of ACC 154–5
no one-size-fits-all solution 164–5
options for the future 170–2
outdated basis of civil claims 148
overview 12, 13
practical problems 147–8
promotion of innovation and other competing interests 19
reality of no-fault regime 168–70
Singapore
absence of proactive approach 152
legislative changes 150–1
potential issues unaddressed 151–2
United Kingdom
contributory negligence 160–1
insurance 160
LRC consultations 161–2
radical new approach 161
statutory provisions 159–60

Autonomy
autonomous vehicles *see* **Autonomous vehicles**
contractual consent 204, 210, 213
digital information fiduciaries 128, 134
future implications of AI development 20–2
medical AI 191, 194
personal data as a proprietary resource 95, 108, 111, 114

B

Big data
AI digital asset management (DAM) systems 242
dampening of public confidence and trust 5
global phenomenon 4–5
growing importance 1
impact of technological change in SE Asia 117–18
medical AI 174
on-going tensions 5

Blockchain technology in land administration
completely trustless system 17
correlation with economic prosperity 253–4
essential features of blockchain technology
centrality of hash function 255
distributed ledger of participating users 255
immutability of blockchain 256–7
limited impact on land administration 258–9
proof-of-work system 255–6
public and private blockchains compared 258
importance of compatibility with property law
effectiveness of hard-fork solution for theft 268–9
India's move from common law system 266
public and private blockchains compared 270
rectification of register 269
Torrens system 266–8
motivations for adopting technology
addressing lack of trust 271–2
avoidance of mismatches between problem and solution 270–1
example of Singapore 273–5
government abuse of powers 272–3
improvements to workflow and transaction time 275
transparency and privacy 272
need for conclusive record of land ownership
Georgia's approach 263–5
India's national effort to modernise 261–2
knock-on effect of gaps 261
land dispute problems in India 259–60
need for a different emerging technology 265
overall progress of India's national programme 262–3
overview 12, 12–13, 16–17
promotion of innovation and other competing interests 20
'theory meets practice' 275–6
underlying difficulties 254

C

Confidentiality
see also **Privacy**
breach of confidence 122–3
information fiduciaries 126, 130, 135
obstacle to data-sharing 50
personal data as a proprietary resource 93–4, 99, 102
PPDA requirements 67

Consent
contractual consent
how to ascertain agreement in practice 208–18
impact of technological developments 199
law of unilateral mistake 219–23

theoretical considerations in law of contract formation 205–8
'theory meets practice' 223
underlying problem 200
data protection under PDPA 76
data pseudonymisation in South Korea
2020 amendments to 2016 Guidelines 30–1
stipulated exceptions 29–30
formation of conventional contracts 12
not the sole criteria for responsible use and management of data 8
Contracts *see* **Algorithmic contracts**
Contractual consent
how to ascertain agreement in practice
agency principles 213–17
autonomous algorithms 217–18
deterministic algorithms 208–12
non-deterministic algorithms 212–17
law of unilateral mistake
relationship between mistake and contract formation 219–20
Singapore approach 220–3
'theory meets practice' 223
theoretical considerations in law of contract formation
assent 206–7
content of choice 208
intent 207
offer and acceptance 205–6
underlying problem 200
Copyright protection
case for propertisation of personal data 78–9
Singapore 48–9
COVID-19
data trusts 65
impact on digital assets
other gaming-related assets 233
overview 228–9
virtual currencies 230
medical AI 174–5
need to balance privacy against other factors 118
obstacle to data sharing 51
public interest considerations 99–100
use of personal contact tracing data 22

D
Data protection
benefits and challenges of AI 87
criticisms of data-driven global tech companies 118
data pseudonymisation in South Korea
consent principle 28–31
debates prior to 2020 amendments 31–4
enforcement agencies 27
key legislative amendments 25–6, 28
statutory framework 26–7
theoretical and practical perspectives 38–45
General Data Protection Regulation (GDPR) *see* **General Data Protection Regulation (GDPR)**
inherent limitations of existing solutions
breach of confidence 122–3
contract law 119–21
legislative regulation 123–4
need for systematic and integrated approach 124–5
tort law 121–2
lessons from COVID-19 118
on-going tensions 5
overview 8
under PDPA 75–6
Data pseudonymisation in South Korea
consent
2020 amendments to 2016 Guidelines 30–1
general principle 28–9
stipulated exceptions 29–30
debates prior to 2020 amendments
need for de-identification 31–4
pseudonymisation under 2020 amendments 34–8
enforcement agencies 27
key legislative amendments 25–6, 28
overview 8
statutory framework 26–7
theoretical and practical perspectives
contract tracing of COVID-19 42–4
failure to address diverse risks 39
failure to draw line between pseudonymisation and anonymisation 41–2
potential conflict with other legislations 42
process of pseudonymisation 40–1
prospects for expanded concept of pseudonymisation 44–5
role of designated data linking agencies 41
scope of 'scientific research purposes' 39–40
significance of GDPR 38
Data-sharing
see also **Data trusts**

autonomous vehicles 150, 152
COVID-19 and public interest 99–100
routes to regulation and governance
data trusts as alternative 56–7
EU approach 53–4
problems of inflexibility 55
risk of over- and under-regulation 54–5
risk of poor fit with general regulation 55
Singapore's approach 56
solving the problem
need for suitable regulatory system and governance 52
respect for restrictions 53
trust of stakeholders 52
underlying obstacles
claims to ownership 49–50
competing interests 48–9
confidentiality 50
COVID-19 51
ethical interests 51
inadequacy of legislative measures 51
overview 47
privacy claims 50
public interest 50–1

Data trusts
see also **digital information fiduciaries; Digital information fiduciaries**
as alternative regulation 56–7
governance mechanism for data-sharing 68
governance to achieve trust
operational decisions of custodians 63
origins of trust based on external regulation 59–60
role of constitution 60–2
legal structure
as charitable trusts 58
cooperatives 58–9
importance of constitution 59
propertisation of personal data 57–8
separate from data sharers 57
outsourcing of compliance issues 64–8
overview 9
personal-data-as-property-model 88
two main issues 68

Digital assets
AI digital asset management (DAM) systems
impact of increasing data 242
privacy and security issues 243–4
uses 243
different types
emails and personal files 234–5
other gaming-related assets 232–4
potentially high-value tokens 240–2
social media accounts 236–40
virtual currencies 229–32
impact of COVID-19 228–9
increasing importance 225
influence on development of private law 18–19
international regulation 249–50
overview 12, 15–16, 225–8
potentially high-value tokens
accounting definitions 245–6
practical concerns 244–5
taxation 246–9
US approach to digital assets 240–2
promotion of innovation and other competing interests 20
self-regulation 250–1
'theory meets practice' 251–2

Digital information fiduciaries
see also **Data trusts**
contemporary issues
'hard and fast rules' not always best 143
increasing regulation 142–3
need for closer partnership with courts 143
development of concept as comparison with doctor-patient relationship
duty of disclosure 142
fiduciary regulation and negligence distinguished 141
preliminary issues 139–41
new way of thinking 118–19
overview 9
under Singapore and Malaysian law
benefits and remedies for consumer 139
interplay with regulation 136–8
reliance on discretion 133–6
summary of Harding's doctrine 131–2
two possible bases for introduction 142
underlying concept of 'information fiduciaries'
core ideas from US literature 126–8
legal difficulties 129–30
merits and shortcomings 128–9

E

Emails and personal files 234–5

EU law
AI defined 2–3
autonomous vehicles
contributory negligence 164
EC review 162
insurance and claims settlement 162
interpretive guidance 162–3

liability under PLD 163–4
municipal legislation 164
data-sharing
problems of inflexibility 55
risk of over- and under-regulation 54–5
routes to regulation and governance 53–4
General Data Protection Regulation (GDPR) *see* **General Data Protection Regulation (GDPR)**
governance and strategic frameworks for personal data 71–2
sui generis database right 49

F

Fiduciaries *see* **digital information fiduciaries**

G

General Data Protection Regulation (GDPR)
data-sharing 53–4
data subject's right of access 142
data trusts 64–7
influence on South Korean legislation 26, 30, 38
international benchmark 9
interplay with digital information fiduciaries 136–8
personal data
case for propertisation of personal data 78–9
comprehensive attempt to regulate personal data 91
ethical guidance 73–5
prohibition of human profiling 72
treatment of personal data as personal property 87–8
'privacy by design' 125

I

Information fiduciaries *see* **Digital information fiduciaries**

J

Japan
Apple-Google exposure notification scheme 43
autonomous vehicles
academic report on JALSA 157–8
amendments to primary legislation 158–9
forward-looking stance 159
modification of existing rules 156–7

K

Korea *see* **South Korea**

L

Land administration *see* **Blockchain technology in land administration**
Legal personality
AEVA approach to autonomous vehicles 171
contractual consent 218
future implications of AI development 20–2
main issue for discussion 17
private law issue 12
truly autonomous algorithms 218
Legislative regulation
autonomous vehicles
EU law 162–4
Japan 158–9
Singapore 150–1
United Kingdom 159–60
data pseudonymisation in South Korea
consent principle 28–31
debates prior to 2020 amendments 31–4
enforcement agencies 27
key legislative amendments 25–6, 28
statutory framework 26–7
theoretical and practical perspectives 38–45
data-sharing
inadequacy of current measures 51
need for suitable regulatory system and governance 52
routes to regulation and governance 53–7
data trusts
governance to achieve trust 59–60
outsourcing of compliance issues 64–8
General Data Protection Regulation (GDPR) *see* **General Data Protection Regulation (GDPR)**
general inadequacy 8–9
inherent limitations of existing solutions for privacy and data protection 123–4
interplay with digital information fiduciaries 136–8
personal data
main focus on content 70
need for appropriate model of ethical decision-making 70
Singapore
autonomous vehicles 150–1
baseline standard of protection of personal data 91

case for propertisation of personal data 79–81
inherent limitations of existing solutions for privacy and data protection 123–4
interplay with digital information fiduciaries 138
PDPA as regulatory or protective function for consumers 110–15
PDPA does not confer ownership 70
personal data as a proprietary resource under PDPA 106–10
protection of personal data under PDPA 75–6
US approach to digital assets
emails and personal files 234–5
leader in legal and regulatory innovation 227
potentially high-value tokens 240–2
social media accounts 236–40
taxation of tokens 246–9
virtual currencies 230–1

M

Malaysia
COVID screening 174–5
inherent limitations of existing solutions for privacy and data protection
legislative regulation 124
tort law 121–2
medical AI
giving of medical advice by medical AI 189–92
importance of tort 177–8
mixed healthcare system 176
omission to utilise medical AI 184–6
possibility of errors 177
potential bias and inaccuracies 186–8
reasonable reliance on third parties 182–4
standard of care 178–82

Medical AI
alternative bases for tortious liability
adaptation of existing principles 193
independent contractor defence 195–8
non-delegable duties 195–8
vicarious liability 194–5
Clinical Decision Support Systems (CDSS) 174
comparative overview 175–6
influence on development of private law 17–18
overview 12, 14
possibility of errors 175
predictive analysis 174
promotion of innovation and other competing interests 19–20
reduction of diagnosis time 175
Singapore and Malaysia
giving of medical advice by medical AI 189–92
importance of tort 177–8
mixed healthcare system 176
omission to utilise medical AI 184–6
possibility of errors 177
potential bias and inaccuracies 186–8
reasonable reliance on third parties 182–4
standard of care 178–82
'theory meets practice' 198
use across broad spectrum of services 173

Mistake
algorithmic contracts 12, 14–15
relationship between mistake and contract formation 219–20
Singapore approach 220–3
medical AI 179
registration of title 267

N

New Zealand
autonomous vehicles
approved users 155
no-fault liability 155
possible need for future adjustments 155
role of ACC 154–5
consumer trust 7
personal data as a proprietary resource 95–7

P

Personal data
as asset or 'currency' 70
criticisms of data-driven global tech companies 118
General Data Protection Regulation (GDPR)
comprehensive attempt to regulate personal data 91
ethical guidance 73–5
prohibition of human profiling 72
general distrust of AI 72–3
impact of technological change in SE Asia 117–18
implications for data subjects 73
importance 69
propertisation of personal data *see* **Propertisation of personal data**

as a proprietary resource
emergence of personal data as multi-dimensional resource 115–16
integrated perspective from several theoretical approaches 105–6
objections to property analysis 97–101
overview 92
PDPA in Singapore 106–10
position at common law 92–7
property as a 'bundle of rights' 102–3
regulating the use of economic resources 103–5
regulatory or protective function for consumers 110–15
rights in relation to 'things' 101–2
reluctance to cede control to suppliers of digital devices and services 91
role of AI 69–70
Singapore
governance and strategic frameworks 71–2
protection under PDPA 75–6

Personal files 234–5

Personal Information Management Systems (PIMSs) 88

Privacy
see also **Confidentiality**; **Data protection**
AI digital asset management (DAM) systems 243–4
blockchain technology in land administration 272
COVID-19
and data sharing 99–100
need to balance privacy against other factors 118
digital information fiduciaries *see* **Digital information fiduciaries**
inherent limitations of existing solutions
breach of confidence 122–3
contract law 119–21
legislative regulation 123–4
need for systematic and integrated approach 124–5
tort law 121–2
obstacle to data-sharing 50
on-going tensions 5
PDPA in Singapore 79
'privacy by design' 79
implementation of a systematic approach 125
potential for greater efficiency and accuracy 70
Singapore 75

Private law
autonomous vehicles
Australia 153–4
comparative approaches 149
difficulties of existing negligence framework 165–7
difficulties of proving breach (standard of care) 148–9
inadequacies of strict and product liability 167–8
Japan 156–7
New Zealand 155
no one-size-fits-all solution 164–5
options for the future 170–2
outdated basis of civil claims 148
United Kingdom 160–1
data trusts as alternative regulation 56–7
development influenced by AI and technology 17–19
importance 1
inherent limitations of existing solutions for privacy and data protection
breach of confidence 122–3
contract law 119–21
legislative regulation 123–4
need for systematic and integrated approach 124–5
tort law 121–2
medical AI
adaptation of existing principles 193
giving of medical advice by medical AI 189–92
importance of tort 177–8
independent contractor defence 195–8
mixed healthcare system 176
non-delegable duties 195–8
omission to utilise medical AI 184–6
possibility of errors 177
potential bias and inaccuracies 186–8
reasonable reliance on third parties 182–4
standard of care 178–82
vicarious liability 194–5
need for closer partnership between legislatures and courts 143
need for property and property law to fit the Fourth Industrial Revolution 77
personal data as a proprietary resource
integrated perspective from several theoretical approaches 105–6
position at common law 92–7
property as a 'bundle of rights' 102–3

regulating the use of economic resources 103–5
rights in relation to 'things' 101–2
range and scope 12–13
Propertisation of personal data
basis for data trusts 57–8
case for propertisation
copyright protection compared 78–9
need for property and property law to fit the Fourth Industrial Revolution 77
purpose and objective of PDPA and GDPR 79–81
treatment of data and computer material under CMA 81–2
effect and impact of personal data as form of property 89–90
inheritance of social media accounts 237
overview 9
personal data as a proprietary resource
emergence of personal data as multi-dimensional resource 115–16
integrated perspective from several theoretical approaches 105–6
objections to property analysis 97–101
overview 92
PDPA in Singapore 106–10
position at common law 92–7
property as a 'bundle of rights' 102–3
regulating the use of economic resources 103–5
regulatory or protective function for consumers 110–15
rights in relation to 'things' 101–2
usefulness of property rights in personal data and deployment of AI
effects on use of AI in relation to personal data 87–9
strengthening rights of data subjects and control over personal data 82–7
Proprietary resource *see* **personal data as a proprietary resource**
Public health
Contagious Disease Prevention and Control Act 27
impact of COVID-19 118
on-going tensions 5
subordination of privacy concerns, 99
Public interest
COVID-19 and data sharing 99–100
data trusts 58
obstacle to data-sharing 50–1

S
Singapore
autonomous vehicles
absence of proactive approach 152
legislative changes 150–1
potential issues unaddressed 151–2
blockchain technology in land administration
motivations for adopting technology 273–5
Torrens system of land ownership 267
case for propertisation of personal data
copyright protection compared 78–9
Law Reform Committee approach 90
purpose and objective of PDPA and GDPR 79–81
treatment of data and computer material under CMA 81–2
copyright protection 48–9
COVID screening 174–5
data-sharing 56
digital information fiduciaries
benefits and remedies for consumer 139
interplay with regulation 136–8
overview 9
reliance on discretion 133–6
summary of Harding's doctrine 131–2
inherent limitations of existing solutions for privacy and data protection
legislative regulation 123–4
tort law 121–2
Law Reform Committee
case for propertisation of personal data 90
misuse of private information 143
medical AI
giving of medical advice by medical AI 189–92
importance of tort 177–8
mixed healthcare system 176
omission to utilise medical AI 184–6
possibility of errors 177
potential bias and inaccuracies 186–8
reasonable reliance on third parties 182–4
standard of care 178–82
mistake in algorithmic contracts 220–3
personal data
baseline standard of protection of personal data 91
governance and strategic frameworks 71–2
PDPA as regulatory or protective function for consumers 110–15

PDPA does not confer ownership 70
as a proprietary resource under PDPA 106–10
protection under PDPA 75–6
pseudonymisation of data 43
'Smart contracts' 200
South Korea
data pseudonymisation *see* **Data pseudonymisation in South Korea**
digital assets 233

T
'Theory meets practice'
algorithmic contracts 223
autonomous vehicles
difficulties of existing negligence framework 165–7
inadequacies of strict and product liability 167–8
no one-size-fits-all solution 164–5
options for the future 170–2
reality of no-fault regime 168–70
blockchain technology in land administration 275–6
challenges 2
data pseudonymisation in South Korea
contract tracing of COVID-19 42–4
failure to address diverse risks 39
failure to draw line between pseudonymisation and anonymisation 41–2
potential conflict with other legislations 42
process of pseudonymisation 40–1
prospects for expanded concept of pseudonymisation 44–5
role of designated data linking agencies 41
scope of 'scientific research purposes' 39–40
significance of GDPR 38
digital assets 251–2
main issues for discussion 17
medical AI 198
overview 10–11
overview of private law and technology 12–13
Tokens *see* **Digital assets**
Torts *see* **Private law**
Trust
see also **Data trusts**
blockchain technology in land administration 271–2
data collection and use 7
data-sharing 52
digital information fiduciaries
development of concept as
comparison with doctor-patient relationship 139–41
Harding's doctrine 131–2
general distrust of AI 72–3
multi-faceted concept 5–6
preservation by wider community and institutions 7–8
as a 'process' 6

U
United Kingdom
autonomous vehicles
contributory negligence 160–1
insurance 160
LRC consultations 161–2
radical new approach 161
statutory provisions 159–60
development of information fiduciaries as comparison with doctor-patient relationship
preliminary issues 139–41
inherent limitations of existing solutions for privacy and data protection
breach of confidence 122–3
tort law 121
risks of over- and under-regulation for data-sharing 54–5
United States
autonomous vehicles 167, 169, 171
concept of 'information fiduciary' 128–9
concerns over misuse of data 5, 7
contact tracing 43
control of identity 78
digital assets 171
emails and personal files 234–5
potentially high-value tokens 240–2
social media accounts 236–40
taxation of tokens 246–9
sectoral approach to data protection 27

V
Vehicles *see* **autonomous vehicles**
Vicarious liability
contractual consent 218
medical AI 194–5
Virtual currencies *see* **Digital assets**

www.ingramcontent.com/pod-product-compliance
Ingram Content Group UK Ltd.
Pitfield, Milton Keynes, MK11 3LW, UK
UKHW020135290926
15471UKWH00003B/501

9 781509 946822